THE TRUTH REVEALED

An Abridged English Version of Kalematul Haqq

Volume 3

Written by Hamid Bin Shabbir

Translated by Mir Baqar Alikhan, Syed Hamid Razvi
& Kaniz Fatima (Shabbir) Alikhan

The Truth Revealed – Volume 3 of 3
An Abridged English Translation of Kalematul Haqq

ISBN: 978-1-927930-66-3

Written by Hamid Bin Shabbir
Translated by Mir Baqar Alikhan, Syed Hamid Razvi & Kaniz Fatima Alikhan
haqqrevealed@gmail.com

Published by the Islamic Publishing House (www.iph.ca)

Cover Design and Typesetting by Islamic Publishing House

Contents

Preface

بِسْمِ اللهِ الرَّحْمٰنِ الرَّحِيْمِ

In the name of Allah, the All-beneficent, the All-merciful

Little do we realize the Blessings and Bounties of Allah ﷻ which He showers upon us but which we take for granted without thanking Him with the thanks that are due unto Him. This is due to our ignorance of His Exalted status. In fact, Allah ﷻ has stated this very same in His Holy Book in various places, for instance in Sura Al-Hajj wherein He states: "Ma Qadrullaha haqqa Qadrihi ... They estimate not Allah His rightful estimation" (22:74): and so also in a few other chapters. In effect we, in our limited human capacity cannot fully appreciate or comprehend His True Essence. Even the holy Ahlul Bayt ﷺ have indicated this in their litanies, for instance the holy fourth Imam states: "Tongues are unable to praise Him to the fullest extent, and reason incapable of knowing His Essence."

In like manner, this concept can be extended to the holy Prophet ﷺ and his Ahlul Bayt ﷺ in that, we can praise them but cannot do justice to their exalted status. We substantiate this statement by referring to yet another prayer which Imam Ali ﷺ recited on the night of the Prophet's ﷺ migration from Mecca to Medina, when he asked Ali ﷺ to sleep in his bed so that he could safely undertake his journey. Ali ﷺ immediately agreed and recited a prayer; the relevant part of which is as follows: "I seek the shelter of Allah through the Grace of the Prophet and his Ahlul Bayt on whom You shower Your blessings; and I rely on my love for them as a shield against any harm being done to me whether apparent or latent, for I know I will be safe in a castle surrounded and protected by this 'love and attachment' that I have for them...."

For the edification of the readers, the concept of Ahlul Bayt was established after the holy matrimony took place between Imam Ali and the Lady of Light Fatima daughter of the Prophet and the subsequent births of their two sons Hassan and Hussain.

The verse (33:33) of "The Mantle" in the holy Quran attests this fact, to which the Prophet has also left a well-accepted tradition about these four members of his family being the ones known as the Ahlul Bayt. The notion of the "Holy Five" was introduced to the Ummah in general from thereon.

However, the reference to the Holy Five has been in the old scriptures dating back up to 5000 years.

My Father-in-Law, the Late Hamid Bin Shabbir has pointed out this very fact in his monumental Urdu work, *Kalematul Haqq (The Word of Truth)*. In his extensive research he discovered that Prophet Noah before setting sail upon the turbulent waters during the Deluge, had affixed a plaque on his Ark which bore a 'prayer' on it seeking the help of God through invoking the names of these Holy Five to help him safely accomplish the mission upon which he had been directed by God. This plaque was discovered by archeologists about 75 years ago and is currently retained in a museum in Russia. That prayer was in an ancient language which was finally deciphered after many months of research; and the gist of this has been noted in his original book as follows: "O my Lord, my Helper. Keep my hand with Mercy and with Your holy bodies: Mohammad, Alia (Ali), Shabbar (Hassan), Shabbir (Hussain) and Fatima. They are the biggest and most honourable. The world was created for them. So help me by these names." (For anyone wishing to gratify their curiosity, they can refer to Volume 2 of *The Truth*

Revealed, pages 113 to 117, or check this out on the YouTube in their archives for confirmation).

Because my father-in-law (in the absence of any computers or electronic assistance), had spent over 35 years in his research and manual compilation, it was truly a herculean task for which he was nonetheless rewarded by the extreme popularity and demand of this book by the Urdu speaking audience of the Indian subcontinent.

However, the fact that the Urdu text was not being embraced by the youth, it was decided by us to do an English translation albeit in a summarized form.

Unfortunately, this task was not undertaken by us till after his demise in 2002, and the first volume was published in the year 2004. It's sequence, the second volume was published ten years later, and now by the Grace of God, we are in the final stage of publishing the third volume, which also was delayed too long due to the onset of the Covid situation and its resulting fallouts.

This 3rd Volume encompasses the period of the three early Caliphs and ends with brief synopsis of the Twelve Imams of the holy Ahlul Bayt 🕋 in accordance to the Shia faith. It also includes in detail, the confiscation of the Estate of Fadak by the early Caliphs, which had been given as a gift to his beloved daughter Fatima 🕋 by her father the Prophet 🕋. It then goes on to describe the trials and tribulations encountered by Imam Ali 🕋 right from the time of the demise of the Prophet 🕋 to the end of his Caliphate and martyrdom.

This foreword would be incomplete without mentioning our close and dear departed friend Syed Hamid Razvi (and his wife Zehra) with whom we spent many hours on a daily basis for two years or more in the course of this translation. Last but not least, my better half Kaniz Fatima, (elder daughter of late author) who spent countless hours not only in the translation, but also in typesetting these three volumes over a span of past several years.

We pray for acceptance of our efforts in the presence of our Lord and Master the Twelfth Imam عجل الله فرجه who though is in occultation but is aware of our sincere endeavours.

Mir Baqar Alikhan (Son in Law)
Retired Engineer

Foreword One

Just as the rare Narcissus flower cries for its lack of recognition in a garden full of many species and blooms, it is similarly possible for the "not so discerning persons" to overlook a gem in the arena of literature when confronted with several other books stacked in a Library.

About 30 years ago, my father Majid Sahib* (*a term of respect), bought me a book and asked me to study it carefully. This was in the early stage of my life when I was hopeful and learning to become a 'Public Speaker' in the way of spreading the message of Islam within our local community. I became totally enthralled in the study of this book which was, so to speak, 'decorated' with various subjects and titles; and offered engrossing debates in advancing the virtues of the Holy Ahlul Bayt ﷺ; and backing these up by citing countless examples of homage paid by the Western Intellectuals to the Prophet ﷺ and the Imams from his Noble Family.

The Proofs and Evidence presented in connection with the arguments regarding the Khilafat following the demise of Prophet ﷺ were penned with such conviction, that the open-minded reader after its sincere perusal 'could not live without being influenced' by this book. And this is precisely what happened to me! The more I got into the depths of it, the more my appetite grew for gaining further knowledge from within its two covers. And that Book was *Kalematul Haqq*: a book illumined by the rays of Haqq (Truth) and its Author was the respected and revered person named (Syed) Hamid Bin Shabbir.

It is an accepted fact that death comes to all; but it also cannot be denied that death comes to '*the person*" but **not** to "*the personality*".

The Late Hamid Bin Shabbir Sahib was one of those blessed with an all-rounded personality that had many brilliant facets: excelling in diverse fields of worldly as well as spiritual Achievements. He spent most of his life in defending the "Right" (Haqq) and was dedicated to upholding it at all costs; and <u>that</u> precisely is why he is still 'alive and active' today: His written document is a definitive proof of his life and service. Humans are naturally created to do something "creative" in this world, but fortunate are those who, despite being in Government or other important occupations, use their valuable studies to turn their natural tastes and inclinations into writing and compilation of important evidence which bring about a change in the character of the society itself.

The Late author was not only a 'Haji' from the religious point of view, but also a successful Judge, well equipped with a worldly education. He was also an author of several books and an Excellent Poet. I still remember that in 1999, I partook in a debate organized by the **Lucknow Christian College** at the "Fair Field Hall" on the Topic of: "**Kerbala Can Change the Course of Time**". I prepared my speech using this same book and became the winner of that competition! After that, my devotion to this book increased and so did my love for its author.

Several years later in 2011 when I visited the city of Hyderabad to deliver a speech at a Majlis (Religious Gathering), I met Mr. Askari Rafiq (who also hailed from Lucknow but had settled in Hyderabad), and Mr. Mir Baqar Alikhan: both of whom were the two sons-in-law of the Late Hamid Bin Shabbir Sahib. I was overjoyed to meet two such close relatives of the person whose book I had studied and whom I had admired for so long.

Mr. Mohammad Askari Rafiq has since passed away, but prior to his demise for many years he invited me as an orator to conduct a series of five large gatherings (Majlis e Aza) regularly *every year* which he used to organize annually in Hyderabad with great sincerity and love, for commemorating and mourning the

Martyrdom of the Lady of Light Hazrat Fatima Zehra 🕌, the beloved daughter of the Holy Prophet 🕌.

Since his sad demise a few years ago, his worthy son Dr. Asad Rafiq, a resident of Chicago, has been conducting these mourning sessions annually also in Hyderabad. It was after this year's session of these gatherings that his Aunt, Mrs. Kaniz Fatima (wife of Mir Baqar Alikhan), and the elder daughter of the Late Author, requested me to pen a few lines as a foreword to be included in the 3rd Volume of *The Truth Revealed*: their English version of *Kalematul Haqq* which they have translated in a beautiful manner and provided a valuable resource for those not familiar with the Urdu language.

In concluding, I pray to the Lord Almighty to reward all those involved in getting this English version together, for their joint efforts in the compilation and printing of this important and edifying as well as an extremely interesting and beneficial version for the English-speaking readers. May Allah 🕌 give them strength and guidance.

Peace on All.

From a humble slave of God, who feels Blessed to get the Dust from the Feet of the Holy Ahlul Bayt 🕌 (*Khakpaye Ghulam e Ahlul Bayt*): Orator and Speaker (Zakir),

Syed Samar Haider Zaidi Al-Wasti
Currently residing in Lucknow, India.
3 Shabaan 1446 AH
2nd February 2025

Foreword Two

While I am not qualified to critique my father, Mr. Hamid Bin Shabbir's monumental work, *Kalematul Haqq*, I have been directed to pen a few words on the circumstances leading up to the creation of this exhaustive treatise on key aspects of Islam's historic evolution.

My father's rise from a mixed Shia/Sunni background to a level of high Irfan (Marefat`) of the Holy Ahlulbayt is indeed meteoric. Most people blindly accept the religion of their forefathers, while this practice is shunned by Allah the Almighty (Quran: 2:170).

Though Musawi Syeds, my paternal ancestors chose not to highlight their sect, possibly due to the persecution of Shias that was rampant at different times in history; so much so that several members of our family married into families practising the Sunni faith.

Consequently, my father, since childhood was exposed to different views on religion. Even before he was a teenager, he had finished reading books on the biographies of our holy 14 Infallible Ahlebait, and being an extremely intelligent and inquisitive person, not to mention a just human being (who went on to become a judge whose judgments were never overturned in higher courts), he set out to find the truth for himself at a very early stage of life.

'*Do not mix truth with falsehood nor conceal the truth while you know*'. (Quran 2:42). This was my father's guiding principle, as he suspected all along that there was a blatant mixing of truth and false propaganda!

While he was an extremely busy person (a judge, an ace hunter, a voracious reader, a poet, a father of 6 children and a learned student of classical music), his primary objective in life was to find the true Islam towards which he invested 35+ years of research, (which included long trips to remote places to collect *a single piece of evidence and/or reference*) which he later incorporated into his manuscripts which he wrote incessantly. It should be noted that there was no internet, no Wikipedia etc.

As to how he gathered such immense amount of knowledge under those circumstances is, to say the least, mind boggling. Few persons are endowed with an untiring capacity of sustained continuous mental effort - the human mind reaches a stage of saturation beyond which effective progress cannot continue. My father was one of those rare individuals who had the untiring tenacity and drive to keep on working on any project that he had set his mind upon, to the stage of not being content till the result was achieved to his satisfaction!

As youngsters we were lucky enough to be with him during school holidays, in remote districts where he was a Sessions Judge. I remember the arduous routine he had of coming home from work late, praying (Namaz), a quick supper and on with the dictation of his researched content to his faithful scribe, Mr. Muhammad Safder, late into the hours every night.

His careful research into important events in the history of mankind from the prophesies in ancient scriptures, to the 'Dawat e Zul Asheera' [Invitation by the Prophet ﷺ to the Hashimite clan], followed by the persecution of the Prophet in Mecca, his migration to Medina, the defensive battles, the last Haj, the amazing gathering at 'Ghadeer e Khum', the Prophet's last sermon, the tragic events surrounding the Prophet's demise, the incident of Saqifa, the atrocities inflicted by the 'Muslims' on Imam Ali ؑ and the rest of the holy family, right up to the tragic and horrible massacre and events of Karbala, laid bare the fact that there were only a handful of true believers among those around the Prophet ﷺ. Most were hypocrites (Munafiqoon). The great sacrifice (Zibhe Azeem, Quran 37:107) by the lord of Martyrs: Imam Hussain ؑ laid bare for all to see the hypocrisy of most of the Muslims soon after the demise of his holy Grandfather.

Kalematul Haqq originally addressed the Urdu speaking audience. However, thanks to my brother-in-law the brilliant Mr. Mir Baqar Alikhan and his wife, my amazing sister Kaniz Fatima Alikhan and their close friend Syed Hamid Razvi, and their tireless efforts involving many years, this treasure of knowledge is now available to the English-speaking community at large.

May the almighty accept the sincere efforts of all the personalities involved in this monumental task and grant them an honourable position in 'Deen' and 'Duniya' by the grace of the 14 Infallibles. Ameen!

Ali Abbas Syed, MD., FRCP (C)
Ret'd Anesthesiologist (Author's third son)

Translator's Word

It is with a deep sense of humility and thankfulness that I, Kaniz Fatima, have now been able to bring the final chapters of my late father's book to a closure and send it for a final publication.

Ever since the date of his demise over 20 years ago, this project had become an integral part of my life, wherein I was committed to extend the knowledge contained within the covers of his Urdu work *Kalematul Haqq* (which had been instrumental in converting many of its readers to the Path of the holy Ahlul Bait ﷺ) to the younger English speaking generation, so that they too could benefit from, and raise their Ma`arefat of the Infallible family of the Noble Prophet of Islam, Mohammad e Mustafa ﷺ.

My inspiration for undertaking this weighty task as a family venture was a 'letter of acknowledgement' which my father had received in my presence, and which had been sent to my father in his lifetime by an unknown stranger from a remote part of India, wherein he had written to say that he had awoken one morning after seeing a strange dream where (he believed) he was given a message from the Imam of Our Time ﷺ himself to the effect: "*Today a Noor [Light] will arrive at your home; and we have observed (endorsed) its contents*". He went on to write that while he was perplexed about the significance of this dream, to his utter surprise later that same day, he unexpectedly received a parcel delivered by the postman and sent by a friend which upon opening, he found it to be the Urdu volume of *Kalematul Haqq!* (Details given in Introduction Section of our English Volume 1).

For the edification of the readers, I had requested my brother Dr. Ali Abbas Syed FRCP(C), husband Mir Baqar Alikhan (P.Eng (C)/UK) and lastly and more importantly, a noted Scholar, Orator and Speaker from the younger generation of our time and resident of Lucknow, India: Syed Samar Haider Zaidi Al-Wasti to express their opinions in brief to shed light on random features and factors contained in this translated volume.

In closing, all thanks are due to Allah ﷻ and to the Imam of Our Time ﷿ for having given all those of us involved in its compilation, the time, health and fortitude to undertake and fulfill this project.

"So he who has done an atom's weight of good shall see it". (Holy Quran: 99:7).

Kaniz Fatima Alikhan (Daughter)

Introduction

KALEMATUL HAQQ: THE TRUTH REVEALED

Volume III [Continued from Volume II]

With a view to acquaint the reader with the sequel of events listed at the conclusion of our last, Volume II of *The Truth Revealed*, we wish to encapsulate in a nutshell the following facts for the benefit of our reader as hereunder:

Immediately after the demise of the Prophet ﷺ, Umar ibn Khattab announced that anyone who "so much as *whispered*" that the Prophet was dead would be killed!

In accordance with his long-conceived plan of preventing Ali ؑ from becoming the next Leader of the Ummah, he approached his brother-in-law Abu Obeida ibn Jarrah and offered him the Caliphate, which the latter refused.

Umar then immediately went over to Abu Bakr, and together they proceeded with haste to a place called 'Saqifa Bani Saada' to implement their strategy, without **any** qualms about abandoning their duty **and** personal obligation of joining in and performing the last (funeral) rites of their Apostle.

Being confident that Ali ؑ on the contrary, would be engrossed in attending to the Prophet ﷺ's burial and hence not be present at Saqifa to claim *his* rights, he Umar, along with some like-minded persons, initiated his plan to install a Caliph without any loss of time.

The first rationale he proffered for taking this action with such haste was that the Meccans [Qureishites] being from the same tribe as the Prophet ﷺ had greater rights over the Medinites [Ansars] for occupying the Office of the Caliphate.

Several attendees however, objected to this suggestion, claiming that if this was the case, then Ali ؑ was closest in relationship to the Prophet ﷺ and should be the rightful Caliph.

Arguments boiled over and a melee ensued; and in this confusion, Umar fearing that matters could get out of control, immediately took hold of Abu Bakr's hand saying: "Give me your hand; I, for one, offer my fealty to you as the Caliph". Uthman immediately followed and did likewise; and so did Abdur Rahman ibn Auf, Abu Obeida ibn Jarrah and Maaz ibn Jabal. A few others present at the premises also followed suit. Thus, based on a handful of allegiances, Abu Bakr was declared to be the Caliph.

Abu Bakr's period of Caliphate lasted for a little over two years and when the time of his death approached, *he* **nominated Umar** to be the next Caliph. To this effect, he dictated his will selecting Uthman as his designated scribe, albeit that in those last moments of his life he was in a 'semi-conscious' condition where he was constantly falling 'in and out' of a swoon!

Umar, upon being thus nominated, occupied the seat of Caliphate for a decade but was known to be incessantly contemplating as to **whom he should appoint as the next Caliph after him**. He toyed with various names such as Abu Obeida ibn Jarrah (a grave digger by profession), Maaz ibn Jabal and even 'Saleem' – a freed slave of Abu Hudaifa. But as most of these 'contemplated nominees' died during his own lifetime; these plans came to naught.

Eventually, when Umar himself was caught in the throes of his own death, he nonetheless continued to the end (of the proverbial 'last breath') with his persistence and relentless determination to ensure that **Ali** 🕮 **would be deprived of the Caliphate.** He appointed a committee (*Shura*) which was biased in favour of Uthman; and as such, his machinations succeeded, and Uthman became the third Caliph.

Uthman held this position for a little over twelve years and in the latter part of his Caliphate, in anticipation of his own eventual death, he also made his own will nominating his brother-in-law

Abdur Rahman ibn Auf to be the successor after him, so that Ali ﷺ would again be passed over for this office. His will, however, was not implemented due to the extreme degree of his unpopularity among the public in the last years of his Caliphate, which eventually resulted in his assassination at the hands of a rebellious Ummah.

The allotment of the Caliphate was always conducted according to an understanding within a 'certain group' among the companions as 'an exchange of favours' among themselves in a *quid pro quo* manner; and Ali ﷺ was **intentionally** excluded by their manipulative conspiracies on all occasions. Under these conditions of such murky politics, had Ali ﷺ chosen to press for his own rights, he would no doubt have been assassinated at the hands of the conniving elements present within the so called 'inner circle' of the Ummah.

Referring to the foregoing events, Ali ﷺ himself summarized the sequence of their actions in a nutshell when he said: "*You have all ensured that the reins of Caliphate will once again change hands among yourselves and have denied me of my rights*".

Finally, according to Umar's own admission, he himself affirmed at some point during his Caliphate that: "Abu Bakr was elected as a Caliph *in haste* so that **someone else** would **not** be nominated to whom we would then have been **forced** to pay our allegiance. In any case, we did not wish to see the Prophethood **_and_** Caliphate both going into the same family [of the Apostle] as that would have raised the status of the tribe of Bani Hashim even higher and given them a sense of superiority over the rest of the tribes in Arabia."

Chapter IX

A Brief Account of Some Heart-Rending Atrocities Inflicted upon the Ahlul Bayt ﷺ After the Demise of the Prophet ﷺ

9.1: The Issue of Fadak and Denial of Paternal Inheritance of Fatima ﷺ

Among the various occurrences which were responsible for breaking Hazrat Fatima Zehra ﷺ's heart, were the painful incidents such as the installation of Abu Bakr as the Caliph at the Secret Counsel of *Saqifa bani Saada*; the non-acceptance of Ali ﷺ's claim to the Caliphate; and additionally the threats, followed by an actual act of bringing fire to burn her House down while she and her entire family were still residing within! Along with these atrocities however, the event that takes prominent position as the most significant act of oppression inflicted upon her was the denial of her personal property of Fadak, and the ruling by many 'Prominent Companions' in the Ummah against her rightful ownership.

Fadak was an extremely fertile area of land watered by several natural springs, abounding with many gardens of date palms, figs, and other fruits. It was situated at about a three days' journey from the city of Madina. There were also several villages in its close vicinity.

When the Jewish fort of Khyber was conquered at the hands of Ali ﷺ, the Jewish community around the area of Fadak became fearful and apprehensive; overawed by the bravery, courage, and chivalry of Ali ﷺ. In a gesture to indicate their willingness to establish peace, as well as appease the Prophet ﷺ they presented him with this fertile plot of land known as 'Fadak' as **a *personal*** *gift* to him from their entire community. This is clearly referred to in the Holy Quran by Allah ﷻ in *Surah Hashr: "And whatever Allah restored to His Apostle from them, **you did not press forward against it on any Horse or a riding Camel** [as in battle]; but Allah gives authority to His Apostles against whom He pleases, and Allah has power over all things. Whatever Allah has restored to His Apostle from the people of the towns, it is for Allah and for the Apostle, and for [his] Near of Kin and the Orphans and the Needy and the Wayfarer so that it may not be a thing taken by turns among the rich of you; and whatever the Apostle gives you accept it, and from whatever he forbids you, **keep back**! And fear [the Wrath of] Allah; Verily Allah is severe in retribution."* (Chap 59: 6-7).

Considering the foregoing Quranic verses, Fadak was **not** part of a 'War Booty' which any Muslim from the Ummah could lay a claim to. It was purely a personal gift presented to the Prophet ﷺ by the Jews as a peace offering; and referring to this very fact Allah ﷻ sent clear instructions as to its disbursement, by *specifically* stating that since it was **not conquered** by the Muslims in any Military Campaign with soldiers riding on horses or mounted on camels' backs to achieve its victory, it was the Prophet ﷺ's prerogative to distribute it as per His command.

Consequently, in compliance with the revelation of a similar verse in Chapter 30: Surah Rome: *"Then give Thou to the Near of Kin, his due and to the Needy and the Wayfarer...."* (30:38), the Prophet ﷺ immediately awarded this Land of Fadak to his daughter Fatima ﷺ, gifting it to her in the form of '***Hiba***' as **her** *individual property* (and also that of her two sons Hasan ﷺ and Husayn ﷺ). Several eminent Sunni scholars such as Suyuti;[1] Hakam;[2] Salabi;[3]

---

[1] Tafseer Durre Manthoor, Vol IV, Pg 177, Egypt 1314 AH.

[2] Kanzul Ummal, Vol 1, Pg 228.

[3] Tafseer-ul Kashful Bayan.

Hafiz ibn Marduwiya and the author of "*Tarikh-e-Rauzatul Safa*"[4] along with many other famous scholars such as Ibn Asakir (tradition through Abu Sayeed Khudri), Sulaiman Balkhi Hanafi in his treatise[5] and many other historians have all categorically stated that Fadak was given by the Prophet ﷺ to his daughter Fatima Zahra ؑ who thereafter <u>personally handled and managed this property,</u> *even* <u>during the lifetime of her father the holy Apostle</u> ﷺ.

The income from this property was collected each year over a period in three instalments. Fatima ؑ would only keep one day's worth of it's income for her own personal expenses, while distributing the rest of it among the widows, orphans and other indigent persons; irrespective of the fact that in order to meet her own domestic expenses, she would often have to raise money to supplement her household income by manually grinding wheat in her Stone-mill at a nominal charge from other residents within her community. Regardless however, her ownership of Fadak was nonetheless acknowledged and accepted as a confirmed and documented fact by all those around her.

After the demise of her revered father the holy Prophet ﷺ, Abu Bakr who had been declared as the Caliph at *Saqifa Bani Saada*, confiscated this property and expelled the employees who were under the service of Fatima ؑ at Fadak. This property was then annexed to the State as being part of the Public Treasury. Tabari in his "Tarikh" mentions in detail the contents of the letter written by Abu Bakr to the employees of Fadak after its annexation, directing them henceforth to stop the remittance from this property to Fatima Zahra ؑ, and to send it instead to the Public Treasury under **his** Express Orders.

---

[4] Tarikh-e-Rauzatul Safa, Vol II, Pg 377, printed by Naval Kishore.

[5] Yanabul-Muwaddah.

9.2: Ayesha Instigates her Father Abu Bakr to Expropriate the Property of Fadak from the Estate of Fatima 🖼️

The German author Kurt Frischler in his book 'Ayesha: After the Prophet' has stated the following on this subject: "Fadak was the property of the Prophet who awarded the same to his daughter Fatima in his lifetime. Her husband Ali used to administer the income from this Estate. But as soon as the Apostle passed away, Ayesha asked her father to take this property away from Fatima saying that 'there is no inheritance from the Prophets, and Fatima should be denied this inheritance'.

Had there been no animosity or jealousy in Ayesha toward Fatima, then the property could have remained with Fatima; but it was not so."[6]

9.2a: Fatima 🖼️'s Bid to Reclaim Fadak as her Personal Property

The Estate of Fadak consisted of a vast area encompassing the following:

1. The Date Palms of the Tribe of Bani Nazeer
2. The Land given by the Ansars of Madina.
3. Seven Orchards known as "The Gardens of Mohriq".
4. One third of the Land of "Vadi-ul-Qara" and some of the other surrounding areas. The details of these are referenced in "Tehsarul Bukhari"[7]

---

[6] Ayesha After The Prophet – by Kurt Frischler.

[7] Tehsar-ul Bukhari Part XI, - Book of 'Jihad-wa-Siyar', Pg 76; Section XII – Pg 62.

After the confiscation of Fadak, in a bid to reclaim legal ownership of her property, Fatima ﷺ filed a formal complaint against the Authorities. In this matter she took with her Imam Ali ﷺ, her two sons Imam Hasan ﷺ and Imam Husayn ﷺ, along with Umme Aiman the housemaid of the Prophet ﷺ [since his childhood] as her witnesses. Abu Bakr demanded proof that this property was given to her by her father [the Prophet ﷺ]. In response, Fatima Zahra ﷺ presented Umme Aiman as her first witness. The latter upon taking the witness stand questioned Abu Bakr as follows: "Do you bear witness that the Prophet ﷺ said that I am one of those who will surely go to heaven?" Abu Bakr replied: "Yes, I confirm this." Upon hearing this she stated: "I now bear witness that the Prophet ﷺ awarded this Land of Fadak to Fatima ﷺ as her personal property (*Hiba*)".

Imam Fakhruddin Razi in his book 'Tafsir-e-Kabir' and Baladhuri in his 'Futooh-Al-Baldaan' have both stated that a slave girl of Ayesha the Prophet's widow, (known by the name of "Riyah") also came forward and testified in favour of Fatima ﷺ. According to 'Habib-us-Siyar' and 'Ma`arij-un-Nabuwah' it is recorded that apart from this verbal evidence, Fatima ﷺ also produced written documentation in court, as proof of her ownership of the said property.

Allama Syed Mohammed Saleh Khashfi Tirmizi Hanafi ibn Mir Abdullah Mishkeen has recorded the details of the proprietorship of Fadak in Hazrat Fatima Zahra ﷺ's name in his book titled: 'Manaqib-e-Murtazavi'[8] in the following words: "After the Conquest of Khyber, Imam Ali ﷺ went towards the precincts of Fadak on the instructions of Prophet ﷺ, to draw up a peace treaty as the inhabitants of that area had already expressed their intent to

---

[8] Compiled in 1037 AH and presented to the Moghul Emperor Shah Jahan.

make terms peacefully and not to engage with the Muslims in any further confrontation. It was at this point that Angel Gabriel 🕊 descended and informed the Prophet 🕊 that Allah 🕊 had decreed that any Gift that was being offered by the people of that area as an endowment in the way of Allah 🕊 and His Apostle 🕊, should be forthrightly awarded to Hazrat Fatima 🕊 and her two sons Hasan 🕊 and Husayn 🕊. In accordance with this Divine Command from Allah 🕊, the Prophet 🕊 had a document drawn up which he then personally presented to Fatima 🕊; **thereby establishing her rightful ownership to the property of Fadak in his own lifetime.**"

This very document was eventually produced by Hazrat Fatima Zahra 🕊 in the Court of Abu Bakr when she presented her claim to Fadak. This fact has been verified by Sibte-Ibne Jauzi in his research and supported by Nuruddin Ali bin Burhan Halaby Shafei in his book 'Aln-Nisaan-al-Uyoon'.

When Abu Bakr examined this document, he issued a Writ sanctioning the reversal of ownership of Fadak to Fatima 🕊. When Umar saw this turn of events, he asked Abu Bakr: "How do you propose to feed the Muslims?" Thereafter he snatched the document from Abu Bakr, spat upon it and tore it to pieces; he then threw it on the ground and stamped upon it! This incident is also described in detail by ibn Hadid in his Book of History.[9]

Bukhari[10] relates that Abu Bakr denied Fatima Zahra 🕊 her inheritance of Fadak along with some of her other properties. Umar did likewise. Uthman on the other hand, when he became the Caliph, awarded Fadak to his brother-in-law Marwan as his 'personal estate' which generated an ongoing income for the latter's exclusive use. Moreover, Abu Bakr even concocted a

---

[9] Tarikh- ibn Hadid, Vol II, Part 17 Pg 307.

[10] Taysur-al-Bukhari, Part 16, Kitab-ul-Jehad wa Siyar, Pg 63.

tradition stating that he had heard the Prophet ﷺ saying that: *"Nahno Ma`asherul Ambiya La Naris wala Nurus, wama taraknaho Sadaqa: We from the group of prophets do not inherit nor do we leave any inheritance. Whatever we leave is for charity."* However, he could produce no other witness to second this 'so called' Prophetic Tradition, and no other person came forward to support him on this either.

Hazrat Fatima ﷺ refuted this statement and denied that the Prophet ﷺ had ever said anything which would go contrary to the edicts of the holy Quran. She then proceeded to quote several Quranic verses herself, which clearly illustrated how the previous prophets had not only inherited from each other but had also passed on their inheritances to their posterity. Among the many verses that she recited to prove the Legitimacy of the previous prophets' Rights of Inheritance, were a few that were related to Zakariya ﷺ who in spite of old age had actively prayed for a child that would become his heir after him: Surah Aale Imran: *"Zakariya prayed to His Lord: O Lord grant me from Thee a good offspring (heir)..."* (3:38). And from Surah Ambiya: *"O Lord! Leave me not alone without an issue though Thou art the best of Inheritors."* (21:89). Then again, from Surah Marium: *"And verily I fear my kindred (cousins) after me, and my wife is barren, therefore grant me from Thyself an heir who shall inherit me and inherit from the family of Jacob (Yaqoob) and make him one, My Lord, with whom Thou art well pleased".* (19:5-6); and elsewhere about Hazrat Sulaiman ﷺ stating: *"...And Sulaiman was Dawood's heir...."* These verses clearly confirm that not only do prophets inherit from each other, but they also pass on their inheritances to their offspring, or else Zakariya ﷺ would certainly not have prayed to Allah ﷻ to grant him a child who would become his inheritor.

A significant point to be noted here is that whenever the holy Book discusses the inheritance of 'Ilm' (**Knowledge** and/or the

'**Book**'), the instructions are extremely <u>specific</u>. But where 'Ilm' is not mentioned then the inheritance *specifically pertains to ownership of a materialistic or Worldly Commodity.* This is confirmed by the noted Sunni scholar Allama Fakhruddin Razi in his 'Tafsir' where he writes that in verses five and six of Surah Marium, the use of the phrase ('*Yarsoni wa Yarso'*) particularly relates to the inheritance of physical property rather than **Knowledge** (Ilm)' or the **Book** (Kitab)'. This is further confirmed by the fact that ibn Abbas, and another exegete Hasan, as well as Zahak, and some other companions who were present on that occasion, expressed their surprise at such a Hadith quoted by Abu Bakr which was in *total* contradiction to the holy Quran; and one which none of these companions had ever heard before!

Allama Fakhruddin Razi quotes in his 'Tafsir'[11]on the authority Hasan the Exegete, who was present in the court of Abu Bakr on that occasion; that "inheritance" in the holy verses quoted by Fatima Zahra ☙ distinctly referred to the inheritance of worldly property and **not to 'Ilm'** (connected to spiritual inspiration or profound knowledge), because the benefaction of 'Ilm' is directly awarded by Allah ☙ to whoever **He chooses;** *and not necessarily handed down in posterity.* As such, Allama Razi writes that all companions present on that occasion *also understood that any mention of "Inheritance" by Fatima ☙ was alluding to the physical property and not to any spiritual endowment.* Likewise, even Abu Bakr, when he quoted his novel and singular Hadith of "No Inheritance" (which had never been heard by anyone before), also clearly meant his denial to be about worldly wealth and property and not 'Ilm' or something spiritual.

Additionally, well-known Sunni scholars such as Baidawi, Allama Baghavi, Zamakshari, ibn Jarir-e-Tabari and others; when

---

[11] 'Tafsir-e-Kabir' – Allama Fakhruddin Razi, Vol 6, Pg 402.

they discuss about inheritance, they allude to 'material property' and not to 'Prophet-hood' or 'Knowledge'. As an example, to illustrate the inheritance of property by prophets and their children, we quote from Quran that Hazrat Sulaiman ﷺ inherited One Thousand pure-bred horses from his father Hazrat Dawood ﷺ; which he, Dawood ﷺ had received as a gift from his father in his own lifetime. But as for his **Prophethood (Knowledge)**, Hazrat Sulaiman ﷺ had already been endowed with this by Allah ﷻ *during the lifetime of his father Dawood ﷺ itself*, rather than it being passed on to him later as an "inheritance" after his father's demise.

In the case of the 'tangible' property of **Fadak**, the rationale behind Fatima ﷺ's claim was to establish the fact that this property was **not** "an inheritance" which she was requisitioning in the court after the demise of her parent; but rather, that **it was her own 'personal property already under her ownership'** as it had been a Gift/ *'Hiba'* bequeathed to her by her revered father, the Prophet ﷺ, **during his own lifetime.** As such, she was only claiming what was already hers! Additionally, she pointed out that notwithstanding the fact that she was claiming her **own** property of Fadak **back** based on her having been *awarded this property as 'Hiba'* by the Prophet ﷺ in his lifetime; but **even had this not been the case** and *the matter were to be argued on "grounds of Inheritance,"* then, she reasoned, she would *still* have been entitled to inherit it because she was the *sole* surviving heir of her father!

In some narrations it is stated that when faced with the proof of her rights of *'Hiba'* Abu Bakr not only got convinced and ordered the return of Fadak to Fatima ﷺ, but also issued a document to this effect. But Umar intervened and said that "Fatima was only one-woman bearing witness, but they needed other witnesses to confirm the fact". Abu Bakr accordingly changed his mind and asked Fatima ﷺ to produce additional witnesses. The document issued by Abu Bakr was snatched from her by Umar who then spat on it, tore it up, and stamped on it after throwing it upon the ground! Tabari[12] commenting on this display of unwarranted behavior by Umar writes that some people present in court enquired from Abu Bakr as to **who** [?] was the *de facto* ruler; to which Abu Bakr replied: "It is Umar; although the people have paid their fealty to me!"

It is worth considering that in light of the manifold Quranic references quoted by Fatima 🌸, does such display of Abu Bakr's behaviour measure up to Islamic standards [?] and what will be the resultant impressions created in an "unbiased" reader's mind upon reviewing the entire circumstances? Rather than giving our own opinion, we refer here to a quote from Maulana Abul Ala Maudoodi[13] which he had based upon a reliable tradition from 'Kanzul Ummal'[14] wherein it is stated that: "The person who is appointed to a position of authority for the Muslim Ummah but decides the affairs among them **contrary to the Book of Allah 🕋, incurs Allah's Wrath and His Curse...**"!

9.3: Rejection of Hazrat Fatima 🌸's Claim for Fadak and Non-Acceptance of Hadrat Ali 🌸 and Hasnain 🌸 as Witnesses

Lady Fatima 🌸 brought Hazrat Ali 🌸, Imams Hasan 🌸 and Husayn 🌸 and Umme Aiman as her witnesses. But Umar came forward again and said: "Ali's evidence is unacceptable because he is her husband. Hasnain 🌸, her two sons are still minors and hence their

---

[12] 'Tarikh-e-Khulufa' – by Tabari, Part 3, Pg 240.

[13] 'Khilafat wa Mulukiat' – by Maulana Maudoodi, Pg 72.

[14] 'Kanzul Ummal' – Vol. 5, Tradition No. 2505.

evidence is also not valid. Umme Aiman's statement is only that of one woman and her evidence as such is incomplete without another [!]; therefore, the claim must be denied, and Fadak and other associated properties are not to be granted."

Baladhuri in his book 'Futooh-Al-Baldan' records that when Abu Bakr demanded evidence Fatima 🕮 presented Ali 🕮 but Abu Bakr said he needed another witness, to which she 🕮 presented Umme Aiman as the second. Thereupon Abu Bakr said that the witness of one man and one woman was insufficient, as the 'Shariah' demands two men, or one man and two women. Based on this he could not accept her claim, because even her two sons were minor in ages and unacceptable by his standards.

It is an instinct in every child to hold a parents' possession dear to the heart. The attachment is not solely for the monetary value but rather, it is an attachment for sentimental reasons as well. Fatima 🕮 was hurt not only because she was denied her father's inheritance contrary to the practices of all previous Prophets inheriting *as well as* leaving behind inheritances; but rather, the real blow to her sentiments was that her claim was deemed <u>invalid</u> **despite the earlier announcements by the Prophet 🕌 that she was the Leader of All The Women in the Universe (*Sayyedatul Nisa-al-Aalemeen*)**! Moreover, the holy Quran had also certified her as being the most pure and sinless person according to the *Ayah Tatheer* – the Verse of Purification: (33:33). Despite possessing all these credentials, her claim was labelled by both Abu Bakr and Umar as being "Flawed and Fallible"!

Furthermore, Ali 🕮 who had been endowed with the title of '*Qaseem-ul-Jannah wan-Naar* - The Allocator of Heaven And Hell' by Allah 🕌 and His Prophet; and while Imams Hasan 🕮 and Husayn 🕮 had been given the title of "*Sayyedai-Shabaab-e-Ahle-Jannah* - The Leaders of The Youth of Paradise", they were yet all rejected and their evidence was "judged" to be "unacceptable" by these two sheiks wielding authority in the Court of Caliphate!

By comparison, a case involving the Prophet ﷺ's companion Jabir ibn Abdullah Ansari had once been ruled in his favour based *on his solitary statement alone* [!] the rationale being offered that he was a 'trusted **Companion** of the Holy Prophet' and as such, *needed no other witnesses to back him up*! Such type of "double-standard behaviour" clearly illustrates that in contrast to others, the noble family of the Holy Prophet ﷺ was being *intentionally* disparaged and insulted and being subjected to a derogatory treatment after the demise of the holy Apostle.

At this stage we appeal to the seekers of 'Truth and Justice' to carefully examine a few pertinent facts noted below, to arrive at a fair assessment of the social conditions that were created by the changing behaviours of these "close companions and prominent members" of the Ummah:

1. The status of Fatima ﷤: She was given the titles of '*Sayyedatun Nisa-ul-Aalemeen* - Leader of The Women on The Universe' and '*Khatoon-e-Mehshar* - The First Lady of The Day of Judgment' by Allah ﷻ and His holy Prophet ﷺ. Additionally, she was endowed with a certificate of 'Immaculate Purification' in the Holy Quran (Chapter 33:33) wherein Allah ﷻ Himself bore witness to her truthfulness!

2. For the Guidance of the Ummah she was equal in status to the holy Prophet ﷺ, particularly so for the women among the Muslims. She was also gifted with a distinctive quality by Allah ﷻ of being able to invoke 'His Authority' and/or wield special powers which were rendered under her control by His Command.

3. As previously mentioned, along with her **absolute purity,** her unique trait of being **sinless** had also been verified by

the Almighty Lord in the 'Verse of Purity' known as '*Ayah Tatheer*' (33:33) of the holy Quran.

4. In his prophetic statements made on several occasions, the holy Prophet ﷺ had often referred to her as being **part of his 'Self'**: '*Bizzatun Minni*'; and he was known to always stand up and greet her whenever she entered in his presence and receiving her honourably whenever she joined him.

5. According to a tradition noted from Ayesha in 'Mishkat al Masaabi', the 'Father and Daughter' were so alike in their gait and mannerisms that it was difficult to differentiate or find any variance between the two of them from a distance.

6. As regards Ali ﷺ, he was given the appellation of being the 'Lord and Master (*Maula*) of the Believers' by the Prophet ﷺ and invested with the credentials of being '*Lisaan-Ullah*' - the 'Word of Allah' and yet his testimony was rejected.

7. In another oft repeated, unanimously accepted tradition, the Prophet ﷺ had consistently made his companions aware that "*Truth is with Ali and Ali is with Truth*" and also "*Truth follows Ali-e-Murtuza wherever he goes*".

8. In addition, several noted Sunni scholars such as Hakim in his 'Mustadrak', Dailami in his book 'Firdous ul Akhbar', Tabarani in his 'Al Kabir', Ibn Jauzi in his 'Usdul Ghabah' and many others have taken an authentic tradition from Ammar ibn Yasser wherein he says that the holy Prophet ﷺ said: "*O Ali! Heaven is for the one who befriends you **and acknowledges you as truthful**, and **Hell is for the one who** holds enmity toward you **and Denies your Veracity.** On the Day of Judgment, you will be the one who will decide the fate of the people between Heaven and Hell.*"

Considering the foregoing, it is now le ft to the readers to determine the Fate of **those persons** present in the court that day, who ruled against Ali 🕮's evidence and pronounced it to be "unacceptable"!

Even the testimony of Umme Aiman, the wife of Zaid and the mother of Osama bin Zaid was rejected and deemed "incomplete" despite her having been vouched by the holy Prophet 🕮 as *one who was among the 'Dwellers of Heaven!'*[15]

It is also recorded in 'Mishkat al Masabi' [Chapter: 'Manaqib-e-Ahle-Bayt-un-Nabi'], that Ayesha herself had stated: "Apart from the Prophet 🕮, I have not seen a person more truthful than (his daughter) Fatima."

The sincere scholar is once again requested to contemplate and decide upon Abu Bakr's decision to deny Fatima 🕮 a property which was already in her possession, and which had been awarded to her by her revered Father during his own lifetime. Notwithstanding these witnesses and several other evidence which had been produced by Fatima 🕮, common sense dictates that the prophet 🕮 **would have** left her *some worldly property* because of the Quranic injunctions (17:26, 30:38) which had already been sent to him commanding him to "*award to his relatives what is due*". But even if such an Order had not been sent, it stands to reason that the Prophet 🕮 would have given some inheritance to his only surviving child; more so because he had utilized and spent *the entire fortune* of the mother of his daughter, Lady Khadija 🕮, for the propagation of Islam in its' earlier days.

Then again, considering the clear Quranic instruction: "*Give to the kin her due*" is it conceivable that the holy Prophet **would have NOT acted** upon it? Most certainly he obeyed this Command of Allah 🕮 as it was a well-known fact among the residents that Fatima 🕮 was duly in possession of the property of Fadak while her father the Apostle of Allah 🕮 was still alive. In any case, also

---

[15]Traditions according to countless Sunni Scholars.

from the general societal point of view, it is a universally accepted fact that '*possession is Nine-Points-out-of-Ten*' *in the eye of Law*! Despite all this, why then was she dealt with as being a 'False Claimer'? Was there any justification in the treatment meted out by them to a personality who was certified by Allah 🕮 as being 'Truthful and Sinless' beyond a shadow of a doubt?

It would have been a different situation had the property **not** been in her possession, and Fatima 🕮 had filed a claim for it, in which case asking her to bring in witnesses as evidence could have been excused. But this was not the case. The property was *already* in her possession and to confiscate it from her and **then** demand that *she* produce evidence to establish her claim is against the "*Sharah*" and beyond any form of Earthly Justice. It is not as if we have **now** taken up this issue 1400 years later and labelled it as an "Injustice", but rather, Fatima Zahra 🕮 *herself* had taken this matter up because *she* had considered it to be an Injustice to herself at the hands of those who had taken hold of the reins of 'power'; to the extent that she was so displeased by their actions that she did not speak to either Abu Bakr or Umar for the remainder of her short life. She even left a will to the effect that these two should not be allowed to participate in her funeral when she died.

It is deplorable and inexcusable, not to mention a downright **disgrace** for the religion of Islam that these two persons who claimed to be the "representatives of the holy Prophet 🕮 after him" treated the infallible members of the very same Prophet's family in this demeaning manner. Close family members who had been accepted as being the most truthful by Divine approval from God Himself.

In 'Sunan-e-Abu-Dawood' its writer puts forth an argument that when any evidence is presented by a reliable and truthful person before any 'fair-minded Judge', the statement of that single truthful person is accepted as being 'sufficient'. In this respect he cites the case of Khuzaima ibn Thabit Ansari, wherein he relates a tradition concerning the Prophet ﷺ himself, who accepted solo evidence given by the former where, considering the past record of his truthfulness, the Prophet ﷺ accepted Khuziama's evidence as being equivalent to that of "two people". This was in the matter related to an Arab who after having sold a Camel to the Prophet ﷺ turned around and claimed that the camel was (still) his private property. The Prophet ﷺ asked for witnesses, and Khuzaima stepped forward and said: "O Prophet! I am certain that this Camel belongs to you, because I am sure about your truthfulness and infallibility!"

Allama Jarullah Zamakhshari while discussing the origin of the title of the 'Twin Witnesses' given to Khuzaima, writes in his book 'Rabi-al-Abrar' that once a Jew demanded the return of a loan from the Prophet ﷺ, who replied saying that he had already returned it in full. The Jew insisted upon bringing a witness. The Prophet ﷺ asked the congregation as to who would come forward from among them and vouch as his witness? Again, Khuziama volunteered saying: Ĭ am ready to be a witness on your behalf". The Prophet ﷺ in turn said: "But you were not present at the time of the dealing, so how can you be a witness for me?" To this he replied: "O Prophet! When we have believed in the _Revelations_ that you have recited to us, then how can we distrust your word in other (ordinary) matters?" Khuziama's evidence was accepted; and thenceforth he came to be known as "_Zul-Shahadatain_ – the man worth the weight of two witnesses"! This same incident is recorded by Naishapuri in his 'Tafsir'.

Ali Muttaqi[16] has written that the Prophet ﷺ, as well as Abu Bakr, Umar and Uthman were known to decide cases based on the

---

[16] 'Kanzul Ummal'- 'Kitab-us-Shahadat – (Book of Evidence), Vol 4, Pg 6.

evidence given by a single person, **provided** the person took an oath about his own truthfulness and veracity.

Maulana Shibli[17] cites several incidents regarding Umar when he was content to accept the evidence of a single person as being 'sufficient' for making his decisions, not just once but on an ongoing basis; and states that he continued to rely on this methodology on many of the day-to-day cases during his reign. We once again appeal to the unbiased and fair-minded reader to contemplate about the evidence given by Fatima ॐ, Ali ॐ, Hasain ॐ and Umme Aiman RA being rejected by the court as being '**unacceptable**', in spite of the fact that the evidence was not coming **from a single lone person**, but from a whole group of honest individuals! What else was needed?

It will not be out of place to cite here an incident which occurred during the Caliphate of Ali ॐ when on his way to Siffeen, he lost his armour. Upon search, it was discovered to be in the possession of a Jewish person. When questioned, as to how he obtained this armour, the Jew simply stated that 'since it is in my possession it is mine' at which point the matter was brought before the Judge (*Khazi Shari*) for a decision. The *Khazi* asked Imam Ali ॐ to produce his witnesses. Imam Ali As replied that he would present his son Imam Hasan ॐ and his slave Qamber. The *Khazi* stated that Imam Hasan ॐ's testimony could not be acceptable being that of a son's for his father. Imam ॐ replied: "I am surprised that you will not accept the evidence of Hasan who along with his brother Husayn has been designated as the 'Leader of the Youths of Paradise' by Allah?" Upon hearing this, the Jew exclaimed in a loud voice: "Verily this armour belongs to Ali ॐ!"

In any case, this incident clearly illustrates the fact that the relationship of the witness should be overlooked in cases where

---

[17] Al Farooq – Maulana Shibli, Pg 486-487.

the character and truthfulness of the person bearing witness is well established. This is also the universally accepted "norm" in all legal cases dealt with throughout the world.

Ibne Abil Hadid the author of "Sharah Nahjul Balagha" writes that he once asked his tutor Ali bin Farqi (who was a teacher in an Islamic school of Baghdad) as to whether Lady Fatima ﷺ was not a truthful person? The teacher replied in the affirmative that indeed she was most truthful. He then asked him: "If this was so, then why did Abu Bakr while being aware of her truthfulness, reject her claim with respect to Fadak?" Upon this, the teacher gave a meaningful smile and said: "Had Abu Bakr acknowledged her claim for Fadak based on accepting her as a '**Siddiqa**' (the 'Most Truthful'), then she would have been back the very next day and claimed the right of Caliphate for her husband Ali ﷺ; and based on his own acceptance of her veracity in the one matter, he Abu Bakr, would have had **no choice but** to also honour her word in the matter of the Caliphate and vacate it in favour of Ali ﷺ! It was solely due to this consideration in his own self interest, that he deemed it necessary to reject her claim."

9.4: Acceptance of Jabir's Claim Without Resorting to any Witnesses

During the Caliphate of Abu Bakr and shortly after the rejection of Fatima ﷺ's claim in the matter of the Estate of Fadak, Jabir ibn Abdullah Ansari put forward his own claim on a share of the booty received from Bahrain. Jabir said that the Prophet ﷺ had promised him a certain amount from the money which was expected to be received from Bahrain. It is reported that Jabir was eventually paid three times of what he had asked for. The rationale given was that: 'being the companion of the Prophet ﷺ his word was reliable and trustworthy' [!] The details of this are recorded in the books of

Bukhari, Muslim and Tabaqat ibn Saad, that Jabir claimed that the Prophet ﷺ had said that when the money (*Maal-e-Ghanimah*) is received from Bahrain, he Jabir, would be given a share from the booty. When the money eventually arrived after the demise of the Prophet, it was announced that anyone laying claim to their share should come forward and collect their portions. When Jabir approached with his claim, Abu Bakr voluntarily gave him three times his share <u>without demanding any witnesses</u> from him, simply because he was a trusted companion of the Prophet ﷺ! Jabir had only asked for 500 Dirhams as the promised amount, but Abu Bakr gave him an additional One Thousand, making it three times more than his claim!

These same three sources[18] have recorded another confirmed fact that the Prophet ﷺ's headgear (*Amama*), his cloak and his sword, along with his mule were all given to Ali ؏ as part of his inheritance after the Prophet ﷺ's demise. Furthermore, they have also written that none of the Muslims raised any objection or demanded that these be taken back from Ali ؏ and distributed among others as 'charity'. The question that arises here is that if these items were not an *'Inheritance'* but **charity** (*"Sadaqaat"* as per the Hadith quoted by Abu Bakr), then why was it that no one came forward demanding that these bequests not be given to Ali ؏ as 'Charity' is forbidden on him; but rather, they be given away to others entitled to receive 'charity' from the possessions left by the Prophet ﷺ, since according to Abu Bakr, 'Inheritance' was something that "no prophet leaves behind"? It clearly stands to reason that had the Prophet ﷺ left no heir, and these bequests had been a part of his *"Sadaqaat"* (charity), then someone or the other from the Muslim Ummah would've certainly expressed a wish to have them as a 'blessed souvenir' for themselves; or, at the least,

---

[18] Bukhari, Muslim and Tabaqat ibn Saad.

demanded that these items associated with the holy Prophet ﷺ be stored in the Public Treasury as a mark of respect, and not given to Ali Ibne Abi Taleb. One must ponder as to why this endowment to Ali ﷺ was treated as an 'Inheritance' rather than charity, and what was the reason or criteria on which the distinction was made with respect to the property of Fadak?

The answer is that it was solely for the purpose of denying a lucrative property to Fatima Zahra ﷺ, that this false tradition about "non-inheritance" was concocted, because this same rule of "non-inheritance" was clearly not applied to the wives' of the holy Prophet ﷺ. The various chambers belonging to the wives of the Prophet ﷺ were individually allotted as "inheritance" to them after his demise. In fact, these dwellings even came to be associated with their names such as the 'House of Umm Salma, House of Ayesha, House of Hafsa' and so on and so forth. If those houses were not considered as part of their inheritances from the Prophet ﷺ, then even the widows of the Prophet ﷺ should have been ordered to evacuate; and these properties should have been turned over to the Public Treasury. But this did not happen. In fact, they continued to live in them to the end of their lives, and these became their personal properties which were eventually passed down to their relatives as "inheritances" upon their individual deaths.

Interestingly, none of the wives were asked to produce any evidence to prove that the chamber allotted to each one of them was in fact under their individual ownership! The fact of their "being in possession of their piece of property" was taken as sufficient proof of their ownership! Yet the property of Fadak, regardless of the fact of it being in the **sole possession of Fatima Zahra** ﷺ was nonetheless confiscated by those very same persons who, [wielding their newfound authority] ruled that the wives were entitled to their share of inheritance **but not the daughter!**

By comparison, we note that in the year 86 AH when the Omayyad Caliph Waleed bin Abdul Malik wanted to expand the Masjid-e-Nabawi ﷺ, he issued an edict to evict the descendants of the family of Ahlul Bayt ؑ: Hasan bin Hasan (also known as Hasan-e-Musannah) and his wife Fatima bint Husayn ؑ living in its adjacent premises. The order was to forcefully remove their personal belongings from the house and if they refused to vacate: to demolish the house right over their heads! On the contrary, in a similar situation, when Hajjaj bin Yousuf ordered that the relatives of Umar occupying the house of Hafsa bint Umar to be removed from *their* house because of the intended expansion of the same Mosque, the same Waleed over-ruled Hajjaj and issued an order that the house be left intact as a mark of respect to the descendants of Umar ibn Khattab![19]

However, the treatment meted out to Fatima ؑ's property was in direct contrast to the foregoing. On the face of it, this may appear to be due to the lucrative revenue generated by Fadak, but the main reason was political intrigue. As noted in 'Tabaqat-Ibne-Saad'[20] Abu Bakr gifted the entire region of Al-Jorf to Zubair, and Umar further awarded the entire property of Al Ateeq to him! Eventually when Zubair ibn Awwam died, his personal wealth was estimated at 520,000,000 Dirhams! He had eleven houses in Madina, two in Basra, one in Kufa, one in Egypt and a huge landholding in Gaza. [Ref: Bukhari].

Apart from Zubair, Talha and Abdur Rahman ibn Auf, Uthman the third Caliph, had also accumulated untold amount of wealth that was distributed to their inheritors; to the extent of hacking **logs of solid gold** down into pieces using axes; to the extreme

---

[19] Jasb-al-Quloob, Pg 173; Wafa-al Wafa, Pg 363; Tarikh-e-Ahmadi, Pg 345.

[20] 'Tabaqat ibn Saad' – translated by Abdullah Imadi, Part 5, Vol 2, Pg 57.

limit that the very hands of the 'hackers' got bruised and blistered from the effort required!

The widows of the Prophet ﷺ were also showered with enormous amounts of wealth and were also assigned a pension of 24,000 Dirhams each. The travesty of behaviour by these Caliphs is that despite the Quranic Injunction of "*Muwaddat*" (Love) towards the Ahlul Bayt, and several Prophetic enjoinders to adhere to them, the treatment meted out to them was exactly the opposite! It was obviously part of a well conceived intrigue to behave towards the Ahlul Bayt in a manner such that it would diminish and belittle their status, so that the Muslim Ummah would eventually pay scant heed to their position; while simultaneously they continued their efforts in working towards strengthening the position of those who had usurped the power into their own hands.

A review of these incidents of history and the severe circumstances that were brought into play by the 'people in power' which engulfed the holy family such as: the burning of the Door of Fatima ﷺ's house, throwing the rope around Ali ﷺ's neck and forcibly dragging him in their attempts to coerce him to pay his fealty to Abu Bakr; and the adoption of other similar oppressive actions to debase the family of the Prophet ﷺ eventually paved the way to the Great Tragedy of Kerbala, where the grandson of the Prophet ﷺ and his faithful band of devoted companions were brutally massacred; and the sacrilegious and heinous act of actually beheading the grandson of the holy Prophet ﷺ **most astoundingly** became acceptable to a majority of the Muslim Ummah! These acts were surprisingly conducted by some of those who had been _companions_ of the Prophet ﷺ, along with many others who were considered to be "pious" and even known to be the "*Huffaz-el-Quran*" - [those who memorized the Quran by heart]!

To add insult to injury, the ladies of the household of the Prophet ﷺ along with their *children*, were taken captives and marched through the streets from Kerbala to Damascus being tagged as "Prisoners of War", denied of their shawls and veils [*Hijabs*] as well as their 'outer cloaks' which were generally regarded as an essential part of formal gear of any person from a respectable family background.

The route that was chosen was the longest possible one to flaunt and parade them through the maximum number of cities to humiliate them; and to display the severed head of Imam Husayn ﷺ and his companions as being that of "Rebels".

In conclusion, we ask our fair-minded readers to reflect not only upon these atrocities but also the ones that were perpetrated by all three earlier Caliphs upon the family of the Prophet ﷺ immediately after his demise. which undoubtedly set a precedent for the later generations to follow up with their own brand of atrocities against this holy household.

Human decency demands, (not to mention that it is also a moral obligation) for us to comfort and console the orphans and treat them with kindness. Hazrat Fatima ﷺ's age according to the Sunni scholars' description was 24, while according to the Shia sources she was barely 18 years old at the time of the demise of her revered father ﷺ. At this tender age of being orphaned, she was denied her inheritance; the Estate of Fadak bequeathed to her by her father was confiscated; fire was brought to her house; a loud and harsh voice was known to have threatened her and the inmates of her house with dire consequences for non-compliance of the new Caliph's orders; and finally the burning door to the entrance of her house was forcibly broken down and thrust upon her, crushing her between the wall and the heavy fallen door; resulting in not only her ribs being broken but simultaneously also causing her to abort the child she was carrying in her womb [!]; while also causing other physical injuries which eventually lead to her death [martyrdom] at a young age in her youth.

Contrast this behaviour to another incident[21] which occurred not too far into the future when the orphaned daughter of Usama ibn Zaid paid a visit to the Omayyad Caliph Umer ibn Abdul Aziz. He placed her in a position of honour in his own seat, sat respectfully in front of her and gave her whatever she asked for! This was the daughter of a "*slave* of the Prophet ﷺ" whereas the treatment meted out to the *daughter* of the Prophet ﷺ by the two Sheiks [Umar and Abu Bakr] is worthy of reflection with an open mind and a fair and impartial contemplation about their harsh and callous behaviour.

9.5: Another Review on the "Concocted Tradition" Related by Abu Bakr

In rejecting Hazrat Fatima Zahra ﷺ's claim to her property of Fadak, as discussed, Abu Bakr announced a hitherto unheard-of Hadith (tradition) quoting the holy Prophet ﷺ as having said: "We group of Prophets [Ambiya] neither inherit nor leave behind any Inheritance. Whatever we leave is only for charity (*Sadaqaat*)."

As far as Hazrat Ali ﷺ, Fatima ﷺ and Abbas ibn Abdul Muttalib were concerned, they never accepted this tradition and rejected it as being false and a lie! In 'Sharah-e-Nahjul Balagha'[22] ibn Abil Hadeed relates from Abi Jafar Naqib Yahya ibn Muhammad Basri that: Ali, Fatima and Abbas never accepted this tradition and in one voice always **denied it as being a lie**. This is supported by the writer of 'Mashiraat-un-Nisa'[23] where he states that Hazrat Fatima

---

[21] Allama Jalaluddin Suyuti – quotes a tradition from Abu Umer.

[22] 'Sharah-e-Nahjul Balagha', Part 16, Pg 318 – Allama ibn Abil Hadeed.

[23] 'Mashiraat-un-Nisa': Vol 2, Pg 26, - printed in Egypt.

🌺 said the following: *"O Group of Muslims! Listen carefully: that you have denied me from my father's inheritance! O Son of Abu Qahafa, does Allah not approve of one inheriting from their fathers? Most certainly you have lied in this matter!"*

The foregoing is reiterated by another reliable Sunni scholar Hafez Abu Bakr Shahaab who writes[24] that Ali 🌺 and Fatima 🌺 and Hazrat Abbas RA never accepted the Hadith of **"Nahno Ma'asharal Ambiya..."** and argued that *"how could it be possible that the Prophet 🌺 would relate this tradition to others, but conceal it from us, when we are his inheritors and as 'family' we were the ones most affected by this?"*

Again, in another famous book 'Tafsir-e-Kabir'[25] Allama Fakhruddin Razi writes: "In this matter, since Ali, Fatima, and Abbas were the persons to be affected by this; they would have also been the most deserving to have been taken into confidence by the Prophet. They were also the most educated, knowledgeable, and pious persons; *whereas Abu Bakr* was **not** from amongst the ones' who would have been impacted by the terms and conditions of this Hadith. Therefore, since Abu Bakr was **not** one of those who would inherit from the Prophet anyway, **why** would the Prophet have discussed this issue with the **one person who was not connected with the matter of his inheritance in *any way whatsoever*, and *why* would he 🌺 not have told this to the persons who were his *direct* descendants and his **actual** inheritors?"

This so-called tradition has also been rejected by several Sunni scholars as being contrary to the Quranic precepts and injunctions. We will later cite a reference of a Sunni scholar in connection with this matter. First off for now, let us review as to how it is possible

---

[24] 'Nasaheh Kafiya' – by Hafez Abu Bakr Shahaab; Pg. 136, - printed in Bombay.

[25] Tafsir-e-Kabir- by Allama Fakhruddin Razi, vol 3, Pg 230.

to regard this 'Inheritance' as not being an inheritance, but rather, as being a 'Charity'? On the one hand, we have the oft repeated and universally accepted tradition from the Prophet ﷺ wherein he has categorically stated that Charity (*Sadaqa*) is forbidden (*Haram*) for his relatives. This being the case, how was it possible that the Prophet ﷺ would leave them in a situation wherein they would be forced to accept charity?

According to some other Sunni Scholars who try to defend this action, they say that Abu Bakr had announced that "he would keep the property intact under his control; but distribute the revenue among the relatives of the holy Prophet". But then again, this contravenes his own ruling; for, as per his own Hadith, such a distribution would have been '*Sadaqa*' (Charity).

By doing this, **did** Abu Bakr intend to give '*Sadaqa*' to the descendants of the holy Prophet ﷺ, which according to the Prophet ﷺ was forbidden to them? Why is there this contradiction in his behaviour in dealing with the property of the Prophet ﷺ by denying his daughter under the ruling that the Prophet leaves no "inheritance" on the one hand, while on the other hand stating that he would *distribute the revenue* from that very same property to the Prophet's family as *not being charity but their "rightful share of inheritance"*? How can these two conflicting and inconsistent arguments of 'double standards' be justified?

As far as the issue of the inheritance by the prophets is concerned, it should be noted that the Prophet ﷺ himself had inherited his father's house. Moreover, the holy Quran contains several verses dealing with the inheritance of several prophets such as Isaac inheriting from Abraham: Joseph inheriting from Jacob, Solomon from David and Yahya (John the Baptist) from Zacharias (Zakariya) etc. It stands to reason then that it is **impossible** that the holy Prophet ﷺ would contravene such Quranic injunctions and establish a precedent on his own. This concocted tradition without any doubt is false and has been categorically denied by the Ahlul Bayt of the noble Prophet ﷺ whose truthfulness and infallibility has been certified by the holy Quran (33:33).

9.6: Controversy over Fadak "Insoluble": According to Some Sunni Scholars

Some Sunni Scholars state that the inheritance left behind by the prophets is only that of "Knowledge" and not of any chattels and/or property; and to this end they advance the argument that Prophet Solomon ﷺ only inherited knowledge from his father David ﷺ. In response to this we will cite the Quranic verses from Surah Ambiya (78-79) wherein Allah ﷺ specifically mentions a case about "some people's sheep grazing in a field, and Solomon and David *jointly* giving their judgment in this matter" and the verse further goes on to add that "**to each of them We granted Wisdom and Knowledge**". This shows that "Knowledge" was given by Allah ﷺ to both, the Father and Son **simultaneously** in their joint lifetimes itself, and it was **not passed on to the son as an 'Inheritance' after the death of the father;** thereby illustrating that the physical encumbrances like property and chattels are what actually get passed on as an "inheritance" from father to child *after* the demise of the parent, while "Knowledge" is given at anytime by Allah's Will!

"*And Dawood and Sulaiman when they gave Judgment concerning the field when the people's sheep pastured therein by night, and We were bearers of witness to their judgment. So, we made Sulaiman to understand it; and to each one We gave Wisdom and Knowledge....*" (21: 78-79).

In addition, in support of the fact that a prophet's offspring **does** inherit from the father, we quote a few verses from the same Surah Ambiya (89-90) and also from Surah Mariam (3-6) where Prophet

Zakariya ﷺ prayed for a child who would inherit him, and Allah ﷻ granted him his wish!: "*And Zakariya, when he cried to his Lord: O My Lord! Leave me not alone; (though) Thou art the Best of Inheritors! So, We responded to him and gave him Yahya, and We made his wife fit for him*" (21: 89-90).

And again: "*When he (Zakariya) called upon his Lord in a faint voice, he said: My Lord! Surely my bones are weakened and my head flares with hoariness; and My Lord I have never been unsuccessful in my prayer to Thee. And surely, I fear my cousins after me; and my wife is barren, therefore grant me from Thyself an heir who should inherit me and inherit from the children of Yaqoob, and make him My Lord, one whom Thou art well pleased with.*" (19: 3-6).

In connection with the inheritance of property from a prophet to his heirs, Allama Saleh Kashifi Tirmizi Hanafi in his book 'Kaukab-e-Durri' (page 391) quotes another book titled 'Maqsad-e-Aqsa' which records that Angel Gabriel descended and revealed to the Prophet ﷺ that "Allah ﷻ desires that Fadak and the surrounding property be given to his daughter Fatima, and to Hasan and Husayn, which is their right". The Prophet ﷺ immediately called Fatima ﷺ and signed and handed over the papers to the property, awarding the same to her. This document was later produced and given by Fatima ﷺ to Abu Bakr as proof of her ownership of the property during her claim which she filed in his court. But this of course as recorded by history, was rejected by **both the Sheiks** and her claim was denied.

Another Sunni scholar Shah Abdul Haq-Mohaddis Dehlavi writes the following in his book[26] regarding the Fadak case:

"The most difficult decision for a scholar is to make a ruling on the Case raised by Janab-e-Sayyeda ﷺ. If we accept that in fact,

---

[26] Ash`Hetul Lamaat Shar-e-Mishkat – Shah Abdul Haq Dehlavi, Vol 3, Pg 453, printed by Naval Kishore, India.

this was an authentic tradition, albeit one which she had not heard before, but supported by some other companions, then when she did hear it, why was she so annoyed with Abu Bakr? Even if she was upset with him before hearing this Hadith, then why did she not reconcile with him after hearing it? Why did she remain furious with him to the extent that she never spoke to him and avoid any association with him for the rest of her life till her very death?"

It is obvious that Abdul Haq-Muhaddis Dehlavi has deliberately twisted the facts by stating that 'some companions confirmed this tradition'; because many Sunni scholars are unanimous in their opinion that Abu Bakr was the sole narrator of this tradition with none to second him! It was only later that Umar, Abu Obaida ibne Jarrah, Salem the slave of Hudaifa and Maaz ibn Jabal came forward to support this tradition for their own ulterior motives. This was the same group of the very five persons who always supported Abu Bakr and were instrumental in making him the Caliph. In history they are referred to as the 'People of The Agreement' – ('Ashaab-e-Moahida') and were the same people who had sworn (and collectively signed) on an agreement in the precincts of the Kaa`ba to keep the Caliphate away from the Ahlul Bayt of the Prophet ﷺ. Hence this sort of confirmation by these conspirators can never be regarded as being equivalent to the confirmation by any of the other companions. In any case, Shah Abdul Haq Dehlavi has eventually acknowledged that the case of Fadak and the matter of Fatima ﷻ is beyond his comprehension!

Maulawi Sadruddin Hanafi in his book 'Riwah Al Mustafa' has in all fairness, accepted that many heinous and woeful atrocities were inflicted upon the daughter of the Prophet ﷺ immediately after his, ﷺ's demise. He writes: "After the death of Prophet ﷺ, Fatima ﷻ suffered several calamities, such as the issue of Fadak, the miscarriage and still birth of her child, the threat of Umar towards the Hashemites while they were assembled in her house and her protest and pleading to the *'Ansaars'* (Medinites) for support. These are significant incidents which resulted in casting a long shadow into the future of the Ummah and are all weighty issues which are best left undiscussed.

Her last will and testament that certain persons should not be allowed to attend her funeral attests to the fact that she departed from this world sad and heart broken. It can be interpreted or justified in whatever way one chooses, but the fact remains that her bewailing lamentation and Elegy with which she addressed her father, resounds to this day wherein she moaned: *"O Father! After you such atrocities have been visited upon me that had they had befallen on bright days, they would have turned into dark nights!"*

9.7: Shahed Zaeem Fatmi's Expose on the Usurpation of Fadak and Concocted Tradition

The distinguished and truthful Sunni scholar Shahed Zaeem in his thesis "Ali ibn Abi Taleb and His Political Opponents" published in a Lucknow journal[27] writes as follows: "By taking refuge on the strength of an entirely concocted tradition, the holy Prophet ﷺ's one-and-only, and most-beloved daughter Fatima had been denied her rightful inheritance from her father. This is a great tragedy. Sayyeda Fatima Zahra ؑ was only asking for her right. To *deny* her this rightful share based on a *single* tradition that was concocted leaves one totally baffled. This was the first concocted tradition which was introduced into the canons of 'Islamic Traditions' by none other than the First Caliph of Islam; and thereby setting the precedent for many other falsified and spurious traditions to follow by traditionalists in the later generations. To

---

[27] Sarfaraz Lucknow, Dated 2nd August 1977, Pp. 14-15.

deny the Ahlul Bayt from their rightful inheritance, he invented a tradition which was contrary to several Quranic verses and many Religious Edicts. Whosoever attempted to raise his voice against this clear injustice and obvious oppression was silenced under the threat of execution. Not only were the rights of Fatima ﷺ denied, but based on this fabricated tradition, Fadak and its surrounding area was also confiscated. These were properties which had been given to his Ahlul Bayt ﷺ by the Prophet ﷺ during his own lifetime."

He then further continues:[28] "But even if the entire Muslim Ummah were to unanimously accept this tradition, it still cannot abrogate or invalidate any **Quranic Edict.** A tradition **simply cannot** overrule the Injunctions of the holy Quran; and the Quran is not dependant on any individual like Abu Bakr or Umar for the interpretation of its verses! Where and in which section of the Quran are there verses that dictate or justify the denial of Muhammad ﷺ's family from their rightful inheritance? During the Caliphate of Umar, he (Umar) awarded the Governorship of the best and most fertile area of the then prevailing 'Islamic Empire' to the two sons of Abu Sufiyan[29] - the notorious enemy of Islam. How is it that this action of Umar did not cause any ripples among those with a 'sense of honour', or even *offend* **any one** of the so-called honourable people, nor did it ruffle their feathers? Nobody seems to have objected to these two brothers being bestowed with this favour, when they had neither participated in the battle of Badr nor taken part in the '*Baith-e-Rizwan*' - the Fealty paid to the Prophet ﷺ "under the tree" during the Treaty of Hudaibiyah. Nor did they

---

[28] Pages: 17-18, - 46.

[29]Translator's Note: Umar made Yazid the elder son of Abu Sufiyan as the Governor of Syria; and when he died during the plague, his younger brother Muawiyah was given the same post again by Umar ibn Khattab.

have the honour of emigrating with the Prophet ﷺ from Mecca! Why has no person, *scholar or otherwise*, not dared to raise any objection to this unjustified benevolence by Umar, or even commented against him? If the rights of inheritance could be denied to the Ahlul Bayt of the holy Prophet ﷺ, then how can there be any justification for the bestowal of favours on these two sons of Abu Sufiyan?

This political manoeuvre by Umar cannot ever be justified under any pretext. He granted the best and most fertile area of the Arabs to the Omayyads; and this was a deliberate conspiracy to transfer the power to a tribe which was an inveterate enemy and rival of the Prophet ﷺ and his family. This was the biggest obstacle for the Banu Hashem and laid the strongest foundation for the ascendancy and rule of the Omayyads, which began with the Caliphate of Uthman bin Affan.

The moment Uthman bin Affan sat on the seat of the kind and benevolent Prophet of Islam, he began his own brand of 'benevolence' by lavishing his kith and kin with all sorts of favours in the form of monetary and landed estates; and installing characterless persons to important official posts. He even went to the extent of appointing the despicable rogue Marwan bin Hakam as his special Vizier and confidante. No one could dare to criticize or say anything against him because of his policy that 'being kind to the relatives was the essence of Islam'! However, when it came to the family of the Prophet ﷺ, '**denying them their rights' becomes the essence of Islam!** When Amir Muawiyah appoints his depraved son Yazid as his successor, it is *at the most* regarded by some as a 'judgmental error'; but when Sayyeda Fatima ﷺ puts in a claim for her father's inheritance, it is deemed to be un-Islamic, and the Caliph is justified in rejecting the same! **I spit on such double standards adopted by the world!**" [Shahed Zaeem Fatmi].

9.8: Displeasure of Fatima 🕊 Against Abu Bakr and her Last Will Forbidding him to Attend her Funeral

A tradition related by Ayesha[30] states that: "After the demise of the Prophet, and the decision taken by my father Abu Bakr, with regards to the property of Fadak, Fatima was extremely annoyed with him (Abu Bakr) and remained so, till her death and never spoke to him again for the rest of her life! She also willed in her last moments that he should be kept away from attending her funeral!"

In the translation of Bukhari[31] by Waheed-uz Zaman, while discussing various Quranic verses the author clearly admits that this concocted tradition finds absolutely no support in the holy Quran. The inheritance of worldly goods by the prophets is clearly established in the Quran, and no further discussion is required on the subject. People of common sense will realize that this was a false tradition because the holy Prophet 🕊 can never say something which was contradictory to the Quranic injunctions. The scholar concludes his opinion on this subject by stating that: "No matter, whatever may be the case, Abu Bakr should not have behaved the way he did. On the contrary he should have had the decency to tell the Prophet's daughter: 'Everything belongs to you; take and choose whatever you wish. We are here to obey and serve you!'"

Another prominent Sunni scholar Maulavi Obaidullah Bismil Amritsari in his book 'Arjahul Mutaalib' writes similarly, stating that: "It was a great offense and an 'Error of Judgment' by denying the claim of Sayyeda Fatima 🕊 to her property of Fadak."

---

[30] Tayser Al Bukhari, Part 17, Kitab-e-Maghazi, Pp. 21-23.

[31] Bukhari – translation by Waheed-uz Zaman, Kitab ul Farayez, Ch 27, Pg 91-92.

Shamsul Ulema Nazeer Ahmed who as such displayed no special regard for either the Prophet ﷺ or his family in any of his views or practices, nonetheless, ended up writing the following in his book 'Ummah Atul Ammah': "Those destitute and starving persons who benefitted from Fatima's father and rose to high positions of prominence because of him, should **never** have forgotten his benevolence and denied her her rightful inheritance. It is the norm that when one has done a favour which is good for a nation, the people of the nation remain grateful and under a sense of obligation for several generations. Here was the Prophet who made these destitutes and robbers into kings; turned rogues into civilized humans; idolaters into true believers; illiterates into educated persons; the uncouth and unmannered into polished and respectable people, and beasts into human beings [!]; yet the recompense for these benevolences that was meted out to his ﷺ's children, grandchildren and the ladies of his family was so abhorrent and deplorable that the entire Islamic world weeps over their maltreatment to this day and will continue to do so till the end of this world!"

Daylami, Tabarani, Hakim, Abul Ala and Abu Naeem narrate from Hazrat Ali ؑ that the Prophet ﷺ often used to say: "*O Fatima! Verily Allah ﷻ is pleased with your pleasure and angry with those who make you angry.*" But unfortunately, with the passing of time, and the circulation of distorted versions of historical events, the people have gotten used to the berating and demeaning comments made against the family of the Prophet ﷺ over the generations by biased and prejudiced writers; to a point where the Ahlul Bayt ؑ have been stripped of their honoured status, and are regarded by a majority of Muslims in the same light as that of any common person. Little do they realize that this attitude is completely contradictory to the Quranic edict where Allah ﷻ has commanded us to love and revere the Prophet ﷺ's Ahlul Bayt as a compensation for his ﷺ's efforts in bringing His Message to the Ummah: (42:23).[32]

But the Almighty be Praised, there **are** still many who **do** revere the holy family and speak the truth! The great Sufi saint of the Indian subcontinent Khaja Moinuddin Chistie has expressed his sentiments about the usurpation of the rights of Fatima ﷺ in a short poem in the following manner:

"*Woe! They were Unbelievers at heart, though they uttered 'Allaho Akbar' in a Resounding Voice!*

They killed the Family of the Holy Prophet but professed to accept his brother Ali as their Fourth Ruler!

They Usurped the Rights of Fatima Zahra: The 'Apple of his Eyes',
Yet shamelessly avowed they were followers of her Father's Faith!"

It is a fact of history that by showing her displeasure against the two Sheiks [Abu Bakr and Umar], and by her expose` of the truth, Fatima ﷺ clearly identified the friends and foes of Allah ﷻ and His holy Prophet ﷺ. This action of hers will function as a beacon for generations and serve as a benchmark for the identification of Truth from Falsehood; and all Muslims will remain indebted to her to the end of time!

Because of his given word and his commitment to adhere to the instructions of the holy Prophet ﷺ "*to bear the trials after his (ﷺ's) death with patience and forbearance*", Ali ﷺ had foregone his own claim to the Caliphate which was rightfully his. Had Fatima ﷺ not revealed the clear distinction between right and wrong, the entire 'Episode of Usurpation' would have remained hidden under the dubious cloud of falsified propaganda and the issue of Ali ﷺ's right to Caliphate would have been lost in the pages of history! But it was the Prophet ﷺ's daughter Fatima Zahra ﷺ, who exposed the

---

[32] Quran; 42:23: - "Say I do not ask from you any reward, but love for my near relatives..."

faces of the hypocrites amongst the so called close companions in the Ummah; and it may well have been for this very same reason that with his prophetic vision the holy Prophet ﷺ had sounded the warning that: *"Whoever infuriates Fatima, infuriates me, and whoever infuriates me, infuriates Allah; and Fatima's displeasure will incur the wrath of Allah!"*

It is a pity that many of the disciples of this Sufi saint Khaja Chistie, do not pay heed to his words or relate to the views of their leader with respect to the rights of Fatima ﷺ; and remain ignorant about the atrocities inflicted on the holy family by those who to all intents, may have uttered the *"Kalema"* by their lips, but yet had kept their unbelief hidden within the deep core of their hearts!

9.9: Sermon of Hazrat Fatima Zahra ﷺ

We will now include a summary encompassing the gist of the sermon delivered by Hazrat Fatima Zahra ﷺ in support of Ali ﷺ and herself with respect to the usurpation of their rights. This sermon was primarily addressed to Abu Bakr, but periodically she also referred to the Muslims who had gathered around and were present on that occasion. This sermon is documented in several books of Shia and Sunni alike, and is acknowledged for its authenticity by several notable Sunni scholars known for their credibility and reliability, such as:

1. Abu Bakr Ahmad bin Abdul Aziz Jauhari in his book: *'Kitab al Saqifa wa Fadak'*.
2. Muhammad bin Muslim bin Qatiba Dinawari in his book *'Kitab ul Imamat was Siyasat'*.
3. Masoodi in *'Muruj az Zaheb'*.
4. Allama ibn Abil Hadid in his *'Sharh Nahjul Balagha'*.
5. Sayyed ibn Tawous and Sayyed ibn Abi Taher in their book *'Kitabul Balaghat Un Nisa'*.

6. Ibne Atheer in his book *'Nihaya'* [The Ultimate]; and also by the author of *'Kashf Al Ghammah'* among others, who have all quoted this sermon partially or in its entirety in their independent writings.

It is reported that Hazrat Fatima 🌸 dressed herself in some of the apparel of her revered Father 🌸 such as tying his *'Amama'* – [his head scarf] over her own veil and draping his cloak around her shoulders. She entered the Masjid surrounded by her maid servants like Fizza and Umme Aiman, along with a group of other women of her family and advanced with a stride that was highly reminiscent of the holy Prophet 🌸. The length of the cloak at times entangled with her feet, but other than that there was no difference between her gait and that of the holy Prophet. She entered the Masjid where Abu Bakr was seated in the position of a Caliph with a group of Meccans and Medinites [*Mohajirs and Ansars*]. A white sheet of cloth was drawn as a curtain between her and the men present. Before beginning her speech, she let out a deep and sorrowful sigh, upon hearing which the whole assembly began to wail and weep alongside with her! She then began her sermon in the name of Allah 🌸 and after praising Him and His Prophet 🌸 she reminded the people of the Divine Instructions, the religious edicts, and their obligations in following the same.

After elaborating on the favours conferred upon the Muslims by her revered Father the Prophet 🌸, she launched into her speech: [An abridged form of it is presented hereunder]:

"No sooner was the Messenger taken away by the Almighty Lord, you people reverted to your old animosities and resorted to hypocrisy. The fabric of Islam has been rent asunder and is in tatters. The misguided ones have taken control of the reins of Islam and Infidelity has become the norm of the people; and the Camel of Infidelity has started its call. Satan has raised his head and called out and you have readily responded to this call. You have started yearning for worldly

*gains and have been quick in this respect! Then he [Satan] antagonised you against the righteous people and found you to be a willing partner. Then you unhesitatingly usurped somebody else's rights and in following Satan's commands you forcefully took someone else's share into your own house. This, even though your fealty to the Prophet and your commitment of obedience had been made by you in the very recent past! The pain of his departure was still fresh, and the agony of his loss had not yet healed. Even before his burial was complete, Satan beckoned to you, and you promptly obeyed. This was done by you on the pretext of prevention of a 'breakdown of law and order', but **you** brought about the breakdown of law, leading to mischief, revolt, and tribulation by **your** very hands!*

Beware that the Fire of Hell will soon surround the Infidels. You have strayed so far from understanding the True Faith that you will never be able to redress the deviations that have crept into the Ummah. How far beyond your capabilities are the understanding of the Islamic Affairs [!] and how little is the knowledge you possess; and how can you hope to correct the various problems (enigmas) dealing with the multifaceted spheres (issues) of the Ummah? Satan has misguided you, although the Book of Allah is amongst you. The edicts of this book are clear and distinct, and its signs are obvious, and its orders are evident. But you insist upon ignoring it and have thrown it behind your backs; and turned away from it in disgust! You have gone against it and issued orders contrary to the Book of Allah; but be aware that the severe punishment and retribution for the unjust is not too far from being meted out by the Almighty God!

Woe unto those who have shaken the very foundations of Islam and turned the Ark [Ship] of Prophethood away from its real destination. They have snatched the reins of Caliphate away from the person who was the most knowledgeable and worthy to be the guide; and the one who was cognizant with both the Spiritual and Material

*matters of Islam. Why have you turned away from this Guidance?
Why are you so vehemently turned against Ali? This surely is a great
loss! Most certainly it is due to the severe sharpness of his sword which
he wielded [on orders of the Prophet] in his defence of Islam, along
with his strict and austere adherence to justice and uncompromising
attitude in the implementation of Divine Laws.*

*I swear by the Almighty! That if you had obeyed Ali, he would
have kept you united and made you walk an extremely easy path,
protecting you from any difficulty, sorrow, and trial. He would have
led you to the springs of pure and pristine waters from which you
would have returned completely satiated. But you did not have the
patience to wait for the disruptive behaviour and disorderly conduct
to abate. On the contrary, you fanned the flames of mischief (Fitna)
and ignited the fire that was started by Satan. You proceeded to
extinguish the Light of Religion and resolved to do away with the
chosen conduct (Sunnah) and rules established by the Prophet ﷺ. You
wanted to revert to the days of ignorance and hid the garments of the
true and shining faith, replacing them with the dark cloak of
infidelity. You have only accepted Islam outwardly, but your actions
are purely those of Hypocrisy. You hide behind bramble screens and
dense veils of furtive conspiracy and are hatching designs against the
Ahlul Bayt and the descendants of the holy Prophet. We have been
bearing the pain inflicted by your actions with the fortitude one
shows in bearing the pains of wounds inflicted by a dagger and an
arrow that sinks in the flesh.*

*Now you have started thinking in terms that I am not entitled to
the inheritance of my Father's property! Do you wish to follow the
laws that prevailed during the dark ages before the advent of Islam?
Who is more competent to command than Allah? For those of the true
faith I say: Do you not know my rights? Yes, **you** know; and this is
as clear as the midday sun for you that I am the Prophet's daughter!
Then you, Muslims, do you consent to my inheritance being usurped*

*by you and the son of Abu Quhafa? Is it ordained in the holy book that **you** should inherit your father's property, and I should not? This is a calumny and a false invention. Have you deliberately renounced the Book of Allah by ignoring it and thrown it behind your back?*

For in this very Book are distinct verses wherein Allah ﷻ says that Hazrat Sulayman ﷺ inherited from his father Dawood ﷺ (David); and that Hazrat Zakariya prayed for an offspring (Yahya) who would inherit him, as well receive his rightful share as a descendant of Jacob - Yaqoob ﷺ. Do you claim to understand the Quran better than my revered father or the son of my uncle [Ali ﷺ]? So be it! If you take possession today of the region of Fadak like taking hold of the rope and saddle of a she camel; then, on the Day of Judgment O Abu Bakr! You will be the accused, and God is a good Judge, and Muhammad ﷺ will be a Claimant of his Right and the place of Trial will be the Field of the Day of Qiyamah! On that day those who worship falsehood will suffer and repentance on that occasion will not be available. A Time is fixed for everything. You will soon know on who will descend the humiliating punishment, and for whom will be Eternal Peace." [After saying this, Sayyeda Fatima ﷺ turned towards the Ansars (Medinites) and addressed them as follows[33]:

"You 'group of young men' - the 'guardians and the custodians' of Islam, how can you condone all that which is happening against me? How can you overlook the injustice? Did not my father, the Prophet of Allah ﷺ say that the respect and regard due to the parents should be observed by their issues? But how soon you have introduced this heresy in your faith and followed the dictates of your desires and your passions? Although you possess the ability to defend us from the oppression and injustice from which we are suffering, yet you remain

---

[33] Part of the contents of the above translation of Hazrat Fatima ﷺ's Sermon has been taken from the booklet of Sermon, courtesy of Dr. M. M. Taqi Khan, Professor and former Chief Scientist of India.

indifferent and inertly compliant. You have the capacity to restore to me what I am demanding. Do you content yourself merely by saying 'Muhammad has died' as if this was not a great calamity in your view? Indeed! It is a great calamity and a disaster that has left a great gap.

A fissure has emerged in what was previously bonded and united. The earth has been darkened by his death, and the Elect of God's creatures are sunk in grief. The sun and moon have lost their lustre, and the stars have wandered from their course. All the hopes that were founded on him are dispelled, and the hearts of mountains are melting with grief. People have lost the respect and esteem for sacred places and their inhabitants. This is a great calamity which cannot be compared to any other. There exists no other event so rapid and so swift in its disastrous effect! This has been mentioned in the Book which you peruse day and night and recite eloquently and loudly. It has been plainly stated therein that calamities have befallen on prophets before Muhammad. They were real and preordained, and Muhammad is a Prophet. They were prophets before him too, so if Muhammad dies or is slain, will you revert to your former faith of the dark and ignorant age? [Quran]. Those who have thus reverted will not be able to harm the Almighty and He will soon reward those who are thankful to Him.

*O Bani Qila! [Men of the Tribe of Khazraj] – O Ansars of Muhammad, it is regrettable that my inheritance is tampered with, and the property usurped; and you are sitting and watching. You are hearing me and are present; and my speech has overpowered and stunned you, and you have all become aware of my plight. You are here in large numbers; you have the power, and you are armed with swords and shields. My voice is reaching your ears, but you do not respond! You hear me clearly, but you are apathetic and uncaring, and doing nothing to redress the wrong that is being done to me, though **you have** the strength to combat my enemies and are* *renowned as being champions of what is 'good and right' and in defending it.*

You are among those elect people that had been lauded for being supporters of the Ahlul Bayt. You have fought against the Arabs and suffered hardships of war. You have fought against outsiders and valiant opponents. We have always commanded you and you have obeyed. The mills of Islam started moving and the world benefitted from the pristine values of Islam. The voice of Polytheism was silenced, and the door of Falsehood was closed; the fires of Kufr, Disbelief, Disorder and Mischief were extinguished. The affairs of the community were brought into order by the introduction of the True Faith; and now after the Truth has triumphed and the clear path been established, why are you wondering and dumbstruck? Are you turning away from it? After the declaration and proclamation of the Truth you are turning back and retreating. Will you become polytheists again after embracing Islam? Will you shrink from the encounter with those who have broken their vows and were prepared to expel the Prophet? They are the very same people who fought with us. Are you frightened of them? Though indeed Allah is more to be feared, provided you are believers and on the true path.

Be Aware and Listen: I am watching you and find that you have taken to repose and luxury; you have removed him who best knew the teachings of the true faith and the affairs of the Caliphate in solving its problems and difficulties. No doubt you have fallen into a life of ease and comfort. You have emerged from poverty and are now rich. In the process, you have strayed from the true religion and assumed a new mould. To summarise, you have torn the garment of Islam which you had put on and spat out the drink which you swallowed thinking it was sweet. But remember this: that even if all of you who inhabit this world renounce Islam and become infidels, this will not affect Allah. Know then, that whatever I have said, I have done so being fully aware of the renunciation of your support for us, *which has become embedded in you, and is now a part of your nature. I realize the treachery which you are nursing and concealing in your bosoms, by which I know that you **will not** respond to my call. Whatever I have said here-to-fore has erupted and flooded out from my grieving heart and was an expression of the agony of my soul and the overflow of my indignation and anger, to relieve the torment of my mind. My objective was to resolve the controversy, and you are all now aware of the facts.*

Now take charge of this She-Camel of Power and rule! But mind that its back is broken, and its legs are wounded. These effects are long lasting and permanent. It is a sign of Allah's Wrath to your eternal shame. It will fling you into the Fire lighted by Allah which will rise from your feet up to your hearts and envelope you; therefore, remember that whatever you are doing is being witnessed by Allah and is before His Eyes. Persons who have inflicted these cruelties and injustices on me will soon realize to what doom and awful place it will lead them into. I am the daughter of that Prophet who used to warn you about the dire punishment that awaits evil deeds. Now do what you choose, and we shall do what we think is fit; and you shall wait for that Day of Reckoning and so shall we likewise, Await."

Upon hearing this address of Fatima Zahra 🌸, the Caliph of the day cried: "O Daughter of the Prophet of Allah! Undoubtedly your revered father was compassionate and kind to the Muslims and a blessing for them, while a terrible visitation and a castigation and horror for the Unbelievers. Indeed, if we look for nearness of relationship to him, among women we shall find him to be only your father, and not the father of any other woman in the world. Among the men, only your husband is his brother whom he preferred over all men; and placed him over all other devotees, followers, and friends. Your husband has indeed succoured and aided him on all occasions and in all great matters. Blessed and fortunate are those who are friends and devotees of the Ahlul Bayt.

Only the evil, ill fated and cruel persons will be hostile to them. You are the pure and a beloved member of the Prophet's family and household, and you are our guide to goodness and Heaven. O You, the Best of Women, and the daughter of The Best and Greatest Prophet, you are true in your word, and above all others in intellect, understanding and wisdom; and you shall not be deprived from your rights, nor prevented from speaking the truth. I swear by God that I have never gone beyond the commands of the Prophet, nor have I done anything without his permission.

Allah is my witness, and His testimony is sufficient that I have heard the Prophet declare that: 'We Prophets leave no inheritance either in gold or silver, or land and property. We Prophets only leave as inheritance the Scripture, our Wisdom, Knowledge and Prophethood. Whatever we possess at time of death would pass on to our successor in the leadership (Wali-ul-Amr), and he is entitled to dispose of it as he deems it fit. What you are claiming now, the Fadak, we have set apart for maintenance of war horses and for buying weapons with which the Muslims are to fight and wage war against the Unbelievers, Traitors and Rebels. Even this I have not done on my own accord, but with the aid and consent of the *Ijma* (general body of Muslims). All my property and my life itself are at your disposal. I shall not spare them or hold them back from you. You are the chief and the leader of your Father's followers and the scared and pure head of your descendants. No one can deny your high rank and status or consider your origin and devotion as commonplace. Your commands prevail on my property and all that belongs to me; then do you think that in this respect I have done anything immoral and hostile against your father?'

Upon hearing this long reply from Abu Bakr, Fatima 🕮 said: "*May Allah be praised! My Father never did anything contrary to the Book of Allah, nor did he ever oppose its Edicts. He followed the verses of the Quran in their entirety. In your insidiousness you have wrongfully accused my father. Are you attributing falsehood to the Prophet of Allah and by this means have joined together to commit deceit and fraud against him?* **This conspiracy after his death is akin to the plans which you people had hatched to assassinate him during his lifetime.** *The Book of Allah is the Final Authority and its verdict is articulate, decisive, evident and just. According to this holy Book the son of Zacharias (Yahya) inherited from his father and was an heir to the progeny of Yaqoob. Also, Prophet Sulayman inherited from his father Dawood ﷺ. Therefore, the rule of inheritance established by Allah for male and female heirs also applies to me. Whatever is described in the Book of Allah negates the arguments of the liars and explains the question clearly and dispels all doubts* (regarding inheritance) *in the minds of generations to come. Your ambitious aspirations have caused you to camouflage your avaricious motives and presented your evil function as being attractive to the public. Hence, I have no recourse but to bear this burden with extreme patience. I seek the help of Allah ﷻ against your conspiracies".*

Abu Bakr replied by saying: "God is true, and so was His Prophet and so is his daughter. You are the mine of wisdom and the abode of blessings of God. You are a source of guidance, a pillar of faith, a beacon of mercy and the direction of true faith and a clear proof of righteousness and of Allah's existence. I am convinced of your truthfulness and believe in whatever you are saying and cannot deny whatever you have stated; but between you and me there are many Muslims who have made me their ruler, and whatever I have confiscated from you is with the consent of these Muslims. It is not my high-handed decision taken singularly, to acquire this property, nor had I insisted on doing this; and these people will testify to this fact".

On hearing this statement of Abu Bakr, Fatima ﷺ turned towards those same people and addressed them saying: *"O You*

Group of People who have succumbed so readily to the words of falsehood and overlooked this dastardly act, do you not ponder on the holy Quran? Or is your intellect locked up? Most certainly your hearts have been steeped in your misguidance resulting in your condoning the despicable actions which have corrupted your Power of Observation and Sense of Justice. The interpretations that you have been provided with are flawed; and the conclusions derived are the worst possible in the way of bringing about harm and mischief. This is what you have adopted, rather than Truth and Justice. By Allah! You will find this burden extremely heavy to bear and the culmination to its ultimate fruition will lead you to no end of trouble. When the veil is removed from your eyes then you will see the horror that lies ahead, where you will find yourselves surrounded in a dark forest of abomination and disgrace; and a terrible punishment from God Almighty will be inflicted upon you such as you had never suspected; and at that time the devotees and worshippers of evil will suffer the consequences of what their hands had wrought and their deeds had accumulated."

After this she turned to the tomb of the holy Prophet ﷺ and recited a poetic verse in which she said: *"O My Venerated Father! After your demise so many calamities have befallen upon us that had they had fallen on the Bright Days they would have turned into Dark Nights; and had they had fallen upon the Mountains they would have disintegrated into smithereens."* She then continued: *"O My Revered Father! After you departed, we were subjected to such severe atrocities which would not have happened had you been alive. Without you we are like a garden without rain whose plants and flowers have withered away due to the scorching wind of the evildoers. When they saw that you ﷺ were no longer around us, they ignored our rights, debased our position, and confined us into such straightened circumstances which left us with no room to exercise our options. It would have been better if we had passed away before you. Your nation is in total disarray and has deviated from the true path."*

On hearing this heartrending speech many members of the crowd present howled aloud and cried in shame; but it, nonetheless, had little or no effect on the Two Sheiks. She then reasserted her claim of inheritance in yet another bid to gain her rights. Upon this Abu Bakr asked her to provide witnesses, whence Ali 🕮, Hasnain 🕮 and Umme Aiman all again presented their evidence which were accepted by Abu Bakr. However, on the instigation of Umar, Abu Bakr changed his mind and again rejected her claim.

At this juncture, Fatima 🕮 addressed the Two Sheiks and said: *"If I narrate a tradition to you from the Prophet 🕮 will you admit to remembering it and act upon it?"* They both replied in the affirmative. She then asked them on oath and said: *"Have you not heard the Prophet say: 'Fatima's pleasure is my pleasure; her anger is my anger. Whoever loves my daughter and pleases her, then he pleases me; and whoever angers Fatima angers me."* Abu Bakr and Umar both acknowledged that they had indeed heard this from the Prophet 🕮. Then she continued and said: *"Allah 🕮 and His Angels are witnesses that both of you have Angered and Displeased me. Whenever I shall meet the Prophet 🕮 I will complain against you both; and in every prayer of mine I shall invoke Allah's curse upon you."*

When Abu Bakr heard this statement, he ran out weeping profusely; and when the crowd ran after him to console him, he said: "You people are happy among your families and have abandoned me to face up to this dire catastrophe." Nevertheless, all such empty words kept floating around, and despite all such display of emotion, her rights were never restored to her.

Heartbroken and dejected, Fatima 🕮 returned to her home. She is known to have then asked Ali 🕮: *"O Abul Hasan! What was the reason that kept you so quiet in my affair? Was it due to some instructions which my revered father had whispered into your ear on his deathbed? You are the same bold person who had destroyed many a brave and valiant warrior, but here, you remained silent in the presence of those faint-hearted persons who had constantly run for cover from every battlefield!"* Ali ⚔ replied: *"O Daughter of the Best of Creation! You know that I was never slack in the affairs of the religion, and I have always done whatever was the Will of Allah. I did not shirk from claiming my due rights; and I have also always fulfilled the commitments that I made with your esteemed father. I have now fulfilled the promises which your revered father had taken from me before his death. Therefore, you beseech the Almighty Lord for your case and bear up to these injustices inflicted upon you with patience".*

9.10: Foul Language used by Abu Bakr Against Ali ⚔ and Fatima ⚔

Allama Abil Hadid in his treatise 'Sharh-e-Nahjul Balagha'[34] has recorded that when Fatima ⚔'s rights were denied by Abu Bakr, commotion and unrest ensued in some sectors of the Muslim Ummah upon which he, Abu Bakr, mounted the pulpit and in a heightened state of anger and annoyance and issued a lengthy statement using extraordinarily foul language against the daughter of the Prophet ⚔ and his cousin Ali ⚔. That statement has been recorded as an entire paragraph by this scholar, but which we, the translators, have refrained from quoting here for the sake of decency and the respect which is due unto these two noble personalities of the holy family.

---

[34] 'Sharah-e-Nahjul Balagha' – Vol 4, Pg 80, by ibn Abil Hadid.

Those interested and wish to get details of this can refer to the original text of "Kalematul Haqq' – Second Edition, Vol 1, page 690.

9.11: Issue of "Fadak" During the Later Periods

After the confiscation of Fadak from Fatima 🕊 by the first Caliph, the third Caliph Uthman awarded this same property to his brother-in-law Marwan bin Hakam for his personal use. Later when Umer ibn Abdul Aziz became the Caliph, he returned Fadak to Imam Muhammad al-Baqir ibn Ali ibn al-Husayn 🕊 from the family of the Ahlul Bayt of the Prophet 🕊.

It is recorded in the 'Sharah' of Abil Hadid that when this event occurred, the nobles in his regime objected to this saying that he had opened the 'door of criticism' for the two Sheiks Abu Bakr and Umar. To this objection Umer ibn Abdul Aziz replied: "Fadak was in the possession of Fatima 🕊 when the government confiscated this property despite her having objected to this and brought in Ali 🕊, Hasan 🕊, Husayn 🕊 and Umme Aiman as her witnesses; claiming that Fadak was her property which had been in her possession from during the lifetime of her revered father 🕊. It was below the status of Fatima Zahra 🕊 that she would make a false claim. Her word by itself was sufficient and there was no need for any further evidence from any other person. Hence by returning Fadak, I have acted in a just manner and been true to her position which justice demands; and I hope that on the Day of Judgement Fatima 🕊, Ali 🕊 and Hasan 🕊 and Husayn 🕊 will intercede on my behalf."

Later, during his period of caliphate, the Abbaside Caliph Mutawakkil re-confiscated Fadak from the household of the Prophet 🕊 and awarded it to his personal barber! Some of the later Caliphs again took it back and gave it to the Fatimids, but then again others retook this property and awarded it to others for their personal use. This 'to-and-fro' process continued back and forth among the successive Caliphs for an extended period, and subsequently ultimately remained away from any of the descendants of the holy family.

9.12: Burning of the Door of the House of Fatima Zahra 🕌

Alongside the confiscation of Fadak, there was the horrific incident of Umar proceeding to the abode of Fatima 🕌 and threatening to set fire to her house. It is a documented fact that Umar gathered some like-minded people around him and arming himself with firewood he approached the house of the Prophet's daughter with a threat to burn down her dwelling. Maulana Shibli Nomani in his book 'Al Farooq' accepts this incident as being a factual truth. In this connection he says: "Umar during the pre-Islamic period was extremely short tempered and was known by all to be the 'incarnation of anger' and this habit remained with him even after his conversion to Islam. So, it was very feasible, and not beyond his terse and autocratic nature, that he would have perpetrated such an atrocity and committed this horrendous act".

Professor Abdul Ali in his book 'Caliph Ali' has also expressed a similar opinion. To quote:

"Umar's threat to set fire to Fatima's house if Ali did not come out was typical of the man."

Several other books have delved into this incident in greater detail, describing the action of Umar in bringing the fire to the house of Fatima 🕌 and knocking the door down on her in his attempt to force an entry when she responded to his call from behind her entrance door. This was at a time when she was in a state of pregnancy and carrying a child in her womb, whom the Prophet 🕌 prior to his own demise, had already selected a name (for the child, though still unborn), as 'Mohsin'.

The physical and mental trauma sustained by Fatima ﷺ during this incident lead to the miscarriage of her pregnancy. As a result of this, combined with the physical injury of broken ribs caused by the fall of the heavy door on the side of her body, she subsequently became so weak and unsteady that for the rest of her short life she had to resort to the use of a cane to support herself. In addition to the brutality inflicted upon her of being pushed behind the burning door, watching her young children being traumatized by the smoke-filled atmosphere around her, as well as simultaneously being a witness to the indignity of seeing her husband Ali ﷺ being dragged out of the house with a rope around his neck; all these atrocities proved to be a further cause of severe agony and mental shock-and-pain for her in her weakened condition. Sadly she passed away within a very short period after these calamitous incidents, at the tender age of 18 years.

Majority of the Sunni scholars preferred not to delve into the details of these atrocities and glossed over the facts by simply stating that her death was caused by the severe shock and distress at the passing away of her beloved father. Nonetheless, there are some Sunni scholars who had a conscience which guided them to break away from their biases and adhere to the truth. In doing so, they acted in accordance with the Quranic injunction "*Do not mix truth with falsehood, nor hide the truth while you know it!*" (2:42)

In this connection the following Sunni scholars have recorded their comments in their individual works: Imam Abul Fatah Mohammed bin Abdul Kareem Shehrastani in 'Kitabul-Milal wa Nahl'; and ibn Hazam in his comments in the preface of this same book;[35] Salahuddin Khalil ibn Aibak As-Safadi in his book 'Wafi bil Wafiyaat'; Ibrahim ibn Yasar in his book 'Urfu al Fiza' etc. have all

---

[35] 'Commentary of Kitabul Mihal wa Nahl' – by ibn Hazam; Pg 73, Printed in Egypt 1373 A.H.

similarly written that Ali 🕮 was dragged from his house, and the door of his house was set on fire, and when Fatima 🕮 came to the door protesting this atrocity, she was squeezed between the wall and the door in such a manner that her ribs got crushed and she lost the baby 'Mohsin' whom she was carrying in her womb.

Similarly, Allama Sayyed Saleh Kashfi Tirmizi Hanafi in his book[36] after first listing the names of the children of Fatima 🕮 writes as follows: "Mohsen 🕮 was her last child who was sadly aborted as a result of the injury inflicted upon her, which consequently lead to her early martyrdom." Here the use of the word "*Martyrdom*" by this writer is worth noting, as it throws light on the situation that prevailed; and the circumstances under which she passed away. Ibn Abdullah in his 'Kitabul Aqad' and Zahabi in his book 'Mizan ul Etedal' have likewise given a similar description of the horrific events that were perpetrated after the demise of the holy Prophet 🕮.

Maulwi Sadruddin has expressed his thoughts[37] on these incidents as follows: "After the death of the Prophet 🕮 there were several atrocities that were committed against Fatima 🕮 such as the confiscation of the property of Fadak and the loss of her unborn child. The treatment of the Muslim Ummah towards her was such that she wept and complained about it constantly; and often wailed on the evil turn of events upon her after the deep loss of her revered father."

Allama Mufti Shah Sayyed Muhammad Saheb Ashrafi Gilani, Mohaddis-e-Kachowi: who was the Head of 'The All India Jamaat-e-Raza-e-Mustafawi Bareilly' and also the Chairman of the 'All

---

[36] 'Manaqib-e-Murtazavi' – Allama Sayyed Saleh Kashfi Tirmizi Hanafi - Pg 236.

[37] 'Ravahey al Mustafa' – Maulwi Sadruddin, Muhammadi Press, Kanpur; Pg 36 -37.

India Sunni Jamaat- ul-Ullema – Bombay', in his treatise 'Haqqa-ke-Bina-e-La Ilahast Husayn' ['In Truth, The Foundation of *La Ilaha Illallah* is Husayn'] has stated that: "Hazrat-e-Butool Tahera Fatima Zahra ﷺ' s extent of pain and heartbreak can be surmised from her own couplet when she wailed and cried out: *'If the calamities that befell upon me had fallen on bright days they would have turned into dark nights.'* If this 'concise couplet', were to be expanded into an essay by any expert in text, **the pens would have dried up** but the depth of details of her grief would still not have been deciphered or described!"

Not only was she mentally and physically tormented by the Muslims, but she was also prohibited from expressing her grief by crying out in an audible manner. The people complained that her weeping disturbed their work and livelihoods, and that she should cry either by night or by day. As a result of this objection, she would often leave her house and go away some distance from her neighbourhood in the mornings and sit under a tree and wail. But after a short time, the so called followers of the Prophet of Islam even hacked and *cut this tree down*; as a result of which Hazrat Ali ﷺ moved further away from the city and its inhabited areas, and constructed a room for her to which he used to take her in the morning where she would cry over her misfortunes; and he, Ali ﷺ would fetch her back home in the evenings. This place later came to be known as *'Bait-ul Huzn* – The House of Sorrow'. The famous Sufi saint of India Khwaja Ajmeri in deference to the grief inflicted on Hazrat Fatima Zahra ﷺ composed a quatrain in which he invokes the Almighty Lord for the forgiveness of his own sins in the following manner:

"O Lord, I invoke You by the depth of the Weeping Heart of Fatima,

O Lord and for the Sake of The Lamentations and Wailings of

The Chief of Womankind.

And by Your Own Benign Grace and Merciful Kindnesses,

Pardon my sins by the intercession of the Martyrs of Kerbala!"

There are confirmed and authenticated narrations from Bukhari and Muslim that after the multitude of atrocities that were meted out upon her by Umar and Abu Bakr, Fatima ؏ was so pained and annoyed with them that *she never spoke to either of them again as long as she lived.* She also made a will that they should not be allowed to attend her funeral.

In accordance with her wish, when she passed away from this life a short time later, Ali ؏ refrained from informing them about her death. He had her casket taken out in the darkness of the night and buried her body before the break of dawn. It is said that he prepared two or three (and some traditions say up to 40) graves around the area of *Jannatul Baqi* [the Medinite graveyard] to camouflage her actual grave so as to prevent anyone from defiling or violating the sanctity of her burial ground; which clearly indicates that there was a fear and/or an expectation that her grave could be desecrated!

Shams-ul-Ulema Nazir Ahmed Saheb notes in his book[38] as follows: "The person who was most devastated by the death of the Prophet ؖ was Fatima ؏. Her mother had passed away early in her life and the Prophet ؖ had occupied the dual role of a father as well as a mother. And what a father he was! One who was the Sovereign of the World and the entire Realm of Faith and Religion. The loss of the 'protective shade' of such a father, the denial of Caliphate to her husband Ali ؏, along with the confiscation of Fadak and the rejection and loss of her claim for her inheritance by the court, were such dire calamities that had they happened to any

---

[38] 'Royaa-e-Sadiqah' – Nazir Ahmed, Pg 153.

other person they would have been driven to take their own life. But it was a credit to her enormous patience and courage and fortitude that she bore these calamities bravely; but nonetheless, could not long survive the shock and its resulting trauma. Whatever the number of the few months and days that she survived, she never forgave or spoke to those persons responsible for inflicting these hardships upon her; and is known to have willed that *these persons should not be allowed* to participate at her funeral.

Even if we grant that her anger was a little excessive, but she being the only daughter of the Prophet ﷺ was able to command a special status. And then again, even if Ali were not considered as being right for the Caliphate, they could have given him a *nominal* post of a Caliph while still retaining the reins of power in their own hands. But if this idea of giving Ali the Caliphate was a bit far-fetched, they could still have given the Estate of Fadak to Fatima ﷺ to keep her happy, as this would not have caused any harm to anybody in any great manner.

The essence of the so-called tradition that 'We Prophets do not inherit nor leave any inheritance; whatever we leave is for Charity' – then this being the case, the handing over of Fadak to her would have been a 'Sadaqa' (charity); and the onus of accepting it as 'Charity' would have then fallen upon **her**. Fatima ﷺ being a 'Sayyeda' would not have partaken of this charity which was *Haram* [forbidden] to the Prophet ﷺ and his progeny, and thus the Sheiks would have been free from blame of not offering any charity to her and still have retained their hold on the entire area of Fadak under their control!

It is a great pity and a cause for great sadness that after the death of the Prophet ﷺ, the treatment meted out to his family was so insulting and demeaning to their dignity that it gradually had the effect of diminishing the status of the Prophet ﷺ's noble family to such an extent that it ultimately paved the way to, and culminated in the Tragedy of Kerbala! An incident so abhorrent that it has no parallel in the history of mankind! This in turn has left a monumental blot on the character of the Muslims to such a towering degree that they have suffered a 'Loss of face in Humanity' for all time! **This** was the payment that the Ummah gave as their 'recompense' to the Prophet ﷺ for his efforts in the way of Allah ﷻ by directly contravening the Quranic injunction of (42:23)[39]: and far from 'loving' her, they meted out the most deplorable treatment to the only daughter of the Prophet of Islam!" [End of Quote].

In 'Mishkat-ul-Masabih'[40] there is a narration by ibn Ayyub that the Prophet ﷺ said: *"On the Day of Judgment the Angels will announce: "Ó People! Lower your gaze and close your eyes, as Fatima [daughter of Prophet Muhammad ﷺ] is going to cross the Bridge of Siraat!' She will cross this Bridge in the blink of an eye accompanied by 70,000 slave girls and Houris."* No doubt[41] this and other such traditions were recounted by the holy Prophet ﷺ to impress the high status of his beloved daughter Fatima ﷺ on the minds of the people; in the hope that they would pay her the respect that was her due, even after his demise.

In the same book on page 141 there is a tradition narrated on the authority of Ayesha that "Fatima resembled her father in her bearing and her gait so much that it was difficult to differentiate

---

[39] "Say (O Muhammad) I do not ask from you any recompense save the love of my near relatives. And whoever earns good We give him more of good therein; surely Allah is Forgiving and grateful". (42:23)

[40] 'Mishkat ul Masabih' – translated by Maulvi Qutubuddin, Vol 4, Pg 145, 141. Ch. 'Babul Fitan'.

[41] Translator's Note: The obvious reason for these kind of constant pronouncements by the Prophet ﷺ was to make his Ummah aware of the high position of Fatima ﷺ.

between them from afar. And he ﷺ used to refer to her as 'a part of his body and soul'. Whenever she came into his presence he would rise and greet her and would make her sit in his spot".

Contrast this respect accorded to Fatima ﷺ by Allah ﷻ on the Day of Judgment together with the Prophet ﷺ's during his own lifetime on the one hand, to the behaviour of Umar and his companions on the other, in taking the fire to burn her house down, throwing a rope around the neck of her husband Ali ﷺ and dragging him by force in order to get him to pay fealty to Abu Bakr! Additionally, also compare the behaviour of Abu Bakr in rejecting her claim by falsifying her evidence and not accepting the witnesses of Ali ﷺ and his two sons Hasnain ﷺ in this matter.

Hence, keeping in mind the Day of Judgment which is inevitable and when one and all of us will be ordered to lower our eyes and pay the respect (which is her due) to the noble personality of Fatima Zahra ﷺ, let every seeker of 'Fairness and Truth' be aware to not simply be satisfied in recognising her high position, *but also being vocal* in speaking out about the atrocities committed against her by the Muslim Ummah under the watch of the two Sheiks.

9.13: Enmity of Ayesha Toward Fatima ﷺ

The extract given below has been taken from a book written by a German author Kurt Frichler in his book '**Ayesha After The Prophet**' translated in 1933 AD which illustrates the intense animosity which Ayesha harboured against Fatima ﷺ. Following is the condensed text:

"Ayesha was always antagonistic toward Fatima. This trait was present even before she married the Prophet. After her marriage, this animosity intensified even further, and she became the worst enemy of Fatima. When Fatima became the mother of two sons Hasan and Husain, this jealously turned into an outright rancour and hatred. She never entered the house of Fatima even once after her marriage to the Prophet. On the contrary Fatima, who was truly kind and pleasant by nature, always greeted Ayesha and kept the channels of communication open with her; but Ayesha was always curt with her and kept her responses very brief and non-committal. The Prophet's deep and intense attachment and love for his only daughter was one of the causes for her own intense jealously. She would be most happy when leaving for a trip outside the city of Medina as that implied that she would not have to put up with the sight of Fatima coming to her father's home!

When Fatima became the mother of Hasan and Husain and Ayesha witnessed the Prophet's deep attachment to his grandchildren she became a mortal enemy of Fatima. Any display of affection by the Prophet to his daughter or her children affected her adversely. It was a normal practice of the Prophet that whenever he returned from his travels, he would first stop by at the house of his daughter and greet her with the words *'As-Salaam Alaikum Ya Ahley Bayt un-Nabi - Peace be upon you, O people of the House of the Prophet!'* before proceeding to his own home. This annoyed Ayesha ever more, who used to openly say that she did not like Fatima or her children, and that she resented Fatima's visiting the Prophet's house! With the demise of the Prophet, she saw an opportune moment to give full vent to her animosity and 'get even with Fatima'. Consequently, seeing the field wide open, she spared no effort in urging, aiding, and abetting her father Abu Bakr to seize the Caliphate for himself. The driving force behind her instigation was again her enmity towards Ali, Fatima, and their children.

After Abu Bakr became the Caliph, Ali ﷺ once questioned him as to whether he was aware of the financial hardships of the Muslims of the Ummah? And if he was aware, then why was he not doing something about it? He further elaborated saying: *"I am speaking on the principle of Islamic justice as to whether it is fair that the wife of the Prophet ﷺ is entitled to a lavish stipend of 12,000 dirhams whereas the daughter of the Prophet and his grandchildren who are from his loins do not receive even a single dirham?"* Abu Bakr contritely replied that this was not intentional but had been due to an oversight on his part that he had forgotten the entitlement of Ali and his wife and children; but henceforth he promised he would arrange to send 48 sacks of wheat annually for Fatima and her children's consumption. But in reality, not a single sack of wheat was ever sent, because as soon as Ayesha became aware of this decision, she vehemently objected and stopped it from being executed. Shortly thereafter the daughter of the Prophet passed away; but even had she survived, Ayesha would have ensured that not a single grain from the quantity of wheat committed would have entered the house of Fatima!" [End of quote].

9.14: Ayesha's Enmity was one of the Causes of the Death of Fatima ﷺ

Referring to the book mentioned in the previous section, the author Kurt Frichler continues on Page 56 of this same book 'Ayesha After The Prophet' he writes as follows: "What was the reason that Fatima passed away when she was still in the prime of her youth? There were two factors: One was the sadness and shock of her father's demise along with the events that ensued; and the second was the intense animosity of Ayesha towards her, her husband Ali, and her children. A month after her father's death Fatima fell ill. Nevertheless, she was still capable of walking to her father's grave assisted by her maid Fizza and her two sons. Progressively her condition worsened. Antar, the slave of Prophet Muhammad recounts: 'As her health deteriorated, she was unable to continue this practice. I was observing that she was getting weaker by the day, and apart from Fizza, another lady by the name of Asma bint

Umais came to assist her in her daily household chores. I will never forget that day when the sun was about to set, and the room was shrouded in darkness. The children (two boys and two girls) were present in the house. They were all wailing and embracing their mother, while Asma was trying to keep them away from her. The boys stood on either side of their mother weeping and the two younger girls were crying and clinging to their mother's bosom. Asma was trying to console them and ease them away from her. The walls of her chamber and the entire structure itself appeared to be mourning with them! Fizza lighted a lamp and entered the room followed shortly by Ali who upon entering the room and seeing Fatima's condition also began to weep and shed tears.

Fatima, who was also crying gained control over herself and addressed her husband saying: 'O Abul Hasan! I am leaving this world very soon. My children have recently been deprived of the loving companionship of their grandfather and will also now lose their mother. This will make their hearts very vulnerable; and motherless children are very tender-hearted and hurt easily. Please ensure that their hearts are protected from any severe sadness so that they do not miss their mother. O Ali! Hold my funeral without any loss of time and bury me in the middle of the night as I do not want anyone who has shown animosity toward me after my father's death and hurt me by their enmity, to partake of my funeral or even visit my grave.' Ali began to weep profusely, to the extent that all of us also began to wail loudly (when we saw Ali crying out loudly). We saw that Fatima's lips started to move again, and we fell into a silence to hear what she was saying, and I heard her last words invoking salutations upon Gabriel and on the Angels of Allah: As Salaam Alaika Ya Gabriel, As Salaam alaika Ya Malaaikatal Rabbi!

The children realized that their mother was no more, and they started wailing and clinging to their mother's lifeless body. Ali ﷺ

who while weeping out loudly himself, gently separated them and turning to me said: *'O Antar! You have heard Fatima's last words that she wished to be buried at night itself; and for those who have hurt her after the Prophet's death should not even be allowed to come close to her grave or funeral? Fetch the people to dig her grave, while I will give her the ceremonial bath and shroud her'.* I then brought two persons, and we had the grave prepared. Ali and his Uncle Abbas, along with Asma bint Omais, the maid Fizza and the children brought the body out from the inner chamber. The funeral prayers were performed, and her body was escorted and lowered into the grave by Ali ﷺ.

After the burial Ali broke out emotionally and cried: *'O Fatima! I swear by the Lord, your death has darkened the world for me and your departure has left me without support or patience! I will never forget this calamity for the rest of my life.'* He then asked me, Abbas, and Fizza to take the children home. I requested Ali to be allowed to stay behind as I had served her in her father's house since her birth. He acceded to my wish, and I stayed behind while the others took the children home. Both Ali ﷺ and I sat near the grave all night, and Ali kept saying: *'O Prophet! The treasure which you had entrusted with me on my wedding I have returned to you. Fatima is lucky that she has been reunited with you. I wish that I could be as lucky to be with you at an earliest moment as well!'* Ali ﷺ then started praising the Almighty Lord and imploring to Him saying: *'O Allah! Whatever You have Willed for me, I am content with Your Decision; and accept your Decree to the extent that I have acquiesced and submitted myself to bearing the loss of Fatima from my side. I only implore You to give me the strength and beg You to give me the fortitude to bear this great calamity which has befallen me.'*

We remained at her graveside all night, and with the breaking of dawn we offered our morning prayers close to her grave; and once again sat by the graveside till the time of sunrise. Ali ﷺ then bade his tearful goodbye to Fatima 🕮 and we departed back to the house".

9.15: False Tradition of the Marriage of Umme Kulthum to Umar

In a bid to lower the position of the Ahlul Bayt 🕮, a false tradition was coined and circulated that Umar ibn Khattab married Fatima 🕮's youngest daughter Umme Kulthum 🕮 when she was only six years in age, while he, on the contrary, was quite an old man! The lady known as 'Umme Kulthum' who was married to Umar was the daughter of Asma bint Umays born to her from her second marriage when she was the wife of Abu Bakr. Her first marriage was with Ja'far e Tayyar 🕮 the brother of Imam Ali 🕮. When he got martyred in the Battle of Muta, she was wed to Abu Bakr, from whom she had two children: Umme Kulthum and Mohammed bin Abu Bakr. After the death of her second husband Abu Bakr, she got married [for the third time] to Imam Ali 🕮; and these two children accompanied her to the house of Imam Ali and were brought up under his guardianship.

Ayesha was instrumental in arranging for her stepsister Umme Kulthum's marriage to Umar; and this is recorded in 'Kitab al Bawariq' whose author quotes two sources[42] supporting this fact. Similarly, in 'Kashful Ghammah'[43] it is recorded that the third wife of Abu Bakr was named Habiba bint Kharja Ansar. When Abu Bakr died in 13 AH, she was pregnant with a child which she delivered some months later in 14 AH whom she named Umme Kulthum. She is the one who is supposed to have married Umar in his later life when she grew up. Coincidentally, all three wives of Umar

---

[42] 'Istiyab' by Ibn Birr; and 'Kanzul Ammal' by Mullah Mohammed Taqi.

[43] 'Kashful Ghammah' – page 488, printed by Siddiqui Press Lahore.

happened to be named 'Umme Kulthum'. It is quite possible that these common names gave rise to this confusion.

The first wife of Umar – Umme Kulthum was the daughter of Jarul Khazaiyah. Umar had two sons from her: Abdullah and Zaid. After Umar converted to Islam, this woman refused to convert with him and was consequently divorced by Umar[44].

Umar's second wife was also named 'Umme Kulthum' and was commonly known as "Umme Kulthum bint Abi Mo'eeth." She was initially married to Amr ibn Aas and after her divorce, later got married to Umar.[45]

The third wife was 'Umme Kulthum bint Jamila' - the daughter of Asim ibn Thabit[46].

Apart from these three women which we have given references thereof, the fourth wife of Umar was also called 'Umme Kulthum' – bint Abu Bakr from his wife Asma bint Omais, as discussed and clarified earlier. The concoctors of false traditions took advantage of this confusion of identical names and fallaciously (or erroneously) documented that the last 'Umme Kulthum'' was the daughter of Ali ﷺ and Fatima ﷺ.

Fatima ﷺ had four children: two boys Hasan ﷺ and Husain ﷺ, and two daughters Hazrat Zainab and Hazrat Umme Kulthum ﷺ. Her fifth child Mohsin was martyred while still in her womb, due to the miscarriage brought about by the heavy fall of the door upon her when her house was attacked by an unruly and disrespectful mob of prominent companions' (Sahaba) of the Prophet ﷺ! Her older daughter Hazrat Zainab ﷺ was married to Abdullah ibn

---

[44] 'Tarikh e Kamil' – bu OIbne Atheer, Vol 3, Pg.22; 'Asabah' – Pg. 343; also 'Sahih Bukhari'.

[45] 'Tafsir e Kabir' - by Fakhruddin Razi; Vol 8, Pg 191; 'Sahih Bukhari'- Vol 3, Pg 76; and 'Qatlani' – printed Naval Kishore Press, Vol 4, Pg 349.

[46] 'Tarikh e Khamis' – Vol 2, Pg 251, printed in Egypt.

Ja'far-e-Tayyar 🕮 and her younger daughter Hazrat Umme Kulthum 🕮 got married to his brother Mohammed ibn Ja'far-e-Tayyar 🕮.

The foregoing was a brief account of facts in support of denial of the false tradition of Umme Kulthum 🕮 the daughter of Fatima 🕮 being married to Umar. There are many books which have gone into greater detail on this subject. We will only list a few of these as follows:

1. *Risala Kanz-e-Kulthum,* complied by Syed Ali Azher, Raees -e- Khajwa.
2. *Risalaye–Shareh Kanz-e-Kulthum* by Maulana Syed Sajjad Husayn.
3. *Kitab-e-Naziyeh Athna Ashari* by Mirza Ahmed Kamil Dehlawi.
4. *Qaul-e-Mousooq* by Barkaat Husayn Sajjada Nasheen Khankha.

9.16: Compilation of Quran by Uthman Authorizing the Copy of Zaid Ibn Thabit While Rejecting the Copy Compiled by Ali 🕮

The first two Sheikhs, Abu Bakr and Umar attempted to put together a unified version of the Quran but were unsuccessful. When Uthman became the Caliph, he issued orders that anyone having any portion or segments of the written Quran should submit it to the government officials. This was a positive attempt at gathering the fragmented verses which were spread haphazardly among the elders of the Ummah. Imam Ali 🕮's complete compilation of the holy Quran was also petitioned. A committee was appointed by Uthman consisting of Zaid bin Thabit, Abdur Rahman ibn Zubair, Sayeed ibn Aas, Abdullah ibn Harith bin Hisham.

It is to be noted that of these men every single one of them were against Hazrat Ali ﷺ. They then selected a specific version which was officially approved for publication, all other copies were ordered to be burnt, while the version compiled by Ali ﷺ was rejected and returned to him. This, despite the innumerable traditions from the Prophet ﷺ and several verses from the Holy Quran itself, linking Ali ﷺ with the Quran: As an example, the following tradition in which the Prophet ﷺ stated: *"Ali is with the Quran and the Quran is with Ali. They will never separate from each other until they meet me at the Pool of Kauther"*.

According to a hadith recorded by Mulla Jami in his book 'Shawahed al Nabuwah' Ali ﷺ's command of the Quran was such that he would complete the recitation of the **entire Quran** in the time it took him for mounting his horse and placing his foot from one side of the stirrup to the other!

Ali ﷺ's own declaration: *"Ask me about anything before you lose me. I will tell you about everything, including the Book of Allah. I will tell you where each single verse of it was revealed, with reference to when, where and why and on what occasion it was revealed: whether on land or mountain, water or air; on earth or the skies; along with the external and internal* (Zahir and Baatin) *meanings and nuances of every verse!"*

On another occasion Ali ﷺ has said: *"My example is like that of the Pole Star around which everything revolves. The Fountains of Knowledge originate from me and the lofty elevation and stature of my knowledge is such that no 'bird of (anyone's) imagination' can ever aspire to scale up to even the lowest to its height."*

He ﷺ has further stated that the entire Quran is encompassed in the Seven Verses of the Opening Surah of *Al Fateha*; which are further condensed into the word of *'Bismillah'* at its beginning; which is again compressed into the alphabet *'Ba'* of 'Bismillah' – and **this** ultimately is encapsulated into the '**Dot**' beneath the *'Ba'* of '**Bismillah**' – And he then added: *"I am the 'Dot' beneath the 'Ba' of 'Bismillah'!"*

According to Khwarzimi and Tabarani who both narrate from Abdullah ibn Masood that the Prophet ﷺ taught him 70 chapters of the Quran, while the rest he learned from Imam Ali ؑ. Ali ؑ's knowledge of the Quran was God given, and the Quran itself bears witness to this fact. Ref: Surah Raad: *"And those who disbelieve say: You are not a Messenger!' Say (to them O Prophet): **Allah is sufficient as a witness between me and you and the one who has complete knowledge of The Book."** (13:43). In this verse the one who is referred to as "one who has complete knowledge of the Book" is none other than Ali ؑ! This verse was revealed when Ali ؑ was only 11 years old!

These kinds of verses are supported by various traditions from the holy Prophet ﷺ wherein a few of the oft quoted ones being: *"Ali is with the Quran, and Quran is with Ali"*; *"I am the City of Knowledge and Ali is it's Gateway"*; *"I leave behind you two precious and weighty Entities [of faith]: the Book of Allah and my Ahlul Bayt. These two will never separate from each other till they meet me at the Pool of Kauther"* and many other similar statements endorsing Ali ؑ's knowledge of the holy Quran.

Another verse of the holy Quran points to Ali ؑ as being the 'Inheritor of the Book': *"Then We gave the Book for an Inheritance to those whom We chose from among Our servants...."* (35:32). But the irony of the situation was that despite all these virtues and testimonies in favour of Ali ؑ from the Prophet ﷺ and the holy Quran itself, **his** version of the compilation of the Quran was rejected and the version compiled by the Committee set up by Uthman was accepted and endorsed as the Official Copy! Allama Jalaluddin Suyuti writes that "Ali ؑ was the sole person who had collected a full version of the holy Quran and presented it to the Prophet ﷺ in accordance with the sequence of revelation".

Muhammad ibn Sireen writes that "had this version [compiled by Ali ﷺ] reached us, we would have gotten hold of a book of immense value to us". In 'Tabaqaat ibn Saad'[47] and 'Riaz-un Nazarra'[48] both the scholars state that "Had this version reached us we would have retained the verses in the sequence of revelation; and the chapters in their proper order, without any errors or confusion over the vowels and articulation of the various nuances and intricacies of the holy verses". The present version now in circulation has a mixture of verses that were revealed some in Mecca and some in Madina all put into the same chapters; and these 114 chapters have been arranged according to their individual lengths: with the longer ones being placed at the beginning and the shorter ones comprising of the last 30 chapters been placed at its end.

Dr Taha Husayn in his book 'Fitnatul Kubra' also criticizes the method of compilation used by Uthman by stating that he selected such persons to collect the official version who were not suited do so; and ignored many close companions who were known to be 'Qaaris' in the very lifetime of the Prophet ﷺ and knew the whole Quran by heart. One such person was Abdullah ibn Masood who was ignored, and the task was entrusted to Zaid bin Thabit who was a mere minor during the time of the Prophet ﷺ; while many of the other venerable companions also knew the Quran from memory. He concludes that this method adopted by Uthman is subject to some doubts.

---

[47] 'Tabaqaat ibn Saad' - Vol 2, Pg 101.

[48] 'Riaz-un Nazarra – Vol 2, Pg 168.

9.17: Deficiencies in the Quran According to Some Scholars

It will not be out of place here to discuss and review whether there were any changes made in the collection of the Quran, and if so, whether they affect the content of the holy Book.

Every sect of Islam accepts the fact that the verses were not arranged in the sequence of their revelation. Several Sunni traditionalists opine that some verses that were revealed in Mecca are part of the Medinite chapters, and some of the later revelations have been listed in the earlier part of the Book and visa versa; and they also state that parts of some verses were not only corrupted but also deleted.

The opinion of the Shia scholars is that except for the change of sequence of the verses, there was nothing deleted or added to the text; and this in fact, is the *Original Book*; and that the change of sequence does not affect the 'Completeness' nor the 'Spirit' of the holy Quran. It may cause some confusion in grasping its meanings and cause some difficulty in identifying those verses which were superseded by later verses; but according to the Shias, the exegeses given by the holy Imams of the Ahlul Bayt 🕊 are sufficient to guide us to their correct meanings. These Infallible Imams have instructed us to adhere to the Quran **as it exists** in its present form, and follow its injunctions without reservations, as the explanations and elaborations given by them will be sufficient to guide us to the correct meaning.

Some Sunnis level the criticism at Shias saying that the 'Shia Quran' has been changed and consequently the Shias do not believe in the version of the Quran as it exists amongst the Muslim Ummah today! However, this is far from the truth, and it is solely among the Sunni schools that this subject of the 'changes' (*Tahreef*) is mentioned and/or discussed. Hence the onus is on the Sunni

Schools to prove or disprove this allegation. The Shias, however, are content to accept the Quran in its present state without question, *especially so,* considering their Imams' ﷺ's injunction for their followers to adhere to it "as is".

In Surah Hijr Allah ﷻ states: *"We have sent down the Zikr and we are its Guardian"* (15:09). According to the Sunnis the word *'Zikr'* in this verse in their opinion refers to the Holy Prophet ﷺ, and that the Almighty Lord has promised to *safeguard His Prophet* rather than the Book, and protect him from his enemies, just as He has stated in other verses elsewhere in the Quran for instance: in Surah Talaq: *"O men of understanding that believe! Allah has indeed revealed to you a reminder: An Apostle who recites to you the clear communications of Allah..."* (65:10-11). But Allama Fakhruddin Razi in his 'Tafsir e Kabir' and other venerable Sunni scholars such as Baidawi and Suyuti debate that the word *'Zikr'* can be interpreted for either the holy 'Book' or the 'holy Prophet' depending on the context. Consequently, these types of interpretations when presented to the public have resulted in adding to their confusion in understanding the Quranic verses.

Apart from the foregoing confusion, another controversial point was also introduced by others, further adding to this dilemma by putting forth arguments about the *number of alphabets* contained in the Quran. Various scholars like Suyuti in 'Durre Manthur' and Fakhruddin Razi in his 'Tafsir' have given these numbers to range from anywhere between 200,000 to 330,000! They further go on to say that the chapters of *Falaq* and *Naas* were not even a part of the Quran, but that the holy Prophet ﷺ had given it to them as a 'Talisman' for protection against Evil. Suyuti goes even further: as far as to say that the opening chapter of Surah Fateha was also not part of the holy Quran! In his 'Durre

Manthur'[49] he records a narration by Ayesha which states that "when she used to read the Surah Ahzab (Chapter 33) during the time of the Prophet ﷺ it had 200 verses. But when Uthman published his version, there were only 73 verses!"

In 'Musnad of Ahmad ibne Hanbal'[50] there is another quote from Ayesha in which she states that she used to recite some verses of the Quran and keep them under her pillow, which were eventually "eaten by a domesticated goat, when she herself was busy tending to the illness of the holy Prophet ﷺ." To add to this confusion, Abdullah ibn Umar also stated that what is presented as the Book today is not the whole Quran, because according to him many verses were lost.

Other than these, the books compiled by various other Sunni scholars abound with discourses relating to the changes about the additions and deletions of verses in the present Quran. According to ibn Abil Hadid, Ayesha used to say that Uthman should be killed because not only had he made many changes in the present version of the Quran but had also burnt the other various authentic copies of the Quran!

9.18: Ayesha's Opinion about Uthman Making Changes to the Quranic Text

Quoting Kurt Frischler again from in his book 'Ayesha After the Prophet' wherein he writes on page 396, that: "Ayesha tried her best to install Talha as the Caliph after Umar, but when she failed in this attempt, she made a pact with Uthman giving her allegiance to him to keep Ali away from the Caliphate. Uthman in turn

---

[49] 'Tafsir Durre Manthur', Suyuti – Vol 2, Pg 106; and in 'Itqaan' – Vol. 2, Pg 25.

[50] 'Musnad-e-Ahmad- ibne Hambal' – Vol 6, Pg 269.

promised to raise her pension from 180,000 Dirhams to 500,000 Dirhams annually. However, after becoming the Caliph he reneged on this promise and thereby brought upon himself the wrath of Ayesha who became his arch enemy. To expose and get even with Uthman [and in order to be more effective as a speaker] she mounted a camel and went out in public to deliver a fiery speech, addressing them as 'O holy warriors of the Army of God! This Uthman has made a lot of changes and alterations to the Book of Allah on the pretext of collecting the Quran. This is an unpardonable sin; hence it is mandatory upon you who are the soldiers of the Holy Army, to avenge this sin by removing him from his office. Should he resist, kill him, and relieve the Muslims of this tyrant!"

9.19: Shia Scholars do not Subscribe to the Belief that the Quran has been Altered

Most of the Shia Scholars are of the opinion that there have been no changes made in the holy text which could have impacted on its meanings or negatively affected its 'Essence or Spirit'. Allah ﷻ Himself has promised to preserve and protect the glorious Quran in various verses, for example: In a 'Guarded Tablet' (*Lauh-e-Mahfooz*): Surah al-Buruj, (85: 21-22) as well as in Surah Waqiya (56:77-80) wherein He states: *"Most certainly this is The Quran in a 'Tablet well Protected' (in an elevated place) which **none shall touch** save the Purified Ones. A revelation from the Lord of the Worlds!"*

To be noted here is the fact that Allah ﷻ states that *"none shall touch it save the purified ones"*. Here the meaning implied in the word "TOUCH" is esoteric in nature; in that, only those with a deep understanding of the true knowledge of its 'Text' and its 'Essence' are the only ones who can understand the implicit and explicit meanings of the esteemed Book. The holy Prophet ﷺ and his holy progeny were the ones who had truly imbibed the essence of the holy Book and as such, *they are the ones* referred to as the "*Purified Ones*".

Normally speaking, it is a daily occurrence that all sorts of people: Muslims and non-Muslims alike, whether in a state of ritual purification or not, touch the Book on a regular basis; so, this obviously does not connote the real meaning that is alluded here: that "*none can touch it except the purified ones*". It obviously points toward a deeper and more significant meaning alluding to the fact that the Glorious Quran was revealed on the 'Heart (*Qalb*) of the Holy Prophet ﷺ' and was understood in like manner by his Infallible Ahlul Bayt ؏; and *this* is the real inference to the *Essence* of the Quran which cannot be imbibed by any, other than those designated as the 'Purified Ones' by Allah ﷻ!

As far as the misconception about the alterations in the Quran is concerned, the Shia scholars put forth the argument that since Allah ﷻ Himself has taken it upon Him to protect its integrity, there is no possibility whatsoever that the Quran has been changed. To this end we quote a few verses randomly from the Quran. For instance, in Surah **Al Fatah** (The Victory): "*Yureedoona Ayn-yubaddelu Kalaam-Allah: They desire to change the Word of Allah, say: By no means shall you achieve....*"(48:15): Also, in Surah **Nisa**: "*Minal Lazeena haadu yuharrefoonal Kalema anm muwadhey-hi.: There are those who alter words from their places.... O You who have been given the Book! Believe that which We have revealed, verifying what you have (4:46-47).*" Then again, as a guarantee against any corruption creeping into the holy verses of the Quran, Allah ﷻ in Surah **Hijr** (The Rock) clearly and unambiguously states: "*Inna Nahno Nazzal naz-Zikra, wa Inna lahu la Haafezoon... Surely We have revealed the Reminder and We will most surely be its Guardian*" (15-9).

Considering the above, we are now faced with the task to examine and see how the Almighty Lord has arranged to protect and guard His holy Book. Towards this purpose we see that in *(Surah **Fatir**)* He states that He has elevated some 'Elite People' who have been chosen by Him to inherit His Book: *"Thumma Aurathnal Kitab al-lazeenas-Tafaina min Ibaadena.... Then We gave the Book for an inheritance to those whom **We** Chose from among Our servants. (35-32)*. On the authority of this verse the holy Prophet ﷺ announced the famous tradition known as the *Hadith-e-Thaqalain* in which he said: *"I leave behind me Two Weighty Entities (Important Heritages) among you: The Quran and my Ahlul Bayt. They will not part company with each other until they meet me at the Pool of Kauther"*.

Hence those who attach themselves to these Infallible 'Chosen Personalities' have no doubt that the Quranic verses were ever lost or altered. Throughout the Islamic history, all the Infallible Imans from the Ahlul Bayt ﷺ of the Prophet ﷺ have advocated to their followers to **accept the Quran in its entirety in its present form, as it has not been altered or modified.** The Shia scholars are, therefore, are completely free from doubt regarding this matter. We give below the opinions expressed by some venerated and famous Shia scholars on this subject:

The great Shia scholar Sheikh Saduq records on page 28 of his famous book *'Risalate-e-Etehqadaat'* ['A Treatise of Beliefs'] that "there is no doubt in my mind whatsoever about there being any alterations or omissions in the Holy Book; and that whatever is contained 'between the two covers' of the present version is most certainly the Quran in its entirety. Those people that say that there were more chapters in the Quran which are now missing are liars". The only observation which this Sheik has made is that there were two [2] sets of Suras [chapters] which were so connected with each other, that if they are being recited in the daily ritual prayers, they should be recited together in conjunction with each other. These are chapters 93/94: **Ad-Duha** (The Glorious Morning) and **Al Inshira** (The Expansion); and secondly, chapters 105/106 **Al-Feel** (The Elephant) and **Al Quraish** (The Tribe of Quraish).

Allama Tabari in his 'Tafsir-e-Majma`ul Bayan'[51] is in complete agreement with the foregoing.

Allama Sayyed Murtaza 'Alam-ul-Huda' - another venerable Shia scholar, also reinforces the point that the holy Quran is complete; and is also of the same opinion as Sheikh Saduq that there are no changes [be it addition or deletion] in the actual text of the Holy Book. The other notable scholar who endorses this same sentiment is Allama Sheik Muhammad bin Al Hasan Tusi in his renowned book 'Minhaaj-us-Sadiqeen'. He argues that it is not possible that the Prophet ﷺ would have asked us to adhere to a Quran which was incomplete. In addition he relates a tradition from Imam Ja'far al-Sadiq ؏ [which has also been referenced in several books like 'Kitab ul Bayan, Kitab Al-Kafi, and Mahasin-e-Ayoob bin Harith], that the Imam ؏ used to say that *"any tradition which is brought to your attention should be compared in light of the existing Quran; and if it goes against the Quran, it should be rejected, because everything is contained within this Quran"*. This is further proof for us that the Quranic text is intact and complete.

However, among the various arguments raised by the Sunni scholars, one of the objections brought forward is that "since the Shias believe that the first three Caliphs were 'dishonest usurpers', then how can they trust that the existing Quran which was collected by Caliph Uthman was not tampered with, and/or altered, and is in fact, the original Quran?" To this the Shias reply that neither Uthman nor the committee appointed by him, *personally* "wrote" any of the verses of the Quran but rather, they merely

---

[51] 'Tafsir-e-Majma`ul Bayan' – Allama Tabari, Vol 1, Pg 5.

collected the various "*Suras* and *Ayats*" (chapters and verses) from different sources; including the inputs from numerous "*Qaaris*" (Reciters of the holy verses) spread all over the Islamic lands. Furthermore, there were many "*Huffaz*" (persons who had memorized the holy Quran in its entirety) present during that period, along with thousands of other laymen who *also knew* a great many verses by heart; to the extent that it is believed that even the Infidels who had not converted to Islam, were also familiar with a great many Quranic verses. Additionally, it is to be noted that the Quran was constantly being recited for 43 years by the Muslim Ummah, and its various verses containing admonitions and injunctions were in current usage by many of the populace who either had the *complete* Quran, or a great many of its verses committed to memory. Thus, when the 'Order for Compilation' was issued, all submissions from varying sources were reviewed and incorporated into the final "approved version".

In connection with the belief that the Quran could retain its pristine purity and authenticity while being compiled under the authority of [so to speak], an "Usurper Caliph", the Shias put forth the analogy that if Musa ﷺ could be raised from his infancy to adulthood under the "*Baatil*" (Pervert) forces in the house of Pharoah, and still retain his purity, then it is not to be wondered at that the Book of Allah ﷻ would also be given the same protection under the leadership of a person who was unsuited for the position!

9.20: Refusal of Ayesha to Allow the Burial of Imam Hasan ﷺ Near the Grave of his Grandfather - the Holy Prophet ﷺ to the Extent of Issuing an Order to Rain Down Arrows on his Coffin

Imam Hasan 🕮, the first grandson of the Prophet 🕮 was a replica of his holy Grandfather 🕮 in his mannerisms, his looks, and his physical form. It is a great injustice of history that he was denied his right to Caliphate by the connivance of the accursed Muawiyah. The Imam's last wish was to be buried near his holy Grandfather the Prophet 🕮, but *"if this was not possible for any reason"* he intimated with an almost prophetic foresight [!], *his request would then be to be buried in the graveyard of **Baqi** near the grave of his paternal grandmother Lady Fatima bint Asad 🕮.*

Upon his death according to his last Will, when his coffin was taken to the place near the Prophet 🕮's grave, a group of persons intercepted and stopped the funeral procession from proceeding further. Attempts by the procession to disregard their objection and proceed toward the burial site resulted in a barrage of arrows being showered upon them, of which about 70 got embedded in the revered corpse of Imam Hasan 🕮. Upon being asked the reason for this loathsome behaviour, the reply was that Ayesha had issued orders to stop them from coming any further. Imam Husain 🕮 approached Ayesha to obtain her permission, but she denied it saying that the area was in <u>her</u> property, and she would not allow Hasan 🕮 (the grandson of the Prophet 🕮) to be buried there.[52]

In the two books: 'Nasikh-al-Tawarikh' and 'Jela-el-Uyoon' it is written that: "Ayesha was adamant in her refusal stating: 'I will not allow Hasan to be buried here, as long as there remains a single hair on my head!' She then ordered the group from Bani Ummayya to shoot their arrows on the coffin; and it is recorded that as many as 70 arrows pierced the dead body of Imam Hasan 🕮".

---

[52] 'Rauzatul Manazir' by ibn Shahnah Hanafi; 'Usdul Ghaba' by ibn Athir and 'Hayatul Haiwan' by Damiri.

It is worth noting that in several other reliable historical references[53] it is recorded that Ayesha readily and most willingly agreed to have Abu Bakr and Umar buried next to the Prophet ﷺ, but adamantly refused this honour being granted to one of the most favourite of his family members: his beloved first grandson Imam Hasan ؑ, the one whom Allah ﷻ and the noble Prophet ﷺ had declared to be One of the Two Leaders of the Youths of Paradise!

Jalaluddin Suyuti[54] narrates from Saad ibne Musayyab that Abu Bakr had willed that he should be buried alongside the Prophet ﷺ and his wish was duly conducted. Out of deference however, he was laid with his head aligned with the Prophet ﷺ's shoulder. In the same book it is stated that Umar, when his time came near, also sent word to Ayesha that when he died, he would like to be buried next to his friend Abu Bakr. Ayesha responded that though she had reserved this spot for her own eventual burial, she would give preference to Umar over herself; and his request was also conducted. The Persian version of the book 'Jasbul Quloob' records the foregoing incident in greater detail: "This behaviour of Ayesha, however, is not to be gleaned over lightly. It is *very significant* because we can clearly surmise the intense animosity that Ayesha had towards the family of the Prophet ﷺ; in that, while the outsiders were granted permission to be buried close to the Prophet ﷺ, his favourite grandson, his own flesh and blood who was designated by Allah ﷻ and His Prophet as being the 'Leader of The Youth of Paradise' was denied this honour! It is quite normal for

---

[53] 'Tazkirah' by Sibte ibn Jauzi; 'Isbatul Wasiya' by Masudi; 'Sharah-e-Nahjul Balagha' by ibn Abil Hadid; 'Rauzatul Zo'a' by Khudawand Shah; 'Asim-e-Kufi' translated by Ahmed bin Muhammad-e-Hanafi, and 'Tarikh-e-Abul Fida.

[54] 'Tarikh ul Khulafa' – by Jalaluddin Suyuti, Pg 93.

family members to be buried in a communal area of a graveyard, and a request to this effect by Imam Hasan ☙ was not abnormal and should have been conducted with **even greater respect and care**.

Ayesha's refusal to comply to their request demonstrates an extremely unbecoming conduct for the 'Mother of the Muslim Ummah' (*Ummul Muslemeen*) in displaying this sort of irrational behaviour; unless of course, as in this case her extreme hatred and jealously towards the daughter of the Prophet ☙ overpowered her reason and common decency. Her cold-blooded order to shoot arrows on a dead body when there was no disturbance or demonstration of any aggression from the funeral procession, is another example of **her degenerate and inhuman behavior** towards the holy family of the Prophet ☙; and the children of Fatima Zahra ☙! The fact that the people also **actually conducted** such a drastic order by Ayesha, is a clear illustration of how far the Muslims had been swayed against honouring the Prophet ☙'s family, so soon after his demise!"

Justice Amir Ali with reference to Ayesha in his book 'Spirit of Islam' has the said the following: "This lady [Ayesha] had always borne an inveterate dislike towards the son-in-law of Lady Khadija (Ali)".

In another book 'Historian's History of The World'[55] the following comment has been recorded with reference to Ayesha: "... Meanwhile Ayesha, who had caused so much discord and bloodshed, finally had her years numbered upon the Earth in the year 56 Hijra. One of her last acts of vengeance was refusing a sepulcher to the body of Hasan and carrying her malice even beyond the grave by denying his expressed wish to be buried at the side of his Grandsire Muhammad; insisting that the Mansion was

---

[55] 'Historian's History of The World' – Vol 8, Pg 176.

hers so that Hasan, in spite of being the Prophet's beloved first grandson was consequently interred in the ordinary burial ground."

In 'Tabaqat ibn Saad'[56] it is narrated on the authority of Muhammad ibne Umar that "Ayesha used to observe the use of her veil when the grandsons of the Prophet ﷺ, Hasan ؑ and Husayn ؑ happened to be within her presence. Ibn Abbas objected to this practice and told her that this behaviour was contrary to "*Fiqha*" - Islamic Jurisprudence. No other wife of the Prophet ﷺ adopted this behaviour".

In the book 'Thaysarul Bukhari'[57] it is stated that on the contrary, Ayesha did not observe the use of her veil in the presence of her male slave, whereas it was mandatory for her to do so! In her journey towards Basra with the intention to instigate the Battle of Jamal, she went hundreds of miles away from her residence in the company of two men: Talha and Zubair, in clear contempt and violation of the Edicts of Allah ﷻ and the Orders of the Prophet ﷺ; thereby demonstrating clearly the extent of her hatred and jealously against Ali ؑ and his children!

In several reliable books[58] it is mentioned that when Ayesha got news of the assassination of Hazrat Ali ؑ, she was so elated that she burst into a poetic ecstasy and fell into a 'prostration in thankfulness' (*Sajdah Shukr*) for having received this news in her lifetime! Dr Taha Husayn[59] writes that at least two reasons can be traced and identified as the cause for Ayesha's enmity towards Ali ؑ: "The first was beyond Ali ؑ's control; in that, he was married

---

[56] 'Tabaqat ibn Saad' – Vol 8 Pg 50.

[57] 'Thaysarul Bukhari' – Section 10: "Kitab-al-Shahadat" – Pg 75.

[58] 'Tarikh e Tabbarri' – Vol 6, Pg 87, First Edition, Eygpt; 'Maqatil us Sibtain' by Abul Faraj Isphani; 'Hayaat ul Haywaan' by Damiri.

[59] 'Fitnatul Kubra' – Dr. Taha Husayn, Vol 2, Pg 321.

to the only daughter of the Prophet 🕌 and she bore him two sons Hasan and Husain 🕌 who came to be known as the children of the Prophet 🕌 and who continued his legacy by being acknowledged as his progeny; and Ali 🕌 happened to be their father! Ayesha herself had no children from the Prophet 🕌, whereas later in his life Ummul Momineen Maria Qibtiyyah bore him a son Ibrahim, during the last years of his life. This was additional cause for her to fret over; and the fact that she herself remained barren and childless haunted her to the end of her life. The second reason was that after the death of Abu Bakr, his widow Asma bint Umays got married to Imam Ali 🕌 and moved into his household along with her young son Muhammad bin Abu Bakr (Ayesha's stepbrother), who was consequently raised by Ali 🕌 as his own son under his tutelage and guidance. These were the two main reasons for Ayesha's hatred for Ali and his children."

Allama Amar Abu Nasr writes on page 35 of his book that: "Ayesha used to constantly complain against Fatima 🕌 to her father Abu Bakr but did not dare to do so before the holy Prophet, as he used to dote over his daughter intensely and would undoubtedly have rebuked Ayesha severely had she attempted to criticize Fatima in his presence."

In like manner, Shams-ul Ulema Nazeer Ahmed in his book 'Ruya-as-Sadiqa' has openly written that Ayesha was always against Fatima 🕌 and she used to hate her children and everyone else connected with her family. This was no secret; and she herself officially announced this fact in the Battle of Jamal; thus, leaving no room for any of her supporters who may wish to absolve her of this unbecoming trait! This sort of behaviour cannot be viewed as being merely at the level of an internal family squabble, but was a clear violation of the Quranic injunction (42:23) to love the family of the holy Prophet: (*Muwaddatah fil Qurba*), as well as acting against the famous tradition of '*Hadith e Saqalain*' ordering the

Ummah to remain attached to his '*Two Weighty Heritages*' – The Quran and his holy family (*Itrat*).

The foundation of 'Enmity' sowed toward the family of the holy Prophet ﷺ by Ayesha has continued over the centuries to this present day. No member from his progeny died a natural death; beginning with the first grandson of the Prophet ﷺ being poisoned and his dead body being desecrated by a barrage of arrows; while the second grandson was brutally martyred in the scorching plains of Kerbala and his body trampled under the hooves of the enemies' horses! Every other descendant from the progeny of these holy Imams were similarly poisoned or put to death unnaturally at the hands of the Ummah following in the footsteps laid down by their enemies of the earlier generations.

It is recorded by Yaqubi[60] that when Ayesha mounted a mule to personally intercept the funeral procession of Imam Hasan ؑ, her nephew Qasim the son of Muhammad ibn Abu Bakr addressed her saying: "O Aunt! We have yet to recover from the ignominy of the Battle of Jamal when you were mounted on a Camel; let us not now disgrace ourselves by going into a Battle of The Mule"!

9.21: Dialogue Between a Slave-girl and Sunni Scholars about the Burial of Abu Bakr and Umar near the Grave of the Prophet ﷺ

This debate took place in the Court of Haroon al-Rasheed and has been recorded in several reliable books; and more recently in a book by Maulana Ragheb Husain[61] who writes that there were many eminent Sunni Scholars present in the court of Haroon, such

---

[60] 'Tarikh e Yaqubi', Vol 2.

[61] 'Manazeray Husayniya' – published in Lucknow, India, 1972.

as Qazi Abu Yusuf, Ibrahim bin Khaled Aouni, Imam Shafei and others when this incident took place.

The name of the slave-girl was Husniyyah. She put forward the following question: "When during his own lifetime, upon receiving the command from Allah ﷻ that all doors leading into the Masjid be closed, the Prophet ﷺ had accordingly ordered all doors leading into the mosque to be closed and sealed off; except his own door and that of Ali ﷺ's: which meant that the rest of the homes were separated from being within the precincts of the Masjid-e-Nabawi. This being the case, then on what authority were Abu Bakr and Umar given permission to be buried next to the Prophet ﷺ's grave when there is also a Quranic Edict that nobody should enter the Prophet ﷺ's house without his permission?"

Imam Shafei replied: "The Sunnis believe that Ayesha and Hafsa granted the permission each for their own fathers as part of the 'Meher' (Husband's Settlement) due to them from the Prophet." To this Husniyyah replied: "But according to the verse in Surah Ahzab (33:50) which instructs '*O Prophet do not go near your wives until you first pay them their dowries (Meher)*' hence the '*Meher*' would have already been paid a long time ago! This being the case, where was the question of the land also being part of the '*Meher*'?" To this question Abu Yusuf interceded: "I personally believe that Ayesha and Hafsa received this land as part of their 'Inheritance' being the wives of the Prophet". Husniyyah promptly responded: "Ayesha's own father Abu Bakr had said to the Prophet's daughter Fatima ﷺ at the time of dispute of Fadak that he believed that the Prophet had said, 'We Prophets leave no inheritances.' So, under what pretext have these two wives used this land and awarded it for the burial of their fathers?"

After this, Husniyyah proceeded further with her argument, and reminded them to: "keep in mind the fact that at the time of his demise the Prophet ﷺ had left behind nine wives, one daughter and an uncle, Abbas. The property left behind by him ﷺ consisted of small apartments measuring about 6 '*hands*' in length and 4 '*hands*' in width. According to rules of Islamic Jurisprudence (*Shariah*) the wives are each entitled to 1/8ᵗʰ of this total land area left behind. When distributed among the 9 wives, it would amount to only a 'handful' of space for each wife. This being the case, it is evident that only a mere tiny portion of the land used for their fathers' graves could be considered as their inheritance, while most of it would clearly appear to have been **usurped from others' share and forcefully appropriated!**" Abu Bakr after the incident of Saqifa had occupied the seat of Caliphate and inflicted all sorts of oppression upon the Ahlul Bayt and the Bani Hashim. At the time of his burial the Bani Hashim did object to Abu Bakr being buried next to the Prophet ﷺ but their protest was to no avail. When Imam Hasan ﷺ wished to be buried next to his grandfather, Ayesha objected and had arrows rained down on his coffin! Therefore, their being buried next to the Prophet was no honour for Abu Bakr and Umar, except another example of their oppressive behaviour in life and in death!"

The Sunni scholars were speechless by this argument and could not offer any argument in their defense.

9.22: Incident Regarding Ayesha while on a Journey Through a Hamlet known as "Ifk".

A few people among the Sunni Jamaat are of the opinion that the accusations levelled against Ayesha about her waywardness are true, since all the Sunni 'True Books' have recorded narrations which point to Ayesha's straying from the path of fidelity. **But Shias are unanimously opposed to this view because** they strongly believe that any such accusation against the wife of the holy Prophet ﷺ is demeaning and a disrespect not only to the lady in question, but also to the holy Prophet ﷺ himself. In support of their stand they quote a verse which was revealed in *Surah Nur:* *"And why did you not, when you heard it, say: 'It does not beseem us that we talk of it; this is a serious slander'; Allah admonishes you that you should not return to the like of it ever again, if you are believers."* (24:16-17).

According to Shia scholars, the **incident of Ifk** was a simple matter in that Ayesha was accidently left behind when they broke journey at a place called Ifk and ended up spending the night alone in distress. The next day she was discovered by one Safwan ibne Ma'atal who escorted her back to the caravan, on account of which some people began to spread rumours which hurt the Apostle of Allah ﷺ a great deal, and consequently the verses quoted above were revealed.

There are many versions of this same incident recorded in the six 'True Books'. We quote here the version recorded in Sahih Bukhari in Ayesha's own words as follows: "It was the practice of the Prophet ﷺ to draw lots as to which one of his wives' would accompany him whenever he went out of the city on his missionary duties. On one such occasion my name had been selected. I accompanied him along with his entourage. Midway through the journey, the caravan stopped for a brief rest. I got off the palanquin and wandered into the woods to relieve myself on a call of nature. On the way back I realized that my necklace had broken and dropped somewhere. I went searching for it. When I returned, the caravan had already left! [It was traditional for the men accompanying the caravan to dismount the ladies' palanquin from the camels' backs and then stay away from the scene when the caravan stopped; and only return after a reasonable time to remount the palanquin, without witnessing the 'mounting and dismounting' of the ladies].

Since I was quite light in weight, the palanquin bearers assumed I had remounted and set off on their onward journey. When thus left alone, I wandered and spent the night alone in distress. But as per the usual practice, I knew that someone would stay behind from the caravan to do a quick check and ensure that nothing had been left behind. On this occasion the person charged with this duty was Safwan bin Ma'atal who returned in the morning to ensure that everything was accounted for. He was known to me; and had himself also seen me in the past, prior to the order of *Hijab* being imposed. He recognized me and recited the Quranic verse: '*Inna Lillahey wa Inna Elaihey Rajeoon – We are from Allah and to Him we return*'. I related to him my reason for being left behind and he respectfully mounted me on his camel and walked alongside, holding the reins of my ride till he escorted me all the way back to the caravan which was close to approaching the city of Medina. Many people started pointing fingers at me; and my uncle 'Mastah' [Abu Bakr's maternal brother] started accusing me of wayward behaviour. The Apostle ﷺ was displeased by this and chastised Mastah and imposed the related penalty on him for spreading false rumours."

The Quranic verses of Surah Nur (24:16-17) were revealed after this incident, and the Shia Scholars are thus of the implicit opinion that in this respect Ayesha is beyond reproach.

It is however, most regretful that a majority of the 'True Books' including Bukhari and Muslim have quoted this incident in a different and most derogatory manner; along with many other books which have also done so on the authority of Ayesha herself and which we found to be extremely vulgar and hence, have purposely omitted in our discussion, as some of them border on lewdness and obscenity.

It is incredible and most disgusting that the authors of the 'True Books' would talk about a wife of the holy Apostle in a manner which is abhorrent, demeaning and disrespectful to the status of the holy Prophet 🌸 himself! For instance, in 'Fateh Bukhari'[62] a tradition is recorded that one 'Abu Salmah' quotes that he and one of Ayesha's brothers went to her questioning her about the way the Prophet 🌸 performed his ritual bath? Rather than explain verbally, (they have written that) in response to their query Ayesha ordered some water and physically demonstrated to them by taking a bath herself [!] under the watchful eyes of the two men; albeit she had a transparent screen hung between them!

Dr. Ghulam Jilani Barq in his book 'Two Islams'[63] questions the rationale, or indeed any need, for this sort of demonstration [of a ritual bath] by Ayesha, and asks how could it possible that when any normal individual will not allow his wife to expose herself in such a provocative way to strange men; the Prophet would tolerate his wife to act in such an abandoned and unbecoming manner? Did Bukhari not feel any sense of shame in writing such things about the Prophet's wife? Furthermore, did not Ayesha possess the ability to describe the procedure verbally rather than physically expose herself indecently to outsiders?

Another distasteful incident where Dr. Barq has expressed his disgust is where Bukhari has recorded that Abdul Rahman bin Auf once approached Ayesha and asked her as to when would a ritual bath of ablution become mandatory for a man? The disgusting details which have been documented not just by Bukhari alone, but also by some of the other six 'True Books' are in the form of incredibly shameful conversations which are of such debased and sunken levels that no self-respecting woman would conduct herself in such manner with strange men; and would in fact think it below her dignity to engage in such vulgar detail. In addition to the above two instances which are comparatively mild, there are

---

[62] 'Fateh Bukhari' Vol 1, Pg 29 .

[63] 'Two Islams' – Dr. Ghulam Jilani Barq, Pages 76 & 137.

several other despicable and repugnant traditions recorded on the authority of Ayesha which, out of a sense of decorum we have refrained from translating. The readers if interested can refer to the following books:

1. Sahih Bukhari, Vol 1, Pg 29.
2. Muwatta – Pgs 16 and 89.
3. Sahih Muslim Vol 1, Pgs 460 & 473.
4. Sahih Bukhari: Chapter on Fasting (Saum) Pp 226-227.
5. Sahih Bukhari: Chapter of Menstruation (Haiz) Pg 22.
6. Sahih Muslim – Vol 3, Pg 72: Chapter on Haiz.
7. Kalematul Haqq (Urdu Edition) Pp 719-721.

Dr. Barq also states[64] that none of the other wives of the noble Prophet ﷺ were known to be involved in pronouncing such abhorrent details or delving into such demeaning activities.

Why would Ayesha become an exception and take it upon herself to be the "self-appointed spokeswoman and **sole authority**" to tackle such coarse and abasing topics which were unfit to her position as one of the wives of Allah ﷻ's chosen Apostle? He further emphasizes that no respectable person could bear to have the name of his wife associated with such sordid discussions. He goes on to add that the holy Quran itself has also confirmed that these two wives: Ayesha and Hafsa caused the holy Apostle ﷺ no end of domestic grief; being involved in devious intrigues to the extent that Allah ﷻ chastised them in *Surah Tahrim* (66:3-5).

Apart from what we have just discussed, it had become Ayesha's second nature to harbour extreme animosity against every single family member of the Holy Prophet ﷺ, especially as stated earlier, against Fatima Zahra 🌸 for whom she nursed a burning jealousy; and also Ali 🌸 against whom her enmity was

---

[64] "Two Islams" – Dr. Ghulam Jilani Barq, Pg 171.

such that ignoring Quranic Edicts <u>and</u> *several* injunctions of the holy Prophet ﷺ, she came out all the way to Basra at the head of an army in the company of Talha and Zubair to do battle against the Caliph of the time Ali ﷺ the Successor of the Holy Prophet!

Even after the end of that battle, known as the 'Battle of Jamal' in which her army was defeated, she refused to go back to Madina, until such time as Ali ﷺ threatened to *"use that particular Authority (power) delegated to him by the holy Prophet ﷺ whereby he could divorce any of the Prophet ﷺ's wives if he found their behaviour to be unbecoming in what was expected from them as 'Ummul Muslimeen'!"*

This acrimonious and vengeful behaviour against the house of Ali and Fatima ﷺ continued all her life right up to her own death. At the time of the death of Imam Hasan ﷺ, the first grandson of the Apostle ﷺ, she came out mounted on a mule to prevent him from being buried next to his grandfather; and ordered the showering of [no less than 70] arrows on his corpse in her determined effort to prevent his burial!

Her lifestyle had become very lavish. It is recorded that she was extremely fond of expensive clothes and jewellery; and was pampered by a large number of gifts and jewellery, not to mention a generous pension endowed upon her by the 2nd Caliph Umar of 180,000 Dirhams from the Public Treasury; which she yet complained was not enough; so Talha stepped forward to give her an additional 1000 Dirhams per month out of his own pocket!

During the hot months she would move to the cooler climes of the Hejaz, and during the cooler season she would come back to live in Medina. The Third Caliph Uthman had promised to give her an additional 500,000 Dirhams upon becoming the Caliph. However, he reneged on this promise as he was far too busy promoting the wealth and well-being of his own relatives from the Omayyad clan. This made her an arch enemy of Uthman, and she got enraged to such an extent that she conspired with Talha and Zubair to put an end to his life. Following this, as discussed earlier, she went after Ali 🌸 in the Battle of Jamal. Finally, her anger turned towards Muawiyah, and she started interfering in his activities to such an extent that Muawiyah who was "a master in his chosen field of manipulation and deception" turned the tables on her and had her murdered in a most surprising manner!

9.23: Muawiyah's Murder of Ayesha by Deception

Towards the end of her life, Ayesha had started planning to install her nephew Abdullah ibn Zubair, the son of her elder sister Asma bint Abu Bakr as the next Caliph of the Muslims. Her main goal in the Battle of Jamal (Camel) had been to kill Ali 🌸 and make her nephew the Caliph. Meanwhile, Muawiyah on the other hand, after the Battle of Siffeen had planned and conducted the assassination of Imam Ali 🌸; and thereafter declared himself the 'Ruler of Shaam' and Caliph of all the Muslim Ummah! Soon after, he started obtaining the fealty of various influential people for his son Yazid to succeed him as the next Caliph after him. Towards this end, he arrived in the city of Medina from Damascus to obtain the allegiance of Abdullah ibn Zubair and many other prominent Muslims. Ayesha upon becoming aware of this was extremely upset and began to bad mouth Muawiyah.

This episode is recorded in the authentic Sunni book of history 'Habib-us-Siyar'[65] in the following manner:

"When Muawiyah arrived in Medina and began a campaign to install his own son Yazid as the next Caliph, he approached Abdullah ibn Zubair, among other prominent Muslims, to pay his fealty to Yazid. When Ayesha got wind of this, she got upset at the thought of her own nephew being pushed aside in opposition to

---

[65] 'Haibib-us-Siyar' Part 3, Vol 1, Pg 58.

her well laid plans. She started cursing and bad-mouthing Muawiyah. He, under the guise of pacifying her, invited her to one of his relatives' houses. There he had a pit dug which he got filled with raw Lime (Calcium Oxide); and had its opening camouflaged by laying some rickety sticks and deceptive straws over it; covered by a carpet and a chair for her to sit on! Upon her arrival, when Ayesha stepped forward to take her allotted seat on the chair, the rickety carpeted floor collapsed, and she fell into the deep pit! Water was immediately ordered to be brought and poured into the gaping hole and her body got scorched from the ensuing heat and got burnt and dissolved in the resultant chemical reaction! It is thus that we find no actual grave for her up to this day!"

9.24: Ayesha's Wealth

To quote the German author Kurt Frischler in his book 'Ayesha After the Prophet'[66] he records as follows: "Ayesha who had been instrumental in installing Umar as the Caliph after her father's death still wielded enough influence over Umar to order him around. She told him: 'I am not obliged to live in the way you are living in a stringent lifestyle. It is my desire to live in an ornate palace. In summer I want to be in cooler climes and in the hot season I wish to move to Bilaaqh [which was on the hills]. I want to partake of delicious food and wear expensive silken dresses and live in a grand house filled with many maid servants in a lavish style. When the rules laid out by the Apostle do not prohibit self adornment and decoration, then why should I not indulge myself with good jewellery around my head, neck, ears, hands, and fingers? And why should I not get one fifth of the 'Spoils of War' of the Muslim army? I need this money to spend my life in luxury and happiness.'

---

[66] 'Ayesha After The Prophet' – Kurt Frischler, Pg 322.

At this Umar asked her if she had any other wish, to which she replied: 'Yes of course! My other wish is to get all the golden jewellery and precious stones that we got as War Booty from the Sassanid Kings which Saad ibn Abi Waqqas has sent to Medina from Madayen, which should all be given to me!' Umar replied saying: 'If I give you just the ornaments of the ladies' jewellery alone, they will fill up many trunks' to which Ayesha responded: 'Do you think I do not have enough trunks? All the ladies' jewellery from the spoils of war should be given to me'!"

Kurt Frischler further goes on to say that one Ibn Hisham who oversaw the Public Treasury during the time of Umar, said that he, Umar ibn Khattab ordered me to give 180,000 Dirhams annually to Ayesha as her annual pension. This was in addition to all the jewellery and precious stones that came from the vault of the Iranian monarch Yazdajard from Madayen.

Similarly, Ibn Hisham also recounts that the jewellery given to Ayesha consisted of eleven Tiaras, one hundred Necklaces, several pairs of Earrings encrusted with diamonds, pearls, and other precious stones, which were all sent to her. Ayesha further demanded that the Bracelets and Anklets that were included as part of the booty should also be delivered to her.

Ibne Hisham was asked by someone as to what was the value of the jewellery that was given to Ayesha by Umar, to which he replied that it would be a hundred million Dirhams!! In closing, Kurt Frischler quotes ibn Hisham as saying: 'As long as I remained the Comptroller of the Public Treasury during the lifetime of the 2nd Caliph, I regularly paid an annual stipend of 180,000 Dirhams to Ayesha as her pension".

In the book 'Tabaqat ibn Saad' it is mentioned that Talha used to pay an additional amount of 1000 Dirhams per month to Ayesha from his own pocket!

Chapter X

A BRIEF ACCOUNT OF EVENTS THAT OCCURED AFTER THE ACENSION OF IMAM ALI ﷺ TO THE CALIPHATE

10.1: Ascension to the Caliphate of Imam Ali ﷺ

After the assassination of Uthman, the people flocked around Imam Ali ﷺ saying they wished to pay allegiance to him as their next Caliph. Imam Ali ﷺ ignored their pleas saying it was not up to them, but to the people who partook in the Battle of Badr to make this decision. He further stated that the Affairs of the State should not be conducted in private homes but openly in the public domain. Subsequently the 'people of Badr' came forward and pronounced him to be the most deserving person for the Caliphate and paid their fealty to him.

Al-Masoodi[67] writes: "A special and close companion of the Prophet ﷺ, Hudaifa e Yamani[68] who was at this time living in Kufa, was overjoyed upon hearing the news of the election of Ali ﷺ as the Caliph. Although he was suffering from a severe ailment at the time of receiving this news, he nevertheless proceeded to the Masjid in Kufa and gathering the people around him he announced: 'Thank God that I have lived to see the day which marks the ascension of Ali ﷺ to the position of Caliphate! O Allah! Be a witness that I am offering my allegiance to Ali ﷺ as my Caliph". He then ordered his two sons Asad and Safwaan to go and join the ranks of Ali ﷺ and pay their own fealty to him. It is

---

[67] Al-Masoodi – History, Vol 2, Pg 215.

[68] Hazrat Hudaifa was famous for being a confidant of the holy Prophet ﷺ and was often referred to as 'The Keeper of Secrets of the Apostle ﷺ".

recorded that Hudaifa passed away seven days after this event. Both his sons joined Ali ؑ's army and achieved martyrdom in the Battle of Siffeen fighting on the side of Imam Ali ؑ.

Various authors have consistently recorded in their accounts that Imam Ali ؑ was extremely reluctant to accept the mantle of Caliphate, because, with the passage of time people had deviated so far from the true teachings of the holy Prophet ﷺ that if he took charge, he said he would adhere so strictly to the 'Truth' that they would not be able to tolerate his Justice. He further added: "If I were to be your Caliph, I will not care about personal views and will lead you according to the Commands of Allah ﷻ, irrespective of the opinions of others. I will not care if any person(s) were annoyed by my code of Divine Justice and will not bow down to anyone's threats or pleas."[69]

Despite Imam Ali ؑ openly warning them about his "no compromise" attitude was he to become their Caliph, people **insisted** upon him to accept their allegiance. He then reluctantly agreed and asked them to assemble in the Masjid of the holy Prophet ﷺ. The first one to pay his fealty was Talha ibn Obaidullah followed by Zubair ibn Al-Awwam. Rest of the people soon followed suit. However, there were some notable exceptions from amongst prominent names such as Abdullah ibn Umar, Saad ibn Abi Waqqas, Abu Saeed Khudri, Zaid bin Thabit, Hisan bin Thabit, Saeed bin Zaid, Osama bin Zaid, Kaab bin Malik, Muhammad bin Muslimah, Noman bin Basheer and Abu Musa Asheri as well as a few relatives of Uthman bin Affan.

A short while after taking their oaths, Talha and Zubair however, both renounced their allegiance to Imam Ali ؑ and

---

[69] Ref: "Tarikh e Tabari", Vol 5, Pg 156; Muhammad ibn Yusuf al Kanji As-Shafei – "Kifayat-ut-Talib"; Muhammad Abu Bakr Khan Malihabadi – "Islam and Bani Ommayya" – Pg 28, printed 1385 A.H.

crossed over to the side of Ayesha to join her in Basra, concurring with her in holding Ali ﷺ responsible for the assassination of Uthman, and demanding revenge for his blood.

Suyuti writes that when Ali ﷺ heard of this turn of events regarding Ayesha preparing a force to confront him with this accusation, he also prepared himself and proceeded to Iraq. The Battle of Jamal eventually took place in Basra during the year 36 A.H. in which 18,000 lives were lost.

This was followed by the Battle of Siffeen in the very next year in 37 Hijra, in which Muawiyah confronted the forces of Ali ﷺ but, though he was overpowered to the point of **losing the battle**, the connivance and cunning machinations by some notorious persons in Muawiyah's army at the eleventh hour, notably that of Amr ibn Aas by parading copies of the holy Quran on the spears caused total confusion among the rank and file. The battle was brought to a halt using their crafty artifice and an 'Arbitration Council' was appointed. This Council was again perfidiously manipulated by the unscrupulous Amar ibn Aas by implementing a calculated move which achieved its goal and failed to resolve the issue, and Muawiyah remained secure in his seat of power in Damascus!

Shortly thereafter a *third group* known as 'Kharijites' emerged and revolted against Imam Ali ﷺ, which resulted in the Battle of Nehrawan. But, as with the case of the Battle of Jamal, the Kharijites were also routed and defeated by Imam Ali ﷺ. However, **one of these Kharijis** by the name of Ibn Muljim, escaped and came to Kufa; and ironically, **he** was the one who struck Ali ﷺ a fatal blow on the head by his sword some years later in the year 40 Hijri, while Ali ﷺ was prostrated in his morning prayers in the Masjid of Kufa during the month of Ramazan; which culminated in his martyrdom on the 21st day of that sanctified month.

In summary, during the brief period of four and a half years of his Caliphate, Imam Ali ﷺ was constantly harassed and opposed by various groups and was simultaneously also kept utterly busy in warding off the many relentless and under-handed machinations and on-going intrigues of Muawiyah; and these gave him no respite or peace of mind and kept him embroiled in striving against multiple conspiracies on many fronts during the fleeting time that he was a Caliph.

10.2: State of Affairs of Muslims at the Time of Ali ﷺ's Ascension to the Caliphate

We will now attempt to give a glimpse of the upheavals and intrigues and the general state of unrest that was prevalent in the society at the beginning of Imam Ali ﷺ's Caliphate. This will be referenced by excerpts and quotes from some authentic and illustrious Sunni scholars, starting with Dr. Taha Husayn in his book 'Fitnatul Kubra'[70] in which he has recorded the following: "Uthman was fond of living a sensual and worldly life. He began to construct many palaces for himself in and around the city of Medina. People then began to follow his example. As a result of various conquests by the Muslims, many lands were acquired, and many slaves and slave-girls were brought over; and the newly rich Muslims began to indulge themselves in lives of worldly luxuries." He further writes: "When the Fourth Caliph (Imam Ali ﷺ) acceded to the seat of Caliphate, he attempted to rectify this sad situation of the Muslim Ummah. But the main obstacle in his struggle was the lack of spiritual attachment of the Muslims and, their lust for a life of indolence and worldly pleasures".

Dr. Sir Muhammad Iqbal has described this decadent scene of indulgence of the Muslim Ummah in one of his poetries as under:

"I recant to you the History of Muslim Nations,

---

[70] 'Fitnatul Kubra' – Dr. Taha Husayn, Pp. 475-477.

First striving hard with their swords and shields.
Next their Dalliance into lives of Sheer Extravagance...."

Allama Abu Nasr in his book 'Ali and Ayesha' records on page 105 as follows:

"The Ummayyads had become so strong that they had almost established their own independence in Syria under the rule of Muawiyah; and they were assisted and advanced in this cause by Uthman who himself was an Ummayyad, hence fortifying the arm of Muawiyah with his own unstinting support. It was in this unsettled environment that Ali ﷺ was given the Caliphate. This event immediately resulted in old animosities coming to the fore, adding further fuel to the fires of rancour. For instance, the reaction of Ayesha upon hearing the news of Ali ﷺ's election: 'Oh! that the sky had fallen upon me before I heard such News' [!] and the like, which subsequently lead to her conspiring with Talha and Zubair, resulting in the Battle of Jamal. Simultaneously Muawiyah started getting ready to do battle with Ali ﷺ and began to ravage sundry lands under the rule of Ali ﷺ. Small raiding parties were dispatched by him to different towns to start skirmishes and plunder the areas, bringing back booty to his coffers in Syria, while at the same time scaring and instilling a sense of fear amongst the general population for the price that they'd pay for showing any loyalty to Ali AS! One of the chief perpetrators of this criminal activity was Busar ibn Artata under the command of Muawiyah, who had consequently become so blood thirsty after slaying countless followers of Ali ﷺ that he ended becoming mentally deranged and eventually died in a mad condition, wielding his sword night and day, while confined inside his house!

Alongside these raiding skirmishes by Muawiyah's hired ruffians, the Khawarijites also started similar raiding attacks, to the point that when one stopped its raid, the other started theirs! In short it seemed like these two had agreed upon a secret pact to burden Ali ﷺ with any number of problems to force his hand and prevent him from conducting other state-related affairs. Even those who initially were the supporters of Ali ﷺ were enticed by Muawiyah by gifts and endowments to such an extent that they gradually switched over to his camp".

Dr. Taha Husayn[71] further writes: "Ali ﷺ was a favourite of the Prophet ﷺ right from the tender age of his infancy to early childhood and beyond. He brought him up like his own son and kept him by his side to an extent that when he received the command from Allah ﷻ to announce his prophethood to the population at large, Ali ﷺ was alongside with him as a child of about 10 years old. He was the first to pray by the side of the Prophet ﷺ and Lady Khadija ﷺ when Islam was first proclaimed. With the passage of time, in all the early defensive battles of Islam the Prophet ﷺ chose Ali ﷺ as his commander, and Ali was *instrumental in achieving all the victories* by the nascent Islamic army. On numerous occasions the Prophet ﷺ announced his love and attachment for Ali ﷺ. When he migrated to Medina from Mecca, he chose Ali to sleep on his bed and entrusted him to distribute the Trusts given in his safekeeping individually back to each of the Meccans. In Medina, he selected him as his 'brother' when establishing the 'Muslim Brotherhood'. He gave the hand of his only beloved daughter Fatima ﷺ in marriage to Ali ﷺ. In the famous Battle of Khyber after several failed attempts by various companions and other persons from the Muslim army, the Prophet announced that he would give the Flag (banner) the next day to 'one who loved Allah ﷻ and His Prophet, and who in turn was loved by Allah and him, ﷺ!' When setting forth on his 'Expedition to Tabuk' he left Ali ﷺ behind as his vicegerent saying: *'O Ali! Your position to me is as that of Aaron to Moses, except that there will be*

---

[71] Ibid. – Pp. 307-308.

no prophet after me.' At the time of his last pilgrimage, he officially announced before the largest gathering of Muslims ever: *'Ali is the Master of those whom I, ॐ is the master of'* and he further added: *'O Allah! Be a friend of one who is a friend of Ali and be an enemy of one who is an enemy of Ali!"*

Taha Husayn goes on to add that "Umar who was familiar with Ali ॐ's many faceted virtues often said that when it came to Islamic Jurisprudence, none could excel Abul Hasan ॐ. In short, the excellent qualities of Ali ॐ are countless; and even though many of his companions were opposed to him they nonetheless were left with no option but to accept his superiority over them in every aspect. Many Sunnis by and large, are all convinced about the superior qualities and characteristics of Ali ॐ while the Shias of course are all unanimous in their agreement about this and they adore Ali ॐ as their Imam!"

Indeed, when later in our upcoming pages we discuss these qualities in more detail, we shall see that the excellences of Ali ॐ in all fields of knowledge and every other virtue far exceed and surpass all our expectations!

10.3: Political Policy of Ali ॐ

When examining the political affairs prevalent during the Caliphate of Ali ॐ we must keep in mind the policy and practice undertaken by the holy Prophet ॐ himself. The cardinal aim of the Prophet was not to establish a worldly state but rather; to establish a 'Code of Life' wherein the Command of Allah ॐ and the Islamic Way of Life would be established for the betterment of the society *in this world as well as the next.* In pursuing this objective, his aim was to leave behind an *exemplary role model* by his own behaviour along with the Book of Allah ॐ for the guidance of the Ummah. His descendants, the holy Ahlul Bayt ॐ also adhered to these principles and followed in his footsteps in their entirety, which is confirmed by the famous tradition known as *'Hadith-e-Thaqalayn'*. This is a tradition which was delivered by the Apostle on more than one occasion, but more significantly during the time of his last pilgrimage wherein he announced: *"I leave behind you two 'Weighty Entities' – the Book of Allah and my Ahlul Bayt (family). If you hold on to these Two you will never go astray."*

In all his struggles against the Infidels and Polytheists, his 'intent and purpose' was never to establish a worldly state. It was purely for safeguarding and instituting the Islamic principles. The conquest and/or expansion of the state was never his aim. In all his dealings it was his practice to adhere to Fairplay, Justice, and Honesty. There was not even a shadow of dishonesty, or intent to cheat, or achieve a thing through cunning and connivance. The age-old practice of others that '**All is Fair in Love and War**' was a complete antithesis of the politics practiced by the Prophet ﷺ. Ali ؑ adopted this very same philosophy in all his political affairs and his was a moto of: *"Fair means for a good End"*.

Ibne Abil Hadid writes that Hazrat Ali ؑ used to say: *'Had I not been careful about piety and justice, then I could have been the most cunning achiever in the entire Arab world!'*

Professor Abdul Ali in his book 'Caliph Ali' writes on page 9: "About him the verdict of historians is that he was 'born ahead of his time'".

Major General Akbar Khan the former Commander in Chief of the Pakistani Armed Forces, writes[72] in his book: 'Hazrat Ali ؑ As an Amir':

"In fact, the study of the period of his life outlines the struggle of the great 'Mujahid' who in the footsteps of his 'Noble Leader' wanted to establish a 'Commonwealth of Muslim Nations' according to the Vicegerency of God on Earth; and whose

---

[72] "Hazrat Ali ؑ an Amir' – by Major Gen. Akbar Khan, Pp. 19-20.

personality, due to his lifelong association with the Apostle, conveyed an impression which made him seem like a replica or a 'second self' of the holy Prophet himself! Hazrat Ali as a Caliph and companion of the holy Prophet Muhammad ﷺ was endowed with an enlightened mind and was a genius in the affairs of Government."

Going back to Dr. Taha Husayn[73], he writes elsewhere that: "The general population had become far more interested in worldly affairs than in religious concerns. In this environment Ali ﷺ and his two sons along with a small group of sincere companions seemed like total strangers; in that, they were going against the majority in strictly adhering to the true Islamic practices. In these turbulent times Imam Ali ﷺ was known to say: *'By God! I have neither strayed from the true path, nor has anyone gone astray because of me!'* Despite the difficult events, Ali ﷺ adhered to his principles and none of the number of intrigues or stratagems could sway him even slightly from the true path. His commitment to achieve the pleasure of God and adhere to the end results would lead to **a choice of life or death**, but he never comprised on the principles of Islam regardless of the consequences. Ali ﷺ's policies were based strictly on Islamic principles, whereas Muawiyah was completely on a worldly plane. Ali was carrying on according to the Will of Allah, whereas Muawiyah was striving for the World. Those that subscribed to the school of 'deceit and fraud' joined the ranks of Muawiyah and only a small group was left to side with Ali ﷺ."

Allama Abu Nasr writes on pages 99 through to 103 that Ali ﷺ wanted the Muslims to follow in the footsteps of the holy Prophet ﷺ but they had already broken into sects; and each sect wanted to rule and obtain worldly power. In this connection he quotes the

---

[73] "Fitnatul Kubra" – Dr. Taha Husayn; Vol 2, Pp. 309-333, 426-427 & 490.

French historian Sedillot as saying: "One would have expected everyone to bow down in reverence to this grand personality of Ali and offer him unstinting support. But this was not to be. Talha and Zubair and Ayesha rebelled against his authority. Then he had to face the opposition of the Omayyads. He could have easily overcome these obstructions by his own cunning and by being indiscriminate in his behaviour; but this was not in his character as he was far above these loathsome traits; and this simply was not Ali!"

Professor Abdul Ali in his book 'Caliph Ali' has observed the following: "Ali lived for the Muslims and the cause of the holy Quran, Muawiyah lived for himself and for the pleasure of the world. So, their paths were opposite. That Muawiyah's path was wrong and paved with malice and selfishness was clear to every right-thinking person."

Reverting to Dr. Taha Husayn[74] he further reiterates that "Ali ﷺ's personality was such that he adhered to the Truth in 'Word and Action' **at all costs**. He was never discouraged by lack of supporters. He was so sure of his adherence to his cause that he would not hesitate to go ahead singlehandedly to tackle any obstacle. The then prevailing political environment favoured Muawiyah and his worldly outlook. Nevertheless, this did not deter Ali ﷺ from adhering to his lofty principles. He was totally disappointed by the lethargic attitude and behaviour prevailing among the Muslims, and he would constantly admonish them to mend their mode of existence. [To illustrate the then prevailing atmosphere Dr Taha Husayn has quoted two brief sermons delivered by Imam Ali ﷺ to the people the first of which is as follows]:

---

[74] Ibid – Pg 408 - 479

*"When you are asked to fight in the way of Allah you shrink from this task. You prefer the present life over the Hereafter. You are neglectful of the day that you will die. Your hearts have been hardened. In the times of peace, you roar like a lion of the plains, and yet when you are required to participate in battle in the way of God you run away like a scared fox! You are losing your territories but are unaware of this danger. Your enemies are spending sleepless nights (in awe of you) but you yourselves are in a state of stupor of indifference! I have certain rights over you, and if you obey me, I will guide you to the right path and relieve you from your state of ignorance. Considering your previous fealty, **be faithful to, and respond to my command** and trust me to guide you to what is best for you."*

In the second instance Ali ﷺ delivered a sermon in a similar vein in which he chides the Muslims thus:

"I do not believe that you are sincere in your word, and are full of idle talk, but slow in action. By your behaviour you have disappointed me to such an extent that I could do without your help. I do not believe that you are sincere in your commitment. May the Lord 'part-company' between you and me. If you persist in your deviated ways, soon you will be utterly disgraced, and the 'sword of injustice' (Muawiyah) will be hanging over your heads and you will be engulfed in calamities. You will have a tough time finding food in your own homes, and atrocities will be showered upon you. Only then you will pine for my return and realize my worth and wish for my guidance!"

In his endeavour to awaken the conscience of the public, Imam Ali ﷺ invited their tribal chiefs and clearly acquainted them with the prevailing conditions and pointed out to them their responsibilities to mend matters and get the people of their tribes to fulfill their obligations. He pointed out that the Caliphate was thrust upon him by these very same people, who soon turned their backs upon the duties associated with their fealty to him. Ali ﷺ then went on to add: *"My patience has now worn thin, and I know that they will not reform their ways. I have given them enough time and tolerated their infidelity but now I am deeply disappointed with their behaviour. I will not wait for their help. I will take whoever comes with me and if there are no volunteers, I will go ahead towards Syria even if I must fight singlehandedly in the Path of Allah and sacrifice myself!"*

This speech had a profound effect in shaming the tribal chiefs into action. A large force was gathered to help Ali ﷺ; but as events dictated, before he could proceed to Syria, Ali ﷺ was assassinated through the devious and cunning plans of his enemies while he was offering the morning prayers in the Masjid of Kufa!" Little did the Ummah realize what a colossal loss they had incurred in the untimely death of a supreme being whose care and concern for others was foremost in his mind, even above that of his own well being and comfort!" [End of quote].

Irrespective of the turbulent times and the war mongering factions claiming a major portion of his time, he nevertheless did not neglect the other responsibilities associated with his office in bringing about a just government dedicated to the upliftment of the general society. He apportioned his time into three clear responsibilities:

1. Religious Matters
2. Political Affairs
3. The War Effort.

All these areas of responsibility received his full and undivided attention. On the religious front he set aside time to lead the daily congregational prayers, delivered sermons on subjects such as piety and character-building, and in general, making the public aware of their duties and obligations towards Allah ﷻ and their fellow humans. He set aside time to answer questions and guide people personally on various matters. He was their Imam, Guide and Teacher and he set a shining example for them to follow. He encouraged them not only in improving their personal traits, but also their social behaviour in their interaction with fellow humans. He strictly enforced honest and fair dealings in trade and ensured that no one was shortchanged because of tampering of Weigh Scales or the like. When he wished to purchase something for his personal use, he would seek out a trader who was unacquainted with his position, just in case the person made any undue concessions for him due to his status as being the Head of the State. He showed no favouritism in matters of distribution from the Public Treasury and practised utmost care in being equitable in his disbursements. He shunned away from the pelf and pomp of his position as a Caliph and often dealt with merchants in an anonymous way when purchasing his own essential needs. During the day he would care for the needy in satisfying their needs: religious or otherwise. When the task of distribution of funds from the Public Treasury was completed, he would have the floor swept clean by someone or do it himself personally, then offer a prayer of two cycles ('rakats') and go down into a prostration of thankfulness to Allah ﷻ.

As several historians have acknowledged in their writings, Imam Ali ؑ's actions and words were highly thought-provoking and deeply penetrating, reaching into the very depth of a person's soul. He was completely straight forward in his speech and dealings and there was no trace of deceit in his character. He was sincere in his actions and dealt with justice and impartiality with everyone, irrespective of their position or status. As far as his Governors were concerned, he dealt with them with justice and fairness as he did with everyone else. The good governors he encouraged to do better, and those that did not measure up, he tried to reform. He sided with the good and chided the wrong. An example of this is illustrated in a letter written by him to Abdullah Ibn Abbas who had been appointed by him as the Governor of Basra.

When news reached Imam Ali ﷺ that Ibn Abbas had misappropriated funds from the Public Treasury in Basra and gone off to the city of Mecca he wrote thus: *"I had appointed you and given you a trust because I found you to be most worthy of this in my judgement. But now you have betrayed that trust. You have deserted me and joined ranks with my enemy. You have forsaken your responsibility to the Ummah and appear to have been working for the worldly benefits of your position. In effect, you have lunged towards the acquisition of worldly wealth with the alacrity of a hungry wolf jumping on a herd of sheep to satiate its lawless desire! Fear God! And remember the Day of Judgement. Return the property that you have acquired unlawfully back to the Public Treasury. I will deal with you at the first opportunity that I get and ensure that the properties obtained by illegal means are returned to their owners at the earliest instance!"*

10.4: Prophet ﷺ's Statement that: 'He Fought the Infidels, and Ali will Fight the Hypocrites'

In the following two chapters of the Holy Quran: *Tauba* (9:73) and *Tehreem* (66:9) it was revealed: *"Ya Ayyohaln Nabi! Jaahadil Kuffar wal Munafeqeen: O Prophet! Strive hard with the Infidels and the Hypocrites!"* When these verses were revealed, the Prophet ﷺ only had occasion to face the Infidels during his lifetime; and the second part of the injunction about 'fighting the Hypocrites' was fulfilled by Imam Ali ﷺ many years later, during his own period of Caliphate. The holy Prophet ﷺ had previously predicted this himself and had stated that *Ali ﷺ's was the only true path, and those who would oppose him would be manifestly in error [hypocrites]!* In this context a well-known tradition has been related by

Khawarzimi on the authority of the close companion Abuzar e Ghaffari quoting the holy Prophet ﷺ:

"I swear by the One who holds my life in his hands, there is a person amongst you who will fight for the **Interpretation of the Holy Book** against a faction of people who will be reciting the 'Kalemah' but will be hypocrites at heart; in the very same manner that I fought the Infidels during the **Revelation** of the Quranic Verses. People will taunt and criticize him, but this will not deter him." When questioned by Abu Bakr and Umar as to who was the person that would fight the Infidels, the Prophet ﷺ pointed towards Ali ﷺ who was at that moment engaged in repairing the Prophet's ﷺ's shoe and said: 'The one who is repairing my shoes.' He then further reiterated that Ali ﷺ will fight the Hypocrites in the same way as he himself had fought the Infidels in his lifetime".

Similar traditions are found in several authentic Sunni books such as:

1. 'Musnad' by Ahmad ibn Hanbal, Vol 2, Pg 32.
2. 'Al Mustadrak' by Al Hakim, Vol 3, Pg 113.
3. 'Riaz un-Nazara' – Vol 2, Pg 191.
4. 'Usdul Ghaba' by ibn Al Athir, Vol 4, Pg 26.
5. 'Kanzul Ummal' Pg 33 and 'Izaratul Khifa' Pg 256.

Abu Bakr ibn Marduwiya relates a tradition from Ali ﷺ that when the second verse of Surah *Ankaboot* (29:2) *"Do men think that they will be left alone and not be tested?"* was revealed, I asked the Prophet ﷺ: *"O Apostle of Allah! How will this test come to pass?"* The Prophet ﷺ replied: *"The people will be tested on* **your** *account; so be prepared for the events".*

Another example in this vein is that after the revelation of verse 41 from Surah *Zukhruf* (43:41): *"For even if we take you away, we will extract retribution from them"* the Prophet ﷺ said: *"After me, Ali will avenge (me) by confronting the Hypocrites."* This interpretation is confirmed by the hadith related to Jabir ibn

Abdullah Ansari in Dailami's 'Firdous al Akhbar' and Suyuti in 'Durre Manthur' as well as by Abu Bakr ibn Marduwiya. The same tradition is related by Hafiz Abu Naeem through the authority of another close companion Hudaifa-e-Yamani. All these traditions collectively state that the Prophet ﷺ said: *"After me, Ali will avenge me by confronting the Nakiseen, Qasiteen and Mariqeen."*

Ibne Asakir relates from Abu Saeed Khudri and ibn Qatata that the holy Prophet ﷺ said: *"There will be a fight against these three groups, and you should join in the fight **against** them."* At this people asked him as to who will lead the fight, and he replied: *"It will be Ali who will fight these groups and Ammar-e Yasser will be with him and will be martyred at the hands of the Hypocrites."* Ibn Abbas similarly relates a tradition from Umme Salama that Ali ﷺ also said that he would fight with the *Nakiseen* in Jamal, *Qasiteen* in Syria, and *Mareqeen* in the Battle of Neherwan. Other similar references in this connection are related through many other close companions of the holy Prophet ﷺ as well; for instance, it is recorded that when Abu Ayyub e Ansari was questioned by some as to why he was fighting against those who professed to be Muslims, he replied that he had been instructed by the Prophet ﷺ to side with Ali ﷺ on such occasions.

Maulana Abu Ala Mawdudi writes the following in his book[75] 'Khilafat wa Mulukiat': "All the jurists, historians and exegetes are united in saying that Hazrat Ali was justified in fighting against all those who opposed him in the battles of Jamal, Siffeen and Neherwan. Considering the verse (49:9) of Surah *Hujurat*, Ali was justified in his action because he was a Just Leader (*Imam e Adil*) and it was not permissible to rebel against him. In my knowledge there is no jurist or traditionalist who can oppose my view on this subject; especially the scholars of the Sunni Hanafi School who are

---

[75] 'Khilafat wa Mulukiat' – Abu Ala Mawdudi, Pp. 338-342.

all unanimous that Ali was on the Right Path, and it was wrong of these groups to go against Ali. All those who opposed him, had deviated from the faith of Islam. Those who took up the sword against Ali on the pretext of avenging the blood of Caliph Uthman had no justification whatsoever. The jurisprudence is clear and there is no room for justification to support the deeds of Talha and Zubair and Ayesha. All of them should be ashamed of their deeds regardless of their positions or status!"

10.5: Ayesha's Complicity in the Assassination of Uthman

Before commenting on the above issue, we would like to remind the reader that Ayesha had become extremely antagonistic toward Uthman when, after having promised her a significant increase in her pension, he had reneged on his promise as soon as he became the Caliph. Rather than adding our own thoughts at this point, we refer the reader to the relevant facts described by Asim e Kufi in his book[76] as follows: "Ayesha returned to Medina after performing the Hajj. En route she was received and greeted by Obaidullah ibn Salmah (also known as ibn *Kalb* – [*Son of A Dog*]!). Ayesha enquired as to what was the latest news. He replied that people have killed Uthman. Ayesha asked: And then what happened? Obaidullah replied: 'People have paid allegiance to Ali as the Caliph.' Ayesha then exclaimed: 'Oh! That the sky would have fallen, and I had not lived to hear this News! I swear by God! They have killed Uthman unjustly and in vain! An injustice has been done in the shedding of his blood. One day in the life of Uthman was better than the whole life of Ali! I will not rest until I have avenged the blood of Uthman!' Obaidullah asked her in surprise:

---

[76] 'Tarikh' by Asim e Kufi, Pg 160.

'Why do you speak thus? Did you not say yourself earlier on, that there is nobody on the face of this earth who is more pious than Ali? Why have you gone against him now and why are you averse to his ascending the Caliphate? Did you not previously encourage people to assassinate Uthman by telling the people to kill the 'Old Infidel'? Now what has transpired that you are saying something different?' Ayesha admitted that earlier on she had indeed said what he claimed about Ali ﷺ, but 'upon hearing the news that he was now elected to the Caliphate had caused her to change her views!' In short, Ayesha then returned to Mecca along with Talha and Zubair and began to conspire against the Caliphate of Ali."

It is worth noting that where the Prophet ﷺ in his lifetime had said [on the Day of the Battle of Khandaq] that: "*A single stroke of the sword by the hand of Ali, was superior to the worship of "Saqelain': the entire creations in both worlds,*" completely putting this aside, Ayesha goes totally against it and says that 'One day in the life of Uthman was better than the entire life of Ali!'

Tabari has also recorded similarly concerning Ayesha's reaction to the news about Imam Ali ﷺ's ascendency to the Caliphate. The author Henry Smith Williams in his book 'Historians' History of The World' has similarly noted the following: "Though she [Ayesha], had notoriously shared in the conspiracy against Uthman, she now proclaimed herself to be the 'Avenger' and denounced Ali as being the perpetrator of his, Uthman's death. Joined with her were Talha and Zubair who were aware and knew the falsehood of Ayesha's allegations."

The historian ibn Khaldun writes that Ayesha in her bid to oppose Ali ﷺ, came out and made a general announcement that if anyone was sympathetic to the cause of Islam and wished to avenge the blood of Uthman, *but had no means of transportation,* would be given an animal to mount and ride upon to join in on the public demonstration.

Washington Irvine in his book "Successors of Muhammad" writes that "Ayesha was an age-old enemy of Ali, and this enmity had increased to such an extent that she was now ready to mobilize an army to dislodge him! On the other front, Talha and Zubair were themselves hankering after the Caliphate, and they were being helped by Ayesha in their efforts towards this end. Both had previously approached Ali with a false display of friendship, pretending to be sympathetic to him, though in their hearts they nourished an enmity; with Talha requesting the Governorship of Basra while Zubair expressed his wish to be made the Governor of Kufa. Ali declined saying that he needed their presence in Medina to assist him in the day-to-day affairs. They eventually abandoned Ali ﷺ and left for Basra to join Ayesha in her undertaking. Ayesha had also instigated Hafsa and Umme Salama to join her in this nefarious act. Hafsa was willing but was restrained by her relatives. Umme Salama refused outright and warned Ayesha not to go ahead as planned and reminded her of the Prophet ﷺ's admonition that "*Ali ﷺ was his Caliph in his lifetime and even after his death*". She also reminded her of a prophecy which the Prophet ﷺ had made stating: '*One of my wives will go astray and be at (a place called) Hawab where the dogs will bark at her.*' He had then fixed his gaze at Ayesha and said: '*O Humaira, be careful that **that** woman may not be any other than you!*'"

"Ayesha however, ignored this admonishment of Umme Salama and equally of some others and proceeded in her set path. She was accompanied by Talha and Zubair. During their journey when they reached the precincts of Hawab the dogs came out in unison and surrounded her palanquin and, as prophesized by the Prophet ﷺ, began to bark at her. She became very agitated and she herself now reminded Talha and Zubair of the saying of the holy Apostle that one of his wives will be on the wrong path and the dogs of Hawab will bark at her. Talha and Zubair, in their attempt to calm her convinced her, along with fifty other men all swearing falsely, that this was not the township of Hawab. Ayesha was pacified". [Tarikh e Tabari].

Dr. Taha Husayn[77] further writes: "Ayesha was not soft like her father but possessed the extreme aggressiveness of Umar. On one occasion when Uthman was berating Abdullah ibn Masood, Ayesha had no qualms about screaming from behind her curtained partition and hurling verbal abuses at Uthman! Recognizing this ambitious streak in Ayesha, when Muawiyah learnt of the plot of Ayesha in conjunction with Talha and Zubair in her outward intent of 'avenging the blood of Uthman', he acquainted them with his promise of support from Syria and Egypt. He advised them to take over Basra and Kufa so that Ali ﷺ is confined only to the area of Hejaz and would not be able to withstand the attacks from the East and the West. When this happens, the coordinated strengths of these three forces would render Ali ﷺ restricted and helpless and create a state of instability for him. Thus Ayesha, Talha and Zubair fell into the trap of the Umayyads and proceeded to Basra. Upon reaching Basra, she sent letters to some prominent people of the town requesting their support and assistance in avenging the blood of Uthman; at the same time promising them that they will proceed to Kufa and take it over; thus, bringing all of Iraq under their control. In this way they will have Ali ﷺ surrounded, and the rule of the three will begin; that is: Talha, Zubair and Muawiyah, and those who supported their cause would be generously rewarded.

But the response she got from most of them was that if Uthman was murdered because he was guilty as a tyrant, then they were not interested in his revenge; but if he was killed unjustly, it was up to Uthman's relatives to take up the cause. Since they were not

---

[77] 'Fitnatul Kubra' – Dr. Taha Husayn, Vol 2, Pp. 320-321, 343-351.

present at the time and place of his death, they refused to get involved!

Letters in a similar vein had been sent by this trio to Syria, Kufa, Yemen and Medina. One of these letters thus written by Ayesha was obtained by Zaid ibn Sawhan a resident of Kufa, who took this letter and read it aloud at the local City Square to the public and then added his own remarks: "O People! Hear this letter out and consider the implications of it! Ayesha is asking us to do that which had been disallowed to her, and she had been instructed as one of the *'Ummuhatul Muslimeen* (wife of the holy Prophet ﷺ) *to stay in their homes!'* But on the contrary, she has taken it upon herself to do what was ordered for us men, that is, to go out and do battle in the way of God until such time as a controversy was suppressed. She has reversed the roles and now is taking the garb of a leader to create mischief and revolt (*Fitna*) against the rightful Caliph, when it is specifically forbidden in Islam."

While Ayesha was still in Mecca, Malik-e-Ashtar, the Commander-in-Chief of Ali ﷺ's forces and his principal supporter, had written to her in the following words: "You are a wife of the Prophet ﷺ and as such worthy of a respectful position. Allah ﷻ has ordered you to remain confined to your abode. It would be proper for you if you stay indoors and not strip the Veil off your face and come out into the open. If you disobey and expose yourself in the battlefield, then I will personally feel responsible to wage war against you till such time as I arrange for your return to your house in accordance with the injunction of the Almighty Lord!"

When the news reached Imam Ali ﷺ that Ayesha had already left for Basra with an army, he also proceeded in the same direction. Enroute when he halted at a place called Rabzah, he got further news that Ayesha had now arrived in Basra, so to dissuade her from her untoward action, he sent the following letter to Ayesha:

"It is not befitting for you to have come out of your house and undertaken this mission. It would have been more worthy of you if you had remained indoors in your own abode as commanded by Allah ﷻ, for, what concern is it for a woman to come out as a leader of an army? You have no reason to be in a battlefield. You claim to have the mission of getting justice done for Uthman who was from the Omayyad clan; so, it is up to them to avenge his blood. You are from a different clan which is from the Bani Tameem and have no tribal connections with them. The persons who have instigated you to do this have incurred a grave sin. I advise you to Fear Allah and guard your respect and chastity and return to your home"

When Ayesha's army reached the outskirts of Iraq, Saeed ibn Aas, Marwan bin Hakam, and a few others came to the elders of Ayesha's army and asked: 'Where are you proceeding?' Upon being told the reason for their mission, they said 'The persons that you are looking for to avenge the blood of Uthman are very much in your own army. Kill them and go back home!' [By this they implied that Talha, Zubair and Ayesha were the actual culprits].

Along with the letter written to Ayesha, Imam Ali ؏ had also dispatched similar letters to Talha and Zubair admonishing them against undertaking this mission:

"You profess to seek justice for Uthman, while the son of Uthman himself is alive and would be the proper person to take up this cause. You are from Quraish while Uthman is from the Bani Omayya. By getting involved in this, you have become guilty of dragging 'your mother' (Ummul Muslemeen) into the battlefield against the command of Allah ﷻ Who has ordered her to remain in the seclusion of her own home." But despite all these admonishments of Ali ؏, the trio did not deter from their self-proclaimed mission. On the contrary, Ayesha responded: "I will not leave this place until I am successful in achieving my purpose."

Some later remarks by Dr. Taha Husayn[78] in describing the Battle of Jamal: "Ayesha with her loud and shrill voice was heard inciting and urging her followers to do battle; and after the death of Talha and the exit of Zubair from the battlefield, her loud orders for the soldiers to fight to the bitter end were heard over the tumult of the warring armies!'

10.6: Review of the Behaviour of Talha and Zubair

Right from the incident of 'Saqeefa Bani Saaida' Talha and Zubair were prominent in demanding the right of Ali ﷺ to the Caliphate; to the extent of announcing that they would not put their swords back into their sheaths till such time as allegiance was paid to Ali ﷺ!

With the passing of time when Abu Bakr was nearing his death and appointed Umar for assuming the Caliphate after him, they again remonstrated to Abu Bakr: "You are now on your way to meet your Creator, how will you answer Him for appointing a harsh person like Umar as the Caliph over us?" They continued with this attitude of supporting Imam Ali ﷺ even up to the point of the appointment of Uthman: raising their objection against the process of selection of Uthman by a 'Shura' [Consultative Body] formulated by Umar and brought about by the connivance of Abdul Rahman ibn Auf.

The only reason they backed off and remained silent was due to the huge bribes paid to them to hold their peace. When this largesse eventually ceased, they began to oppose him and became his open enemies. Most historians have said that these two played a leading role in bringing about the downfall and ultimate demise of Uthman. When Ali ﷺ was elected as the 4th Caliph, these two were among the first who came out to pay allegiance to him. But

---

[78] Ibid, Pg 354.

when the Governorships of Basra and Kufa were denied to them, they left Ali 🕮 and joined forces with Ayesha and came out in the battle of Jamal against him!

Professor Abdul Ali in his book 'Caliph Ali' has expressed his opinion as follows: "Zubair and Talha's complicity with those rebels that had attacked Uthman was strong. Zubair was lukewarm, but Talha was openly inciting the rebels against Uthman. It was obvious from their behaviours that both were more interested in gaining either the office of the Caliphate for themselves' or, failing that, looking out for their own self interests in some other ways, rather than having any true loyalty towards Ali 🕮".

In like manner Dr. Taha Hussain has presented his view that "the careers of Talha and Zubair were consistently full of conspiracies according to the current policies of their time, swaying in unison to the political conditions best suited in their own self interests. Talha's own son Muhammad bin Talha was known to admit that 'his father participated in, and had his hands tainted with the murder of Uthman; and it is strange that he is now active in avenging that same blood by going against Imam Ali!' But to me, it is *even more surprising* that according to many narrations from the Sunni sources, these *same two persons are supposed to have been given* the "Good News" by none other than the Prophet 🕮 of being among 'the **ten selected** persons' (*Ashra e Mubbasharra*) who are guaranteed a place in Heaven"!

Moving along, we will now give a brief account of the Battle of Jamal. Uthman bin Hunaif was the governor appointed by Ali 🕮 in Basra. When Ayesha arrived there with a huge army, Uthman bin Hunaif with his small contingent of soldiers could not withstand the onslaught of Ayesha's large army and was consequently defeated. Ayesha's army not only plundered his State Treasury but also personally humiliated him by having his beard plucked out hair by hair [!] in open view of many; after which he was most ignobly chased out of Basra.

Bukhari[79] in brief, relates through Abdullah bin Ziad Asadi that when Imam Ali 🕮 got news that Ayesha was encamped in Basra, he sent his elder son Hasan 🕮 and his companion Ammar bin-Yasser to Kufa to gather some people for the forthcoming battle of Jamal. Imam Hasan 🕮 mounted the pulpit [while Ammar-e-Yasser stood with him on the lower tier] and gave a resounding speech stating that Allah 🕮 was testing the people as to whether they would follow His path or opt to go with Ayesha; briefly summarizing the activities of Ayesha (the wife of the holy Prophet 🕮) against Ali 🕮: the Caliph of her time! This speech was much applauded, and they partially succeeded in rounding up a small group to join Imam Ali 🕮 in Basra.

The battle lines were arrayed in Basra around the middle of Jamadi-ul-Akher, 36 Hijri. Abdullah ibn Zubair egged his army on to fight Ali 🕮 and thus avenge the blood of Uthman. Imam Hasan 🕮 replied from the opposing side with an eloquent speech which stirred the emotions of the people on both sides. Regardless, Ayesha was unmoved and highly incensed and refused to talk to Imam Ali 🕮 or negotiate in any way, saying that it was impossible to win any argument against him.

Justice Amir Ali's comment on this issue is as follows: "He Ali, had earlier nearly sacrificed his own sons in an endeavour to protect Uthman. This lady (Ayesha) had always borne an inveterate dislike towards the son-in-law of Khadija, and now this feeling had gone into a positive hatred. She was the 'life and soul of the insurrection' and she herself accompanied the insurgent troops to the field riding upon a camel. The Caliph (Ali) in his characteristic aversion to bloodshed sent his cousin Abdullah ibn

---

[79] 'Bukhari' – Ch 29, Pg 548.

Abbas to adjure the insurgents by *reasoning with every bit of obligation of the Faith* to abandon their intention of war, but to no avail."

A famous Sunni scholar Shamsuddin Fakhozi was once asked; "Was not Ali the killer of Uthman?" His reply was: "If this was so, then woe unto Uthman! For anyone who gets killed by Ali, or kills Ali, goes straight away to hell!"

When Ali ﷺ was convinced that the opposition army was not going to resolve the matter in a peaceful way, he delivered the following sermon to his army in which he described a whole code of behaviour for the warring soldiers:

"O my Companions! As much as I could, I tried to dissuade the opposition army from escalating matters any further; and warned them about the uncalled-for destruction of life and limb which comes from fighting wars. I appealed to them to have mercy on their kith and kin and stay away from this battle. In my life I have experienced many a war, and I have grown up in the battlefield. You may have forgotten, but I am the same Ali who has decimated their ranks and killed their leaders. The sword which I wield in my hand now is the very same with which I have beheaded many of their leading warriors. Besides this, I possess a 'strong and resolute will'. I am not afraid of meeting death which is certain, and I know that if one does not die in the battlefield, he will die in the home. It is far better to die on the battlefield defending the Cause of Allah ﷺ than dying in our home. I swear by Allah in Whose Hand is my life, that a thousand wounds delivered to my body are far easier for me to accept than dying like a woman in the bed."

Ali ﷺ paused and then called aloud to his army:

"Do not to initiate the battle. Do not pursue anyone who flees the battleground. Do not disrobe the fallen or the injured person. Do not take as slaves or chattels their men or womenfolk. Do not plunder the personal belongings of the defeated or fallen soldiers." Then he raised

his head towards the skies and said: *"O Allah! You be my Protector and Guide. You know that Talha and Zubair had pledged their fealty to me and are now arrayed against me in this battle!"*

He had no armour on his body except for the shirt he was wearing and a robe draped over his shoulders and a cloth tied like a turban on his head. He was mounted on the Prophet 鷺's mule called 'Shehba'. He moved and placed himself between the ranks of the two armies and called out for Talha and Zubair to come out. Talha did not respond, but Zubair came forward, at which Ali 鷺 asked him: *"O Zubair! What is your reason for wanting to fight against me?"* Zubair replied: "To avenge the blood of Uthman," at which Ali 鷺 unhesitatingly responded: *"That blood is dripping from the swords on your side!"* He then went on to remind Zubair about at least two different occasions when the Prophet 鷺 had predicted that he, *'Zubair, would fight against Ali 鷺; and had warned him that he should beware of such a day because he would be on the wrong side and whoever will rise against Ali will go to hell'.*

Zubair acknowledged the truth about this and withdrew from the battlefield saying he had forgotten the Prophet 鷺's words and swore that he would retract immediately. Seeing this, his own son Abdullah along with Ayesha began to taunt him and suggested that his oath to withdraw from the battlefield could easily be compensated by giving charity or freeing a slave; and urged him to take up arms against Ali 鷺, failing which he would be viewed by all as a weak-kneed coward. Zubair reacted to these taunts and picking up his lance he took up a stance to attack Ali 鷺's army. When he started moving through the ranks of his army, Ali 鷺 ordered his forces not to retaliate and let him ride through the entire length of the battlefield unharmed. Despite repeated taunts by his son and other companions of his army about being faint hearted and a coward, Zubair eventually withdrew from the war zone and went away taking shelter in the house of a person called

Umer bin Harmuz-al-Majashi who hosted him for a time, and then killed him.

As for Talha, Imam Ali ﷺ also addressed him in the same eloquent manner as that of Zubair, and he also withdrew from the battlefield. In response, Marwan bin Hakam shot an arrow at him that got embedded in his leg and he eventually died from this wound. Another tradition relates that after sustaining the leg wound, Talha called his slave and departed from the warring area. While still on his way, he encountered a person who was from the army of Imam Ali ﷺ and his sincere follower. Talha asked him to stretch his hand so that he could indirectly in absentia, renew his fealty to Ali ﷺ before his death. Imam Ali ﷺ was saddened upon receiving this piece of news.

Despite the desertions of these two prominent persons, Ayesha insisted on continuing her battle and urged her army to rain down arrows on Ali ﷺ's forces which resulted in a few casualties; upon which his army asked for permission to retaliate. Ali ﷺ calmed them down saying that his army will not be guilty of initiating the war. He then asked for someone to fetch the holy Quran and called out to his army at large as to who would volunteer to go into the battlefield during the enemy and request them to refrain from their mischief and abide by the Quranic injunctions. He warned them that whoever undertook this task would die. A person known as 'Muslim' stepped forward and volunteered to do as Ali ﷺ bade him. He went forth and was martyred as predicted. Ali ﷺ continued to show restraint, but after him, two more persons were killed due to arrows being rained upon his army from the enemy forces. Finally, after these three persons were killed, there was no excuse left not to retaliate back in response. In a clear voice Ali ﷺ declared: *"O Allah! Be witness that I have not taken the first move to initiate this battle"* and the fight then began in earnest.

Dr. Taha Husayn has recorded the same in his book but also adds, that seeing the unbecoming behaviour of Ayesha, some soldiers from Ali ﷺ's army began to mock her by saying that "mothers are expected to be kind to their progeny, but in spite of her being the '*Ummul Muslimeen*'- (Mother of Muslims), she was subjecting the men to death and the loss of limbs and disfiguration!" Ayesha was so incensed that she picked up some stones and pebbles and uttering some angry words, threw them on those men in retaliation. At this she was again taunted that "it was not she who threw the stones at them but it was the hand of Satan that did so"[!] in direct opposition the Quranic verse: "*Wama Ramalto...*" referring to the fact that when the holy Prophet ﷺ had done such an action it was considered to be not him but Allah ﷻ who threw the stones at the enemies; but since she was now going against the Prophet ﷺ's and Allah ﷻ's injunctions she was being swayed by Satan!

Allama Umer Abu Al Nasr on page 164 of his book 'Ali and Ayesha' described Ali ﷺ's army as being composed of 1000 warriors under the command of Hazrat Abu Ayub-e-Ansari. Similar numbers of 1000 each were under the respective commands of Malik ibn Ashtar; Khozaima ibn Thabit Ansari; Ammar ibn Yasser; Abdullah ibn Abbas and Qais bin Saad bin Ibada. Along with these, many other venerable companions of the holy Prophet ﷺ also accompanied him. His own three sons Hasan ﷺ, Husayn ﷺ and Muhammad-e-Hanafia ﷺ were in his proximity, as was his nephew (and son-in-law) Abdullah ibn Jafar-e-Tayyar ibn Abi Talib ﷺ. The Standard Bearer of his army was his son Muhammad-e-Hanafia ﷺ, while Imam Hasan ﷺ was given charge of the right wing, and the command of the left wing was under Imam Husayn ﷺ. The Leadership of the Foot Soldiers was given to Muhammad ibn Abu Bakr.

This battle took place on a Thursday, the 10th of Jamadi-ul-Akhir 36 A.H. From Ayesha's army of thirty thousand, more than half were killed. From Ali 🕮's army of twenty thousand, about a thousand were martyred. Ayesha was mounted on a camel called 'Al Askar' and by various narrations, about sixty or seventy persons lost their hands merely while holding the reins of her camel! It was only when her camel was brought down that the battle came to an end! The soldiers of Ayesha's army began to flee from the scene of battle. Ali 🕮 ordered his army not to pursue those who fled, nor to disrobe those who were injured or dead. After ascertaining that Ayesha was not injured in any way, he ordered her brother Muhammad ibn Abu Bakr to escort her from the battlefield and had her lodged with due respect, along with a lady-in-waiting called Safia bint Harris, in the house of the widow of Abdullah ibn Hunaif Khazai.

The next day he sent Abdullah ibn Abbas to convince Ayesha to return to Medina. However, she refused and stayed on. The following day he sent Malik ibn Ashtar, again to no avail. On the third day Ali 🕮 himself went personally to the house, where he 🕮 met Ayesha who was sitting with the widow of Abdullah ibn Hunaif Khazai - a leading citizen of Basra, but got killed fighting on the side of Ayesha. Upon meeting her, Ali 🕮 addressed her by saying: *"O the one who has caused a split among the people and divided friends from each other and has orphaned the children of Abdullah ibn Hunaif! May Allah deal with you as He seems fit! You have always been an enemy to me, but I am not here to berate you for your past behaviour. However, as a wife of the holy Prophet 🕮 it behoves you to return to your home and refrain from any further such unbecoming activities."*

Several reliable books such as 'Tarikh-e-Asim-e-Kufi', 'Rauzatul Ahbab' (Vol. 2), 'Manaqib-e-Murtazawi' (on pages 207-208) and 'Habib-us-Siyar' (Vol. 1) have all recorded that Ali 🕮 spoke mildly to Ayesha advising her that according to the holy Quran the wives of the Prophet ﷺ should remain in the security of their own lodgings and only speak from behind the curtains when spoken to. He reproved her further saying: *"You have committed deeds that are unbecoming with your status. You are aware of my close relationship to and special position with the Prophet ﷺ. Despite this knowledge you have harboured an enmity toward me and have not only encouraged but also befriended those who were inimical towards me. When you have been granted the rank of: "The Mother of the Faithful', why is it that you have gone beyond the limits prescribed for you? Why have you disregarded the Quranic injunction that 'the wives of the Prophet should communicate with others from behind the veil'? But whatever has transpired is beyond recall and is best forgotten. You should now return to Medina and abide in the house allotted to you by the Prophet ﷺ."*

Notwithstanding this sincere admonition, Ayesha refused to return to Medina. In view of this obstinate attitude, Ali ﷺ sent his eldest son Hasan ﷺ to her the next day with a warning that her failure to return to Medina would leave him, Ali ﷺ, with **no option but to exercise '*the Right given to him by the Prophet ﷺ in connection with any* of his wives, which she, Ayesha, was well aware of'**! It is recorded in the books that when she received **this** message, Ayesha was in the act of combing her hair and had barely completed brushing only one side of her head; but rather than continue with her grooming, she immediately abandoned this task halfway and ordered her carriage to be brought post haste to start her journey back to Medina without any further loss of time! When her lady companions insisted on knowing the real reason for this hasty retreat, in light of the fact that she had rebuffed the earlier attempts by Abdullah ibn Abbas and Ali ﷺ in a headstrong and unyielding manner, Ayesha reluctantly admitted that 'on one occasion during the Prophet ﷺ's lifetime I had spoken rudely to Ali

🕮, and the Apostle 🕮 had become highly enraged and turning toward Ali he had said: "*O Ali! I give you full authority to divorce any of my wives **during my lifetime or after my demise,** for any misbehaviour on their part, which you deem as being **unfit!**"*

Thereafter Ali 🕮 arranged for forty women from Basra to accompany her to Medina. He also arranged for her brother Muhammad bin Abu Bakr to travel with the entourage to oversee the safety of the caravan. The women were made to dress in the garb of men and carried a sword with them to give the semblance of an armed guard. When upon reaching Medina Ayesha expressed her vexation against Ali 🕮 at being sent on a long journey in the company of males, the women removed their head gear and revealed their identity!

Ibne Abil Hadid writes that Ali 🕮's noble behaviour in dealing with Ayesha in this instance is totally in contrast to that of Umar. Had she behaved in this manner with Umar, as she had done with Ali, he would have chopped her into several pieces!

Washington Irving in his book 'Life of The Successors of Muhammad' has made the following observation: "Ayesha might have looked for cruel treatment at the hands of Ali, having constantly been his vindictive and persevering enemy; but he Ali, was too magnanimous to triumph over a fallen foe!"

The most unusual feature that reveals itself in this entire episode is that nobody in the history of mankind had *ever given such complete authority* to anyone else to divorce any of his wives! This was a unique act on the part of the Prophet 🕮 who had **consciously** given this kind of exclusive prerogative and power to Ali 🕮 to implement it **both**: *during* his own lifetime and/or *after* his demise!

10.7: Opinion of Edward Gibbon Regarding the Battle of Jamal

In his book[80] 'The Decline and Fall of the Roman Empire' Gibbon has the following comment: "Talha and Zubair were accompanied in their fight by Ayesha the widow of the Prophet, who nurtured to the last hour of her life an implacable hatred against the husband and the posterity of Fatima. The most reasonable Moslems were scandalized that the 'Mother of the Faithful' should expose in a camp, her person and character".

Based on Gibbon's comment, Allama Saleh Kashafi-e-Hanafi in his own book 'Kaukab-e-Durri' quotes Ayesha verbatim (page 126): "The Apostle ﷺ had told me that *Allah ﷻ had given him a pledge that whoever opposes Ali will be thrown into Hell.* I had totally forgotten this tradition when I went against Ali on that fateful day of Jamal. I only recalled it when I was already in Basra."

Allama however, expresses his surprise that it is quite remarkable that on the one hand where she herself has quoted several traditions from the Prophet ﷺ on the merits of Ali including one where she has quoted that *'Ali's love is an integral part of achieving Paradise'*, Ayesha should have forgotten this particular tradition, or indeed any other tradition regarding Ali ؑ at the time of going against Ali in the Battle of Jamal. What is more amazing is that after having remembered this tradition in Basra (by her own admission), she pursued in her intent to battle even after Talha and Zubair had abandoned their own fight! Contrary to giving up her own war, she incited her troops to continue the fight to the bitter end! Even after her defeat in the battle, she adamantly refused to return to Medina and only did so under duress when Ali

---

[80] 'The Decline And Fall Of The Roman Empire'- Edwardd Gibbon: Vol 2, Pg 123.

🌣 issued the threat of using the authority given to him by the Prophet ﷺ to enforce a divorce on his behalf to any of his wives' whom he found to be deviating from the true path!

10.8: Opinion of Fazl ibn Rozbahan Regarding Ayesha

This scholar who has openly displayed his antagonism towards the family of the holy Prophet ﷺ in many of his works, has written one such book[81] titled 'Abthal-al-Baatil' – 'Refutation of Falsehoods' in which he criticizes and condemns many Shiite beliefs [which incidentally have been counter argued by the great Shiite scholar Allama Hilli RA, as well as another notable scholar Allama Syed Noorullah Shustari RA in his book 'Ahqaq-Al-Haqq' ['Consolidation of Truth' in which such baseless criticisms have been exhaustively rebutted!] One such criticism by Rozbahan is that when the 'Verse of Purification' (33:33) was revealed exclusively in praise of the Ahlul Bayt of the household of the Prophet ﷺ as the Shiites and other eminent Sunni scholars accept, Rozbahan states that apart from Ali 🌣, Hasan 🌣, Husayn 🌣 and Fatima 🌣, all the wives of the holy Prophet ﷺ are also included in this verse. He argues that the *"Rijz"* (uncleanness) in this verse implies "major sins" such as polytheism, adultery, fornication, and the like; and does not include other kinds of sins that these persons may have indulged in. Hence, he states that Ayesha's battle against Ali 🌣 was a "minor sin" and thus does not preclude her from being part of this verse of purity, or as being one of the Ahlul Bayt.

At least by giving the fuzzy logic, Rozbahan has admitted that Ayesha **did in fact commit a sin** by going against Ali 🌣, for which she will be answerable on the Day of Judgment.

Maulawi Khaleel Ahmed Deobandi writes the following on page 509 of his book 'Noor-un Ala Noor': "Had *'Imamat'* been

---

[81] 'Abthal-al-Baatil' – Fazl Ibn Rozbahan.

designated as one of the 'Roots' of Islam, then the Battle of Jamal would not have taken place, because then Ayesha would have been labelled as an Infidel for going against the Imam designated by Allah ﷻ. But this battle took place because she had a live hatred and animosity toward Ali ؑ even during the lifetime of the holy Prophet ﷺ. Whether "*Imamat*" is one of the principles of Islam or not is a separate issue; but Ayesha's deep hatred and jealously toward Ali ؑ and his family is a confirmed fact! However, it is beyond any reasonable explanation that on the one hand she had personally been the one clamouring for the death of Caliph Uthman, calling him a 'Jew' and an 'Infidel', but upon Ali ؑ's assuming the reins of Caliphate, doing a complete turnabout of face and marching forward in battle against him, conveniently changing her slogan to 'avenging the blood' of this very same Uthman! Notwithstanding the fact that these foregoing events had all been prophesized by the holy Prophet ﷺ that: "*One of his wives' will venture out from her house and the dogs will bark at her*", and his added warning that "*One who goes against Ali and is killed by him or kills him will go to hell*"; she, Ayesha **consciously** ignored all these predictions and confronted Ali in the Battle of Jamal. In addition, the initial part of the Quranic verse (33:33) specifically forbade the wives of the Prophet ﷺ to leave their houses: "*O wives of the Prophet! You are not like other women, if you are afraid of Allah....remain in your houses and do not display yourselves in the manner of displaying your finery in the days of ignorance....*"(33:32-33). In addition, there was the injunction for them keep aloof from and only speak to the outsiders 'from behind a veil'. But far from adhering to this command, she travelled in the company of Talha and Zubair, accompanied by thousands of male soldiers, albeit she personally had covered herself with a cloak; but the undeniable fact remains that she totally disregarded the guidelines of behaviour specified for her by Allah ﷻ as a wife of the holy Apostle!"

In 'Sahih Bukhari'[82] a tradition is recorded that the Prophet ﷺ on one occasion, had specifically pointed at the house of Ayesha and repeated three times: *"This is the house from which Intrigue and Mischief will originate, and Satan will raise his head from here!"* In the same section of the book another tradition has been recorded from Abdullah ibn Umar, that during one of his sermons which the Prophet ﷺ was delivering in a standing posture, he interrupted his speech, and in the middle of his sermon he pointed at the living quarters of Ayesha and repeated three times: *"The Horn of Satan will emerge from **this** house, and Harm and Intrigue will start from here.'*

When questioned by a lady companion (Maidat e Ghaffaria) about her condition in later times, [after her return to Medina from the Battle of Jamal], Ayesha would get extremely perturbed at the memory of her own ill conceived action, saying she often remembered her father constantly gazing at the face of Ali saying that to do this (looking at Ali's face) was equivalent to performing an act of worship to the Almighty!

Some historians, to defend her reputation put forward an argument that she Ayesha, repented for her action against Ali ؑ [at Jamal] and reformed herself. However, the facts of history reveal a different story, in that not only did she refuse to allow the body of Imam Hasan ؑ to be buried next to the grave of his Grandfather, the holy Prophet ﷺ; but on the contrary she ordered her followers to rain down arrows on the coffin and the funeral procession of Hasan ؑ, in her bid to stop him from being buried there. It is also said that when news of the martyrdom of Ali ؑ in the Masjid of Kufa reached her, she prostrated herself in a gesture of thankfulness for having been alive to hear such welcome news!

---

[82] 'Sahih Bukhari' – Section 12, Pg 68, Subject: 'Kitab Jihad-wa-Seer'; Trans. Waheed-uz Zaman.

It is also a glaring fact of history that none of the other wives of the holy Prophet ﷺ ever left their dwellings after his demise. When given a choice, Hazrat Sauda refused to go for Hajj, saying she had already performed this obligatory duty during the lifetime of the Prophet ﷺ, and preferred to stay within the confines of her own apartment. Hafsa *had* wanted to accompany Ayesha to Jamal but was prevented by her intervening relatives who reminded her of her obligation to stay at home. Umme Salama never emerged from the house after the Prophet ﷺ's death; and forbade Ayesha in vain, from travelling to Basra. Several historians are of the opinion that Ayesha was the only one of the Prophet ﷺ's wives who was an arch enemy of the Prophet's family and was one of the chief architects in preventing the Caliphate from going to Ali ؈ on account of her enmity towards Ali, his wife Fatima ؈ and their noble children.

10.9: Battle of Siffeen

Shortly after the Battle of Jamal, Ali ؈ found himself embroiled in the Battle of Siffeen in the month of Zilhij in the year 36 AH; in which Muawiyah came out in confrontation, taking the same cause of 'avenging the blood of Uthman' a step further as *his* excuse for waging war against Ali ؈. He wanted to get the entire Caliphate for himself. Ali ؈ sent him a letter through his representative, written in a very mild tone asking Muawiyah to reconsider his actions; and instructed his two delegates: Saad bin Qais Hamdani and Shoaib bin Rabi, to persuade and invite him toward the right path of Islam, so that the blood of the Muslims could be spared. Muawiyah ignored this letter, and after three months he returned an envelope containing a blank piece of paper, with an oral message through the two delegates that 'his only answer was that the sword was unsheathed, and it would settle the issue'!

Muawiyah then proceeded with a large army of 120,000 soldiers and encamped on the banks of the River Euphrates at a place called Siffeen, choosing the best watering spots, thereby withholding entry to the river by the opposing army. When Hazrat Ali ﷺ and his army arrived on site, they were tired and thirsty but were denied access to the water by Muawiyah's army. Ali ﷺ ordered his two Generals Malik-e-Ashtar and Ashaas ibne Qais to attack Muawiyah's garrison stationed at the river and retake the watering-post by force. They advanced with a 4000 strong contingent and successfully snatched the water access. Now it was the turn of Muawiyah's army to plead for water! Amar ibne Aas, the evil genius of Muawiyah consoled him that contrary to what *he* did, Ali would **never** deny water to anyone; and advised him to apply to Ali ﷺ for being allowed access to the river. In humiliation Muawiyah sent a group of twelve persons to negotiate with Ali ﷺ, who in his characteristic magnanimous fashion immediately granted the request. This noble action so impressed two of Muawiyah's delegation of twelve: Maqatil bin Zaid and Daud Bakri that they immediately switched sides and paid their allegiance to Hazrat Ali ﷺ. The other ten returned to Muawiyah with the happy tidings of accessibility of water for all and sundry.

Muawiyah now started a war of attrition in the manner of a 'Gorilla Warfare', keeping himself safe within the confines of his tent in a cowardly manner, and hiding behind the ranks of his army. Hazrat Ali ﷺ on the contrary displayed amazing acts of valour in this battle, riding on his mule and going through their ranks as what has been described by many as a 'whirlwind raid', scattering the opposing army in different directions! He eventually arrived at the tent of Muawiyah and challenged him to come out and settle the matter in a One-to-One Single Combat against himself, rather than shedding the blood of many Muslims. Amar ibne Aas, the confidante of Muawiyah supported this proposal, to which Muawiyah replied that 'all knew well that nobody ever lived to tell the tale after confronting Ali's sword!' He sneeringly added that Amar bin Aas must be eyeing the rule of Syria for himself and hence had lent his support to such a proposal, the outcome of which beyond doubt, would be 'certain death' (for him) as Ali's opponent!

10.10: Gibbon's Statement about Siffeen

Edward Gibbon in 'The Decline and Fall of The Roman Empire' has noted the following: "He [Ali] generously proposed to save the blood of Moslems by a Single Combat, but his trembling rival declined the challenge saying that going against Ali ﷺ would be 'a sentence of inevitable death'. The ranks of the Syrians in a single night alone, were broken by the charge of a hero who was mounted on piebald horse and wielded with irresistible force his ponderous two-edged sword. As often as he smote a rebel, he shouted 'Allah Akbar' [God is Victorious!]; and in the tumult of that nocturnal battle, his voice was heard to repeat 400 times that Stupendous Exclamation!"

10.11 Statement of a British Historian Andrew Crichton

Dr. Andrew Crichton in his book[83] 'A History of Arabia and It's People' has endorsed the following comment on the Battle of Siffeen: "Ninety actions or skirmishes are recorded to have taken place, and in these the humanity of Ali was as conspicuous as his Valour. He strictly enjoined his troops to invariably await the first onset of the enemy; and to spare the fugitives and respect the virtue of the female captives. Not a day passed in which he

---

[83] 'History of Arabia and It's People'- by Andrew Crichton, printed 1852, Pg 306.

displayed not some extraordinary feat of personal strength and skill. The bravest leaders of the Syrian host fell in succession by the single prowess of his restless arm: *for Death itself seemed to dwell on the point of his spear and perdition in the hilt of his sword!* The hideous and gigantic warrior Kerreib who could obliterate with his thumb the impression on a silver coin, he [Ali] cleft him asunder with a single stroke from the crest to the saddle bow. Two warriors attacked him in disguise, but with a sweep of his double-edged scimitar, he bisected the middle with such rapidity and precision that the rider remained fixed on the saddle; the spectators concluding he missed his blow, until the motion of the horse threw the body in halves to the ground!"

10.12 More Details on the Battle of Siffeen

In this Battle of Siffeen Muawiyah was adept at hiding himself and was wont to send other warriors to represent him in his guise to conduct the war games. Sometimes he sent Abdur Rahman ibn Khalid bin Waleed, and at times Abala ibn Aur and such others. The Commander of The Faithful Ali ibn Abi Talib ﷺ however would himself come out boldly in the battlefield. At times he would send his Generals Malik-e-Ashtar, Hujr bin Adi Al Kindi, Ziad bin Haseen Al Tameemi, Saad bin Qais-e-Riyahi and Qais bin Saad bin Ibada Ansari also to display their dextirity.

These skirmishes continued through the month of Zilhaj. When the new year of 37 AH dawned with the advent of month of Mohurrum there was a pause in the action, according to the customary Arab tradition. On the 1st of the next month of Safar, Ali ﷺ addressed the Syrian army in the following words: *"O You! The inhabitants of Syria! I invited you to come to the path of Truth and Justice, but you have not paid any heed to my call and have remained belligerent. The Almighty Lord does not love those that betray their trusts...*" But the Syrians again paid scant heed to his counsel.

In preparation for a face off, Ali ﷺ then aligned his forces under various commanders: Malik-e-Ashtar over those who hailed from Kufa; Suhail bin Habeeb over the horsemen from Basra; Ammar-e-Yasser in charge of foot soldiers from Kufa while the foot soldiers from Basra were entrusted under the command of Maaz bin Fadaki. He finally selected Hashim ibn Otabah to be the Standard Bearer carrying the flag of his army; and with this arrangement in place, he proceeded to step forward into the battlefield himself.

Allama Saleh Kashafi Hanafi has painted an interesting word-picture of Muawiyah's personality at the battleground of Siffeen in his book 'Manaqib-e-Murtazavi' in that he says: "Muawiyah came out dressed in the **Garment of Guile and Deceit,** wearing an **Armour of Brazenness,** with **a Sword of Shame** hanging on his belt, strutting about in a cowardly manner whilst taking cover under **a Shield of Dishonour**; then clutching the **Banner of Disgrace** in his hand, he finally entered the battlefield riding the horse of **Animosity and Belligerence.** Thus were the forces of Evil and Justice now arrayed against each other! Nevertheless, his entry into the warzone was short lived, for he promptly made his exit taking shelter behind the ranks of his soldiers!

To maintain a facade of bravery, Muawiyah resorted to an underhanded trick of paying various persons to disguise themselves in his garb and show up periodically on the battleground in hopes of boosting his army's morale. For instance, on one occasion Muawiyah bribed someone called Abdullah ibn Saada Anfardi with a promise of some gold coins and money to disguise as Muawiyah and go out to face Ali ﷺ in hopes of impressing his own army about his boldness as a warrior going out personally to challenge Ali! However, when Abdullah was faced with the mighty sword of Ali, he cried out in fear: 'O Ali, I am not

Muawiyah but have been bribed by him to give false propaganda to his army!' Ali ﷺ held his sword sparing his life and let him return to Muawiyah who in turn became furious with Abdullah for revealing his guise! The next one whom Muawiyah persuaded to venture out in his disguise was Obaidullah ibn Umar ibn Khattab, who, when faced with the lighting flashes emanating from the Zulfiqaar [the two-pointed sword of Ali] scuttled away from the battlefield like a jackal would from its predator!

Notwithstanding the futility of his previous attempts, Muawiyah again bribed and sent yet another person by the name Umru Salaan to face the brave 'Lion of God' in battle. Ali ﷺ however, advised this person to give up falsehood and invited him to come towards righteousness, but when he refused, Ali roared loud the phrase: '*La Howla wala Quwwata Illah Billah – There is no Strength save that of Allah*' and with these words he pinned him on his spearhead and raising him in mid-air asked him as to what he saw. In terror he cried: 'By God! I see the fire of Hell blazing!' and with this he shrieked and fell to the ground, lifeless!"

The same Allama has related many such incidents with respect to the valour of Ali ﷺ and we recount a few more of these hereunder: "Amr ibn Aas and Busar ibn Artah who were sent in battle by Muawiyah got trapped in a situation where they were faced with imminent death at the hands of Ali ﷺ. In desperation they disrobed themselves shamelessly and turning tail took to their heels knowing full well that the 'Lion of God' was too noble to pursue any foe that resorts to such low tactics to save their lives!

During this battle, once when Muawiyah saw that 'The Lion of God' was far afield, he ventured forth to show himself on the battleground. However, when he was confronted by Saeed Hamdani a noted soldier from Ali ﷺ's army, he fled the scene in terror and took refuge in his own tent, to the extent of losing his power of speech for a considerably long while! Seeing this, a seasoned Syrian warrior called 'Mohraq' emerged from the ranks of Muawiyah's army and issued a challenge to the Iraqis as to whether there was anyone 'daring enough' to face him. One Abdul Murad came forward from Ali ﷺ's side but was slain and decapitated by the Syrian and his head displayed around the field to instil fear among the rest of the army! Seeing this, another warrior Muslim bin Abdur Rahman came forward and confronted the Syrian warrior Mohraq, but he too was met with the same fate. Mohraq again shouted for any other who was willing to face him? Imam Ali ﷺ who had been observing these proceedings, changed his attire and came out incognito to accept this challenge.

The Syrian not recognizing Ali ﷺ lunged towards him. The Commander of the Faithful however, with lightning speed severed the arm of his opponent, which resulted in his falling to the ground and losing his life by a swift stroke of Ali's sword. Ali ﷺ then issued a challenge of his own, which resulted in seven warriors coming out from Muawiyah's army but meeting with the same dire fate of instant death by the dexterous wielding of Ali's sword. After this performance, despite Ali issuing further challenges, none dared to come out, having witnessed his lethal prowess, even though none of them had recognized Ali's identity due to his remaining incognito. Ali ﷺ then continued to parade himself between the two armies while waiting for someone to accept his challenge. But none came forward. On the contrary, a murmur began to circulate among the ranks as to who was this 'unknown soldier' who had dispatched such noted warriors with a single stroke of his deadly scimitar!

Muawiyah then summoned one of his slaves by the name of Soub, who was strong and reputed to be a good warrior; and asked him to take on this unknown warrior and kill him. Soub declined saying: 'Do you wish to send me to my instant death? I have studied this unknown warrior carefully and it is obvious that even if the entire army came out to fight him, he would put them all to death!' When none then dared to come out, Ali ﷺ removed the veil and revealed himself, whereupon everyone acknowledged that besides Ali there was no one who could have accomplished the feats that they had just witnessed!"

As the war progressed over the course of time, another incident records the advent of a warrior named Karrieb from the Syrian army who came out: challenged and slew two brave soldiers from Ali ﷺ's army and then threw another challenge at large for further face offs with anyone from the Iraqi army. Upon seeing this, Ali ﷺ girded himself with his sword and armour and approached this person and asked him to identify himself by his name and ancestry; to which he replied: 'I am Karrieb ibne Sabah al Hamiri'. Imam Ali ﷺ responded by inviting him towards the right path saying: *'You appear to be a brave person, and I bid you to save yourself and abandon the misleading way which Muawiyah is deluding you towards and come over to our side'.*

But instead, Karrieb replied: 'O Ali! I have come to fight' and saying this he began to brandish his sword. Thereupon the Commander of the Faithful drew his own sword whence there was a clanging of metal for a bare moment and Karrieb was shortly seen fallen from his horse cut up in two pieces! Karrieb's brother, Harith al Hamiri came out to avenge his brother's death, but met with the same fate in a matter of moments! Four others then came out from the opposing army and were all slain by Ali in quick succession! While Ali ﷺ was inflicting death by his sword upon his opponents, he was heard to recite the following verse from the holy Quran: *'The Sacred month for the sacred month, and all sacred things are under the Law of Retaliation; whoever then acts aggressively against you, inflict injury on him in like manner as he has inflicted upon you, and safeguard yourselves with full awareness of Allah's Laws, and know that Allah is with those who guard against evil.'* (2:194).

The Lion of God then called out to Muawiyah challenging him to come out and face him for a singlehanded combat to settle the issue, thereby saving a lot of Arab blood that was unnecessarily being shed on both sides due to the personal antipathy which Muawiyah had toward Ali. Muawiyah however declined and hid himself in his tent. But observing this act of cowardice from Muawiyah another notable warrior from his army by the name of Urwa Ibne Daud accepted the challenge and confronted Ali. But likewise, he too was soon cut into two by Ali's sweeping blow from his fatal sword. The death of this warrior Urwa had a profoundly demoralising effect on the Syrian army as he was reputed to be an outstanding warrior and one of the bravest from the enemy forces. As none other came out to wage war any further and nighttime was approaching, Ali ﷺ retreated to his side of the battlefield and the fight was left to be continued on for yet another day.

It thereby became a regular practice of Ali ﷺ to periodically disguise himself in different attires and mingle incognito with the soldiers of both sides to gauge the mood of the two armies. On one such occasion when Ali ﷺ was wearing his disguise, he was attacked by Amr Ibn Aas. However, when he was overpowered with lightning speed and pinned to the ground by a spear in a life-threatening stance, Amr immediately realized that his opponent was none other than the formidable Ali. Knowing full well that none escaped death when faced with the sword of Ali ﷺ, Amr also resorted to the cowardly act of lifting his clothes and indecently exposing himself without any trace of shame or embarrassment. The noble Ali turned away from him in disgust and spared him; and Amr escaped with his life, back to his tent on Muawiyah's side.

Muawiyah was highly amused to learn about the low, [albeit 'fast thinking'] tactics of Amr Ibne Aas in saving his life and kept throwing taunts at his cowardice; to which the latter replied that

Muawiyah would have done likewise to save his skin, had he been confronted by Ali ﷺ's death-inflicting sword.

These examples only go to show as to what lengths people went to in taking advantage of Ali ﷺ's noble personality and high principles. Many warriors came forward to do battle with Ali ﷺ, but when faced with imminent death at his hands, resorted to the same cowardly example set by Amr Ibn Aas of baring themselves to save their lives! One such of these was the tyrant Busar ibn Artah, a so called 'brave and notable warrior' from Muawiyah's side who was famous for terrorizing the meek and lowly, and yet who, when death loomed large over him after being overpowered by Ali ﷺ in one of the battles, also did not hesitate to expose his private parts to save his own life!

The battle was often thrown into a lull with none coming forward from the army of Muawiyah to confront Ali ﷺ.

At this juncture, we feel it would not be out of place for us to mention the contribution of a tender aged youth, an eleven-year-old [not having yet reached his teenage] who was introduced to the battlefield by Imam Ali ﷺ.

On one such occasion, when none of the opposing army came forward to confront him, he, Ali ﷺ called his young son Abbas ﷺ aged 11 years and asked him to go forth in his place and face the army of Muawiyah. Though young, he was so tall and well-built that he fitted comfortably into the armour belonging to his father, who covered his son's face with a veil to conceal his identity and sent him into the battlefield to issue a challenge to the enemy's army at large. In response, Muawiyah asked one of his renowned warriors Aba Shasha to take on this youth. The latter protested saying that it was below his status to fight this mere youth, as his reputation amongst the circle of great warriors was such that he was regarded as being equal to a Thousand Super Warriors. Instead, he offered to send one of his seven sons who were all also considered to be formidable fighters, to do quick work on this youth. However, when the first son arrived, he was slain in the twinkling of an eye! The other six sons came forward; and one by one were also quickly put to death.

Aba Shasha was extremely enraged and finally came out himself to avenge his sons. But he too was killed in an instant and met up with his seven sons at the hands of this veiled youth. After this display of valour, the army was so demoralized that none dared to come out to challenge the youth. Even the soldiers from Amirul Momineen 🕮's army were themselves aghast and said that apart from a "Hashimi" youth there could be none other who could display such martial feats and lightening action. Thereupon, when Abbas 🕮 returned to his father, he, Ali 🕮 removed his son's veil and introduced him to the two armies "**Abbas ibn Ali: Qamar-e-Bani-Hashim** - *the Moon of the Bani Hashimites*"!

Going forward, this was a long-drawn-out battle which extended over several weeks and months. It is recorded that there were more than 70 skirmishes that took place during the battle of Siffeen in which Hazrat Ali 🕮 *personally* participated. On one Thursday night which came to be known in history as the *"Lailatul Hareer"*- (*The Night of Intense Heat*), the cry of 'Takbeer' (*Allaho Akbar!*) was said to have been heard in Imam Ali 🕮's resonating voice at least 530 times. It was known by all that it was his 🕮's practice to pronounce this expression every time that he struck an enemy down with his sword! A similar cry of 'Takbeer' was also heard from his brave General Malik=e Ashtar RA 400 times on that same night!

On this night it is also recorded that the undaunted Ali 🕮 actually put a halt to his onslaught on the enemy during the peak of battle, spread his prayer mat between the ranks of the two opposing armies and offered his Night (*Isha*) prayers with an implicit faith in His Creator; while arrows whizzed past him on his right and to his left, yet he remained totally unperturbed and fearless about his own death and continued his communion with the Lord until such time as his prayers ended! It is recorded elsewhere that when someone later asked him in bewilderment "Ya Ali! Was this an appropriate time for offering prayers when the battle was raging in full force?" to which he replied: *"This **Salaat (Prayer)** is the **very reason** that I am fighting for, **to save and keep it alive!**"*

When the morning dawned it was clear to Muawiyah and his cohorts that the battle was certainly lost and that Ali ﷺ's army were victorious. Those that were killed on the side of Muawiyah numbered more than thirty thousand; and his army now appeared to be ready to capitulate. Seeing this, Muawiyah himself was preparing to flee; whence Amar ibn Aas [his chief advisor] devised a cunning ruse and convinced him to introduce the holy Quran onto the battlefield by raising it on the points of the lances of his soldiers, with a cry: *"Let Quran be the Judge between them"*: thereby confusing the common majority as to which side they should align with! Ali ﷺ saw through this ruse and gave a speech to the soldiers explaining that Muawiyah and Amar ibn Aas and those fighting with them had no sympathy or attachment to the Quran and these were the very same people who had abandoned the holy Book and broken their pledges; and he appealed to them not get taken in by this artifice.

Likewise, Imam Ali ﷺ's General: Malik e Ashtar echoed the same sentiments of Ali ﷺ and kept pressing his attack in an implicit conviction that given a little more time, he would achieve a complete victory. However, this was not meant to be, as there were many in his own army who, when faced with the copy of the holy Quran, were thrown into a total state of confusion as to which side they should be on and fell prey to the ploy introduced by Amr ibn Aas. Consequently, the fighting came to a halt and Imam Ali 🕮 by default was denied his imminent victory!

In Muawiyah's army of 120,000 it is reckoned that 45,000 were slain, whereas on the side of Imam Ali 🕮, the loss was confined to 25,000 out of his force of 90,000. There were however, many notable and venerable companions of the holy Prophet 🕮 who fought on the side of Ali 🕮 in this battle and attained martyrdom. Of these Ammar ibn Yasser was one about whom the Prophet 🕮 had predicted that *"he would be slain by the hypocrites"*. Another noted personality was Owais-e-Qarani who despite having attained an advanced age, had come prepared to fight; and subsequently got martyred in this battle. It is stated in 'Tarikh e Khamis' that Hazrat Owais traversed through miles of desert terrain on foot [after his mount had succumbed to the rigours and hardships of the journey and died]; with a backpack of some sweet-tasting water which he presented to Imam Ali 🕮 upon arriving in his presence. He displayed a superior performance of bravery in afflicting the enemy with death and destruction before he also achieved a noble death in fighting for Ali 🕮. Yet another notable companion to be martyred was Khuzaimah bin Thabit-e-Ansari about whom the holy Prophet 🕮 had certified as being *"Zul Shahadatain"*, that is, on account of his honest and truthful character his single witness was equivalent to the witness of 'two persons'. Two sons of Hazrat Hudaifa-e-Yamani [whom the holy Prophet 🕮 had given the title of 'The Keeper of Secrets'], Saeed and Safwan, fought on behalf of their father and were also martyred, as their father had specifically ordered them to always be with Imam Ali 🕮.

There is a tradition recorded in a 'Shawadat-al-Nabuwah' that during the Siffeen campaign a person approached Imam Ali 🕮 while he was stepping into the river for a drink of water; and addressing him he invoked his greetings upon him saying: 'Peace be upon you O The Commander of the Faithful' and 'Leader of the Pious!' ['*Amirul Momineen*' and '*Imam al Muttaqeen*']. Ali 🕮 responded to his greeting. This person then introduced himself as 'Shamoon bin Yohanna' and pointing to a nearby property, he said: 'I am the owner of that monastery, and I have some scriptures which have been handed down through generations to me from the companions of our Nabi Esa 🕮. If you allow me, I wish to read out some of the great qualities which have been mentioned in those manuscripts about a person like yourself. It is written that someday a noble person will camp near this river who will be a close relation of the last Prophet, and he will bring glory and eminence to the religion of the East and will fight against the people of the West. This person will have absolutely no value or attachment of this world. Death in the cause of Allah would be dearer and more acceptable to him than a drink of water is to the thirsty. To help and assist him is to attain the pleasure of God; and to be killed while fighting with him in his cause is akin to achieving the supreme martyrdom in the way of God.' This person, having recognized the excellent attributes mentioned in his holy scriptures as being manifested in the noble personality of Ali 🕮, became a devout Muslim and was martyred fighting on the side of Imam Ali 🕮 on the 'Night of Lailatul Hareer.'

As an aside, we wish to digress a little and comment upon the behaviour of the two sons of the second Caliph Umar ibn Khattab, who despite being aware of the exalted position of Imam Ali 🕮 did not pay their allegiance to him. Abdullah ibn Umar the elder son not only refrained from paying his allegiance to Ali 🕮, but according to Bukhari he paid his fealty to Yazid ibn Muawiyah, the murderer of Imam Husain 🕮; and he also accepted large bribes from Yazid to convince others to pay their fealty to Yazid! Later, he even went on to pay his allegiance to the notorious Caliph Abdul Malik bin Marwan. The younger son Obaidullah ibn Umar was similarly also on the side of Muawiyah and met his death fighting against Ali ﷺ in this Battle of Siffeen. Such was their hatred towards the Ahlul Bayt ﷺ!

Earlier on we had briefly discussed the feats and prowess displayed by Imam Ali ﷺ in various skirmishes individually undertaken by him during the Battle of Siffeen. Our purpose was to illustrate the bravery, strength, valour and lightning speed which the 'Lion of God' had exhibited even at age 60; which was as keen and deft as that which he had demonstrated in his youth (at age 25) in bringing down renowned warriors such as Amr ibn Abduwad, Marhab, Antar, Haaris, Abu Jundal, Waleed, Shaiba, Karreib and others, in the defence of Islam.

We will now again examine the opinions of the two eminent Sunni scholars Dr. Taha Husayn and Maulana Abul Ala Maududi in their respective treatises 'Fitnatul Kubra'[84] and 'Khilafat wa Mulukiyat' with respect to the Battle of Siffeen and its aftermath. They state that had Muawiyah been honest and fair in his dealings, it would have been incumbent upon him to pay allegiance to Ali ﷺ like the others had done; and then bring the heirs of Uthman to demand the investigation or compensation for the blood of Uthman. But it is quite apparent that this issue of revenge for Uthman was not as important to him as was his goal in preventing the Caliphate from reaching Ali ﷺ. This we can clearly conclude from the fact that after the martyrdom of Ali ﷺ, when he achieved his own goal to garner the Caliphate for himself through a so called 'Peace Treaty' with Imam Hasan ﷺ, he completely forgot about avenging Uthman's blood or bringing his assassins to justice!

Dr. Taha has gone into detail in exposing the conniving nature of Muawiyah and the extent to which he stooped to achieve his lowly desires and attain the Caliphate for himself. On page 380 Dr.

---

[84] 'Fitnatul Kubra' – Dr Taha Husayn, Pp. 289 – 546.

Taha summarizes the events at Siffeen as follows: "It should be kept in view that before beginning the Battle of Jamal at Basra, Ali ﷺ had himself ordered that the holy Quran to be brought out into the battlefield; and had requested the opposing armies to abide by its laws so that they should not remain in ignorance about its importance or have any excuse later of not abiding by the injunctions of the Holy Book. Another pertinent point to be considered was the fact that Ali ﷺ was conscious of the relationship of Talha, Zubair and Ayesha with the Prophet ﷺ; and therefore, was required to deal with this matter with extreme care and caution. He reminded them of the Quranic injunctions of not to initiate the battle until all hope of reconciliation was lost. As such, it was only after the army of Ayesha had killed the bearer of the Holy Book sent by Imam Ali ﷺ as the mediator, that Ali ﷺ was left with no option but to respond by a defensive action when the battle was started.

In fact, if Muawiyah and his Syrian companions had been genuine in their intention to bring the Quran as a mediator, they should have begun this process *before* initiating the battle. But they did not do so. On the contrary, even when they were repeatedly reminded of the Quranic injunctions by Ali ﷺ during the battle, they paid absolutely no heed and chose to ignore his advice. Several representatives (*safeers*) were sent by Imam Ali ﷺ to Muawiyah for this purpose, but they were all sent back empty handed. They did not believe in peace or mediation by the holy Book but were intent on doing battle. However, after weeks of warfare, when they were on the point of imminent defeat, they resorted to this ploy of raising the pages of Quran on their lances and thereby creating confusion within the armies and bringing the fight to a halt. Ali ﷺ being the Imam of the time did not fall for this ruse and reminded the people that Muawiyah and his coterie had no attachment to the Quran, or even to the religion of the holy

Prophet ﷺ, and that this was just a ruse to save themselves from the sword and defeat. But most of the confused army did not obey Ali ؏ which lead to the matter being settled through an arbitration by a third party."

Maulana Abul Ala Maududi in his book[85] has categorically stated that: "This introduction of the Quran in the battlefield by Muawiyah was not with the purpose of resolving the matter in consideration of the Quran or bringing it in as an 'Interpretation of the Islamic law', but rather, it was only **a manoeuvre to escape the indignity of a resounding defeat**! Can this ruse be really passed off as an *'Islamic Ijtehaad'* [Jurisprudence]?"

Reverting back to Dr. Taha Husayn, he writes: "This conspiracy did not end here but took a more sinister and devious turn in that, the selection of the two arbitrators Ashath bin Qais and his companion from Yemen who insisted on choosing Abu Musa-e-Ashari as one of the arbitrators; whereas Ali ؏ himself was not allowed to select the person of his choice in the persons of Ibn Abbas or Malik-e-Ashtar. Abu Musa was that person who was instrumental in preventing the people of Kufa from assisting Ali ؏ in the Battle of Jamal. Thus Ali ؏ was not only denied the option of selecting his own representative but was also forced to accept a particular person of whom he did not approve! All these things did not happen "incidentally" but were according to a devious Syrian stratagem.

Ibn Abbas was denied acceptance because of being a close relative of Ali ؏, and Malik-e-Ashtar was denied because he had taken an active part in the battle on Ali ؏'s side and was motivated to achieve victory at all costs! Akhnaf bin Qais from Ali ؏'s side wanted to be alongside Abu Musa to represent Ali ؏'s interests, but this proposal was also denied, insisting that only Abu Musa be

---

[85] 'Khilafat wa Mulukiyat'- Allama Maudadi – Pg 345.

the representative because he had not partaken in the battle on either side. It is indeed strange, and a mockery of justice that they did not apply the same yardstick in the selection of the other arbitrator Amr ibn Aas who not only took part in the battle but was also a constant advisor to Muawiyah in his devious ploys! In summary, Amr ibn Aas was the representative of Muawiyah, and Abu Musa Asheri was chosen to represent Ali 🕮 against his wish.

Several books like 'Khasas-un-Nasai', 'Rauzatul Ahbab', 'Habib-us-Siyar' and 'Rauzatus Safa' have all recorded that when the Peace Treaty was being written after the Battle of Siffeen, the title by which Imam Ali was referred to was *'Ameerul Momineen'* - *Commander of The Faithful.* Amr ibn Aas objected saying: 'Ali is your Ameer, and not ours, and this title should be deleted'. Akhnaf objected strongly, but Ashath ibne Qais agreed with Amr and said it should be removed. While this dispute continued, Ali 🕮 himself took the paper and struck off the title of *'Ameerul Momineen'* and looking up at the sky proclaimed, *"Allah ho Akbar!"* When questioned about his reason for pronouncing the *'Kalemah Tawheed'* Imam Ali 🕮 said that *this incident was like what the Prophet ﷺ had encountered in his lifetime at the time of signing the Treaty of Hudaibiya; when the Meccans had objected to the Prophet ﷺ being referred to as 'Rasoolullah' and had insisted upon having that title deleted! When I refused to delete it, the Apostle of Allah himself took the pen and struck the title and instead inserted the words: "Muhammad ibn Abdullah" and then looked at me and prophesied: O Ali! One day you will be faced with a comparable situation!"*

Abu Musa, besides having no sympathy towards Ali 🕮 was also a thick-headed simpleton. He easily fell into the trap contrived by the cunning strategy of Amr ibn Aas who approached him and said: "O Abu Musa, let us both disown Ali *as well as* Muawiyah; and let the Muslims approve whomsoever they wish to elect." Abu

Musa readily agreed to this proposition. Amr Ibne Aas then pretending to give preference to Abu Musa for his seniority in age, asked him to be the first to announce his decision. Abu Musa again, fell for his deception, and ascending the stage, announced that he as a representative from the side of Ali ﷺ disowned him, Ali, from the candidacy of the office! Amr Ibn Aas then cunningly stepped forward and announced: "O People! You have just seen that Abu Musa has disowned and disqualified Ali from the Caliphate. I accept the decision of Abu Musa and now, as we are left with only the one name of Muawiyah, I install him as Caliph of the Muslim Ummah!"

So, saying, he proceeded to congratulate Muawiyah on his success! Even the simpleton Abu Musa was annoyed at his crafty deception; and while the majority of people were left astounded, only a small group of people protested against it as being a move of downright fraud and treachery and refused to accept the decision; and they continued to regard Ali ﷺ as their true Caliph while the majority went along with the deceit of Muawiyah's side and submitted to him as their new Caliph.

10.13: Battle of Nehrewan

The rebels and the hypocrites did not let Ali ﷺ have any respite from their constant attacks and intentions of doing battle. In 38 AH after the inconclusive Battle of Siffeen, Ali ﷺ returned to Kufa to establish his government. But shortly thereafter, the Kharijites advanced towards Kufa with a force of 12,000 to wage war against Ali ﷺ. He met them with his army at a place called Nehrewan with an intent to stop them; predicting before the start of the battle that his army would lose not more than ten soldiers, while the Kharijites would escape with barely ten remaining from their side! In his customary noble behaviour, he instructed his army not to initiate the attack but to await and see as to what the first move from the Kharijites would be. The battle began with the Kharijites advancing towards Imam Ali ﷺ's army raising a slogan: "*Sareiah! Sareiah fil Jannah – Hurry! Hurry To Attain Paradise!*"

Ali ﷺ split his soldiers into two flanks and surrounded the opposing army, wreaking havoc upon them. The enemies were completely routed, and as predicted by Ali ﷺ, only ten of his soldiers [or by some accounts seven] got martyred and only about ten of the Kharajites survived, while the rest met with an ignominious death. It is said that from the surviving Kharijites two fled to Khorasan, another two towards Yemen and some towards Talmardan. Their descendants are still to be found in these areas.

After the battle, Ali ﷺ insisted upon his soldiers to look for the body of a deformed person with a wasted left hand and with an unsightly growth on the left side of his chest who was killed on the enemy side. After a great deal of searching, they discovered the body and Ali ﷺ thanked the Almighty Lord that this person had met his just fate, as this was the very same person who had accused the Prophet ﷺ of being unfair in his distribution of the war booty after the Battle of Hunain. The Apostle of Allah ﷺ had ignored his accusations twice, but when he did this for the third time, the signs of anger were clearly visible on the Prophet ﷺ's countenance, and he predicted that this would be that noxious person from whose progeny will be born a tribe of people who would be as far away from religion as an arrow is after being released from its bow! They would be fluent in the Quranic recitations, but the spirit of the Quranic injunctions would not go beyond their vocal cords![86]

---

[86] 'Fitnatul Kubra' –Dr. Taha Husayn, Pg 114; 'Sahih Bukhari' – Chap 4, Pg 34 & Chap 12, Pg 229; and Sahih Muslim, Vol 1, Pg 431.

10.14: Opinion of Manazer Ehsan Gilani about the Events at Jamal and Siffeen

Manazer Ahsan Gilani was the 'Head of Religious Studies' at the Osmania University, Hyderabad, India. Along with some other publications, he is also the author of the book titled: "The Political Life of Imam Abu Hanifa". He states the following:

"After the demise of the Prophet ﷺ, wealth and a luxurious lifestyle had become rampant within the Muslim society and Islam was taking a deviated path. People were going astray from true Islamic values and were left with no 'role model' to look up to. At this critical juncture, Imam Ali ؑ stepped forward; and after the Battles of Jamal and Siffeen, he clearly demonstrated to the Muslims the discrepancies and deviations which had overtaken the teachings of the holy Prophet ﷺ, causing confusion and chaos in the attitudes and behaviour of Muslims at large.

It was Ali ؑ and his noble family who responded to the arduous task of taking up the gauntlet of the 'Deen of Islam' and reviving the 'Sunnah' [traditions] and the teachings of the holy Apostle ﷺ; and leaving a legacy behind for the Muslims to follow for generations. It is quite a different matter however that the Muslim Ummah still remains to this day, misguided, and has indeed been unfortunate in not being rightly directed in their beliefs and attitudes despite the shining role models left by the progeny of the holy Apostle."

Chapter XI

BRIEF HISTORY OF THE TWELVE IMAMS OF THE HOUSE OF THE HOLY PROPHET ﷺ AND SOME MIRACLES THEY PERFORMED

11.1: Father of the Holy Imams: The First Imam - Ali ibn Abi Taleb ؏

The birth of the holy first Imam ؏ occurred on the 13th day of the month of Rajab, on a Friday in the 30th 'Year of The Elephant' (*Aam-ul Feel*) 600 AD. This event occurred about 10 years prior to the public proclamation by the Prophet ﷺ of his Prophetic Mission. It is recorded in countless books[87] that as the time of the birth of her child approached, his mother Hazrat Fatima bint Asad ؏ went to the Kaaba to pray for a safe delivery. When she arrived there, the wall of the Kaaba split open and a Voice from within beckoned her to enter. She did so, and the wall closed after her, enfolding her within its four walls. The birth of Ali ؏ occurred shortly thereafter **inside the House of Kaaba.**

Hazrat Ali ؏'s father's name was Imran ibn Abdul Muttalib ؏ and by his '*kuniyat*' [patronymic or pseudonym] he was popularly known as 'Abu Talib'. This was in line with the Arab custom where the father was referred to as the parent of his eldest son. Before the birth of their child, both his parents: Abu Talib and Fatima bint Asad went to the Mount of Abu Qais, praying and seeking

---

[87] 'Al Mustadrak' by Al Hakim; Vol 3, Pg 483; 'Fusool al Mohimmah' – by Nooruddin bin Saleh Maliki; Vol 1, Pg 14; 'Maraj Al Zahiyah' by Masudi; Vol 5, Pg 175; 'Shahadat-al-Aiyni' by Allama Ulusi; Pg 4; 'Bashaara Al Mustafa'- Sheik Muhammad Ahsan Ahmed; Vol 2, Pg 251, and many other notable books by both Sunni and Shia scholars.

guidance for choosing a suitable name for their awaited child. It is recorded that they a heard a resonating sound; and when they looked up they saw a Banner of green light displayed across the sky on which was written the name: "*ALI*" and a voice was heard to say: "*I have given you both a Pure and Infallible child and his name will be associated with My Own Exalted name 'ALA' and he shall be called 'ALI'!*"

In addition to this famous name, his mother by her personal choice called him '**Hyder**' while his father referred to him as '**Asad**'; both of which names connote a 'Lion' in the Arabic locution! After his birth it is recorded that he did not open his eyes for three whole days, even while being held by his own parents. But when Prophet Muhammad ﷺ arrived on the third day and held him in *his* arms, he immediately opened his eyes and locked eyes with him, and after invoking his greetings upon the holy Prophet he started reciting verses from the holy Quran! This recitation of the Quran by him in his infancy should not be cause for scepticism to any person, as on a parallel it is supported as a fact from the Quran itself that Jesus ﷺ also spoke from his cradle as a newborn babe. This miraculous behaviour of Ali ﷺ reciting the Quran as an infant is similarly testified by Allah ﷻ Himself in a holy verse in *Surah Ra'ad* (13:43) that He, Allah ﷻ had endowed Ali ﷺ with the **complete knowledge of the Holy Book** (*Ilm ul Kitab*).

Hazrat Abu Talib ﷺ the father of Imam Ali, had earlier brought up the holy Prophet ﷺ who, having been a posthumous child, had initially been under the guardianship of his Grandfather Abdul Muttalib ﷺ; who in turn, just prior to his own death, had willed that his son **Abu Talib** should thenceforth take on the **sole responsibility of guardianship** of his orphaned grandson Muhammad ﷺ. [Hazrat Abu Talib was the only 'full' brother of Hazrat Abdullah, the father of Muhammad ﷺ]. Accordingly, both Hazrat Abu Talib ﷺ and his wife Hazrat Fatima bint Asad ﷺ took charge as guardians of the young child Muhammad ﷺ and reared him like their own son; [indeed, even better!] in giving him greater preference in everything over their own children! Fatima bint Asad 🌸 specially took on the role of a soft-hearted maternal figure and was extremely attached and tender towards him; even taking precaution to safeguard him in his sleep by constantly rotating and alternating his sleeping arrangements with her own children's during the night, in fear of the probability that someone becoming aware of the exact spot where the young Muhammad ﷺ regularly slept at, may attack and harm him under the cloak of darkness.

Among his other talents, Abu Talib 🌸 was also a poet of renown; and in a book of history recorded by Abul Fida there is a poem which is attributed to Abu Talib 🌸 in which he states:

"O Muhammad! You invited me to Best of Religions: Islam. And I certify that you are indeed the most Truthful and Honest person. I strongly believe that the Religion of Muhammad is the best religion among all religions of the world! Until my last breath I will be your Protector and Supporter and ensure that no harm will come to you in my lifetime from any side!"

In the year 35 *Aamul Fil* Mecca suffered a severe famine. Finding provision for a large family was difficult. By this time Muhammad ﷺ as a young man was financially established in his own business. He, along with his Uncle Abbas ibn Abdul Muttalib approached Abu Talib 🌸 and offered to lighten his burden of caring for his large family. Consequently, Hazrat Abbas adopted his older son Aqeel while Muhammad ﷺ adopted the young Ali 🌸, taking him **under his total care**. Thus, from the tender age of five years, Ali 🌸 came under the protection, guidance, and training of the holy Prophet ﷺ which was a unique privilege that was bestowed upon Ali 🌸 by the workings of Providence!

Referring back to the instance of Ali 🌸 reciting the Quran in his infancy, upon seeing the Prophet ﷺ for the first time three days after his birth: as mentioned earlier, this should not be a cause for any surprise for our readers, because the Quran itself testifies to the fact that when the disbelievers taunted the holy Prophet as being a poet or a magician, Allah ﷻ declared in Surah *Ra'ad* (13:43) that it was sufficient for the Apostle that Allah ﷻ Himself was a witness to his Prophethood along with "*the one (person) who had complete knowledge of the Book*"- which was none other than Ali ibn Abu Talib ؑ! It is to be noted that when this verse was revealed, Ali ؑ was barely nine years old and yet he is vouched by Allah ﷻ Himself as having the knowledge of the **entire holy Quran** ingrained in him since the time of his birth!

This statement, however, should **not be** misconstrued by any that [*Mazallah!*] the Prophet ﷺ did not have the knowledge of the holy Quran and that Ali ؑ recited it ahead of him [!] because by his own statement Muhammad ﷺ had declared that "*he was a Prophet Fourteen Thousand Years prior to the advent of Adam ؑ when the latter was still in a stage of being created with 'Clay and Water'! The "Noor" (Divine Lights) of Prophet ﷺ and his infallible progeny were in a state of adoration and worship of the Almighty Lord __eons__ before the creation of the universe or its inhabitants!*"

Imam Ahmed ibn Hanbal and Allama Jarir-e-Tabari relate from one Afeef-al-Kindi that: "Once I went to Mecca and stayed with Abbas ibn Abdul Muttalib. At the time of dawn, I went into the precincts of the Kaaba. There I saw a young man praying with his face towards the Kaaba. Soon after, a youth came along followed by a lady and they both also joined the young man in offering their prayers. I asked Abbas ibn Abdul Muttalib as to who these three persons were. He replied that the two males were his nephews Muhammad ibn Abdullah and Ali ibn Abu Talib, while the lady was Khadija bint Khuwaylid, who was the wife of the young Muhammad. After this, Abbas added that **these were the only three persons he knew of who followed this new religion.**"

These same two scholars relate another similar incident in their respective works 'Manaqib' and 'Al Kabir' through Abdullah ibn Masood, a venerable companion of the holy Prophet ﷺ, who stated that he personally witnessed a young man with a fair skin and rosy cheeks enter the precincts of the Kaaba through the 'Baab e Safa'. His wavy hair extended down to his ears; and he had dark large eyes and shiny white teeth visible through his thick growth of beard. He had a wide forehead and a high impressive nose conveying the impression of an Elite origin, a very handsome face and a good-looking man with a slim form and a narrow waist. He was accompanied by two other persons: a young boy of five or six years in age and a lady who had her face covered. All three proceeded to kiss the Black Stone (Hajr e Aswad) and performed seven circuits around the Kaaba. Upon enquiring about the identity of these three, I learnt through Abbas that the two males were his nephews – Muhammad ibn Abdullah and Ali ibn Abu Talib; and the lady was Khadija the wife of Muhammad. Apart from them, none other is following this new religion." It is also recorded elsewhere that even at the tender age of two years, Ali ؏ was seen standing and praying beside the holy Prophet ﷺ when he used to be in solitary worship near the holy Kaaba.

Nisa`i, Ahmad bin Hanbal, Hafiz Abu Naeem, Abuzair Usmani, ibn Abi Shaiba, ibn Asim, Hakim, and others have all related a tradition that Imam Ali ؏ used to say: "*I am the servant of Allah and the brother of the holy Apostle; and **I am the Siddique al Akbar** [The Foremost Among the Truthful]. No one has the right to use this title besides me; and anyone who does so is a Liar. I performed my prayers with the holy Apostle ﷺ nine years before anyone else!*"

It is recorded in 'Futuhaat-al Quds' that whenever Prophet Muhammad ﷺ entered the house of Abu Talib ؏ while his wife Fatima bint Asad ؏ was pregnant with Ali ؏, and invoked his salutations on them, Ali 🌸 would also always respond to him from within his mother's womb! Upon witnessing this strange phenomenon Hazrat Abu Talib 🌸 remarked: *"Surely my nephew Muhammad is the last amongst the prophets sent by Allah and my unborn son (who recognizes this fact) will be his Vicegerent."*

An interesting incident has been recorded by Najmuddin Fakharul Islam Abu Bakr bin Muhammad in his 'Manaqib-al-Ashaab' that once when Ali 🌸 was still an infant, his mother left him in his cradle for a short while to deal with some chores. Their house was located on the side of a hill. A large snake made its way into the house and came near the cradle of Ali 🌸. Even at that early stage of being a 'babe in arms' Ali 🌸 caught hold of the serpent in such an iron grip that it died on the spot. When his mother returned and found him with the dead snake, she named him **"Hyder"** which denotes a 'Lion of the Desert'!

It is also recorded in this same book that whenever a child was born to the Qureish in Mecca, Abu Jahl (the uncle of Umar) used to apply the dust from the idols of Kaaba (as an eyeliner) into the eyes of the newborn babies (an antiquated ceremony of baptizing the infant). When he tried to do this with Ali 🌸, he shut his eyes so tight that Abu Jahl despite exerting his full strength and pressure could not succeed in getting them opened! When he persisted in trying to somehow prod his eyes open, Ali 🌸 slapped Abu Jahl with such force that his neck remained crooked for the rest of his life!

Mulla Husayn Waiz Kashifi writes in his book 'Rauzatus Shohoda' that when Ali 🌸 was brought home from the Kaaba, he was wrapped up in a cloth in the Arabic tradition, with his hands strapped by his sides. However, it was soon seen that the cloth was torn apart, and his hands were free! No matter how often he was tied up, he would rip the cloth and free his hands from the bindings! Seeing this, his father Abu Talib 🌸 said that his son possessed the strength of a "Lion" in his arms; and turning to his wife Fatima bint Asad he enquired as to what name she had chosen for him. She replied that she had added the name **"Asad"** (also a Lion) after her own father. When the Prophet ﷺ arrived, he said that the child should be named "Ali" as this was the name selected for him by Allah ﷻ. Both parents concurred that they had also once heard a voice proclaiming that their unborn child should be called "Ali". Likewise, several traditions in various reliable books testify to the fact that Ali ؑ's name had been selected by Allah ﷻ and been revealed to his parents on unique occasions prior to his actual birth!

Even from the tender age of nine or ten Ali ؑ used to accompany the Apostle ﷺ whenever he used to go about in the streets of the city after the announcement of his prophetic mission. The infidels of Mecca, however, would often encourage their children to harass the Prophet at such times by taunting him and pelting stones at him. Ali ؑ soon took it upon himself to ward them off and physically beat them up as well, even though some of them were twice his own size, to the extent that he soon came to be known as ('*Khasm*') 'The Beater'! Shortly thereafter, the children stopped their molesting for fear of being beaten up by the young Ali whom they found to be a formidable bodyguard, constantly trailing the Prophet like his shadow!

As the Prophet ﷺ continued preaching his newly proclaimed religion of Islam, Ali ؑ remained with him in close proximity, walking behind him and following him step by step; and the holy Prophet ﷺ in his turn spared no effort in training and imparting an excellent upbringing to his young protege in every facet of his life and character building; so much so that this child ultimately became a 'mirror-image' of the holy Apostle himself! The 'Light' or '*Noor*' of these two noble personalities of Islam that had been in unison prior to the creation of the universe, remained together in close proximity to each other in this world as well, up until the sad departure of the holy Prophet ﷺ; who ultimately in his death received his last rites, and was also interred into his grave, by none other than his ever faithful companion Ali, the son of his uncle Abu Talib ؏!

Considering the foregoing, it is impossible to comprehend the life of the Prophet ﷺ [nay, his very existence!] without being conscious of his affection and attachment to Ali ؏. They were both as indispensable to each other and as closely bonded with each other, as are the two faces of a coin! To understand either of them fully, one **must** acknowledge the intense love which existed between these two exalted personalities and their closeness and inseparable attachment to each other; details of which have already been described in the earlier chapters of our book.

In brief, many incidents have been recorded in the history of Islam which clearly illustrated the attachment which the Prophet ﷺ had toward his cousin Ali ؏. On one occasion when Ali ؏ had been sent on a mission outside the city, the Prophet ﷺ is known to have sent up a prayer saying: "*O Allah! Do not let me leave this world before I have seen the face of Ali **once more** during my lifetime!*"

When the order from Allah ﷻ came down for all the doors leading into the mosque [*Masjid-e-Nabawi*] to be closed **except those of Imam Ali ؏ and his own,** people criticized the Prophet that he was being biased in favour of his cousin Ali; to which the Apostle ﷺ replied that he was not doing this by his own whim or wish, but rather, it was in accordance with the command of Allah ﷻ!

After the Conquest of Mecca when the Prophet ﷺ was ordered by Allah ﷻ to cleanse the holy Kaaba of the 360 idols located within it, he did not seek the assistance of anybody except Ali ؏ to accomplish this important assignment. [One of the other reasons could quite possibly have been that some of the new converts may have still retained 'some affinity' toward some 'deity' or idol lodged therein, which they may have worshiped in the past]. Ali ﷺ had no such affiliations and thoroughly cleansed the Kaaba of all the idols, to the extent that the Prophet ﷺ got him to mount on his own shoulders to destroy the idols that were placed higher up in niches located close to the ceiling of the Kaaba. When Ali ﷺ jumped down from the Prophet ﷺ's shoulders, he was seen to be smiling, and upon the Prophet ﷺ asking him for the reason of his smile, he replied that though he had descended from such a lofty place, yet no bodily harm had befallen upon him! The Prophet ﷺ replied: *"The question of harm could not arise since the one who raised you was the (Sayyedul Ambiya) - Leader of the Prophets, and the one who helped you descend was Gabriel - the (Sayyedul Malaika) – the Leader of the Angels!"*

Ali ﷺ's diet was extremely simple, and his apparel was also very ordinary. It is recorded in various books [88] that one day Abdullah ibn Abbas enquired as to the reason of his humble attire to which Ali ﷺ replied: *"I feel embarrassed to ask anyone to patch my clothes repeatedly. But this world is transitory, and its pleasures are transient. It is Allah ﷻ's order that the Commander of The Faithful should dress similar to the poorest of the Ummah, so that the poor may not feel inferior, and the rich may try to emulate their leader."*

It is recorded in several books [89] that Ali ﷺ used to go for days without eating a full stomach; and when the pangs of hunger beset him, he would tie a stone around his stomach to alleviate his hunger and even in this state he continued with his thanksgiving

---

[88] 'Riaz-un Nazzara' – Vol 2, Pg 230; 'Tabaqat ibn Saad' – Vol 3, Pg 18.

[89] 'Istiyab'- Vol 2, Pg 478; 'Riaz un Nazzara'- Vol 2, Pg 235; 'Izalatul Khifa' – Pg 276.

to the Merciful Lord, which was totally in line with the training he had received from the holy Prophet ﷺ.

His normal diet consisted of barley bread and water. At times even when the bread became hard and stale, he was seen to be breaking it on his knee and dipping it in water to soften it and make it edible! The left-over pieces of this dry bread used to be carefully put back in the small sack and sealed by Imam ؏. When questioned about the reason for sealing the sack, *he would reply that it was to prevent his children who out of love for him "may moisten it with oil to make it more palatable for me!"* He was not against the consumption of meat but usually avoided it saying that *"one should not make the stomach a graveyard of dead animals"*!

An incident is recorded that once a stranger entered the city of Medina and being hungry after his journey, he proceeded to the Mosque of the holy Prophet ﷺ where he thought he might get some food. There he saw Imam Ali ؏ who offered his own food to the stranger. But finding that the bread was stone hard, the newcomer was unable to partake of the food offered! Seeing this, Imam Ali ؏ directed him to a place where his son Hasan ؏ used to feed the poor and indigent persons of the city daily. Upon arriving there, the stranger was welcomed and seated on the dining area by Hasan ؏. Shortly thereafter, upon noticing a strange behaviour on the newcomer's part, in that, while he was eating, he was simultaneously also saving up some food in his bag; Imam Hasan ؏ intrigued by this action, approached him and asked the reason for this behaviour; while telling him that he need not shy away from eating his fill, nor be worried about saving for his next meal as he could always come back for more. To this the stranger replied that he was stalking up this food not for himself but for a person he had met in the Mosque whose bread had become so hard that it was almost inedible. When Imam Hasan ؏ heard this, tears welled up in his eyes and he explained that "that person" whom he referred to was none other than his own venerable father Imam Ali 🕮 and that was his usual diet!

Ali 🕮 used to repair the shoes of the holy Prophet 🕮 as well as his own. When he purchased new clothes, he used to buy two sets and always give the first choice to his slave Qamber[90] and take the one that was left over. If Qamber chose the cheaper one, Ali 🕮 would insist on giving him the better and more expensive one saying that because Qamber was his junior, the nicer garment would look better on a younger person, than it would on himself at his senior age!

Another noteworthy incident is recorded in the same book[91] in connection with his generosity that on one occasion when a beggar approached Imam Ali 🕮 for some food, he asked his slave Qamber to fulfill his need. Qamber replied that the food was loaded on the camel's back for starting on their mission. Ali 🕮 instructed him to give away the camel along with the food. Qamber said that the camel was tied up as part of a Caravan of many other Camels. Imam Ali 🕮 replied: "Give him the entire Caravan!" Upon hearing this, Qamber instantly dropped the reins of the camels that he was holding in his hands and darted to a corner hiding to take refuge! When asked about his strange action, Qamber explained later that the **'Sea of open-handed generosity'** of his master **Imam Ali 🕮 was at its 'Zenith'**; and since he was holding the reins of the Caravan, he feared that the magnanimous Imam may next also have given **him away** in charity along with the entire Caravan had he had not dropped the reins and darted! **He** Qamber, would then have been deprived from the honour of being the slave of such a Grand and Wonderful Master!

---

[90] 'Riaz-un Nazzarra' – Vol 2, Pg 229.

[91] Ibid, Pg 230.

One day during his Caliphate in Kufa, Ali ﷺ was passing through the marketplace when he observed a vendor of dates closing his shop early and complaining that he had barely arrived and set up his business when he had to close shop and return home to address a domestic emergency. Ali ﷺ despite being the Caliph of the time immediately offered to mind his shop till such time that it took the vendor to go and return after tending to his household crisis!

Mukhtar Muthar al-Basri has recorded another incident that one day Imam Ali ﷺ was making the rounds of the market when he ﷺ saw a slave girl crying. When asked about the reason she said that she had purchased some dates from a vendor which her master upon taking home did not approve of and had instructed her to return them to the vendor and bring back the money. The shopkeeper however, refused to comply and now she was afraid of her master's wrath. Imam Ali ﷺ intervened and asked the shopkeeper to comply as she was only a servant and would be penalized by her master. The shopkeeper was annoyed at this suggestion and pushed Ali ﷺ away physically, asking him to keep out of his affair. Imam Ali ﷺ bore this without retaliation, but the people around rushed to caution the vendor that the person he had just shoved aside was none other than the Commander of The Faithful! The vendor became contrite and trembling with fear he returned the money and apologized to the Imam ﷺ saying that he had not known his position of eminence. Ali ﷺ accepted his apology and mildly chided him that he personally wished for no respect or recognition for himself but only sought to ensure that the merchants be fair and reasonable in their dealings with all their clients!

Another incident of interest relates that during the days of his Caliphate in Kufa, Imam Ali ﷺ was known to take care of a particular person with leprosy who had been abandoned by his family and sent outside the city limits. Ali ﷺ used to visit him regularly, feed him and even wash his clothes! One day Imam Hasan ﷺ happened to pass by the place of this person with leprosy and heard him weeping and wailing aloud. Imam Hasan stopped to enquire the reason for his grief. The person with leprosy replied that it had been three whole days that he had not seen the man who used to feed him and take care of him. Hasan ﷺ asked as to who that person was; the leper replied that he knew not his identity but said that Hasan ﷺ's voice and manner of speech was very much like that of his unknown benefactor. When told that 'that person' in question was his revered father: the 'Commander of the Faithful' who had passed away after being struck by an assassin's sword three days ago, the leper heaved a deep sigh of grief and died from the shock and resultant sorrow!

In short, there are countless incidents recorded that reflect his piety, nobility, generosity, chivalry, magnanimity, compassion, justice and fair play and several other countless qualities endowed in him which are all reflections of the noble personality of the holy Prophet ﷺ. After assuming the Caliphate, when Ali ﷺ lead the congregational prayers for the first time, it is recorded in Sahih Bukhari[92] that people unanimously remarked that they had experienced the same pleasure in performing their prayer in congregation as the one they used to feel while praying behind the holy Apostle!

About his acts of worship, it is stated that he used to offer 1000 cycles of prayers each night and that it was normal to hear him recite 2000 'Takbirs' out aloud every single night. When offering his prayers his colour would turn pale in awe and deference to the Almighty Lord. Seeing his motionless body in prostration people

---

[92] 'Sahih Bukhari' – tradition related by Mutraf bin Abdullah; and Imran bin Haseen.

would often mistake him for dead! The incident of an arrow being embedded in his heal after one of the battles of Islam, is too well known to be repeated here in detail. Nonetheless, it is unanimously recorded by every scholar that the wound in his heal was so painful that Ali ﷺ would not allow anyone to even touch it for cleansing. When consulted, the holy Prophet ﷺ told the people to wait till Ali was offering his prayers; and to remove the arrow during the time that he was in the act of praying; as due to his intense absorption in worship, he would be not even be aware of the arrow being withdrawn or the wound being treated! Accordingly, upon completion of his prayers when Imam Ali ﷺ was apprised of the removal of the arrow from his wound, he was totally astounded!

Ali ﷺ surpassed all his predecessors in his noble qualities; and no other personality in the history of Islam has been given the titles which he has been endowed with by Allah ﷻ and His noble Prophet such as:

1. **Nafsullah** – the Soul of God
2. **Lisanullah** – The Tonge of God
3. **Yadullah** – The Hand of God
4. **Wajhullah** – The Face of God
5. **Ain-ullah** – The Eyes of God
6. **Uznullah** – The Ear of God
7. **Ayatullah** – The Sign of God

All these attributes are beyond human comprehension. Mulla Ali Qoushanjyi was extremely biased against Imam Ali and his family, but nonetheless even **he** has been compelled to write that: "The mind cannot comprehend the eminent qualities and deeds of Ali ﷺ and none of his predecessors come close to any comparison with him!"

In his book titled "Hazrat Ali as An Amir' General Akbar Khan has recorded the following: "To describe the wonderfully illustrious personality of Amirul Momineen Ali ibn Abu Talib is to describe the holy Prophet of Islam, for both these Godly souls were of one and the same Light (*Noor*); and both manifested the Divine attitudes in their personal conduct and character... The wonderful qualities of Hazrat Ali as a 'Man', as the most Faithful Devotee of the Prophet, as the Greatest Defender of the Faith, as a 'Mujahid, as the Commander in Chief of the Muslim Forces, as the Divinely Inspired Scholar, as a Heavenly Commissioned Imam, as a Caliph (Ruler of the Muslim Empire), as an Humble Labourer earning his daily sustenance for himself and his family, as a Social Worker for the Cause and Protection and Maintenance of the Helpless Widows and Destitute Orphans etc., etc.; are so numerous that even after enumerating them in a detailed volume, none can confidently say that he has done full justice to the subject or has drawn a perfect picture of the Great Hero!"

The Quran is filled with countless verses in praise of Ali ﷺ [along with several traditions from the holy Prophet ﷺ in his praise] which we have already discussed in detail in Volume I, chapters 3 and 4 of this book. However, there are some verses that were revealed for the '*Muhajirs*' (Immigrants) and some for the '*Ansars*' (Helpers) that describe their virtues in a collective manner, but it is not likely that they apply to each person individually; and according to Ibn Abbas, the greater probability is that they refer to Ali ﷺ. He has categorically stated: "Wherever a verse begins with the words "*O You who Believe – Ya Ayyohal Lazeena Aaminu...*" it primarily refers to the foremost amongst the faithful: the Commander of Believers, Ali ibn Abu Talib ﷺ!

Apart from the foregoing explanation of Ibn Abbas, there are several verses that single out 'a particular person' and are specifically in praise of '*one and only one*' person; and that person is none other than Ali ﷺ. For instance, in Chapter 13: Surah *Ra'ad* (13:43): "*... Those who disbelieve and say 'Thou art not an Apostle'. Say thou: Sufficient is God as a witness between Me and you; and **he*** *with whom is the (complete) knowledge of the book".* The assertion about '*a male person* in a <u>*singular tense*</u> as **having the complete knowledge of the Holy Book'** exclusively refers to Ali 🕮 alone! When people asked the holy Prophet 🕮 as to who 'that person' was, he replied: [93] *"My brother Ali ibn Abu Talib!"*

It is widely recognized that Ali 🕮 himself used to say: *"Ask me anything about the holy Quran, for I know **when** each and every one of its verses was revealed, **where** it was revealed, **for whom** it was revealed and to whom it applies in general!"* No wonder the holy Prophet 🕮 was fully justified in declaring: *"I am the City of Knowledge, and Ali is its Gateway!"*

Whenever the Caliphs were confronted with any problem, vis-a-vis the Quran or Islamic Jurisprudence, they often used to refer it to Ali ibn Abu Talib 🕮. In Surah *At-Tahreem* which was revealed in condemnation of the two wives of the Prophet 🕮 (Ayesha and Hafsa), Allah 🕮 declares: *"Then verily God is his (Prophet 🕮's) Protector, **and** Gabriel **and** the 'most virtuous male' (**Salehul-Momineen**) amongst the Believers...* (66:4)" In this verse the reference to '*the most virtuous male*' again according to several scholars[94] is to none other than Ali ibn Abu Talib 🕮 **in the singular masculine gender**.

Likewise, in Surah *Hud* (Ch 11:17) where the verse opens with the words: *"Is **he** then who has a clear proof from his Lord and follows him (the Apostle) and is "**Shahedum-Minho**" - a witness from Him (Allah) ...."* Here again the mode of address is in the 'singular male gender' referring exclusively to Ali 🕮. In addition, the "Verse of *Wilayah*" – Chapter 5, verse 55 Surah *Maida*, the

---

[93] 'Tafsir e Husayni; Tafsir e Thalabi; Tarikh ul Khulafa – Jalaluddin Suyuti.

[94] Kalbi, Saadi, Mujahid Abu Saleh, 'Durre Manthur', 'Hulyatul Awliya' and many others.

"*Wali*" who gave away his ring in charity to a beggar while in the position of bending in '*Ruku*' during his prayers (as has been mentioned in this verse), is again none other than Ali 🕌! Innumerable Sunni scholars as previously stated, all concur that all these verses point specifically to Hazrat Ali 🕌 **alone;** specially the last verse, as no other person except Ali 🕌 had performed this act of giving charity while bowing in a state of prayers! However, there are some antagonists who cast aspersions on the merits of Ali 🕌 and raise an objection as to the state of Ali 🕌's concentration in prayers while giving away the ring. To this we say that the One to Whom the prayer was being offered, was best aware of his actions and intent, and **He** was the One who sent down this verse, not just in acceptance of his prayers but also in appreciation of his charitable act!

In like manner, in verse 61 of Surah Aale Imran (3:61) where the word "*Nafs*"[95] of the Prophet 🕌 was mentioned, no one was qualified to be included in this category except Ali 🕌, albeit the implication of the word "*Nufoos*" in the **plural tense** opted by Allah 🕌, gave room for *more than one person* to be accommodated as the '*Nafs*' of the Prophet 🕌 had he so chosen; but nonetheless the Prophet 🕌 singularly only selected Imam Ali 🕌 to represent him under this category!

Similarly in Chapter 2 of the holy Quran when the Apostle 🕌 on the 'Night of *Hijrat*' was ordered by Allah 🕌 to migrate from Mecca in the darkness of the night, and Ali 🕌 slept in the bed of the Prophet 🕌, the verse was revealed stating: *"And among the people is he who sells his Nafs (soul) seeking the pleasure of Allah; and Allah is most affectionate to (His) servants. (2:207)."* Here again there was no ambiguity as it was solely revealed in praise of Ali 🕌

---

[95] Translator's Note: There is no equivalent word for "*Nafs*" in the English language, but it may loosely be referred to as representing the "Soul".

who slept on the Apostle's bed all night on that occasion in compliance to his ﷺ's instructions. Apart from these there are several other verses that praise the Prophet ﷺ's family (the Ahlul Bayt ﷺ) in a collective way in which Ali ﷺ is also included. For instance: Chapter 33 Surah *Ahzab* (33:33) – the 'Verse of Purity'; Chapter 42 Surah *As Shura* (42:23) 'Verse of Muwaddat' – Love for Family of the Prophet; Chapter 37, Surah *As-Saffaat* (37:24) verse of questioning about the '*Wilaya*' of Ali ﷺ, as well as the verse sending Salutations on the Progeny of the Prophet: *"Salam Ala Aale Yasin"(37:130)*; then in Chapter 11 Surah *Hud* (11:73) sending Blessings on the people of the household of the Prophet: *"Rehmatullahey wa Barakaatahu Alaikum Ahlul Bayt"* as well as the entire Chapter 76 Surah *Dahr* was revealed in the praise of the Ahlul Bayt ﷺ.

Apart from these Quranic verses there are several traditions recited by the holy Prophet ﷺ specifically in praise of Ali ﷺ that are found in countless books of Sunni and Shia scholars. Some of these are:

"Man Kuntum Maula fa Aliyun Maula –Of whom I am the Lord and Master, Ali is his Lord and Master."

"Ana Madinatul Ilm wa Aliyun Baaboha – I am the City of Knowledge and Ali is its Gateway."

"Aliyun Minni, wa Ana Minho – Ali is from me and I am from him."

"Ali Sayyedul Arab – Ali is Chief of The Arabs."

"Ali Waliyul Momineen – Ali is the Lord of the Believers;" and many other similar sayings which we have mentioned earlier in chapters Three and Four of this book.

11.2: Martyrdom of the Commander of the Faithful Ali ﷺ

The Martyrdom of Imam Ali ﷺ occurred in the year 40 AH, after almost Five Years into his Caliphate. As was his habit, Ali ﷺ normally used to spend a greater part of his nights in prayers; and during the day he would address the Affairs of the State. About five years after taking charge of the Caliphate, in the year 40 AH, on the 19th night of the holy month of Ramadhan, Imam Ali ﷺ appeared to be unusually disturbed and constantly kept stepping out into the yard under the open sky and looking up at the Heavens, to the point that even his family members noticed and commented on his unusual behavior!

After completing his supplementary morning prayers in his home, Imam Ali prepared himself to leave the house and go towards the Masjid of Kufa for the congregational prayers. Before stepping out he told himself: *"O Ali! Be prepared to meet Death, for today it has its appointment to visit you!"* So saying he proceeded to step out of his house. The domesticated ducks and fowls that were reared in his home spontaneously raised their cries in agitation and coming up to him caught hold of his garment in their beaks, as if they could mysteriously sense the imminent calamity, and so tried to prevent him from leaving home! When some inhabitants of his house tried to chase them away Ali ﷺ remonstrated with them saying: *"Leave them alone because they are already bemoaning my impending death today!"*

Upon entering the Masjid Imam Ali ﷺ engaged himself in prayers and supplications. His cursed assassin Ibn Muljim was already in the mosque (concealing the poisoned sword within his garments), along with some other people who were also asleep. Ali ﷺ awakened them all, including ibn Muljim, and asked them to prepare for the morning prayers. When the congregational prayer which was being led by Imam Ali ﷺ commenced and was still in progress, Ibn Muljim abandoned his own prayer and came out with his bared sword. When Ali ﷺ was in the act of prostration, he struck a severe blow to his head! The assault was severe, and the wound was deep. The Prayers were totally disrupted. The Assassin sped but was chased and caught by others and brought back into the confines of the Mosque. Imam Ali ﷺ suffered from this injury inflicted by the poisoned sword for two days and eventually succumbed to it and passed away from this world on the 21st of Ramadhan. He was 63 years old.

It is stated in 'Riazun Nazzara'[96] that one day Abdur Rahman Ibn Muljim approached Ali ﷺ and requested him for some assistance. Ali ﷺ complied with his request and when the former had left, he told those around him that one day this same man would be his assassin. Upon hearing this, the people asked if he should not be arrested and put in prison right away; but Ali ﷺ replied that the deed had not been committed yet and hence he could not be punished ahead of his crime!

In the same book[97] there is this tradition related by ibn Shahab: "I was on my way to Damascus from Iraq to meet Caliph Abdul Malik ibn Marwan. Abdul Malik took me aside and said that 'I will reveal a secret to you which none other is aware of, and which you will not reveal to anyone. On the day that Ali ﷺ was assassinated, there was fresh blood under every stone in *Bait-ul-Muqaddass'* (Jerusalem). Whenever any stone was moved or turned from its place there was fresh blood underneath! Beside the two of us nobody else knows about this. Do not ever think of disclosing this to anybody.' I kept my promise and did not mention this to anybody till Abdul Malik was alive."

This same episode is recorded in 'Tarikh e Abul Fida' wherein he writes that on the day that Ali ﷺ was martyred there was fresh blood under every stone that was picked or moved from its position

---

[96] 'Riazun Nazzara' – Vol 2, Pg 245.

[97] Ibid, Pg 374.

in Jerusalem. In his well-known book titled 'Spirituality and Islam' Professor M. G. Reynolds has noted the following towards the end of it is third chapter: "The status that was achieved by Ali 🕮 was unique which no other ruler has achieved. His spiritual loftiness along with skillful excellence in administration of worldly affairs, are unparalleled till today. On the day of his martyrdom when the news spread in the City of Kufa along with the Muslims, the Jews as well as the Christians were equally devastated and wept bitterly. Hundreds of women and children who used to be supported by Ali 🕮 were roaming the streets tired and hungry; and once again subjected to a life of poverty and neediness after his demise. When the news of his assassination reached Jerusalem, the Chief Pontiff was affected by the loss so deeply that tears were running down his face for days in sadness! The Jews of the area were saddened to such an extent that the entire town was draped in an aura of gloom for months!"

In the year 1910 AD British Major Inhal while making a speech on the death anniversary of Hazrat Ali 🕮 had this to say: "After the passing away of Ali 🕮, the world lost a Spiritual Guide who was a guide not only for the Muslims but for the entire humanity. His existence was a guarantee of peace and tranquility for all people regardless of their faith or religion. There can be no other person dearer to the hearts of the people than Ali. When his coffin was taken out of the house, the streets were overflowing with mourners from all faiths which included Muslims, Christians, Jews and the Majusis [Fire Worshipers] who wailed and wept bitterly as if one of their own kith and kin had been lost!"

11.3: Opinions of Hitti, Osborne, and Davenport About the Character of Ali 🕮

Phillip K. Hitti has written the following in his book[98] 'The Makers Of Arab History': "Orthodox in religion, Valiant in battle, Eloquent in speech, True to his friends and Magnanimous to his foes, he Ali, became to his followers the paragon of Moslem nobility and Arab chivalry."

Major Osborne has also expressed his thoughts in a similar vein: "The dagger of an assassin destroyed the hope of Islam. With him (Ali) perished the truest hearted and the best Muslim of whom Muhammadan history has preserved the remembrance."

Dr. Davenport in his book has the following comment: "Ali had been in his youth a model of modest piety and energetic loyalty to the Apostle. He was now 55 years of age; genial and charitable, meditative, and reserved. He shrank from a society in which Religion had been displaced by Politics and Devotion by Intrigue..."

11.4: Last Will and Testament of Ali ﷺ

Prior to his death Imam Ali ﷺ made his Will on which he obtained the signatures of all his sons including Imam Hasan and Husayn ﷺ, Hazrat Muhammad Hanafia and others, along with many of his close relatives. He handed this to Imam Hasan ﷺ with the instruction that this should be given to Imam Husayn ﷺ after him. In addition to the foregoing, a separate Will had also been drawn up exclusively for his two sons Imams Hasan ﷺ and Husayn ﷺ; the gist of which has been recorded in 'Tarikh e Tabari'[99] and in Al Kafi'[100] as follows:

"I adjure you to be aware of your responsibilities. Never seek this world but be of such a character and manner that the world will come seeking you. Do not be sad at any worldly loss. Always speak

---

[98] 'The Makers of Arab History'- Phillip K. Hitti, Pg 46.

[99] 'Tarikh e Tabari'- Vol 6, Pg 85.

[100] 'Al Kafi' – Vol 1, Pg 184.

the Truth no matter how bitter it may seem. Always adhere to the principals of Truth and Honesty. Face all adversities with a bold front and constantly work to seek the Pleasure of Allah. **Oppose the tyrant and help the oppressed.** I bid you and all the rest of my children and relatives and all others to whom my message will reach to always have the Fear of Allah in your mind and never be disunited. Settle all your differences with Patience and Justice. Care for the orphans and look after their welfare and needs. Be considerate to the neighbours and pay heed to the holy Quran. None should surpass you in the act of implementation of the holy Quran in your personal lives. Be aware of your Daily Prayers; it is the main pillar of your 'Deen' (Religion). Do not be neglectful of the House of Allah (Kaaba) and never abandon it throughout your lifetimes. Struggle in the way of Allah (Jihad) with your Life and Property. Be Kind and Generous amongst each other. Never tire from inviting people towards good and preventing them from doing bad. Do not let evil mongers gain an upper hand over you. I forbid the clan of Bani Hashim to start a feud over (the excuse of avenging) my blood. At the most, strike my assassin with only one stroke and if he survives, then leave him alone as he has dealt a single blow on me. If I survive, it will be my choice as to whether I will retaliate in kind or pardon him."

To the intelligent observer it will be obvious that Hasnain 🙵 did not need these instructions as they were already endowed and imbibed with these lofty ideals of Islam. Rather, it was for the rest of the Muslim Ummah to pay attention to its contents and adhere to its principles that Imam Ali 🙵 as a responsible Father was fulfilling his duty in leaving a Will behind, which though addressed to his sons was equally designed for the Ummah to follow him.

11.5: Some Miracles of Ali ibn Abi Talib 🙵

The Ahlul Bayt of the Prophet ﷺ were blessed with the gift of performing miracles in a manner like the prophets of the old. There are countless miracles performed by Imam Ali ؏, but only a few of these are described hereunder to illustrate their significance:

1. Mulla Abdur Rahman Jami in his book 'Shawahid e Nabuwah' has recorded that when Ali ؏ used to mount his horse, *he would complete the mental review of the entire Quran* within the time it took for him to place his first foot on the stirrup, to the time that he put his other foot across the horseback!

2. In the same book a tradition is related by Asma bint Umays that when Fatima Zahra ؏ was married to Imam Ali ؏ she was surprised to witness an unusual incident, in that, the Earth was conversing with Ali ؏! She mentioned this to her father the Apostle of Allah ﷺ who replied: *"O Fatima! May you be congratulated! You have been given in marriage to a person who is of pure descent; and you have been privileged to become his wife! Allah has commanded that the Earth remain under the control of Ali and report all the incidents that occur on the face of this Earth from the East to the West!"*

3. Sayeed ibn Abi Taleb in his book 'Kifayat al Momineen' has written a tradition which Allama Sayyed Saleh Kashfi Hanafi has reproduced in his book 'Manaqib e Murtazawi' on page 180 as follows: One day the Prophet ﷺ was laid low with a headache and fever. He mentioned this to Ali ؏ who placed his right hand across the chest of the Prophet ﷺ and prayed thus for his recovery: *"O Ailment! Be gone for you are only a slave of Allah and His Prophet"*. The Prophet ﷺ was immediately relieved of his malady and sat up saying: *"O Ali! Among the distinctive and divine attributes awarded to you by Allah ﷻ, one of them is that all Illnesses and their Remedies have been given under your control!"*

4. The Incident of 'The Re-appearance of The Sun' (*Radde Shams*) has been recorded by several authoritative historians and

scholars such as: Suyuti, Abu Abdullah Muhammad bin Yousuf, Qazi Ayyaz, Hafez ibne Sayyed an-Naas, Hafez Allauddin Mahallati, Hazrat Jami and others in their respective books together with Kamaluddin Mohammed bin Talha Shafei in his book 'Matalib as-Suool' and Allama Yousef Kanji Ash-Shafei in 'Kifayat-ut-Talib' all of whom relate through Asma bint Umays that one day the Prophet ﷺ was resting with his head on the lap of Ali ؏ when he started receiving a Quranic revelation. By the time the revelation (*Wahi*) ended, the sun had set at which point the Prophet ﷺ sat up and enquired: *"O Ali, have you recited your 'Asr' prayers?"* Ali ؏ replied that he *had* offered the prayers conceptually in mind, by gesture and symbolism whilst sitting, so as not to disturb the Apostle ﷺ during the time of revelation. The Prophet ﷺ said: *"Invoke Allah ﷻ with your prayers to bring the sun back for you so that you can perform your prayers in a proper and timely manner."* Ali ؏ prayed; and the sun reappeared back on the horizon [!], and he offered his prayer as per the normal requirements.

A second similar miracle was performed by Ali ؏ when he was on his way with his army for the Battle of Siffeen. By the time it took for the army to cross over the River Euphrates, the sun had already set. On reaching the other side of the river, Imam Ali ؏ raised his hands in prayer and the sun returned on the horizon, thus enabling his whole army to offer their prayers in a proper time and manner!

5. Another incident is also related in 'Shawahid e Nabuwah' on the authority of Ibn Abbas that once when the Prophet ﷺ was on his way to Mecca before the signing of the Treaty of Hudaibiya, he encamped at a place called Hajfa. His companions went in search of water. However, they returned empty handed to report that they *had* found a well but could not get any water because strange and scary sounds were emanating from within, along with 'apparitions of heads floating without bodies' and 'flames of fire darting out'

from the well! None of the companions were prepared to venture any further!

The Prophet ﷺ then designated Ali ؑ to go forth and investigate the matter and get the necessary supply of water. Ali ؑ asked some of the companions to collect the utensils for water and led the group to the well, asking them not to be fearful. Upon their arrival they witnessed the same scary bodiless faces accompanied by frightening noises. When the water bucket was lowered into the well the rope connecting the bucket was mysteriously severed. Ali ؑ asked the companions to fetch another pail from the camp, but they were too mortified to move Sfrom their place!

Seeing this, Ali ؑ unsheathed his sword and jumped into the well! A lot of commotion was heard and finally the voice of Ali ؑ resounded with the proclamation of "*Allah ho Akbar*" after which a calm prevailed. Soon after, Ali ؑ emerged from the well with the bucket filled with water for the army camps. Many *Jinns* which inhabited this well were slain, while many others that survived converted to Islam. Amongst the latter was one *'Zaafer e Jinn'* who many years later offered his services to join forces with Imam Husayn ؑ on the *Day of Ashura* to help him in Kerbala, but Imam Husayn ؑ had thankfully declined to accept this help as it would have given him an undue advantage over his adversary!

Many other such encounters of Ali ؑ with the *Jinns* are recorded in 'Ahsanal Kibaar' and 'Farhat ul Khuds' and 'Manaqib us Saleh' by Kashfi Hanafi and several others: of battles with the *Jinns*, along with Imam Ali ؑ educating them in the Islamic faith and doctrines etc.

6. Suyuti has recorded from various sources that during the Battle of Khyber, Ali ؑ lifted the Gate of the Fort which weighed several thousands of kilograms (2000 mounds) in his left hand alone, which normally, even forty persons jointly would be hard

put to move! After yanking the gate from its hinges, Ali ﷺ used it as a 'drawbridge' to enable the troops of his army to cross over into the Fort; and eventually, he even used it as a shield for himself when the enemies tried to pelt arrows at him from the height of the fortress. He finally flung it so far, that later, even 80 persons collectively together could not move it from the spot where it had fallen!

It is also stated that the door was wrenched with such force that the entire Castle of Khyber shook violently as in an earth tremor, to the extent that Hazrat Safia who was sitting on her couch deep inside the fortress fell face downwards, apparently with such force that she broke one of her front teeth! Similarly, in 'Shawahid e Nabuwah' Maulana Jami writes that the other amazing sight was that "when Ali was transporting the people across the trench by lifting the door of Khyber in his hands, **his feet** were suspended in midair"!

7. Khwaja Bandey Nawaz Gesudaraz Husayni RA on page 138 of his book has documented that even with his eyes closed Ali ﷺ would never injure any of the people of his army while wielding his sword.[101]

8. Another anecdote mentioned in 'Shawahid e Nabuwah' records that when Imam Ali ﷺ had moved to Kufa during his Caliphate, there was a severe flood where the River Euphrates almost overflowed its banks and threatened the township with imminent drowning. People flocked around Imam Ali ﷺ crying for help; upon which the Imam ﷺ donned the Apparel of the Prophet ﷺ along with his Turban and taking his (ﷺ's) staff in hand, he, accompanied by his two illustrious sons, Hasan ﷺ and Husayn ﷺ, proceeded to the river. Then pointing the Prophet ﷺ's staff at the

---

[101] Translator's Note: Contrast this with the "Friendly Fire" casualties of several innocent lives lost today.

river, he ordered the water to recede, which it immediately did; by falling off its level by about a metre or so. The people, however, were still afraid and asked for a further reduction of the water levels which the Imam ﷺ complied with again, for a total of three times in all till the people were calmed and the level had fallen low enough to no longer pose a threat to the inhabitants.

9. Khwaja Nizamuddin Awliya who was a disciple of Fareeduddin Shakarbaar has compiled the quotes and sayings of Khwaja Qutubuddin Bakhtiyar Kaki; and on page 210 of this compilation, he records that: One day an impoverished Jewish person approached Imam Ali ﷺ for some monetary help. Ali had nothing on him to give to this person. He asked him to open his palm and recited a short prayer in the form of 'Salutations on the Prophet ﷺ and his holy progeny', which he repeated ten times and blew this on the person's palm closing it into a fist. He asked him to keep his fist closed till such time as he fulfilled all his needs and requirements. When this person returned to his comrades with his fist closed, they mocked him for being a simpleton in believing that the 'blowing of some words on his palm' would solve his problems. However, when the man opened his fist, there were ten pieces of gold coins in his hand! Seeing this miracle, they were all in awe and many of his Jewish companions converted to Islam.

10. Maulana Jami related from one Habab ibn Abdul Azdi that during the Battle of Neharwan Habab thought to himself that it would be a great sin to kill any of the Kharajites as they were also Muslims. At that very moment word was received that the enemy had crossed the river and was moving towards them; but Ali ﷺ did not concur with the news and stated that this was not so. Subsequently three other persons also came with the same report, yet again Ali ﷺ disagreed with it. At this point Habab told himself that **if** what Ali ﷺ said was true, then he was the true leader. When the reports were later found to be false, Imam ﷺ tapped Habab on

the shoulder and said: *"Habab, now have your doubts been put to rest?"* He then predicted that when the battle takes place, only ten will survive from the Kharajites army and less than ten will be martyred from his side. This outcome also proved to be completely true.

11. It is recorded that once Imam Ali ﷺ was **individually** invited by **40 persons** to partake of an evening meal at each of their independent houses, **all at the exact same time!** Ali ﷺ not only accepted all their invitations but also attended each individual gathering arranged by these forty hosts! Upon meeting each other the next day and discussing among themselves as to how Ali ﷺ had graced their home by his presence, they were incredulous to learn that the Imam had been a guest at everyone else's house also at the exact same time! They started arguing as to how this could be possible because each said that Ali ﷺ was at their own home! To verify the truth, they approached Ali ﷺ himself and questioned him whether he had **really** been present in all the 40 places *at the same time*? Ali ﷺ confirmed this fact to their complete satisfaction; and to add further to their appeasement, when the holy Prophet heard about this event, he stated that Ali was also present in *his company* that evening that very same time! The people dispersed expressing their amazement and loudly proclaiming: *"**(Surely) Ali is the Manifestor of The Most Amazing Traits! (Naade) Aliyun Mazhar al Ajayeb....**"*

12. It is recorded in 'Shawahid un Nabuwah' by Mulla Abdul Rahman Jami that when Ali ﷺ was on his way to Siffeen the soldiers of his army became extremely thirsty as they ran out of water. There appeared to be no sign of water in close vicinity. While searching around they came across the dwelling of a lonesome monk, who upon asking for some water, said that he had none, especially for such a large crowd; but he informed them that if they continued their travels, there was a place at about a distance

of three 'farsakhs' (six miles) away from there where they could find a water source. Ali ﷺ seeing that the soldiers were too tired to move any further, turned his mount to face the Kaaba and went forward a few paces, dismounted from his horse, and asked the people to dig at that certain spot. They did but came across a large slab of stone which proved to be so heavy that none could dislodge it however hard and how many of them tried! Ali ﷺ rolled up his sleeve and taking hold of the rock, he flung it away to a great distance, revealing a spring of sweet freshwater gushing beneath the surface! The entire army was quenched of their thirst and after everyone was satiated, Ali ﷺ covered up the fountainhead, so that it was again camouflaged and hidden from common sight. Seeing this, the monk rushed forward and excitedly addressed Ali ﷺ saying: "You are either a prophet, or a *successor* of a prophet, or an Angel; because it is recorded in our books that only one of the above persons will uncover this hidden water fount!" To this Imam Ali ﷺ replied: *"I am the successor of the last Prophet of God."* Hearing this, the monk converted to Islam testifying that Ali ﷺ was indeed the true successor of the Prophet ﷺ!

In this connection, many renowned scholars while giving an exposition on the seventh verse of Chapter 76: Surah *Hal Ataa* [Aka] Surah *Dahr* of the holy Quran: *"Aiynan Yashrabu beha Ibaad-Ullahey Yu Fajjey-ru naha Taf-jeera.... A Spring from which the servants of Allah drink; (and) which they make to gush forth as they please!"* (76:7) are unanimous in giving their opinion that this incident clearly falls under the manifestation of this verse which would be one such 'Heavenly Spring' of pure water called '**Noor**' which Ali ﷺ and other members of the holy Ahlul Bayt ﷺ could, and did, access and unveil whenever and wherever they wanted; and that the 'Spring' of sweet tasting water mentioned in this incident doubtlessly falls under this category.

13. In the same book, Mulla Jami has recorded that many years after the demise of the holy Prophet ﷺ, Ali ؑ asked some persons to testify as to whether they had not been a witness to the Prophet ﷺ's (well known) declaration at the event of Ghadeer proclaiming: *"Man Kuntum Maula fa Aliyun Maula….Of whosoever I am Master of, Ali is the Master."* Only about a dozen persons, (or some say thirty) present in that gathering, acknowledged in the affirmative. Anas ibn Malik had also been among those who had witnessed that incident and though **now present** in the gathering, refrained from voicing his agreement. When questioned by the Commander of the Faithful about his silence, he evasively answered that he had now become too old to remember the past, at which Ali ؑ responded: *"If you are lying, your face will be disfigured by Leukoderma."* No sooner had these words been pronounced by Ali ؑ, than Anas was afflicted with this disease and white spots started appearing on his face for all to see which he in his shame, tried to hide with his head cover but to no avail! Another companion Zaid ibn Arqam who also knowingly withheld his witness, instantly became blind, and was later known to repent and plead forgiveness of God for the rest of his life.

14. In another book 'Fauhat Al Quds' it is recorded (and this is also confirmed by Allama Saleh Kashafi Hanafi in his book 'Manaqib-e-Murtazawi' on Pg 435), that one day Khalid bin Walid was passing through a wooded area with his contingent of armed soldiers when he saw Imam Ali ؑ alone by himself in a secluded area of the same thicket. Khalid decided to attack the Imam from behind by striking him on his head and approached stealthily, armed with his iron club. Imam Ali ؑ turned upon him with lightening speed, snatched the club from Khalid's hand and twisted it around his neck like a halter!

Countless attempts by Khalid to have this iron halter removed by many different persons later were unsuccessful as none could pry it open! The Ironsmiths were all the opinion that to loosen it, the iron around his neck would have to be heated, which Khalid would not be able to withstand! They were unanimous in their suggestion that Khalid should return to the person who had knotted the club around his neck in the first place! Thereupon Khalid gathered a few venerable companions of the holy Prophet ﷺ and came to Ali ؏ appealing for mercy. The companions also pleaded for his pardon, invoking mercy in the (name of) the 'Soul of the Prophet ﷺ' and implored for Khalid's forgiveness. As was characteristic of him, the Commander of the Faithful out of his magnanimity removed the curled iron bar with his two fingers from around Khalid's neck and set him free!

15. It is found in several reliable books and in many traditions recorded on the authority of Mulla Jami as well as Allama Saleh Kashfi Tirmizi in books such as 'Zohratul Riaz', 'Rauzatul Shohada' and 'Fasalul Khattab' as well as in his own 'Manqib-e-Murtazawi' (pages 480-481) that Imam Ali ؏ had foretold about his own death; to the extent of even mentioning his assassin by name. The author has further recorded that when Imam Ali ؏ passed away, the Angels were heard to loudly proclaim his death and ask everyone to vacate the premises. This was in line with the prediction of Ali ؏ himself that *'After (his) death the Angels would mourn and partake in his funeral rites. A plank of wood would be found in a section of his house, where his body would be placed upon; and the ceremonial ablution (bath of the dead body) would be performed, and his corpse would be scented by the Camphor from heaven and wrapped in the Shroud that would also be sent from Heaven.'*

In keeping with the rest of his prediction, when Imam Ali ؏'s body was placed in his coffin and his children were summoned to bid farewell to their revered father, Imam Hasan ؏ performed the first funeral prayer, while Imam Husayn ؏ performed a second similar prayer. The coffin as predicted, thereafter, appeared to be raised on its own, being lifted by Angels Gabriel 🕮 and Michael 🕮 in the front, while the rear end was supported by Imams Hasan 🕮 and Husayn 🕮. As the funeral procession moved forward, (to the public at large it appeared as if) the coffin was suspended in mid air, as they could not see the Angels holding its frontend. This procession moved in a certain direction and came to a halt at a particular spot. This spot in fact was the very place where the bodies of two previous prophets Hazrat Adam 🕮 and Hazrat Noah 🕮 were buried several years before. Imam Ali 🕮 was laid to rest between these two prophets of God; and his grave (as per his instructions) was camouflaged and completely hidden from public view. For almost a hundred and fifty years these three graves remained concealed; and were only known to the members of the holy Ahlul Bayt 🕮 and their close associates. It was only after an extended length in time that they were discovered. Khwaja Bandey Nawaz Gesudaraz Husayni has also confirmed this and additionally has also stated on page 9 of his hand-written manuscript of 'Jawame Kalam' that in spirit, Imam Ali 🕮 by his miraculous powers was also present at his own funeral with his face covered by a veil!

An interestingly detailed account is given in the book 'Zohratul Riaz' that when Allah 🕮 had commanded Hazrat Noah 🕮 to build an Ark, there were three Tablets which were left over. When Noah 🕮 asked Allah 🕮 as to what he should do with these, he received the following revelation: *"O Noah! A friend of Mine named Ali will be born in the latter days and will be buried here. This will be his place of burial. Keep the Tablets at this location and I shall order the Angels to make this spot a place of their (regular) visitations."*

Over a century later after the martyrdom of Ali 🕮, the Abbasid Caliph Haroon Rashid who became the caliph in 170 AD was out hunting for deer in this area along with his hunting dogs. The deer escaped and took refuge on a certain elevated spot. The hunting dogs stopped in their tracks and turned away; and no matter how hard they were instigated, they would not budge or go up the elevated spot in pursuit of the deer. Haroon was surprised at this unusual behaviour of his well trained canines; and upon making enquiries from the local inhabitants, he was informed by an old man that he had it on the authority of his father and grandfather that the spot where the deer had taken refuge was the grave of Imam Ali ﷺ, the Commander of the Faithful, who was also known as 'Haider'. Hearing this, Haroon paid his own homage to this grave and returned home vowing never to go hunting in that area again.

16. Dr. Mohiuddin Qadri Zor has written in his book 'Hayat e Mir Momin' that Hazrat Shahnawaz Noorul Huda who is buried in the graveyard known as 'Daira-e-Mir Momin' in Hyderabad India, had instructed his relatives that after his death, upon completing his ceremonial funeral bath and enshrouding of his body, it should be left aside as he had been apprised by Imam Ali ﷺ that **he** would himself come to perform his Funeral Prayers. They did as requested. Shortly thereafter, a rider appeared on horseback with a veil over his face and conducted the prayers. When he was about to leave a few people mustered enough courage and asked him as to who he was. The veiled rider replied: *"I am Ali ibn Abi Taleb!"*

A similar incident has also been recorded by Dr. Zor (on page 677) about another holy personage known as 'Shah Chiragh' who is also buried in the same graveyard; wherein this saintly person also had his funeral prayers lead by none other than Imam Ali ﷺ!

17. In the book 'Ahsan-ul-Kibar' and in 'Manaqib' of Saleh Kashafi it is recorded that Salman e Farsi, the revered companion of the holy Prophet ﷺ passed away in the town of Madyan in Iraq during the days of Umar-e-Khattab's Caliphate in Madina. Imam Ali ﷺ who was also present in Madina at that time, informed the people around him that Salman had just died, and as the holy

Prophet ﷺ had asked him, Ali ؏, to perform Salman's funeral prayers he was duty bound to do so, and was leaving for Madyan. After a short absence, he returned to Madina the same day by the noontime (Zohr) prayers. Many including Umar Khattab were sceptical about this and did not believe that this could have happened; to the extent that Umar immediately sent his messengers out to investigate the matter. Those people returned after several days of travel, confirming that the inhabitants of Madyan had vouched to the fact that Ali ؏ **had** indeed been present in Madyan and that he had led the funeral prayers of Hazrat Salman-e-Farsi ؏ at his burial!

18. In the book 'Tazkeratul Awliya' published by 'Jame Millia' in Delhi India, an incident is recorded about a saint who popularly came to be known as 'Bu Ali Qalandar' though his real name was Hazrat Shuja Uddin. It is said that he withdrew from the world and secluded himself like a hermit in a wilderness close to a pond of water. He stood in this pond for several years offering prayers to Allah ﷻ and doing mystical meditation. After many years he heard a voice which told him to get out of the water as he had succeeded in his mission and had achieved his goal. Bu Ali replied: 'Oh Allah! Where should I go? You are the Only One who can take me out of this place'. As soon as he said this, he felt that someone with a powerful grip had caught him by his shoulders and physically lifted him out of the water! In amazement he said, 'I had asked Allah ﷻ to get me out of this spot; who are *you* that have relieved me from my predicament?' The stranger replied: "*I am Ali ibn Abi Taleb*'. On hearing this Shah Bu Ali Qalandar fell to the ground and kissed his feet. He later composed a quatrain in Farsi which is noted below:

Haideram Qalandaram Mastam, Banda-ey Murtuza Ali Hastam.
Man baghair az Ali na Danistam, Huwa Allah, Huwal Ali Hastam?

Roughly translated, the above couplet states:

I am the Mystic of Haider; and the Slave of Murtuza Ali... I know of none other than Ali: that when I call upon Allah for help, Allah Himself sends Ali[102]!!

19. It is mentioned in 'Marij Al Nabuwah' and 'Zohratul Riaz' as well as on page 247 of Allama Sayyed Saleh Kashfi Tirmizi Hanafi's 'Manaqib-e-Murtazawi' that ten days after the demise of the holy Prophet 🙵 a stranger appeared in the Mosque of Madina [*Masjid-e-Nabawi*]. He was carrying a whip in one hand and his face was covered by a veil. He greeted those present and enquired as to who was the successor of the Apostle after his demise. Abu Bakr pointed towards Ali 🙵 and the stranger greeted Ali saying: "Peace be on you, Young Man!" Ali 🙵 replied: "*Peace be upon you, O the Person of the Well, Muzir.*'"

Abu Bakr and all those present were amazed at the response of Ali 🙵. The stranger who was an Arab, asked: "O Young Man, how did you know my name?" Ali 🙵 replied: "*My brother, Muhammad e Mustafa 🙵 had informed me that your name was Muzir and your father's name was 'Daram'. You are now 360 years of age. When you were 100 years old you had gathered your tribe and informed them about the coming of the holy Prophet 🙵; and had asked them to be prepared to accept him (🙵) as their prophet and to subsequently convert to Islam when that happened. Your tribe became angry and turned against you, and threw you into a deep well, where Allah 🙵 preserved your life till such time as the holy Apostle 🙵 passed away from this world. When this happened, Allah 🙵 engulfed your tribe in a devastating flood in which they all perished. Allah 🙵 extricated you from the well and released you from your captivity. You heard an 'Unknown Voice' which apprised you about the demise of the Prophet*

---

[102] Translator's Note: It was after these incidents and specifically after being touched by Imam Ali 🙵 he was known to perpetually emit a pleasant fragrance and hence came to be known as 'Bu Ali' (the Fragrance of Ali 🙵).

and informed you that you will be like one of his companions. You were instructed by the same 'Voice' to travel to Madina and perform a visitation to the Apostle 🌸's holy grave. You have travelled day and night and have gone through great difficulties to reach here." When Muzir heard these facts, he began to weep and enquired as to the identity of the Commander of the Faithful; to which he replied: *"I am Ali ibn Abi Taleb. The holy Prophet 🌸 had predicted that I would meet you, and that I should convey his salutations to you."* Muzir was beside himself with joy upon receiving the greetings of the Apostle of Allah and kissed Imam Ali 🌸 on his forehead. Ali 🌸 asked him to be seated and remove the veil from his face. Muzir did so and a light shone from his face which illuminated the entire Masjid! Muzir then said that he had certain questions which nobody would know the answers to except the Prophet or his Successor. The Commander of the Faithful told him to ask whatever he wished, to which Muzir queried as follows:

1. Who were those 'male and female personages' who had no parents?
2. Who was that 'person' born without a father?
3. Who was that 'female' who delivered a child in three hours?
4. Who was that 'messenger' that belongs to neither Jinn nor Mankind, nor Angels or Animals?
5. Which was the 'Grave' that transported the 'body contained within' to various places?
6. Which is that 'live being' that cautioned its companions to beware?
7. Which is that 'animal' who ate, but did not drink anything?
8. Which is that 'substance' that gave birth to a 'live' being?
9. Which is that 'piece of Earth' that saw the 'sunlight' once, but will never see it again?
10. Who are those 'enemies' that will never be friends?

11. What is implied by the word '**Shaiy**'; and conversely, what does '**La Shaiy**' signify?

Muzir had several other questions which for the sake of brevity, we have left out and only selected the foregoing few; to which Ali ﷺ replied as follows:

1.   *Adam and Eve ﷺ are the two created without parents.*
2.   *Jesus was the person born without a father.*
3.   *Hazrat Mary ﷺ gave birth to Jesus ﷺ in three hours.*
4.   *The 'Heavenly Messenger' that belonged neither to Jinn nor mankind, Angel nor Animal', was that 'Crow' which was sent by Allah ﷻ who demonstrated to Cain (Qabil) how to bury his brother Abel (Habil).*
5.   *The 'Live Grave' which took its inmate on a tour of the oceans was that 'Fish' which had swallowed Jonas (Younus) ﷺ and carried him within its stomach for three days.*
6.   *That 'live being' who cautioned her companions to 'beware of being trampled' was the 'Ant' when she saw Soloman ﷺ approaching with his large army.*
7.   *The body that ate but did not drink was the 'Staff' of Moses ﷺ that swallowed the snakes conjured by the magicians of Pharoah.*
8.   *The 'substance' that gave way to a 'Living being' was that Rock from which the 'She-Camel of Hazrat Saleh' ﷺ emerged.*
9.   *The 'area of the earth' which witnessed the sunshine only once was the bottom of the Sea which parted for Moses ﷺ when he struck his rod and took the Israelites to safety.*
10. *'Life and Death' are the two 'Enemies' that can never be friends.*
11. *The word 'Shaiy' implies a 'Believer' while 'La Shaiy' points to a non-believer.*

When Muzir heard the answers to all his many questions, he got up in reverence and again kissed the forehead of Imam Ali ﷺ and began to sing his praises. He then requested that he be taken to the final resting place of the Prophet ﷺ, upon reaching which, he threw himself on the grave and began to weep excessively. Ali ؏ requested the people to leave because he predicted that Muzir's final hour had approached. Within the hour Muzir's soul departed from his body, and he was buried near the grave of Hamza ؏ in the cemetery of Ohad.

20. It is mentioned in a book 'Fauhat Al Quds' and Allama Kashafi Hanafi has also included the same on page 329 of his book 'Manaqib e Murtazawi' that during the Caliphate of the Abbasids, a resident of Balkh who used to live in Egypt and was a lover of the Ahlul Bayt ؏ used to recite their praise in public. He was once invited by a Kharajite to his home on the pretext of giving him a feast. Instead, when this person entered the house the Kharajite gouged his eyes and severed his limbs, and his corpse was dragged and thrown into a graveyard. At the time that this was happening, Prophet Khizr ؏ was paying his respects at the grave of Imam Ali ؏ in Najaf; and he heard the voice of Imam Ali ؏ from within, instructing him to visit the graveyard in Egypt and to take care of this lover of Ahlul Bayt whose body had been dismembered and thrown there. Ali ؏ then also taught Khizr ؏ different names from the *'Ism-e-Azam'* of Allah ﷻ, that were to be pronounced for healing various parts of the severed body. He was further instructed that when the person was revived from his death Hazrat Khizr should escort him to the main Masjid in Egypt where he would observe a strange phenomenon.

Khizr ؏ abiding by the instructions of Imam Ali ؏ went to the graveyard and after reviving the dead person back to life he took him to the main Masjid as instructed. This person again began to extoll the praises of the progeny of the holy Prophet ﷺ. Similarly, this time again, another person approached him and invited him to his house. Though he was afraid to accept a second such invitation he nonetheless accepted because of Imam Ali ﷺ's bidding. As he proceeded, he perceived that this was the very same house where he had earlier been killed and his eyes gouged, and body dismembered! The host however, told him not to be alarmed as the person who had done the atrocities earlier was his father. He said that though he himself had been extremely averse to the act of his murder, he had been helpless to do anything in protecting him. That same night he said he saw Ali ﷺ in his dream scolding his father saying: *"O Black Bear! You have been unjustly cruel to my friend, and you will be punished in this world and in the Hereafter!"* The host then went on to say that he was very frightened when he woke from his dream; and then to his amazement he saw that his father had indeed been turned into a black bear! Upon seeing him in this state, he had locked him forthwith in a room, to be confined there for the rest of his life! Subsequently this son of the Kharijite became a lover of the Ahlul Bayt ﷺ and an enemy of their enemies.

21. The same scholar, on page 340 of his treatise describes yet another incident which he has extracted from the 'Collections of Makhdoom Jahanian Qudsara.' It is said that during the time of Umar's Caliphate, a person named Thabit was accused of rape and robbery. Umar condemned him to death by stoning. Ali ﷺ heard about this and forthwith went to Umar and questioned him as to why he does not ponder and consider all the aspects of the case before passing this harsh judgment of execution.

The woman who accused this person Thabit was asked by Imam Ali ﷺ to state the truth. She insisted on her story saying Thabit forced himself on her and stole her jewellery which was later found in his possession. Ali ﷺ asked for a staff and a piece of cloth to be brought from his house. He then called for some other woman and asked them to place the cloth on her belly. Holding the staff in his hand, in an audible voice Ali ﷺ said: *"O Embryo! Relate the truth to me!"* A voice was heard from the womb of the woman saying:

"Allah is One, Muhammad is His Prophet and Ali Murtaza is the Successor of the Prophet!" The voice then went on to describe the whole affair of how this woman was extremely fond of Thabit's good looks and his Godfearing nature. She offered herself to him, but Thabit refused to get involved in a major sin. When she was not successful in making him relent, she in her extreme passion offered herself to a slave and got pregnant. She then hid the jewellery in Thabit's possession to implicate him falsely for this crime!" Thabit was released, and the woman was punished according to the Jurisprudence.

Seeing this miracle performed by Ali ﷺ the people were amazed. Umar himself rubbed both his eyes on the hand of Ali ﷺ and declared: "O Ali! You are the true Successor of the Prophet, and nobody else! May Allah ﷺ not keep Umar alive when you are not present to help resolve such matters!"

24. Another interesting incident is recorded in 'Ehsanal Kibaar' on the authority of Abu Laila who said that the Caesar of Rome had sent a lot of gifts for the holy Prophet ﷺ; but by the time the presents arrived in Madina, the Prophet ﷺ had passed away. The Ambassador wrote to Caesar about this and asked for further instructions. Caesar replied saying that he had three questions, and whoever gives the correct answer, the gifts should be given to that person, or else returned to him.

The Roman Ambassador went to Abu Bakr and asked him if he was the Vicegerent of the Prophet? Abu Bakr replied in the affirmative whereupon the Ambassador put forward these three questions to him:

i. What is that which Allah ﷺ does not have?
ii. What is that which cannot be associated with Allah ﷺ?
iii. What is that which is outside the realm of Allah ﷺ's knowledge?

Abu Bakr upon hearing this said in annoyance: "You are talking in the blasphemous manner of an Infidel!" Umar who was also present did not know the answers; and like Abu Bakr, was very harsh in dealing with the Ambassador. Abdullah ibn Abbas who was also present, told them that it was very 'unbecoming of them to be so rude to a person who was [a newcomer in their city and was] seeking some information'. Abu Bakr then addressed Ibn Abbas saying: "Then do you know the answers?" Ibn Abbas replied that though he did not know the answers himself, he knew that Ali ibn Abi Taleb 🖼 would be the one to know them. All of them went en masse to the house of Ali 🖼 who had at that moment just completed the compilation of the holy Quran. The Roman Ambassador repeated his questions to Ali 🖼, to which he 🖼 gave the following reply:

i. *That which Allah does not have is a '**Partner**'.*

ii. *That which cannot be contexed with Allah 🖼 is '**Injustice**'.*

iii. *That which is not part of Allah's knowledge is (their belief) that* **He has a son**[103]*!*

When the Ambassador heard these answers, he promptly took the '*Shahadat*' and became a Muslim saying: "O Ali! You are the true Successor of the Prophet; and handed the gifts over to Ali 🖼 who immediately distributed them among the believers.

25. The same book has another tradition related on the authority of Amar ibn Aas that after the death of Abu Bakr, when Umar became the Caliph, a visiting Jewish scholar asked Umar as to who among them is the most knowledgeable about the Book of Allah and the Sunnah of the holy Prophet? Umar pointed toward Ali 🖼, whereupon the scholar told him: "O Caliph! When you yourself are admitting to the superiority of him over you in knowledge, then

---

[103] Holy Quran: Surah Younus: 10:18 – "Say! Will you inform Allah about something He does not know in the Heaven or on the Earth?"

why are you taking the fealty of the people as their Caliph?" He then turned towards Ali ❧ and asked him a substantial number of questions; and upon hearing all the answers to his various queries, he was overwhelmed and began to weep; and forthwith converted to Islam saying: "I testify that you are the true Successor of the Prophet!" He then unrolled his sleeve and produced an old parchment written in the Ibrani (ancient Hebrew) language which he presented to Ali ❧. Ali ❧ read this scroll and shed tears of joy. When people asked the reason for his tears, he replied: *"This scroll confirms that my name in the Torah has been referred to as 'Habeel' and in the Evangel (Gospel) as 'Meora'."*

26. In a book 'Kifayatul Momineen' by Allama Saleh Kashafi Hanafi there is a narration by Ibn Abbas quoted on page 265 in which it states that during the Caliphate of Umar, a person from Azerbaijan migrated to Madina. He was the owner of a camel which he used as his means to earn a livelihood for his family. One day this camel went berserk and wandered into the wilderness. None could control this animal. People suggested to this person that during his lifetime the Prophet ❧ used to teach special prayers to the people to overcome similar situations. Hence, they recommended him to approach the Prophet ❧'s successor and request these special prayers. Accordingly, this newcomer went to Umar and asked him for the same. Umar said: "Repent!" The person said: "I have done this many times but with no success". Umar then said: "I will write a letter which you should place in front of this camel." The contents of that letter were as follows: "O Group of Jinns and Devils, this letter is from the Commander of the Faithful, Umar; and you should make this camel come to his senses, and do not dare go against my order!"

The person did as instruct, but the camel contrary to the bidding, began to attack him even more severely by biting and kicking him, to the extent that it took many days for this person to recover from the wounds inflicted by this attack, which also left some scars on his face and body. Days later when he regained some strength he again went to Umar, related the whole episode, and begged him to provide him some monetary compensation so he could look after his family. Umar directed Ibn Abbas to take this person to Ali ﷺ. When Ali ﷺ saw this person, he smiled at him and told him to recite a certain prayer in front of the camel. No sooner was this done, the camel became instantly docile and reverted to serving his master as aforetime. Subsequently, the income earned through this camel was more than enough to enrich his master; and in fact, it enabled him to go on a pilgrimage to the House of Allah, from where he also brought some gifts for Ali ﷺ in appreciation of his benevolence.

Several scholars have recorded many more incidents of Ali ﷺ's miraculous deeds performed during the days of the rule of the other Caliphs. But since some of these reported traditions do not reflect well upon the other companions of the holy Prophet ﷺ, we have voluntarily avoided including them in our work, as it is not our purpose to belittle any of the companions.

In the book 'Kitab-e-Mastool' also by Allama Kashafi Hanafi, there are many anecdotes mentioned with respect to a prominent slave of Imam Ali ﷺ named Qamber. The latter was a very tall person; and in one such an incident it is said that he was sent by Imam Ali ﷺ with a letter containing some advice to Muawiyah. When Muawiyah saw Qamber he ridiculed him about his height and asked him if he had any news from the Heavens? Qamber replied: "Yes! The Commander of the Faithful is pursuing you and the Angel of Death is in quest of you!"

Allama Barsi has authored a book titled 'Madinatul Maajiz' in which he mentions that one day a Jinn was sitting in the company of the Prophet ﷺ and Imam Ali ﷺ happened to come by. Upon seeing him, the Jinn exclaimed: "O Apostle of Allah! Protect me from this person!" Upon being asked as to what Ali ﷺ had done, the Jinn replied: "I was in the service of Prophet Soloman, and I disobeyed one of his orders. He asked some Jinns to arrest me, but I overpowered them; whereupon this young man appeared and subdued me and handed me over to Soloman ﷺ. I still carry the mark of the bruise that was inflicted by his strong grip and which is still fresh, despite the lapse of hundreds of years!"

The personalities of the holy Prophet ﷺ and Ali ﷺ (including the rest of the Fourteen Members of the holy Ahlul Bayt ﷺ) are beyond human comprehension; as they were created *before* anything else was in existence: There was no Time or Space; no Sky or Earth, no Angels or Jinns or Mankind! As the holy Prophet ﷺ had himself stated: "*He and Ali ﷺ were created from the same 'Noor' (Light) prior to the creation of anything else";* hence they are above the restrictions of 'Time and Space'. For them to be present in several places at the same instant through variant Ages and Eons of time is not to be questioned. Also, it is **not to be wondered at** when they split the moon into two or complete the recitation of the entire Quran while mounting a horse or bring the sun back on the horizon after it had already set! As the Quran itself states: *"Kulla Shaiyin Eh-saiy naho Fee Imamim Mubeen – Everything have We confined into a Manifest Imam!"* [36:12]. Thus, for these personalities to have control over the Sky and the Earth and the Sun and the Moon was a mere display of their authority over the rest of creation. After the conquest of Khyber when people asked Ali ﷺ as to how he had managed to wrench the Gate of Al Qamus (the Fort of Khyber) with one hand which normally required some 40 persons to open and close it, he ﷺ replied that he did it by the 'Divine Power' gifted to him by Allah ﷻ!

At this point, it is worth mentioning that when Abraham ﷺ was inviting people towards the Monotheistic Faith, he confronted Nimrod and told him that *'his God in the One Who gives life and death to the people'* to which Nimrod replied that he could do the same by pardoning a person condemned to death, or executing an innocent one, causing **his** instant death! Abraham 🕮 then countered by saying: '*My God makes the sun rise from the East'* and asked if Nimrod could make it rise from the West [?] at which Nimrod was totally dumbfounded [2:258]. Considering *this Quranic verse,* we can surmise that one of the signs of being invested with 'Divine Power' is the ability to make the sun rise from the West. Imam Ali 🕮 performed this miracle of making the sun after it had already set, arise from the West **not once but twice** during his lifetime! It was due to these types of, as well as countless other amazing miracles displaying extraordinary powers of Divinity that people mistook him to be 'God incarnate'. One such group which are still in existence and who revere Ali 🕮 as a Deity are known as '*Nusairies*'.

There is a well-known tradition that there was a particular group of people who used to encamp near the *Masjid e Kufa* who took Ali 🕮 to be their God and believed that he was the one who provided their sustenance! When Ali 🕮 became aware of this fallacy, he rebuked them and asked them to repent and reform saying: "*I am also a servant of Allah like you. I eat and drink like you do. If I do good God will reward me; and if I disobey His commands, I will be punished. I am afraid of Him, and I advise you to do likewise".* When they refused to change their stand, he instructed his slave Qamber who was also present, to take them aside and convince them to change their ideas about him. When three days elapsed and they had still not changed their views, Ali 🕮 gathered them and warned them that their refusal to repent would leave him with no choice but to execute them. Upon their persisting with their blasphemy, Ali 🕮 order Qamber to dig a trench and fill it with firewood and light the fire and burn these people alive [as this was the punishment prescribed in Islam for blasphemy]. These people readily agreed to be burnt holding on to their 'belief that Ali 🕮 was an incarnation of God on Earth' rather than deny their devotion and love for him; and voluntarily jumped into the burning trench and died! It is additionally recorded by some others that Imam Ali 🕮 revived them again and questioned them whether they had now changed their mind after tasting the 'chastisement of death and recognizing their True Lord'? They, on the contrary said that if anything, their faith was further reinforced because they were now more convinced that not only could Ali 🕮 make them die but also bring them back to life!

Some Sufis and their reputed scholars have written about some incidents regarding the supernatural displays of Ali 🕮 which border on his deification. For instance, the great Sunni scholar Imam Shafei has a line in one of his poems which says: *"Maata Shafei, Wa Laisa Yadri, Ali Rabbahu am Rabbahu Allah?"* Which when translated reads: *"Shafei died, but could never comprehend: whether his Sustainer is Ali, or is it Allah?"*

Many other great scholars such as Allama Shams Tabrez, Abdur Rahman-e-Jami and Bu Ali Qalander to name only a few, have also composed poetry in similar ways in which they have alluded to his rare attributes and praised him to a level of being 'Divinity Personified', to the extent that it was hard for them to distinguish whether it was 'Ali or Allah' who was their Lord: for, whenever they called upon Allah for help it was Ali who came to their rescue!

With regards to the 'Love' for the Ahlul Bayt of Prophet 🕮, Imam Shafei has written in another one of his compositions that: *"If the Love of the Progeny of the Prophet, the Ahlul Bayt 🕮 is 'RAFZ'* (Disbelief or Dissention), *then let it go on record that I was the biggest and foremost among the 'Rafazis!'*

Then he goes on to say: *"If taking the name of Haider is classed as being a 'RAFAZI' – then be it known that Allah, Mustafa, and Angel Gabriel are all 'RAFAZIS"!*

As mentioned earlier, it is not easy to comprehend the personality of Ali 🕮. He is "Timeless and Spaceless." His name appears from time immemorial in several ancient scriptures of different religions in some form or the other. For instance, many Hindus venerate Ali 🕮; and research of various scholars into the Hindu philosophy indicates that not only do the Hindus respect him for his saintly position, but some even pray to him to have their wishes fulfilled. In this context it is worth recognizing the efforts and scholarly research conducted by a Sunni scholar Maulana Siddique Deendar who has an immense respect for Ali 🕮. He has conducted an in-depth study of the 'Bhagavat Geeta' and other Hindu scriptures which foretell the advent of Prophet Muhammad 🕮 and Imam Ali 🕮; and he has also endeavoured to utilize his findings to unite the Hindus and Muslims in South India alike. In his book 'Sarwar-e-Alam' this scholar writes that in the Hindu scriptures, 'Gunaan Shashtar' (Hindu Philosophy) in particular, Ali 🕮 is identified as 'Ganpati' - the 'Door to Knowledge.' (Baab-ul-Ilm). This is like the famous saying of the Prophet 🕮 where he said that "Ali is the Door to the City of Knowledge."

A tradition was established among many Hindus that when they initiate the education of their children, they place the statue of 'Ganpati' in front as a depiction of entering the doorway to knowledge; and it said that all their textbooks also carry the image of 'Ganpati' which in fact alludes to Ali 🕮's knowledge! He further writes that Ali 🕮 is known as 'Abu Turab' in Arabic [Father of the Earth] and the same appellation ('Sayedu Jaati') is found for Ali 🕮 in the Hindi language. In short, to understand the luminous personality of Ali 🕮 is beyond the grasp of mere humans; because the Prophet 🕮 has himself stated that: "Nobody can understand Allah except me and Ali; nobody can understand me except Allah and Ali; and no one can understand Ali except Allah and me! In this context, Ali 🕮 himself has said that: *"Two types of persons will perish on my account: One who elevates my position to God, and the other who belittles me and bears enmity towards me!"*

It should, however, not be misconstrued that whoever loves Ali 🕮 excessively will be condemned to eternal damnation. On the contrary, considering the many sayings of the holy Prophet 🕮, to love Ali 🕮 excessively is the **essence of True Belief** [*Eman*]. And again, in view of the well-known tradition wherein he [🕮] said: *"To look at the face of Ali ibne Abi Taleb is worship [Ibadat]!"* Then again, many other similar sayings such as: *"True belief will NOT enter one's heart, unless the love of Ali is present in it"*. *"One who has love of Ali in his heart is the one who will be granted entrance into Paradise"* and again: *"A person who reduces the position or status of Ali even to the extent of the size of the 'eye of a needle' will be cast headlong into Hellfire!"* The list goes on.

From all these foregoing prophetic statements it can be argued that no one can profess to be a true believer unless they recognize Ali 🕮 as the real Successor of the Prophet 🕮, believe in his '*Wilayat*' and accept him as being the Vicegerent and Supreme Leader and holiest of the Apostle 🕮's companions. It is to be understood however, that when one examines the various superhuman attributes and overwhelming actions and deeds of Hazrat Ali 🕮, care should be taken not to go over the deep end and assume him to be the incarnation of God Himself!

It is related that once some Nomadic Arabs approached the holy Prophet 🕮 and asked him to define the real concept of '*Haqq*' [Truth] to them. The Apostle 🕮 pointed towards a spot in the corner of the mosque [where Imam Ali 🕮 was completely absorbed in offering his prayers] and said *"there is the bodily personification of Haqq!"* These kind of co-ordinated actions: (of Ali 🕮 standing up for prayer and the Prophet 🕮 directing people toward Ali 🕮), were designed to show the people that Ali 🕮 was the

'Personification of Truth' in the way that God wanted it; but obviously he was NOT God himself, because had he been so, he would not be standing up offering prayers to God!

There is a tradition recorded by Khawarizmi related by Imam Ali ﷺ himself, who said the following: "*When I conquered the Fort of Khyber the holy Apostle ﷺ told me: 'O Ali! I hope that my Ummah will not start saying about you things, which the Ummah of Isa ﷺ says about him! However, O Ali! I can only say that I fear that if I elaborate about your excellences, the people will start taking the dust beneath your feet or the water from your ablutions and using these as a cure for their ailments! You are from me, and I am from you. I will inherit from you, and you will inherit from me. You are to me as Aaron was to Moses ﷺ except that there is no prophet after me. You will discharge my obligations and will fight against the people to maintain my Sunnah. In the Hereafter you will be nearest to me, and on the Day of Judgement you will be my Caliph at the Pool of Kauser. You will cordon off the hypocrites away from the Pool [of Kauser] and you will be the first one to arrive at the Pool and the first one to enter Paradise from my Ummah! Your battles are my battles, and your peace treaties are my peaceful alliances; your secrets are my secrets; your pronouncements will be my pronouncements. You are the Doorway to my heart; your blood is my blood; your flesh is my flesh; your sons are my sons. Truth [Haqq] is with you, and Truth is in your words, and in your heart and in between your two eyes! Faith and Belief are embedded in your flesh and blood. The Almighty Lord has asked me to give you the glad tidings that your progeny will be in Paradise and your enemy will be cast into hell! Your enemy will never be allowed near the Pool of Kauser, while your friends will never be away from it!*'" Ali ﷺ then said that when he heard these glad tidings, he went into a prostration in thankfulness to Allah ﷻ for the countless bounties that He had bestowed upon him!

11.6: Prediction of Abraham 🕊 Regarding the Shrine of Ali 🕊

A British historian has written about the well-known Arab traveller Ibn Jair in his book 'The Travels of Ibn Jair[104] that Hazrat Abraham 🕊 once during his lifetime came to the city of Najaf and purchased a piece of land; and predicted that one day there will be a Shrine constructed at this spot where people will come for pilgrimage and throng to pay homage and attain salvation. Seventy Thousand of them will be sent to Heaven without any questioning!

11.7: Accounts of Miracles at Imam Ali 🕊's Shrine by Ibn Batuta

The world-famous traveller generally known by the appellation of 'Ibne Batuta' whose real name was Allama Maghrebi Abu Abdullah Muhammad bin Abdullah bin Muhammad bin Ibrahim Tanji Andalusi [!] who travelled across the world in the 8th century which included countries such as: Egypt, Ethiopia, Hejaz, India, Iraq, Persia and various other places and compiled memoirs of his journeys under the title of 'Rehlat-e-Ibne-Batuta'. On page 110 of this book, he records the following: "Many miracles have been observed emanating from the Shrine in the city of Najaf, based on which it is established beyond doubt that this indeed is the burial spot of Ali 🕊. Year after year on the night of the 27th Rajab [of the Islamic calendar] which is also known as the '*Night of Ascension of the Holy Prophet* 🕊,' people gather here in large numbers from all over the Middle East, bringing with them the sick and the disabled and leave them near the tomb of Ali 🕊. The congregation then begins to pray and recite the Quran and other related prayers.

---

[104] 'The Travels of ibn Jair' – Text by Gibbs Memorial, Vol 5, Pg 211.

Around midnight or shortly thereafter, all the sick and infirm are miraculously cured and appear as if no malady had ever touched them! A loud chant of '*Allaho Akbar*' goes up, followed by the resounding recitation of their '*Kalemah Shahadah*': "*There is no God but Allah and Muhammad ﷺ is His prophet and Ali is his Vicegerent!*"

To get a glimpse into the sectarian attachment of Ibn Batuta, we quote a further paragraph from his diary in which he states: "We then proceeded from Najaf to Kufa and on to a village called 'Barmalah' where we encamped for the night. All the inhabitants of this village were 'Rafazi' Shias." This statement clearly reflects on the religious beliefs of ibn Batuta himself and shows that despite **not being a Shia** he acknowledges the miracles of Imam Ali ﷺ's shrine!

11.8: Miracle Which Occurred in the Holy City of Najaf on Saturday March 25, 1882; and was Republished in the Indian Newspaper: 'The Times of India' 100 Years later in 1982

This miracle was reported in the City of Shiraz on March 6th, 1882, and then reproduced in 'The Times of India' on the 25th of the same month in 1882. We reproduce the text as stated in the old papers: "SHIRAZ, March 6: - About a fortnight ago Shiraz was electrified by the report that some belated pilgrims having applied for admission into Najaf and been refused by the 'Keeper of the Gate' which, according to standing orders, must be kept closed from soon after dusk until morning, invoked the aid of their Imam by exclamations of 'YA Ali, YA ALI!' and behold – a Miracle! – The gate flew open, and the pilgrims repaired to his shrine to pay their adorations! According to another account the gate fell in utter destruction! When this report became known, the people of Shiraz, inspired by religious enthusiasm, resolved upon getting up an 'illumination' in an expression of their sense of the glorious triumph of their Faith. His Excellency, the Saheb Dewan, the Governor General of Faras however, thought it prudent to postpone the entertainment (celebration) until an inquiry had been made, and authenticity of the report established. The telegraphic reply of a Mushtahed (High Priest) of Najaf not only corroborated the report but spoke of the miraculous recovery of one affected with palsy who had been carried to the shrine for cure. Scarcely a couple of hours had passed when the entire population of the city was in possession of the purport of the telegram".

A Hundred Years Ago

From *The Times of India*
(NOT ISSUED ON SUNDAY, MARCH 26, 1882)

Saturday, March 25, 1882

A MIRACLE IN PERSIA
(FROM OUR OWN CORRESPONDENT)

SHIRAZ, MARCH 6. — About fortnight ago Shiraz was electrified by the report that some belated pilgrims having applied for mission into Najaf and been refused by the keeper of the town to which, according to standing orders, must be kept closed from on after dusk until morning, invoked the aid of their Imaum by clamations of "ya ally ya ally," behold — a miracle — the gate open and the pilgrims repaired to his shrine to pay their orations! According to another account the gate fell down in utter destruction. When the report became generally known the people of Shiraz, inspired by religious enthusiasm, resolved upon getting up an illumination in expression of their sense of the glorious triumph of their fatih. His Excellency the Saheb Dewan, the Governor General of Fars, however, thought it prudent to postpone the entertainment until inquiry had been made and the authenticity of the report established. The telegraphic reply of a mustahid (high priest) of Najaf not only corroborated the report, but spoke of the miraculous recovery of one affected with palsy who had been carried to the shrine for cure. Scarcely a couple of hours had passed when the whole population of this city was in possession of the purport of the telegram,

اخبار ٹائمز آف انڈیا مورخہ
۲۶ مارچ سنہ ۱۸۸۲ کا
اصل انگریزی ترجمہ — اس کا اردو ترجمہ اگلے
صفحے پر درج ہے —

No sooner was the telegram confirming the miracle received, than the city was illuminated and broke into festivities!

11.9: Wrong Judgements of Umar ibn Khattab Corrected by Ali ﷺ and Umar Proclaiming: Had Ali Not Been There, Umar Would Have Perished! – 'Lau La Ali, Lahlaka Umar'

In this section we will cast a glance at some of the legal judgements given by Ali ﷺ during the caliphates of the three previous Caliphs. Many a time there were judgmental errors in the verdicts issued by these three; wherein Imam Ali would intervene and rectify their errors. Some of the times however, the issues would be brought to Imam Ali ﷺ's attention when the defendants would have already been erroneously executed! Umar was careful about handling 'hard to resolve' issues and would often refer such cases for Ali ﷺ's review and abide by his decision before announcing his own decision. It was on many such occasions that Umar announced: "*Lau La Ali, Lahlaka Umar!* - Had Ali not been there, Umar would have perished"! Details of such incidents are numerously recorded in various authentic books.[105] In addition to this, it has been recorded that Umar often used to say: "O Allah! Save me from a day when I am faced with a difficult court case and Abul Hasan is not there to resolve the problem!"[106]

There is a related tradition reported by Yahya ibn Aqeel in 'Riaz un Nazzara' and also in 'Tarikh ul Khulafa' that Umar always consulted Ali ﷺ when faced with difficult problems and often used to say: 'May God not keep me alive when Ali is not around;" and also: "Ali is the most knowledgeable among us and the best

---

[105] 'Riaz n Nazzara'- Vol 2, Pg 194; 'Istiyab' – Vol 2, Pg 44; and 'Izalatul Khifa' Pg 268.

[106] 'Tabaqat ibn Saad'- Vol 2, Pg 102; 'Usd ul Ghaba' – Vol 4, Pg 23; and 'Asabah' – Vol 4, Pg 270.

decision maker".[107] Another similar tradition is recorded in the book 'Istiyab' from Abdul Rahman ibn Awna Al Abdi that his father asked Umar as to which place he should designate as his 'Meeqhat' for starting his lesser pilgrimage of 'Umra' and Umar replied: "Go and ask Ali!" In any event, the books abound with evidence that acknowledge the fact that Ali ﷺ was the most competent; and Ayesha herself used to say that: "In matters of the traditions and 'Sunnah' of the holy Prophet ﷺ, Ali was the most knowledgeable". It is similarly recorded[108] through Mughaira under oath, that Ali ﷺ never made a mistake in any of his decisions!

During the caliphate of Abu Bakr, Khalid bin Waleed once wrote and asked him for a verdict regarding sodomy which was being committed in a certain area. Abu Bakr referred this to Ali ﷺ who gave examples of previous generations guilty of the same crime and ruled that the perpetrators of this sin should be burnt alive. Abu Bakr in turn conveyed this decision to Khalid.

Ibne Birr writes about an incident in his book 'Istiyab' that a companion named Al Qama once asked Abu Bakr the meaning of the Quranic verse: "Ehdinass Siratul Mustaqeem..." as to why Muslims were asking for the "Right Path" when they were already on the right path? When Abu Bakr could not give any satisfactory explanation, Al Qama got disillusioned and went away to Rome and eventually became a Christian. When Abu Bakr came to know about this, he sent his question to Ali ﷺ who unhesitatingly gave references of two Quranic verses and clarified that the actual

---

[107] 'Sahih Bukhari' – Chp 18, Pg 117; 'Sunan ibn Maaja' Pg 14; 'Musnad ibn Hanbal' – Vol 5, Pg 113; 'Kanzul Amaal' – Pg 36; 'Kanzul Haqaiq' Pg 21; and 'Mishkat' – Vol 5, Pg 138.

[108] 'Musnad ibn Hanbal'- vol 5, Pg 113; 'Kanzul Haqaiq'- Pg 21; 'Mishkat'- Vol 8, Pg 136.

meaning of the verse in question is to invoke Allah ﷻ in that: *"He should **keep us steadfast (maintain us)** on the Straight Path."* Abu Bakr dispatched a note with this explanation of Ali ؏ to Al Qama who received it on a day when he was coming out of the church. He immediately accepted the explanation, reverted to Islam, and returned to Madina. On a similar note, ibn Jarir relates on the authority of Abdullah ibn Abu Bakr that when a person Hayyan ibn Manfiz came to Uthman enquiring about the rules applicable in the case of a divorce of a suckling mother; Uthman was unable to tackle the query and approached Ali ؏ for a ruling.

Dailami, Khawarzimi, Al Fazaili, Hafiz us Salafi, ibn Saman and Abul Qasim Mehmood Zamakhshari all relate an incident that: a couple of persons jointly approached Umar and enquired about the rules applicable with respect to divorcing a slave girl? Umar got up from his place and went to the place where Ali ؏ was sitting and asked him the same question. One of the two persons turned to Umar and remarked: "You are supposed to be our Commander, and we came to you; but you have gone over to another person for a ruling?" Umar replied: "It is a pity that you do not know who this person is! He is Ali ibn Abi Talib about whom I bear witness that I heard the Prophet say that *'even if the knowledge of the Seven Heavens and the Earth were put on one side of the Scales and Ali's knowledge is put on the other, Ali's knowledge will be heavier than the rest put together!'"*

In the works of several reliable traditionalists such as Khawarzimi, Darqatni, Muhib ul Tabari and ibn Samah it is recorded from Umar e Khattab that some Arabs quarrelling among themselves came to him for resolving their dispute. He in turn asked Ali ؏ to decide the matter. One of the disputants objected as to why he would decide when he was without any authority. Upon hearing this, Umar jumped down from the pulpit and caught the man by the scruff of his neck saying: "You do not know about this person? He is my *'Maula'* and the *'Maula'* of all Believers; and anyone who does not accept him as his *'Maula'* (Lord and Master) is not a believer!"

Faqih Ganji Shafei in chapter 57 of his book 'Kifayat-ut-Talib Fee Manaqib-e-Ali ibn Abi Talib' relates a tradition from Hudaifa Yamani and this same tradition is also found in 'Noor-ul-Absaar' related on the authority of Saeed ibn Musayyab, that a group of people once brought a person to Umar complaining that when he was asked as to how he began his day, his reply was: "I befriend *'Fitna'* (Mischief) and I abhor *'Haqq'* (Truth) and I confirm what the Jews and Christians say. I believe in the Unseen, and I accept and testify about that which has not yet been born. I pray without performing ablutions; and on this Earth there is a certain 'commodity' that I possess which even God does have in the Heavens!" Umar was nonplussed! He was at a loss as to whether to call him an Infidel or a Muslim! Being out of his depth he approached Ali ﷺ for guidance. After listening to the case, Ali ﷺ said that this person was indeed speaking the truth.

He then went on to elaborate that "*this person admits he loves his 'Aal and Maal' (children and property) which in the Quran Allah ﷻ has referred to as 'Fitna'. He abhors 'Death' which is 'Haqq.' When he says he confirms what the Jews and Christians say, he alludes to that which Allah ﷻ has said in the Quran: ['The Jews say that the Christians are not on the right path, and the Christians says that the Jews are misguided'] and thereby testifies that both are erroneous. When he says he believes in that which he has not seen, he means Allah ﷻ; and as for believing in something that is yet to be born, is his belief of 'Qiyamah' (Day of Judgement) which is yet to happen! His 'prayers without ablutions' refer to the 'Salwaat' (blessings) which he sends on the Prophet ﷺ and his progeny for which it is not necessary to be in a state of ablution; and finally, when he says he possesses a 'commodity' on this Earth which God does have, he means* *that **he** has a wife as a '**Partner**' which can never be applicable to Allah ﷻ!"* Upon hearing these amazing clarifications by Imam Ali ؑ, Umar confoundedly exclaimed: "I seek the protection of Allah and pray that I may not live to see a day when Abul Hasan is not present!"

Various historians and scholars of note such as Muslim, Bukhari, Fakhruddin Razi, Suyuti, ibn Kathir, ibn Abil Hadid, Zamakshari, Qartabi, Sandi Qastalani, Muttaqi, Haakim and many others have recorded several instances which illustrate that Umar was very weak in his knowledge of *'Fiqh'* (Islamic Jurisprudence) as well as in his knowledge of the holy Quran; and would often have difficulty in even grasping simple matters being put to him for a decision. For example, instances cited in relation to the dowry at the time of marriage; the conjugal rights of a wife over a husband; rules of inheritance of childless couples and conversely also about *'Kalala'* – issue of inheritance of a childless person whose parents are both dead; rules of 'major' ablutions in the absence of water, etc.

A popular tradition has been documented unanimously by many scholars that Umar marvelled at the peculiarity of Ali ؑ in giving instant decisions without pondering over the issues or taking time in arriving at his conclusions. When he questioned him about this, Ali ؑ asked Umar to raise his hand and asked as to how many fingers were on his hand? Umar immediately said "Five". Ali ؑ asked him as to how could he reply without any hesitation. Umar said: "Because it is my hand and it is in front of my eyes;" at which Ali ؑ responded: *"In like manner, the knowledge of ALL matters of (Heaven and Earth- Seen or Unseen) is right before my eyes!"*

On page 481 of his book 'Al Farooq' Shibli writes that Umar never took a decision on any problem without consulting with other companions; particularly on issues for which there was no precedent to base his own opinion upon. He further writes on page 482 that Umar never really understood the significance of the 'Peace Treaty of Hudaibiya' in which the Prophet ﷺ had agreed to certain terms in the treaty, which Umar erroneously thought was a total surrender in favour of the Meccans. It was for this very reason that to manifest the true significance of this treaty Allah ﷻ revealed the chapter of *Surah Fatah*: Chapter 48 and referred to this Treaty as the **'Fatah Mubeen'** – 'The Clear or Imminent Victory'.

In the same book Shibli, to illustrate the incorrect judgements and decisions taken by the earlier Caliphs, recounts on page 415, a detailed incident of the murder of Malik ibn Noweira who had refused to pay *'Zakaat'* to Abu Bakr so long as Ali ﷺ was present within the community. In response to his refusal, Abu Bakr dispatched a contingent under the command of Khalid bin Waleed to collect this *'zakaat'* from Malik by force if necessary. Without any warning, Khalid slaughtered the men of Malik's tribe, including Malik himself. On the same night, he also forcefully slept with the wife of the murdered Malik! He then enslaved all the women of this tribe and brought and presented them to Abu Bakr who ordered them to be distributed as slave girls among the Muslims! Later when Umar became the Caliph, he reversed this order of Abu Bakr and set them free. Eventually when these venerable women who had been distributed as slave girls to various Muslim households returned to their own homes, they went back with the shame of having unwanted pregnancies and/or illegitimate children!

The question that now arises and faces us is: Who was correct? Was it Abu Bakr, or Umar? Or were they **both** wrong? This was not a trivial matter to be overlooked, as many Muslims were unjustifiably slain as well as wrongly enslaved; and their society was flooded with illegitimate children who all their lives remained without a status inside their own community!

Another incident which is worthy of note is the one which eventually lead to the assassination of Umar. Moghaira had a Persian slave called Abu Lulu a hand-craftsman, who used to make hand mills and other small articles and for which he was forced to pay a tax of four dirhams to his master daily. Abu Lulu felt this amount was excessive and appealed to Umar for mediation; but the latter dismissed his complaint saying that his master was justified in levying this tax. Abu Lulu was extremely upset by this ruling of Umar; and eventually decided to get even with him. He found an opportunity one day in the recess of a mosque, and using a double-edged dagger which he himself had crafted, he ripped open Umar's stomach and fled the city of Madina. This attack resulted in Umar's death three days later.

It is recorded that on one occasion the Romans sent a delegation to Umar [being the Caliph of the time], with a whole set of questions related to the previous scriptures, including details of the 'Ashaab e Kahaf (People of the Cave); with the challenge that if Islam was indeed a true religion, it should have answers to all these questions. Umar was totally dumbfounded and could not understand even one of the many issues. As per his usual habit he went to Imam Ali 🕮 taking the Romans along with him. Ali 🕮 who was busy writing some document of his own, paused and wrote down the answers to each question without even glancing at, or reviewing the contents of their queries. The Roman delegation was astonished and said that such a feat was only possible by one who knew the Four Scriptures and possessed Divine Knowledge!

Another interesting case which has been recorded in many books of tradition such as Sahih Bukhari, Musnad ibn Ahmed ibn Hanbal, as well as in various works of Hameedi, Sheikh Sulaiman Balkhi Hanafi, Muhammad ibn Yousuf Shafei, Muhibuddin Tabari, Imamul Haramain Muttadid etc who have all noted that in one case Umar had a pregnant woman sentenced to death by stoning, as she was accused of adultery. While she was on her way, she was protesting that she was pregnant and calling out for help. Ali 🕮 having heard her protestations inquired from Umar if he had already passed the verdict? Umar replied in the affirmative. Ali 🕮 then asked Umar whether he had considered the child she was carrying in her womb. Umar said he was not aware of the 'Rules regarding the Unborn Child' and asked Ali 🕮 to give his decision. Ali 🕮 ruled that the woman be spared till the child was born *and* until such time as proper arrangements were put in place for the care and nurturing of the newborn, before the sentence of death was implemented. Umar once again cried out: "If Ali was not present, Umar would have perished!"

Various books such as Haakim in his 'Mustadrak', Baihaqi in his 'Shaab al Eman' and Musafir in 'Ahwal al Akhirah' have a tradition on the authority of Abu Saeed Khudri that Umar was once performing Hajj and Ali 🕮 also happened to be present at the same time. Umar, after completing the circumambulations of the Kaaba stood in front of the Black Stone (*Hajr e Aswad*) and addressing it, called out in a loud voice: "I know you are a mere stone, and you can neither hurt nor benefit me; but I am bound to kiss you because the Prophet did likewise." Upon hearing this, Ali 🕮 chided Umar saying: *"Indeed! This stone is capable of harming or benefitting you, because it will bear witness over you on the Day of Judgement!"* Then he went on to quote a verse from the Quran related to this issue as well as a tradition from the holy Prophet 🕮 that kissing this stone signified the recognition of the *'Tawheed'* – Unity of Allah 🕮. Umar immediately became contrite and once again proclaimed the superiority of Ali 🕮's knowledge over his own saying: "May I not live in a period when Abul Hasan is not present to correct me!"

Hameedi has authored a book titled 'Jama Bainus-Sahih-ain' which is a precis of all the six 'Sahih' books. In it he has mentioned a case of five persons who were brought before Umar accused of adultery. He sentenced all of them to death by stoning. When Ali ﷺ was informed about this, he asked Umar to bring those persons to him; and upon evaluating their background and their crimes on an individual basis, he told Umar that his decision was against the tenets of the Quran. He then went on to explain that one of these five was an Infidel (*Kafir-e-Zimmi*) living under a Muslim rule so he should be executed as he had committed adultery with a Muslim woman. The next was a married man who was a Muslim and should be executed. The third was a bachelor who should be pelted with 100 lashes. The fourth was a slave, and he should be given half the punishment of 50 lashes. The fifth was mentally handicapped and his punishment was 25 lashes. On hearing this verdict from Ali ﷺ, Umar once again resorted to his refrain: "Had Ali not been present Umar would have perished!"

On page 834 of the same book another case is cited (which is backed by other[109] reliable traditionalists) that an insane woman was brought before Umar accused of adultery. He was unsure as to what punishment he should bale out; and took pity on her. Ali ﷺ was consulted and he said that the Prophet ﷺ had said that three types of people should have their judgement deferred as follows:

1. Insane persons till they regain sanity.
2. Minors till they reach adulthood.
3. Persons that are sleeping, till they wake up.

Upon hearing this Umar raised the cry: "Allah O Akbar!"

Ibne Saman and Al Khalqi, as well as Mohib e Tabari in his book 'Riazun Nazzara' all relate a tradition from Hazn bin Abi Al Aswad that on one occasion Umar ruled that a woman who had delivered a child six months after her marriage should be stoned to death.

---

[109] 'Sunan ibn Dawood' – Vol 2, Pg 227; 'Musnad Ahmad ibn Hanbal'- Vol 1, Pg 104; Istiyaab'- Vol 2, Pg 474 and 'Riaz un Nazzara'- Vol 1, Pg 194.

When Imam Ali 🕮 heard about this he stopped him, saying that according to the holy Quran, the period from the conception of a pregnancy to the weaning of the child from a mother's milk is mentioned as being **30** months. In yet another verse of the Quran, Allah 🕮 has stated that the '*period of weaning*' is **24** months; hence it stands to reason that in **rare cases** the ***least period of pregnancy can be*** of only six months duration. Umar withdrew his decision and thanked God for the presence of Ali 🕮 at this crucial hour.

In the same book[110] as well as in 'Manaqib' by Khawarzimi, another incident is recorded that a woman was sentenced by Umar to 'death by stoning' as she had admitted to committing adultery. While she was being led to the site of her punishment, Ali 🕮 stopped Umar and asked whether he had used force or threatened her in any way in extracting her confession. Umar replied in the affirmative. Ali 🕮 then reminded him saying: "*Have you not heard the Prophet 🕮 say that force or threats should not be used in extracting a confession from the accused; and if done so, it is not to be accepted as evidence against the defendant.*" On hearing this Umar reviewed the case and released the woman, and admiringly exclaimed: "It is just not possible for *ANY* woman ever, to give birth to a second Ali in this world"

Again in 'Riazun Nazzara' as well as in 'Mauta' (pages 22 and 28) it is written that once while leading the morning prayer Umar recited two lengthy chapters: Surah: *Yousuf* (12th) in the first cycle and Surah: *Hajj* (22nd) in the second cycle of his prayers, [just as Abu Bakr had once recited the Surah *Baqra* (Chapter 2) also in his morning prayers]; with the result that by the time they finished these lengthy recitations the sun had risen high on the horizon and the time for completing the morning prayers had elapsed!

---

[110] 'Riaz un Nazzara'- Vol 2, Pg 196.

Al Harb Al-Tai reports from Muhammad ibn Yahya bin Hayyan, that Hayyan bin Manqad had two wives: one from the Hashimite clan and the other an Ansari (Medinite). He divorced the latter but died later in the same year. The Ansari wife came to Uthman demanding her share of inheritance from her ex-husband's wealth saying that her period of *"Iddat"* (three menstrual cycles) after pronouncing the divorce had not been completed at the time of his death. Uthman was perplexed and sent her to Imam Ali ☙ who told the woman to stand by the pulpit of the holy Prophet ☙ and state under oath that she had not completed her three menstrual cycles prior to his death. She did so and was included in the inheritance!

It is related in the book 'Fee Al-Manaqibul As-haab' written by Abu Bakr Najmuddin Muhammad bin Al Husayn Ash-Shablani, that during the Caliphate of Umar, two women claimed to be the mother of the same infant boy. Umar had difficulty in resolving the matter and referred it to Imam Ali ☙ who first advised the two women to fear God and for the false mother to withdraw her claim. Neither of them budged from their stand. Ali ☙ asked for a carpenter working nearby to be called over to cut the child into two equal parts, so each woman could be given one half of the child's body! One woman instantly withdrew her claim saying she was the one who had lied, while the other woman merely looked on. Imam Ali ☙ immediately picked the child up and handed it to the one who had withdrawn the claim, saying that she, being the real mother, rather than see her child dead, had preferred to see it alive albeit in someone else's lap!

There are countless such instances recorded in various books from several reliable Sunni scholars such as Tabaqat ibn Saad, Tarikh ul Khulafa, Mustadrik, Baihaqi, Istiyab, Suyuti, Kanzul Amaal, Musnad-e-Imam Ahmad etc. in which they have recounted (giving full references), details of situations where Ali ☙ had assisted and resolved many a problem for Abu Bakr and Uthman in the same way that he had extricated Umar from tricky situations. They have all noted numerous incidents wherein all three of these Caliphs appealed to Ali 🕮 for guidance in difficult matters of 'Fiqh' (Islamic Jurisprudence) as well as on subjects covering a whole spectrum of other issues during their periods of Caliphate; and Ali 🕮 never refused them in their hour of need!

'Musnad ibn Hanbal Vol 1, Pg 100 and 'Kanzul Amaal' Vol 2, page 345 has recorded an incident in connection with Uthman going on Hajj with some of his companions. Haris ibn Abdullah narrates that Uthman was in the state of "Ehram" for Hajj when someone presented him with a meal of roasted partridge which had been shot as a 'game bird' by an arrow. Some of the companions hesitated to eat, but Uthman declared that "since we have neither hunted the bird ourselves nor asked anyone else to hunt it for us; and those that hunted this bird were not in a state of "Ehram", there is no restriction for us to eat from this meat." However, seeing his companion's hesitation he nonetheless decided to enquire if there was anyone present who had a better knowledge about this situation. Ali 🕮 who was in the vicinity was consulted, whereupon he in turn asked whether there were any people present there who had been with the Prophet 🕮 in a comparable situation; if so, to identify themselves. When they stood up, he reminded them of the incident when the Apostle 🕮 had refused to partake some meat of a hunted animal while he was in a state of "Ehram". Twelve witnesses testified to being present at the Prophet 🕮's incident; and Ali 🕮 reminded them that the ruling was that only those persons who were relieved of their state of 'Ehram" could eat such a meat offering!

Of the many unusual decisions taken by Ali 🕮 considering his Divine Knowledge, one is recorded by notable Sunni scholars where they narrate that when Umar entered the mosque one morning he found the dead body of a man dressed as a female, which had been left inside its precincts. Being completely baffled, he sought Ali ﷺ's help who in turn first ordered that the body be buried. He then told Umar that nine months later a child will be found in the same spot who he, Umar as the Caliph, should arrange to be looked after by a wet nurse; and undertake the responsibility for its care and upbringing from the 'Baitul Maal' (Public Treasury). He then added: "*Following this incident, a woman will come to the same Mosque on the Day of 'Eid' (Festival) looking for the child and bewailing: 'Where are you, O oppressed son of an oppressed Mother and a Cruel Father...!' When this happens, you should bring that woman to me*".

As predicted by Imam Ali ﷺ the child was found in the same spot nine months later; and subsequently on the Day of the Festival a young woman appeared and was taken into custody and brought before Ali ﷺ. Addressing her he said: "*I am aware of your situation, but I want you to describe the circumstances leading to your arrest in your own words.*" She confessed that she was the one who had slit the throat of the dead man in question and had dragged his body and left it inside the Mosque. She went on to say that she had been a lonely person whose parents were both dead. An old lady acquaintance of hers taking advantage of her situation tricked her one day by saying that she wanted her to meet one of her woman friends who turned out to be a man dressed as a woman; and one who out of sheer lust had been harbouring evil designs on her virtue for a long time. This same man taking unfair advantage of that opportunity had forced himself on her that day, because of which she ended up with the child. In her struggle to free herself, finding the dagger tied on the belt around his waist, she used it to kill him; then dragged his body in the darkness of the night into the Mosque and left it there!

Imam Ali ﷺ asked Umar to search and locate the old woman who was responsible for this sordid affair and when found, she was sentenced to death for being the architect of this incident of adultery. Umar was again forced into pronouncing his slogan: "O God let me not be alive when Abul Hasan is not there to solve my difficulties!"

Another tradition illustrating Imam Ali ﷺ's Divine Knowledge is found in the book 'Kaukab-e-Durri' by Allama Kashfi Tirmizi Hanafi who in turn has taken the narration from the book 'Ahsanul Kibar', that during the reign of Umar, a faithful companion of the Prophet ﷺ by the name of Abu Abdullah Ansari had passed away and left behind a fairly large inheritance of One Thousand Dinars; and a son aged three years. His widow married another person, and when the boy reached the age of twelve years, he noticed that his mother was giving some of his inheritance money to her husband. The boy pointed out to his mother that she was being unjust to him by dipping into his inheritance. When this woman perceived that her son was aware of her actions, she denied that he was the son of his late father, but that he was a slave who had been bought and named after her previous husband. The boy complained to Umar, but the woman brought seven persons paying them a hundred Dirhams each to bear false witness. Based on this evidence, Umar sentenced the boy to imprisonment.

After four months one of Umar's sons happened to see this boy in a weakened condition with a shackle around his neck. Upon enquiring the reason for his confinement in jail, the boy stated that his father Umar had imprisoned him based on his mother's false charges. Hearing this Umar's son intervened and standing in as a 'Guarantor' brought the boy to Imam Ali ﷺ. When Ali ﷺ saw the boy in his under-nourished condition he instructed his slave Qamber to have him washed and fed and dressed in clean clothes. When he found out that the boy was the son of Abu Abduallah Ansari, he wept as he was reminded of the service that his late father had rendered to the Prophet ﷺ. He then took the boy to

Umar and told him that the boy had been wrongly convicted. Consequently, Umar had the mother, the seven witnesses brought back, and they again repeated their false oaths. Ali ﷺ then sent for a local Medicine Man to come and draw some blood from the mother which was placed in a shallow dish. He then covered the dish with his cloak and recited some special prayer whereupon a voice was heard from the blood in the dish: "O Successor of the Prophet! I am in fact, the mother of this boy; but due to the greed of this world, I gave false statements against him!"[111] Those present were awed and amazed, the miscreants were all punished, and the inheritance was given to the youth as its rightful owner.

Another incident recorded in 'Ahsan-ul-Kibar' and also on page 442 of 'Kaukab-e-Durri' states that a young man approached Umar and said that his mother denies that he is her son. The woman was called, and she brought along her four brothers and 40 other persons as witnesses in support of her position. Umar sentenced the boy to be imprisoned. As he was being led to his punishment, he raised a hue and cry proclaiming his innocence. Hearing this, Imam Ali ﷺ intervened and took the boy back to the court of Umar where he asked the woman as to whether she was the mother of the boy. When she replied in the negative, he asked her if she would allow him, Ali, to be her *"Wali"* (Guardian) in this matter, to

---

[111] Translator's Note: For those who may be a little skeptical about accepting the veracity of this incident, we simply have to look at several verses in the holy Quran where Allah ﷺ has stated that in the Hereafter our own hands and skin etc. will bear witness against us: e.g. Surah Yasin: *"On that Day We shall set a seal upon their mouths, and their hands shall speak to Us, and their feet shall bear witness of what they earned.' (36:65).* In the capacity of being the *'Wali'* of Allah ﷺ and the true *'Wasi'* of Rasool ﷺ as well as being the *'Quran-e-Nathiqh' – The Speaking Quran'*, Ali ﷺ was endowed with the Divine Power by which he could enable even the inanimate objects to speak!

which the woman readily agreed. Ali 🕮 then asked his slave Qamber to bring 400 Dirhams from his house and give it to the woman and when she had accepted it, he told her that as her Caretaker he would pronounce her "*Aqd*" (marriage) with this youth on the dowry of 400 Dirhams. When the woman heard this, she was alarmed and confessed her guilt saying that her brothers had put her up to this ruse so that they could deny the youth of his inheritance and benefit from it themselves. The brothers and the other false witnesses were punished for their involvement in the crime; the youth was reunited with his mother and Umar once again cried out: "Lau La Ali, Lehlaka Umar!"

Another unusual case is recorded in 'Malfuzaat' (Sayings of the Saints) by Maqdoom Jehaniya, as well as in 'Kaukab-e-Durri' page 449 that once a rich merchant died leaving behind his large fortune, a daughter, and three slaves. While in the stupor of death he made an unusual Will that one of his three slaves should be married to his daughter and given the bulk of his Estate; the second slave should be given 1000 Dinars and set free, while the third slave was to be executed! None of these three were identified by name. Subsequently the girl arrived at the court of Umar accompanied by the three slaves. When Umar was confronted with this unusual bequest he was baffled as to how to decide on which slave should be meted with which one of the three stipulations of the Will. He consulted some of his companions who also could not resolve this dilemma.

Collectively they approached Ali 🕮 for a solution. Ali 🕮 assembled the three slaves and in turn, gave a knife to all three slaves with instructions to dig up the grave of their master and sever his head and bring it to him. The first slave refused to accept the assignment and returned the knife back saying he could not do this to his master! The second slave took the knife and proceeded in the direction of his master's grave, but on reconsideration returned saying he could not conduct such a deed either. The third slave took the knife and headed purposefully towards the grave. Ali 🕮 sent some persons after him to stop the slave when he begins to dig the grave open and to return him back to the court.

The slave was brought back; and Ali 🕮 pronounced his verdict that the first slave should be married to the merchant's daughter and be given the bulk of the Estate. The second should be given 1000 Dinars and set free, while the third slave, though he would have been considered to be deserving of a death sentence according to the contents of his master's Will, was to be returned back as a slave under the authority of the daughter and her new husband to do with him as they willed; because under the Islamic Jurisprudence he could not be put to death for this reason alone as no crime had actually been committed by him. In admiration Umar exclaimed: "Whatever the Prophet said in praise of Ali was indeed the truth!"

On page 318 of the same book as well as in 'Ahsan-ul-Kibar' there is a tradition related by one Hasnain ibn Abdul Raheem-e-Tammar that during the Caliphate of Umar the city of Madina was rocked by a severe earthquake. People started to panic and flocked to Umar's house asking him to pray and stop their homes from being demolished; and the city from being destructed. No number of prayers had any effect and the earthquake only grew worse. Umar then took a group of people and went to Ali 🕮 asking him to intercede. Imam Ali 🕮 asked him to bring a hundred companions of the Holy Prophet 🕮 to him out of whom he chose ten, which included the likes of Salman-e-Farsi, Abuzar-e-Ghaffari, Ammar-e-Yasser, and Miqdad ibn Aswad Kindi. He then proceeded to the graveyard of "Baqi" with these selected companions and upon entering its precincts he halted and stamped on the ground three times saying: "What has happened to you today? (Ma laka? Ma laka? Ma laka?" Immediately the quake stopped, the ground settled, and the city was saved! Everyone went back glorifying the praises of Ali ﷺ.

In the book 'Kifayatul Momineen' as well as in 'Ahsan-ul-Kibar' and also in Allama Kashafi Najafi Hanafi's 'Kaukab-e-Durri' on page 323, it is recorded on the authority of Salman-e-Farsi ﷺ that during the Caliphate of Abu Bakr there was a pious lady called Umme Farwah who was an ardent lover of the Ahlul Bayt ﷺ. She used to be openly vocal in singing praises about their lofty position. One day she was aggressively confronted and contested by a wealthy person from within the community. When she countered his arguments with further praises of the Prophet ﷺ's family he beat her so severely that she died. The shocked husband after burying her, complained in the court of Abu Bakr asking for justice, but to no avail.

He then came to Ali ﷺ and while weeping profusely, he recounted the whole affair, and related the circumstances involved. Imam Ali ﷺ asked the husband to take him to the grave of his wife where he performed two units of prayers and incanted some special prayers. The grave soon opened, and Umme Farwah emerged wearing a modest cloak and addressed Imam Ali ﷺ saying: "O My *Maula!* (Lord and Master) The hypocrites wished to conceal the glory of your status, and they punished me for my attachment to you; but they will never be able to swerve me away from you!" Imam Ali ﷺ sent her back to her home with her husband where she lived several years with him and bore several children, some of whom were later known to be martyred on the plains of Kerbala with Imam Husayn ﷺ!

During the last days of his life, the holy Prophet ﷺ used to constantly mention that "*a group had emerged from within his Ummah that was inimical and actively hostile towards (the merits of) Ali ﷺ*". This same group gathered further momentum and began to show itself openly during the Caliphate of Imam Ali ﷺ. It is recorded that one day one such group of hypocrites tried to ridicule Ali ☜ by bringing a coffin in which a youth was made to lie down pretending to be dead: accompanied by his old mother shedding crocodile tears at his loss. They asked Ali ☜ to perform the funeral prayers of the dead lad. Imam ☜ advised them to go back and leave him alone to continue with his own work. They however insisted; and **twice** Imam Ali ☜ declined. When they insisted for the third time, Ali ☜ turned to the mother and asked her whether *she really* wanted him to perform the funeral prayers of her son, to which she [and others in the group] replied: that was the reason why they had come to him! He then proceeded and offered the prayers after which, pointing to the coffin he told them: "*Take this dead person and bury him in his grave.*" They all began to laugh, but soon the laughter changed to shock and awe as they were astounded to see that the youth was indeed dead! The mother now started wailing and weeping in earnest and implored Ali ☜ for the revival of her son as well as her own forgiveness, stating that she had been coerced into being a part of their wicked ruse to belittle him. The kind-hearted Ali ☜ relented and ordered the youth to rise, who also then apologised and repented for his own actions.

An incident during the lifetime of the Prophet ☙ is recorded in several reliable books such as 'Al Mustadrak' of Hakim, 'Al Sawaiq Al Muhriqa' by ibn Hajjar Makki, 'Ahsan-ul-Kibar' and 'Kaukab-e-Durri' which has been related by Abu Bakr where a bull owned by a person gorged a donkey to death which was owned by another person. The owners of both animals got into a dispute and came to the Prophet ☙ for a ruling. He ☙ in turn referred the case to his companions for an equitable decision. They decided that since the issue was between two animals there was no responsibility or onus upon either of the two owners. The Apostle ☙ then referred the matter to Ali ☜, who enquired of the owners whether their animals had been tethered or left free to roam? The owner of the donkey said that his donkey was tied to its post; whereas the owner of the bull admitted that his animal had been left free of its tether and was at liberty to move around. Upon hearing this Ali ﷺ ruled that the owner of the bull was responsible for paying compensation for the donkey as he should not have left the bull free to run amok. The Prophet ﷺ accepted and implemented the decision of Ali ﷺ thereby showing that even in his own lifetime he ﷺ, relied on Ali ﷺ's sense of fairness and clear thinking in always arriving at the correct decision!

Another lighthearted incident from during the lifetime of the Prophet ﷺ is recorded by reliable traditionalists that on one occasion he was seated with his companions and eating some fresh dates but leaving the pits (date seeds) on the mat in front of Ali ﷺ. Taking the lead from the Prophet, the companions also did likewise. The Prophet ﷺ light heartedly remarked: *"Who has eaten the most dates?"* The companions replied: "The one who has the greatest number of seeds in front of him ate the most!" Humorously Ali ﷺ replied: *"On the contrary, the one who ate the dates along with the pits would appear to have eaten the most!"* The Prophet ﷺ smiled and said: *"It is very hard to beat my brother in any contest (of words), because I am the City of Knowledge and he is its Gateway!"*

In the book 'Najmus Saqaib' an incident is recorded on page 124 that upon his death a person left an amount of 1000 Dinars with his friend with the instruction to him to *"give away in charity whatever amount was pleasing to him"* and keep the balance for himself. This person gave away 100 Dinars in charity and kept 900 for himself. The recipients of the charity complained and asked him to share at least half of the total amount with them. The person refused. The case was brought to Ali ﷺ who turned to the man and said that these people were being very fair to him in offering him half of the total amount. But the person disagreed saying that the owner had clearly told him to give away in charity "*whatever was pleasing to him*". Upon hearing this Ali ﷺ ruled that 900 should be given away in charity because "*that was the amount which was pleasing to him* [!] and he should only keep the remaining balance of 100 Dinars for himself as his share!

In all reliable Sunni books of Jurisprudence and history, including the 'Six True Books' (*Saha Sitta*) it is recorded by numerous narrators that Ali ibn Abi Taleb ﷺ was the Best, Most Fair and Supreme judge of his time. In this context we will relate only a few of his noteworthy judgements and conclude our discourse on this subject.

The first incident that we have listed is taken from 'Kanzul Amaal' and from 'Tarikh-ul-Khulafa'[112] on the authority of Zaar bin Habash and deals with two travellers who had settled for lunch. One of them had **three** loaves of bread and the other had **five**. A third traveller was passing by, and they invited him to join them to partake of their meal. He assented. After eating, the stranger left **eight** Dirhams with them as compensation for the cost of his share of the meal. After his departure one of the two friends who had contributed five loaves, kept five Dirhams for himself and offered three Dirhams to his friend. The latter disagreed saying that they should both share the money *equally* because they had both *equally offered to share their entire food*. When they could not agree among themselves, they went to Imam Ali. Ali ﷺ advised the owner of the three loaves to take what was being offered to him in good faith by his companion; but he refused saying he would 'only take what was his rightful share'.

Hearing this, Imam Ali ﷺ said; "*If you really want what is 'rightfully yours' then your share is only one Dirham.*" The person

---

was shocked and said: "By God! How could this be so? If you can prove to me that this is my 'rightful share' I will surely accept it!" Ali ﷺ explained as follows: "*There were 8 loaves between the three of you. Let us assume that you all ate an equal amount. If we break the 8 loaves into 3 pieces each, then we end up with 24 pieces. Assuming all of you ate equally, when we split the 24 pieces among the 3 persons, then you would all have eaten **8 pieces each**. Since you had 3 loaves to start with, your contribution was 9 pieces out of which you yourself ate 8, which leaves you with **only one** extra piece to be shared with the stranger. Your friend on the other hand, had 5 loaves which were broken into 15 pieces out of which he ate 8 pieces but gave away 7. Since the stranger also ate 8 pieces, 7 were contributed by your friend and only one piece came from you. Hence your 'rightful entitlement' is only **one Dirham**.*" Hearing this clear minded and simple argument, the person praised Allah and readily accepted this decision of Ali ﷺ for its fairness and equitable conclusion.

Another **amazing** decision taken by Imam Ali ﷺ is in the instance of *a unique incident* wherein three partners had jointly invested in a business of 'purchase and sale' of live camels. Their monetary investments were in the ratio of **half (½),** one third **(1/3rd)** and one-ninth **(1/9th)** respectively. After the sale transactions were completed and their profits were realized and shared in proportion to their individual investments, there were 17 camels still left over yet to be divided among them in the same proportions. The first one claimed his share as half of the 17 camels which amounted to 8½ camels, the second claimed 1/3rd which came to 5¾ camels while the last was left with his portion of 1/3rd which amounted to a little over 1½ camel! They were in an absolute quandary as to how to bring about an acceptable decision without killing any of their animals! Many others upon hearing about this dilemma also became curious to see how this could be resolved. They approached Imam Ali ﷺ who instantly agreed to solve their complex issue and told the three partners that: "*To your 17 camels I will add one of my own before making the distribution.*" He then ordered his slave Qamber to bring one of his own camels out and add it to their herd, making it to a total of **18 camels**.

Out of these **18**, he gave **9** camels to the partner who had contributed **one half** of the investment. To the next who had contributed **one third** of the money, he gave away **6** camels which amounted to his share of **1/3rd** investment. Finally, from the remaining 3, he away **2** camels to the third person who had contributed **1/9th** of the investment. The total number of camels thus handed over (9 + 6 + 2) was equal to the exact number of **17** [!] with **one** camel **still left over** from the group of **18**! He again ordered Qamber to take his camel back home and tie it to its post!

Each one of the three partners got more than what they had expected; and they, along with the large crowd of spectators that had gathered, were absolutely dumbfounded at the **amazing** competency, impressive proficiency and razor-sharp clarity of Imam Ali ﷺ's decision making powers! They all went away more than satisfied, singing praises of Imam Ali ﷺ!

Muhammad bin Talha al-Shafei has recorded an incident in his book 'Matalib-as-Sawool' **about a famous decision by Imam Ali** ﷺ which has been documented and registered in the chronicles and used as a 'Benchmark' in the annals of 'The Rules of Islamic Jurisprudence' under the title of **"The Ruling of The Dinars"** for all future rulings in similar situations! He writes that a woman once came to Imam Ali ﷺ when he was just about to depart on some errand and had already placed one foot in the stirrup of his mount. She cried out to him: "O Commander of the Faithful! My brother died recently leaving behind an inheritance of 600 Dinars; but I have been given only **one** Dinar as my share. I have come to you for justice on my behalf!"

Without the slightest hesitation Imam Ali replied: *"Your brother must have had two daughters and also been survived by his mother and a wife."* The woman concurred and said: "Yes". Imam further added: *"You must also have 12 brothers who survived him."* She again said: "Yes." Imam Ali 鑫 then said: *"You have already received your fair share, return back home."* Then for her benefit, while nudging his horse to move forward, he explained the distribution of 600 Dinars as follows:

"Two thirds (2/3rd) of 600 Dinars are for his two daughters which is equal to 400.

One eighth (1/8th) is the share of his wife which amounts to 75 Dinars.

The share of the mother is one sixth (1/6th) which is equal to 100 dinars.

The remaining 25 Dinars were distributed two each among the 12 brothers which in total amounts to 24 Dinars, leaving 1 Dinar (half the share of the brothers) for you as his sister!"

This amazing quality of Imam Ali 鑫 in making 'Lightening Swift' decisions with precision and accuracy was the hallmark of the Commander of The Faithful which was evident **time and again** for all to sit up and take notice!

In the same book, another similar ruling on the distribution of an inheritance is recorded which was given by Imam Ali 鑫 while he was delivering a sermon from the pulpit in the Masjid of Kufa. A person entered and called out: "O Commander of the Faithful! My son-in-law recently expired, and his family has given only one ninth (1/9th) of the inheritance to my daughter rather than the one eighth (1/8th) which should be due to her as a wife's share." Without hesitation Imam Ali 鑫 replied: *"Your son-in-law must have left behind two daughters and is survived by both his parents."* The man replied in the affirmative. Imam Ali 鑫 then explained that: *"Because of these circumstances the share of your daughter has been reduced from 1/8th to 1/9th. Be satisfied and do not demand anymore than her fair share which has been given!"*

In a handwritten manuscript by the author of the book 'Najmul Saqib' an incident is recorded on page 204 which occurred during the Caliphate of Ali ﷺ. Two women gave birth simultaneously at the same location. One gave birth to a boy and the other delivered a girl. The girl's mother swapped her daughter with the boy. The mother of the boy complained about this to Imam Ali ﷺ. As there had been no witnesses to this incident, Imam Ali ﷺ order that *an equal amount of milk* from both the two nursing mothers should be taken in identical bowls and each weighed on the scale. He then ruled that the mother whose milk was heavier in weight was the mother of the boy! People witnessing the proceedings were amazed and inquired as to how he had come to this decision? He calmly responded: *"From the Quran."* Intrigued, people again asked: "Where in the Quran?" Imam Ali ﷺ then replied giving reference to the Quranic verse which states that *"the male person's share is twice that of the female."*

Again, in this same manuscript a case is documented about a man who died in an uninhabited area, leaving behind a son and a slave. The slave came to the court of Imam Ali ﷺ and put forth a claim that *he* was the son of the bereaved person, and the son in fact was his slave! The son vehemently disputed this misrepresentation of truth. When neither owned up, Imam Ali asked his slave Qamber to make two holes in a wall and ordered both disputants to place their heads in each hole. (In another version it is stated that he asked both to lie face down on the ground and shut their eyes.) In a resounding voice Ali ﷺ then called out: *"Qamber! Draw your sword and cut off the head of the slave!"* The real son being a master all his life, remained calm whereas the slave immediately panicked and retreated! He was subsequently punished for making his false claim.

The degree and level of Imam Ali ﷺ's mental faculties and his 'all encompassing, accurate and exhaustive perception' under varied circumstances and situations can be gauged from another very interesting tradition recorded in several books: that one day the Prophet ﷺ withdrew into his room and appointed Ali ﷺ to stand by the door with instructions not to admit anyone inside, as he was being visited by different angels. Shortly thereafter, the angels began to arrive in large numbers and conversed with the Apostle of Allah while Ali ﷺ kept vigil. After the angels had all departed, he asked the Prophet ﷺ whether the number of angels who visited him was 320 in all. The Apostle ﷺ asked him as to how he knew of the exact number? Imam Ali ﷺ replied: "*I identified them each by the tone of their voices and sounds of their wings!*"

To illustrate this 'all encompassing' knowledge of Imam Ali ﷺ further, we list the next tradition related from one known by the name of Zadhan that: one day he was sitting with a group of people in the company of Imam Ali ﷺ when they were visited by a group of scholars from the Jewish and Christian communities. The delegation was led by a Jewish head named Jaluth and a Christian leader called Jaleeq. After greeting them, Imam ﷺ conversationally asked Jaluth as to whether he knew the exact number of sects that the Jews got divided into after the time of Moses ﷺ. Jaluth said he was not aware of it and would have to refer to the book before he could answer. Imam Ali ﷺ said: "*Woe unto you! The knowledge should be in your breasts and not between the covers of a book! If the book were to get burnt or lost, how would you deal with the queries that you would be faced with from your people?*" Then he turned his attention toward Jaleeq and asked a similar question to him as to how many sects did the Christians get broken into after Jesus ﷺ's departure. The Christian head promptly responded that there was 45 sects. Imam ﷺ rebuked him saying: "*By God that is a lie! I know the Torah and the Evangel (Taurath and Injeel) better than either of you. Among the Jews there are 71 sects of which only one is on the right path. Among the Christians there are 72 sects of which only one is on the right path. And as for the Muslims, they will be divided into 73 sects of which only one will be on the right path. And these will be my Shias!"*

At one time a group of 10 scholars who were extremely inimical toward Ali 🕮 arrived in his presence with the intention of ridiculing him by assessing the extent of his knowledge. All of them decided to ask him the same question but demanded a different answer for each. Their question was: "Between 'Knowledge and Wealth' (*Ilm* and *Maal*): which of the two is better?" Ali 🕮 immediately replied giving multiple answers of which we have only listed ten:

1. *Knowledge is better because Wealth is the legacy of Hamam, Pharoah and Qaroon, whereas Knowledge is the legacy of the prophets.*

2. *A person must protect his Wealth, whereas Knowledge protects the person.*

3. *Wealthy persons have more enemies, while knowledgeable persons have more friends.*

4. *Wealth dwindles when spent, whereas Knowledge increases with usage.*

5. *A Wealthy person is often viewed as being a 'miser' whereas a knowledgeable person is considered generous.*

6. *On the Day of Resurrection, the Wealthy will have to account for their Wealth, while the one in possession of Knowledge will be free from this kind of questioning.*

7. *With Wealth there is a danger of theft, while Knowledge cannot be stolen.*

8. *Knowledge illuminates the soul, whereas Wealth darkens it.*

9. *Wealth and possessions decay with time, but Knowledge lasts forever.*

10. Wealth induces pride and a superiority complex in a person whereas Knowledge brings about humility and humbleness.

Imam Ali ﷺ further elaborated on the last point by giving the example of Pharoah and Nimrod who on the strength of their Wealth even went to the extent of calling themselves 'God'! These kinds of responses of Ali ﷺ to different situations, were just a small sampling or a mere glimpse of his own extensive knowledge, but if anyone is interested in knowing more about his vast array of knowledge; they should refer to the book called 'Nahjul Balagha' (Peak of Eloquence) which is a compilation of some of his sermons, letters and sayings that were collected by a scholar named Syed Razi; and one will then get a better idea of the sharp wit and superior intellect of Ali ﷺ.

Allama Wahidi in his book 'Fawaij' writes that when the first two verses of chapter 42 of the holy Quran (*As-Shura*) were revealed (42:1-2), they were only conveyed in the form of '*Muqattaat*' ('letter symbols' in a 'short-meter' form): *"Ha, Meem; Ain, Seen, Qaf."* The Prophet ﷺ became extremely sad. When asked for the reason for his sadness, he replied that the denotation of these verses signifies a time when the Muslim Ummah will be engulfed in various adversities. Whenever Abdullah ibn Abbas used to recite these verses, he would always add that Imam Ali ﷺ used to foretell all the calamities that would befall the future generations of Muslims from his in-depth knowledge of these two verses alone! This same statement is confirmed in the 'Tafsir-e-Thalabi'. 'Sahih Muslim' has further elaborated on this with an additional comment that "Imam Ali ﷺ was aware of all the calamities that had already occurred at different locations of the earth in the past, as well as the ones yet to occur in future anywhere on this planet"; and further states that the Imam ﷺ also foretold about which one of the many communities would subsequently perish or survive!

Supporting the foregoing statements, Imam Ghazzali has also written that there is a book titled: 'Jafr Jame Ad-Duniya wal Akhirah' wherein all events and occurrences and details relating to every thing, every occurrence and every phenomenon on earth and the heavens, are stated as being in the "exclusive knowledge of Ali 🕮 as well as the eleven immaculate Imams from his descendants" and that **none** is privy to this knowledge, **nor** can one claim to be aware of this other than these selected personalities; because this intelligence was Divinely *bestowed upon them and them alone!*" Sulayman Balkhi in his book 'Yanabiyal Mawaddah' also records that this fact is supported in the book 'Durre Munnazzim' by Muhammad bin Talha Shafei which reiterates that 'Jafr Jame Ad-Duniya wal Akhirah' contains 1700 pages exclusively devoted to Ali ibne Abi Taleb 🕮, with lengthy compilations of symbols and 'short-meter' forms of secret and mystical icons, the meaning of which cannot be deciphered by anybody but Imam Ali 🕮 and his eleven descendants from the holy Ahlul Bayt AS.

Masoodi, the compiler of the 'Muruj al-Zaheb' fame, in his other book 'Isbaatul Wasiyah' writes on page 92 of this book that Angel Gabriel 🕮 handed a sealed book to the holy Prophet 🕮 and said: "*Allah 🕮 after sending you His greetings advises that this is the Covenant which you had taken and which was witnessed by My Angels. I Allah am witness to the fact that you have read this book and given it to Ali; and you both have promised to propagate the Message of Prophethood; and you both have accepted the undertaking of this Mission.*" After this, Masoodi further writes that Angels Gabriel and Michael and other exalted angels were asked to witness this document. Moreover, Lady Fatima Zahra 🕮, Imams Hasan 🕮 and Husayn 🕮 were also advised of their respective responsibilities to continue the propagation of the Prophetic mission; and they in turn were also made privy to the details of the forthcoming events. Likewise, they were also asked to bear witness and accept this covenant; after which it was sealed with a golden seal and given to Ali 🕮.

The proof of Ali 🕮's infinite knowledge and magnanimous character can be gauged from the fact that even those who were opposed to him used to consult him on various issues; and he would always give them the best possible advice in their interest! It is recorded in 'Kanzul Ummal'[113] that even Muawiyah, despite being his arch enemy used to send questions of jurisprudence and other difficult matters to Imam Ali 🕮 for guidance; and Ali 🕮 never refused and always complied with the correct answers! It is a well-known fact that all three Caliphs when faced with 'hard to resolve' matters and issues always resorted to Ali 🕮 for help and guidance which was given by him unhesitatingly to help them out of any sticky situation. Umar's utterances such as: "O Allah! Do not keep me alive for the day when Abul Hasan is not there to solve my difficulty" and similarly: "If Ali was not there, Umar would have perished" have been recorded countless number of times in the annals of Islamic history by a whole spectrum of varying scholars.

The bias against Imam Ali 🕮 however had taken such a deep rooted and 'blind attachment to others' by many of these very same scholars, that Suyuti for example, in spite of being aware of all the foregoing facts and the multiple occasions when Umar sought help from Ali 🕮 crying: *"Lau la Ali, Lahlaka Umar"*, still writes that 'if the knowledge of Umar was put on one side of the scale, and the knowledge of the rest of the world were put in the other, Umar's side would be the heavier!' He further goes on to state that 'if knowledge were divided into ten parts, Umar would have nine of these, and even in the tenth Umar would have his share!' **How**

---

[113] 'Kanzul Ummal' – Vol 4, Pg 230.

could such exaggerated opinions be expressed, leave alone written and propagated, when these <u>very same</u> statements were made by the holy Prophet ﷺ in praise of Ali ؑ's unlimited knowledge! There is absolutely no room for justification of any such utterances by Suyuti, when he himself has acknowledged that Ali ؑ often corrected the mistakes committed by Umar; and further more, in light of the Quranic verse of *Surah Raad* (13:43) where Allah ﷻ says that *Ali ؑ was the one who possessed the '***Knowledge of the entire book***'* and that, along with Allah ﷻ, *he* was a witness to the Prophethood of Muhammad ﷺ! Moreover, in *Surah Zumar* (39:9) the holy Quran clearly announces that there is "*no comparison between those who possess knowledge and those that are ignorant*"! Yet again, in *Surah Yunus* (10:35) it is again reiterated that the "*one who guides to the Truth is worthier to be followed than the one who needs to be guided*"!

BRIEF ACCOUNT OF THE OTHER IMMACULATE IMAMS OF THE HOLY AHLUL BAIT ؑ

11.10: Second Imam: Hasan ibn Ali al-Mujtaba ؑ

Imam Hasan ؑ was the eldest son of Imam Ali ؑ and Lady Fatima Zahra ؑ, the daughter of the holy Prophet ﷺ. His birth occurred on 15th Ramzan 3 AH. His distinctive quality has been shown as being born after only six months of pregnancy. He was named Hasan. His other titles are Syed, Tayyab, Taqi, Zaki and Mujtaba. By the order of the Almighty and considering the Quranic verse (3:61) he, along with his brother Imam Husayn ؑ, came to be known as the 'Sons of the holy Apostle ﷺ'. The name 'Hasan' was given to him by his grandfather the holy Apostle ﷺ according to Divine instruction from Allah ﷻ. This was on a parallel to the name of prophet Aaron ؑ's eldest son 'Shabbar' in the Ibrani language, which translates to 'Hasan' in Arabic.

In the books 'Musnad ibn Hanbal', 'Darqatni' and 'Nasikh ut-Tawarikh' it is recorded that when Imam Hasan was born Angel Gabriel descended with a Divine Injunction saying: *"O Apostle of Allah! Your relationship to Ali is like that of Aaron to Moses. Hence the names of his children will be in accordance with the names of Aaron's children, namely: his eldest son was Shabbar, his second was Shabbir and the youngest was Mubasshir".* In Arabic these names translate into 'Hasan, Husayn and Mohsin' – the three names given by the Prophet ﷺ to the sons of Ali and Fatima ﷺ. In 'Tabaqat ibne Saad' it is related on the authority of Imran Sulaiyman that 'Hasan and Husayn' are two heavenly names which were not in Arabic usage prior to the birth of these two children.

It is said that both Imam Hasan ﷺ and Imam Husayn ﷺ resembled their grandfather the holy Prophet ﷺ in their own ways, in that, Imam Hasan ﷺ's face and upper part of his body, while Imam Husayn ﷺ's lower portion of his face and body resembled the holy Apostle ﷺ respectively. Among the 'People of the Mantle and/or Blanket' (*Aal-e-Aba*) Imam Hasan ﷺ was ranked fourth and was amongst those included in the 'Verse of Purity' (*Ayat e Tatheer, 33:33*). According to this Quranic verdict he too was also 'Infallible'. He is not only an Immaculate Imam, but according to the well-known Prophetic tradition, he, and his brother Imam Husayn ﷺ are the "Leaders of the Youths of Paradise". A special distinction of these two Imams ﷺ is that **both their parents were Infallible** and this distinction is unique and exclusive to these two Imams alone.

After the martyrdom of Imam Ali ﷺ Imam Hasan ﷺ became the Caliph of the Muslims; but due to the constant intrigues of Muawiyah, he was soon forced to give up his temporal position after a mere six months. The conspiracies of the Umayyads, especially the machinations of Muawiyah and his son Yazid, to have him assassinated or removed continued incessantly to the extent that even his drinking water had to be stored in 'sealed' containers for fear of being contaminated with poison! Ironically however, he was eventually poisoned by this same means of adding poison to his drinking water and killed through the deception of one of his wives' Jodah bint Ashad who was bribed and bought over by Muawiyah with an advance payment of one hundred thousand Dirhams; along with a false promise that she would be wedded to his son Yazid after her husband Hasan ﷺ's death.

Imam Hasan ﷺ's clemency and tolerance (*Hilm*) was such that in spite of being certain of Jodah's heinous act and guilt, he willed his relatives that if he survived, he would deal with her as befits, but in the event that he does not survive, then she should not be accosted with any harassing questions; and no action should be taken against her, leaving the matter to the Will of Allah ﷻ!

He was martyred on the 28th day of the Islamic month of Safar in the year 50 AH. Being aware of the possibility of his life being curtailed early, he had made a Will asking to be buried by the side of his grandfather, the holy Prophet ﷺ. But realizing the prevailing conditions of those turbulent times, he made **a second Will** that if there were any objections to this request of his, he should alternately be laid to rest near the feet of his revered mother Fatima ﷺ in the Graveyard of Baqi.

His foresight about making an alternate Will proved to be prophetic. Its harsh reality unfolded when Imam Husayn ﷺ started to lead the funeral procession to bury his deceased brother in the precincts of the Prophet ﷺ's grave. Ayesha came out with a squad of archers raising severe objection; to the extent of ordering her men to rain down arrows on the coffin of Hasan, albeit he was none other than the Apostle ﷺ's own grandson! It is recorded that 70 arrows got embedded into his revered corpse! Faced with this kind of an antagonistic behaviour from a wife of his grandfather, Imam Husayn ﷺ was compelled to bury him in Baqi (as per the instructions of the alternate Will), by the feet of their noble mother Fatima Zahra 🕮.

Imam Hasan 🕮 was the embodiment of tolerance and forbearance and was well known for his generosity. His 'open house' was legendary and known far and wide for feeding the poor and needy, (or even the well fed) alike. He never ate any meal without having the needy and underprivileged persons also partaking of a meal at his house at the same time. In connection with his forbearance (*Hilm*) a well-known incident is recorded in countless number of books: of a slave once dropping the contents of an entire bowl of hot soup on the Imam 🕮's body and in contrition reciting a verse from the Quran: "*... those who control their anger....*" The Imam 🕮 instantly responded: "*I have subdued my anger....*" The slave went on to add: "*... and forgive...*" Imam 🕮 replied: "*I have forgiven.*" The slave further expanded upon the verse and rejoined: "*... Allah loves those who are kind to others*" and the Imam 🕮 displayed his unbounded kindness by saying: "*I have set you free*" and not only did he release the slave from bondage but also bestowed a pouch full of money as a gift for immediate use and expenses!

Many Sufi scholars are of the opinion that Imam Hasan 🕮, along with the other Eleven Immaculate Imams 🕮 from the progeny of the holy Prophet 🕮, were *cleansed from birth of all impurities* by Allah 🕮 Himself and are the **only** true Leaders and Imams of all Muslims of all times.

In this same vein, the Sufi scholar Abul Hasan Hajwari Data Gunj Baksh (*Murshad-e-Oola*) on pages 86-87 of his book 'Kashful Mahjoob' has included a letter written by the famous Sufi scholar Hasan-e-Basri which he had sent to Imam Hasan 🕮 to clarify a question on the complicated issue of 'Compulsion and Free Will' (*Jabr and Qadr*). Despite being a scholar (*Aalim*) of repute, by his own admission, he states that he does not possess even a small fraction of the knowledge of Imam Hasan ﷺ. Given below is part of that letter written by him:

"The Blessings of Allah ﷻ be on you, O Son of the Prophet ﷺ and the 'Light of his Eyes'. All of you from the *Bani Hashim* are like a 'Boat sailing in the deep seas of Knowledge'. Whoever gets on this boat will be saved and attain salvation in a manner like those who boarded the Ark of Noah. O revered Son of the Prophet! What is your verdict regarding the issue of '*Jabr and Qadr*' which is causing such commotion and controversy among us. The reason for my referring this to you is because you are the son of the Prophet and your knowledge is that which will never diminish or change, because it was given to you by the Almighty Lord Himself. **Your** Protector is Allah ﷻ Himself and by His Order and His Will **you** are the protector of His creatures". The letter goes on further in similar vein but for brevity we have curtailed it at this point, just so to depict the Sufi scholar's view and respect for Imam Hasan ﷺ and his high regard for his knowledge.

An incident is recorded by Data Ganj Baksh that one day an Arab came to Imam Hasan ﷺ and began to abuse him and his family. The Imam ﷺ rather than retaliating in kind, gave him a pouch of money realizing that he must be a stranger in town (who was unaware of his identity); and adding that this money would help him to fulfill his needs, while simultaneously offering his regrets at being unable to give him more, as this was all that he had with him at that moment. The Arab in that instant immediately changed his behaviour saying 'I bear witness that you are a true the Son of the Prophet and you have displayed the same qualities of forbearance and generosity as your noble Grandfather! I was only trying your patience (*Hilm*) and testing your magnanimity!"

Another tradition recorded on page 381 of his book is that a person arrived at Imam Hasan ﷺ's doorstep saying "O Son of the Prophet! I need 400 Dirhams". Imam ﷺ gave him the amount he

needed and re-entered his house with tears in his eyes. His slave
enquired the reason for his tears and the Imam ﷺ said that he was
regretful of the fact that he had not fulfilled the needs of a
disadvantaged person *prior to* him expressing his need!

Imam Hasan ﷺ and Imam Husayn ﷺ were known to have
performed countless pilgrimages (*Hajj and Umra*) on foot. On one
such journey while they were on foot, a caravan of pilgrims
travelling on their mounts met up with them; and out of respect
for their position as 'Sons of the Prophet ﷺ' they dismounted from
their rides and started the journey on foot with them. However,
after a short while itself, they found the going to be tough and slow
and hard on their feet; so they sent word through Saad ibn Abi
Waqqas, (a companion of the Prophet ﷺ who was also a part of
their caravan) that the two Imams ﷺ should also ride with them;
because, in their presence and out of respect for their position, the
rest of the caravan could not get astride their own mounts as long
as the two Imams chose to travel by foot. To this end they even
offered them two of their animals for use as their mounts, but the
Imams ﷺ declined saying they had taken a vow to accomplish the
pilgrimage on foot. However, to save the caravan from further
discomfort (and for the ease of their conscience), the two noble
Imams sent word that they themselves would change their course
and take an alternate route to reach the holy Kaaba, so that the
caravan could proceed on their mounts as per their own plans!

It was the normal habit of Imam Hasan ﷺ to distribute whatever
amount of money or items of value which got accumulated in his
house from time to time; with the result that his house was always
open for the poor and downtrodden to enter and take away
whatever they wished. In any event, the charity of the holy
household of the Prophet ﷺ and his progeny and especially that of
Imam Hasan ﷺ was legendary; and it is small wonder that he,

Imam Hasan 🕮 was referred to as the 'Kareem e Ahlul Bayt' even among the members within the holy household itself.

But despite being aware of all these merits, a majority of the general pubic remained indifferent towards the Ahlul Bayt 🕮 due to the confusion created by the false propaganda of the Umayyads, particularly that of Muawiyah in sparing no effort towards tarnishing the image of Ali 🕮 and his noble progeny. With such prevailing sentiments of the public in his mind, Imam Hasan after the martyrdom of Imam Ali 🕮, while accepting the fealty of the people for his Caliphate delivered a sermon, the introduction of which was as follows: "*All praise be to Allah Who has honoured us with the Caliphate. I have heard from my beloved Grandfather, the holy Prophet 🕮 that there will be 12 Imams from amongst us Ahlul Bayt to guide the Ummah. All of them will be martyred either by the sword or by poison!*" [This prediction came to be true over the course of the Islamic history].

When Muawiyah came to know that Imam Ali 🕮 had been martyred, he sent a contingent of 7000 soldiers under the command of Zahak ibn Qais to attack Iraq. This person appointed several spies all over Kufa and in other parts of Iraq to create disunity among the people, while also offering massive amounts of bribes to obtain their support for Muawiyah. According to several historians, notable chiefs such as Umer ibn Harees, Ashath bin Qais, Hajar ibn Hajar and Sheeth bin Rabia were approached individually to lure them into assassinating Imam Hasan 🕮 in whatever way possible.

The incentive offered by Muawiyah for this heinous act was Two Hundred Thousand Dirhams in cash, along with the command of an army contingent **plus** the 'hand of one of his own daughters in marriage'! The result of these intrigues of Muawiyah was such that the spirit of revolt became widespread, even to the extent of prevailing within the army of Imam Hasan 🕮 itself. This caused some of the rebellious soldiers from within his army to eventually attack the tent of Imam Hasan 🕊, robbing him of his possessions and bodily injuring him in the process. He was lifted on to a stretcher by some of his loyal soldiers and carried to Madayen where he was treated for his wounds. Simultaneously some of the Imam 🕊's commanders were conspiring secretly with Muawiyah on a regular basis, that if he were to make a full-fledged attack they would personally arrest and hand Hasan 🕊 over to him. The atmosphere of intrigue and confusion was such that even Abdullah ibn Abbas a close relative of Imam Hasan 🕊 was bought over by a bribe of one million Dirhams and switched his loyalty and moved over to Muawiyah's camp!

With such prevalent conditions, Muawiyah became confident of the lack of support for Imam Hasan 🕊 among within his own followers, and as such he wrote to him with impunity saying: 'Most of your commanders and trusted people are now under my sway. I suggest to you that there is still time for you to negotiate a treaty with me or else you know what the result will be.'

Such in brief, were the dire circumstances under which Imam Hasan 🕊 was left with little option other than to sign a peace treaty with Muawiyah.

Terms of the Peace Treaty

The terms of the Treaty are recorded by Tabari and other historians, and are as follows:

1. Muawiyah will govern in accordance with the Book of Allah and the traditions of the Prophet 🕊.
2. After the death of Muawiyah the Governance will revert to Imam Hasan 🕊 and then to his brother Imam Husayn 🕊.
3. The 'Shias' of Ali 🕊 will not be harmed or treated badly in Hejaz and Iraq.

4. An annual income of Fifty Thousand Dirhams will be sent to Imam Hasan ﷺ on a regular basis, along with the revenue from certain agricultural estates in Iraq to care for the families of Bani Hashim.

5. No harm will be inflicted on any member of the Ahlul Bayt ﷺ secretly or openly.

6. Ali ﷺ will not be abused or vilified after the ritual prayers or after the sermons given from the pulpits, as had become the normal practice under Muawiyah's rule. (Some historians contend that Muawiyah amended this last condition to read that the abuse would continue but not take place if Imam Hasan ﷺ or other of his close relatives were present!)

Ibne Atheer, Ibn Jauzi, ibn Abdul Birr and Abul Faraj-e-Isfehani and some others have written that while ratifying this Peace Treaty Muawiyah gathered a large crowd and requested Imam Hasan ﷺ to deliver a sermon. A part of it is given below:

"O People! From the first of our family Allah had provided you with Guidance, and now from the last one of our family He is trying to save you from bloodshed. We are the Ahlul Bayt from the Household of your Prophet; and Allah has kept us away from all uncleanliness and has purified us with a thorough purification as only He can do! We are the means of salvation for you and are the pure progeny of the holy Prophet. We are one of the two Weighty and precious Entities which the Prophet left among you: The Book of Allah and his own progeny. Allah has made it mandatory for you to obey us, for obeying us is like offering obedience to Allah! If you dispute with us, it is akin to disputing with Allah and His Prophet! Be aware that only he is the Caliph who follows and implements the Book of Allah and the traditions of the Prophet ﷺ. A Caliph is not the one who is unjust and commits atrocities and rules with his own whims. Such a person will enjoy his rule for a brief period and its intoxication will wear off, but the effects of his sins will linger on...."

In this short sermon Imam Hasan ☀ clearly demonstrated to the people as to **who was** the just Caliph and the real heir to the Prophet ☀ whose obedience and support was incumbent upon one and all. He also exposed Muawiyah as being nothing but a temporal ruler, unfit to fill the seat of Caliphate; but one who had obtained the authority to rule based on a few peace treaty conditions. Hasan ☀ did not pay allegiance to Muawiyah nor did he abdicate from his God given right of being the true heir of the holy Prophet ☀; and by doing so he also made it clear that there is a difference between "signing a treaty and paying one's allegiance".

On this same subject, Dr. Taha Husayn mentions the following in his book[114] that after the ratification of the Treaty with Muawiyah "Imam Hasan ☀ gathered a few lovers of the Ahlul Bayt and addressed them with these words: *'You remain attached to us and continue your love towards us. If I had wanted the pomp and glory of this world, I could have surpassed Muawiyah in my endeavours. But I look at things differently. I wished to avoid bloodshed and loss of innocent lives; and chose to be patient and rely on the Will of Allah. You should also resign yourselves to His Will. Remain in your houses and stay your hands so that the good ones among you will survive and attain peace and get deliverance from the evil ones.'"* Dr. Taha further infers on page 507 that Imam Hasan was waiting for a day when Allah ☀ would relieve the world of the nefarious presence of Muawiyah and the righteous people would again be able to accept the affairs in their own hands. He further states that Imam Hasan ☀ remained in his abode in Madina and was not afraid to express his opinion; and whenever he met up with Muawiyah or the antagonists of Ali ☀ in Mecca, he was

---

[114] 'Fitnatul Kubra' – Taha Husayn, Pg 505.

fearless in giving expression in the defense of his revered father Imam Ali 🕮.

Contrary to the terms of the cartel however, the ink had not yet dried on the Peace Treaty paper when Muawiyah ordered his governors and his army officers to slay all Shias of Imam Ali wherever they found them; destroy their houses and confiscate their properties at random. Nobody was allowed to recite any tradition in praise of Ali 🕮; and if there was one that was recited, then it was to be off set by inventing 10 traditions in praise of the first three Caliphs! But quite appallingly he did not stop at this, because the fire of enmity burnt in his heart to such an extent that he attempted to poison Imam Hasan 🕮 on at least six seperate occasions. He was finally successful in his last attempt which he achieved through manipulating one of the wives of Imam Hasan 🕮 called Jodha bint Ashath; in that, she was made to administer a devastating poison personally sent by Muawiyah which had a deleterious effect on the Imam's liver causing his death. She was paid a bribe of one hundred thousand Dirhams and given a false promise of eventually getting her married to his son Yazid which however, never materialized!

The various earlier attempts to poison the meals of Imam 🕮 had debilitated and ruined his health to such a state that he was forced to drink copious amounts of water to assuage his constant thirst. Knowing that the water was now being kept under a special sealed container next to his bed, Jodha as his wife successfully contrived to infuse the poison into his jug of water, leading to his painful death within a brief time thereafter. Hasan 🕮 expired on the 28th of Safar 50 AH at the early age of 47 years.

Muawiyah had established a communication network of spies from Madina to Damascus, so that he was continuously kept abreast of the happenings in Madina. When the news of Hasan 🕮's demise reached him, he fell into a prostration of thanks proclaiming 'Allahu Akbar' in a loud voice, causing people to inquire the reason for his exuberance. He was beside himself with pleasure and announced that Hasan ibn Ali had been assassinated! Various books such as 'Hayatul Haywan,' 'Usd ul Ghaba' and ibn Atheer among others record that Hasan 🕮 had nominated his brother as his successor and the Imam of the people after him.

11.11: Some Miracles of Imam Hasan al-Mujtaba 🕮

There are many verses in the holy Quran with reference to the holy Ahlul Bayt 🕮 which were discussed earlier in this book. Here it will suffice to mention a few of his miracles. The first which we list is one which has been mentioned in the book 'Shawahed-e-Nabuwah' by Mulla Jami, that one day in his childhood Imam Hasan 🕮 was returning back to his own home after visiting his Grandfather in the evening when the sky suddenly turned quite dark, but by the Grace of Allah 🕮 a light appeared miraculously brightening his path which accompanied him till he reached his home safely.

In the book 'Aalamal Wara' written by Abul Ali al Fazal bin Hasan al Basri there is a tradition related by Ibn Abbas that one day Lady Fatima Zahra 🕮 came to the Prophet 🕮 anxious and worried that her two sons Hasan 🕮 and Husayn 🕮 had been gone for a long time and had not returned home. The Apostle 🕮 prayed for their safe return and no sooner had he done so, Angel Gabriel appeared with the message that he should not be worried about their safety as both the children were in the vicinity of Bani Najjar; adding that they *"both were honourable in 'this world and in the Next' and their father transcended them both"*! When the Apostle 🕮 accompanied by Ibn Abbas went looking for them, they found them comfortably asleep with their arms around each other; with an Angel on each side providing them with a shade from the sun.

The Prophet ﷺ picked them up and brought them to their mother ﷺ.

Another incident from their childhood states that both these two grandsons of the holy Apostle once inscribed some texts on their slates and approached their respected mother asking her to judge as to who had the better handwriting. Not wishing to displease either of them she directed them to their honourable father so that he could be their judge. When they went to him, Ali ﷺ said that in the presence of the holy Prophet ﷺ he could not precede him in deciding the issue. He in turn asked them to go to their revered Grandfather to resolve this matter. The Prophet ﷺ also not wanting to take sides sent them back to his daughter Fatima ﷺ saying that as their mother, she was the best to decide between the two. Consequently, to show her fairness to both, she broke the string of beads from around her neck and scattered it on the ground saying that the one who picks up the greater number of beads would be judged as having the better handwriting over the other! As the children got engrossed in collecting the beads Allah ﷻ sent an Angel down with orders to ensure that **both** the children picked an **equal number** so that neither of them would be disappointed. Towards this end, as the necklace was comprised of an odd number, when both had collected an equal amount, the last bead was miraculously split into two halves by the Angel so that each of them ended up having **the same amount** of beads (or pearls) in hand!

Quoting a tradition from one of the 'Sahih' books, Abu Abdullah Naishapuri has mentioned in his book 'Amali' that one year during their childhood, Hasanain ﷺ on the night before the festival of *Eid* asked their revered mother as to whether they too would have new apparels for the *Eid*, in the same manner that most other children in the city of Madina seemed to be getting ready to don in the morning. Fatima ﷺ spent the night in a state of anguish because she and Ali 🕮 could not afford this minor luxury for their children, and she was perturbed at the thought of disappointing them on the day of *Eid Celebration.*

When the morning dawned and the children approached her about their clothes again, she, to pacify them said that the '*tailor would be delivering them*'. No sooner had she said this than a knock sounded on their door and a person appeared at the doorstep announcing that he was the tailor who had brought the clothes ordered for the two children! Fatima 🕮 surmising that it was her father the Prophet 🕮 who had sent the apparels, went over to thank him. But when he heard the whole story, he said: *"O Fatima! That was not any tailor but the Angel Rizwan from Heaven who had brought the pair of clothes for your two sons as a gift sent by Allah 🕮 Himself!"*

On another occasion, later in his lifetime when Imam Hasan 🕮 was travelling with ibn Zubair, they happened to break journey and lay down to rest under a dried-up palm tree. Ibn Zubair expressed a wish that it would have been nice if the tree bore fruit which they could have enjoyed. The Imam 🕮 asked whether he really wanted to eat some dates, and when he received a reply in the affirmative, he 🕮, raised his hands in prayer whereupon the tree revived to life and instantly got laden with fresh dates which they all partook of. Upon observing this a camel-herder in the vicinity who saw this happening said that he had witnessed a wonderful magic being performed, in response to which Ibn Zubair chided him saying that it was no magic, but a miracle performed through the prayers of the 'Son of the holy Apostle Muhammad'🕮!

It is recorded in various books such as 'Arjah Al Matalib' and 'Nurul Absaar' as well as in 'Hulyat-e-Awliya' by Hafiz Abu Naim Isfahani that after the death of Imam Hasan 🕮 a person went to his grave and began to abuse him. He immediately became insane and began to bark like a dog. It is said that even after he died and got buried the barking sound could be heard emanating from his grave.

11.12: Third Imam: Husayn ibn Ali al-Shaheed 🕮 - The Martyr of Kerbala

Imam Husayn 🕮 was the second son of Imam Ali 🕮 and Lady Fatima 🕮. He was born on the 3rd of Shabaan 4 AH and was named 'Husayn' by his grandfather the holy Prophet 🕮. His patronymic filial appellations were 'Aba Abdullah; Syed Tayyab; Zaki; Sibte Rashid; Al-Marzatallah and Shaheed-e-Akbar' to name only a few. There is a tradition recorded through Ibn Abbas in 'Marij un Nabuwah' as well on page 446 of a book by Allama Syed Kashafi Hanafi that when Imam Husayn 🕮 was born, thousands of Angels visited the house of Fatima 🕮 and after paying their homage to her, presented their felicitations to the Prophet 🕮.

He was martyred on the 10th of Muharram 61 AH on the plains of Kerbala; and according to the verse of the holy Quran that *"Martyrs never die"* he is acknowledge by one and all as being eternal and alive to the very end of time. He is a universally recognized and respected saint to whom people of all races and religions, despite their differences, are united in paying their adoration and loyalty. In the subcontinent of India many Hindus as well as Sunni Muslims maintain individual religious centres especially during the month of Muharram, to commemorate the Tragedy of Kerbala, by displaying the *Alams* (Banner or Flag) which are venerated as symbols of a firm stand by Imam Husayn 🕮 against tyranny and oppression.

Just as the concept of Allah 🕮 as well as the Prophet 🕮 and Ali 🕮 are beyond our human comprehension, in like manner, so are Imams Hasan 🕮 and Husayn 🕮 also in this same category of being 'larger than life' personalities, hence beyond our limited conception.

A tradition related by Buraida is recorded in books such as 'Sahih Tirmizi', 'Mishkat al Masabih, Sahih Nisai' and 'Sahih Sunan ibn Abi Dawood' that one day the Prophet ﷺ was delivering a sermon from the pulpit in Madina when his two grandsons Hasan ؓ and Husayn ؓ while still in their infant stage of childhood, entered the Masjid. He immediately abandoned his sermon, got down from the pulpit, picked them up and jointly seated them on each side of his lap. Later, when he was leading the congregational prayers and went into the position of prostration (*Sajda*), both children promptly climbed onto his back and shoulders. Rather than shake them off, he prolonged his prostration till such time as the children themselves slid off his back!

Similarly on countless other occasions he was known to indulge them in their innocent and childish activities in several diverse ways. For instance, while in a standing posture prior to starting his prayers or in conversation with others, these two children would come and cling to him or run between his legs and he would in fact accommodate their childish games by spreading his legs wide enough to give free run to their innocent playful behaviour. Not once was he ever known to chide or rebuke them. It is not out of place to mention here that these two grandsons were playfully all over him often during his prayers, as well as in his other activities **conducted in view of the public eye** and not restricted merely to his private life when he was within the confines of his own home! It was common knowledge that if he did not see them even for a short while, he would pine for them. He would always hug and kiss them; and many a time he would allow them to suck his thumb. He was known to repeatedly say: "*O! My Beloved Children! You are dearer to me than my own son Ibrahim, because his departure from my life was tolerable, but I could never bear the thought of your separation from me in my lifetime!*"

Giving credence to these sentiments expressed by the holy
Prophet ﷺ in the foregoing section, a tradition has been recorded
by several historians that when the Prophet ﷺ used to travel a
certain path in his daily routine, he would sometimes hear a child
crying from one of the houses. It is recorded that one day the
Prophet ﷺ stopped by that house and requested the mother to
ensure that the child does not cry when he ﷺ, was within earshot;
because he said the sound of her son's weeping was very similar to
that of Husayn ؏'s, adding further that: "... *It pains me a lot when
I hear him cry, as his voice is very similar to the voice of my Husayn
and the thought of Husayn crying is unbearable to me*".

All grandparents love their grandchildren; nevertheless, the
love of the Prophet ﷺ for this grandson was unique; in that,
Husayn ؏ was to become a pivotal figure in the continuation of
his own ideology. His well known tradition: "*Husayno Minni wa
Ana minal Husayn - Husayn is from me and I am from Husayn*"
lends credence to the fact that his Prophetic eye was referring to
the fact that Husayn ؏ would play a key part **in the preservation
and safeguarding of the tenets of Islam** which he ﷺ, as the final
Apostle of Allah ﷻ had brought down for all humanity to last till
the end of time.

There was no limit to the amount of love exhibited by the
Prophet ﷺ for his two grandsons Hasan ؏ and Husayn ؏; and he
also constantly tried to instill a similar kind of love and attachment
for them in others. The amount of love Ali ؏ as a father also had
for these two illustrious sons of his is unparalleled in the history
of mankind. He often used to tell his children from his other wives
that *they were his* progeny, while *these other two* sons born to Lady
Fatima Zahra ؏ were exclusively referred to [by all] as the "*Sons
of the holy Prophet ﷺ*"! The truth of this was borne out by the fact
that he, Ali ؏ later deputed his renowned and distinguished son
Abbas ؏ to represent him in the battle of Kerbala in order to help

Husayn ﷺ who in the capacity of being the 'Son of the Prophet' would stand up against the enemy forces that would come out in opposition to the tenets of Islam propagated by his Grandfather, the holy Apostle ﷺ.

Both Hasan ﷺ and Husayn ﷺ grew up in the same lap of the holy Apostle ﷺ in which **Islam itself** was nurtured. Hence their love for Islam was akin to the love of 'kinship' which one has for the 'next of kin;' and this is why we see that in their later lives, they both sacrificed everything that they possessed in order to safeguard the Mission of their Grandfather, and to keep it alive **at any cost** and to leave it as an excellent model for mankind right up unto the last generation of humanity on Earth.

The display of these acts of affection and love by the holy Prophet ﷺ for his two grandsons were mandated by injunctions in the Quran to clearly show the importance of these two young Imams in the Sight of Allah ﷻ; as well as to demonstrate their exalted position over the rest of the Ummah. Whenever these two siblings mounted on the back of their grandfather ﷺ while he was in prostration during the congregational prayers, Angel Gabriel would descend by Allah's decree, asking him to prolong his prostration and **to remain** in that position till such time as his grandsons dismounted from his back **of their own volition**! In addition, the Prophet ﷺ was also requested *not to take any action to deter the children from their playful ways* due to a concern that their innocent tactics were causing disruptions in the congregational prayers; or worrying about similar situations happening again in future. In other words, this again indicates that it was Allah ﷻ's wish that '**no action be taken that went against the Will of Hasan ﷺ and Husayn ﷺ,** and thus by ordering His Apostle to lengthen his prostration for as long as the two young Imams decided to remain atop his back, [irrespective of the fact that he was leading a congregational prayer with a number of followers behind him], Allah ﷻ clearly implies that abiding by the pleasure of Hasnain ؑ is also counted as being a part of performing Allah's worship!

And indeed, in truth, this was no "child's play"; rather, there was a far greater significance to these acts and a deeper meaning to this relationship than that of a mere family or filial connection.

Allah ﷻ had sent Angel Gabriel on more than one occasion to inform the Prophet ﷺ about the eventual martyrdom of both his grandsons; and specifically, about Imam Husayn ؑ - that he would be beheaded in a most gruesome manner, denied of food and water on the plains of Kerbala. Whenever the Prophet ﷺ received this sort of message, he would weep profusely and hold Husayn ؑ against his chest and would at times even ask him: "*My son! Allah has asked for a great sacrifice from you, are you prepared for this?*" Imam Husayn ؑ would always cheerfully reply that '*yes, he was ready for the test*' and would then go on to quote a relevant Quranic verse from *Surah As Saffat: "O My Father! Do what you are commanded, and Inshallah you will find me of the patient ones...."* (37: 102)[115]!

The martyrdom of Imam Husayn was not a matter of chance or coincidence; but rather it was an 'Event of such an intense and world-shaking Magnitude' that the Prophet ﷺ was consistently preparing Husayn ؑ from a very tender age to bear this supreme test. The fact that all the high-ranking prophets of earlier ages had also predicted this tragic event to their own followers in the past, sheds light on the gravity of this sacrifice which Allah ﷻ Himself has referred to in the Quran as *"Zibhun Azeem: the Supreme Sacrifice."* (37:107-108). This sacrifice of Husayn ؑ in the Way of

---

[115] Chapter 37:102 – As Saffat: "...O My Son, surely, I have seen in my dream that I shall sacrifice you. Consider then what you see. He said: 'O My Father! Do what you are commanded...'"

Allah ﷻ is a great treasure-house of a **'Divine Plan and Intent'** of the Almighty Lord which is beyond the grasp of ordinary humans. The moral and spiritual 'Treasures' contained within it will never end till the Day of Judgment. The more one hears and reads about this sacrifice the more one learns about its multifaceted unique aspects.

Every year during the annual gatherings that are held for the mourning of Imam Husayn ﷺ, one always returns appreciating some **new** precepts from the many **latent aspects concealed** within the 'folds' of this Great Event; and this will continue to be an ongoing process of learning for all Humanity till the end of time! By sacrificing his every single possession to save the religion of his Grandfather Muhammad-e-Mustafa ﷺ, Imam Husayn ﷺ saved it in such an exemplary manner that one can say that the *'Deen'* (religion) of Muhammad is now the *'Deen'* of Husayn ﷺ! In other words, Husayn ﷺ became the 'Saviour of Islam', and for this very reason the Prophet ﷺ had proclaimed: *"Husayn is from me, and I am from Husayn – Husayno Minni wa Ana minal Husayn!"*

The great Sufi saint of the Indian subcontinent Khwaja Ajmeri has composed a beautiful quatrain[116] in which he summarized that Husayn ﷺ is not just the 'Saviour' but in fact **he is** the very 'Foundation' of Islam:

The King is Husayn; The Emperor is Husayn!
Religion is Husayn: The Shelter of Religion (Islam) is Husayn.
He gave his head, but not his hand (in fealty) to Yazid.
*In truth, the Foundation of **'Kalemah: La Ilaha'** is Husayn!*

Along with Khwaja Ajmeri, the famous traditionalist Ibn Abi Shaiba pays homage to Husayn ﷺ in words which when translated

---

[116] "Shah ast Husayn; Badshah ast Husayn; Deen ast Husayn, Deen Panah ast Husayn. Sar daad na daad dast dar dast e Yazid; Haqqah ke bina-e-*La Ilaha ast* Husayn.

depict the venerated status of the Imam Husayn 🕮 as being a 'Proof' of Allah's existence' and 'A Great Sign' of the Almighty Lord! Similar sentiments were also expressed by the highly acclaimed Islamic scholar Ibn Arabi regarding Husayn 🕮. At this stage it is not our intention to discuss the details of the martyrdom of Husayn 🕮 or his lengthy journey to Kerbala, but rather only to reflect on the greatness of the sacrifice which had already been mentioned in the previous scriptures, as well as in the holy Quran. Husayn 🕮 himself used to mention at every stage of his journey to Kerbala that this was the "*Will of Allah which I am duty bound to fulfill.*" We shall reflect on a few of his famous sermons and some acts of his devotion which will reveal the aim of his sacrifice, as well as his own exalted personality. Only a few glimpses of his journey will be described to touch upon his thoughts and the nature of his mission:

It is mentioned in the books 'Fusool-e-Mohimma' and 'Kashaful Ghummah' that Imam Husayn 🕮 used to often express the following sentiments: "*Attach yourself to the Creator and have expectations from none other than Allah 🕮 because only then will you be needless of one who is honest or a dishonest liar. Sustenance is from Allah alone; anyone who relies on others for a livelihood displays a lack of trust in his Lord. And the one who thinks that others beside Allah are sufficient for him has indeed sunk into an abyss. One who has attached himself to Allah 🕮 has in fact detached himself from others. Even if people hurt you, do not bow down to anyone except Allah, who alone is your Provider and Protector. Ask no one other than Him for help. There is none in this world from the East to the West who can alter your destiny save the Almighty. If people come to you for help, consider this to be a blessing to you from Allah 🕮!*"

Regarding the people around him towards the latter part of his life he used to say: "*I am the only survivor from amongst the people I used to love. I am now alone among people who are not well disposed towards me. I do not wish evil for them, but they are the ones who talk badly behind my back. They constantly try to hurt me though I endeavour to help them to the best of my ability. They are aware of the conspiracies that are being devised around me, but they take no action to stop them. On the contrary, when the animosities tend to subside, they fan the flames to ignite the intrigues further. Is it not possible for them to use their good sense to suppress these underhanded plots? Do they not realize that this attitude will be injurious to them eventually? My Lord is sufficient to me, and I am in no need from others because it is unthinkable that Allah's help will not be with those who are being mistreated by others. Even if it can be assumed that this world is a good place, nonetheless the reward from Allah is much greater. Sustenance for everybody is predestined; hence abstain from greediness in this respect. While it is a certainty that accumulated wealth will be left behind when one dies, is it then not foolhardiness to be niggardly (and not be liberal) in giving this wealth in the cause of Allah ﷻ? When we know that death is inevitable, then martyrdom in the path of Allah should also be the best death to aspire for."*

The following is one of the supplications[117] (*Dua*) which Imam Husayn ؏ used to recite daily: *"Fuwazzo Amri Illallah.... O Lord! I have given the reins of my soul into Your Hands and I have dedicated myself to You. You are the sole Protector for me from everyone while nobody other than You can save me from Your wrath (or displeasure)".* Another of his daily invocations was: *"O Lord! All Good and all Blessings originate from You. The Destiny and Power belong to You alone. I seek shelter under Your Strength and Power in all things, and I adhere to the path that You have chosen for me. I hope to tread this path steadily according to Your wishes and hope to do only those things which meet with Your approval. I will not allow*

---

[117] 'Minhaj-ul-Dawaat; Pg 241.

any leeway for my own 'Nafs' (Soul, Ego, Self) to dictate my actions or to stray from Your Path. Nor will I allow any shortfalls in my endeavours in fulfilling my obligations towards You; and I shall walk steadfastly in the direction which You have chosen for me. Keep me under Your Support and do not deny me Your Grace. Do not deprive me of Your Help and do not separate me from the goal which You have determined for me. Lead me on that path so that I can accomplish that which has been destined for me by Your Will. Guide me in my desire to reach that goal for which you have created me."

The foregoing prayer clearly indicates the total determination and dedication of Imam Husayn ﷺ in striving towards achieving that paramount and supreme destiny for which he had been created. Every step which he took in his life was in conformity with achieving that aim in accordance with the Will of God, and for which he dedicated his entire life toward bringing about its manifestation.

Yet another invocation recorded from the holy Imam ﷺ is as follows: *"O Lord! You are my sole Protector and You are my only Support. Help me with Your Lofty Support, which is never tainted by any malice, self interest or fleeting worldly pleasures. Protect me in my times of trials. Save me from getting embroiled in calamities (Fitna) and protect me from being influenced by Satan, or any devilish insinuations and temptations from entering my heart; so that no malice enters my heart against others and let not others think wrongly about me."*

Another famous and very lengthy supplication shown by Imam Husayn ﷺ is known as his **'Dua-e-Arafah'** which reflects his lofty ideals and is usually recited up unto this day by pilgrims going on *Hajj* on the '*Day of Arafah*'. He used to recite this long supplication during the Greater Pilgrimage (*Hajj*) and starts off with the following famous statement: *"O Lord! What has he **gained** who **lost** you? And what has he **lost** who has **found** You?"*

In the last year of his life when he received the intelligence that plans were underfoot by Yazid to have him killed during the rites of *Hajj* by having his agents intermingle with the crowds in the garb of other pilgrims; Imam Husayn ﷺ abandoned his plans of the Greater Pilgrimage (*Hajj*) and changing it into the Lesser Pilgrimage (*Umra*), he departed from the Kaaba on the 8th of Zilhaj 60 AH towards Iraq. Thus started his fateful journey on a path which took him to his ultimate destination of martyrdom on the plains of Kerbala!

If one reflects on the life of Imam Husayn ﷺ it becomes imminently evident that he adhered to lofty principles and spent his life in abiding by the sublime prayers in their practical aspects and personification. When Muawiyah died in 60 AH at the age of 85, he installed his son Yazid as the Caliph. During this period Walid ibn Oqba ibn Abu Sufiyan was the governor of Madina. Yazid immediately upon ascending the 'throne' ordered Walid to obtain the featly of Abdullah ibn Umar, Abdullah ibn Zubair and Husayn ibn Ali ﷺ. In the case of Husayn ﷺ he added that should he, Husayn ﷺ refuse, he should be beheaded! Abdullah ibn Umar who had refused to pay allegiance to Imam Ali ﷺ, eventually did pay his fealty to Yazid albeit after certain 'issues' and 'considerations' were granted to him following several 'back and forth' negotiations. Abdullah ibn Zubair who had ambitions of becoming a Caliph himself, had no intention of paying allegiance, and repaired to Mecca where he took refuge.

Despite the lateness of the hour, Imam Husayn ﷺ was summoned by Walid to his Palace one night with urgent orders to comply. Husayn ﷺ went taking with him a few of the Hashemite youths; the most notable being his illustrious brother Hazrat Abbas ibn Ali ﷺ. However, upon arriving, he instructed his companions to remain at the outer door and to only enter if they heard him raise his voice. He then went in accompanied by the notorious

Marwan bin Hakam. Walid asked Husayn 🕮 to pay his allegiance to Yazid which he refused to do point blank. On hearing this reply from Husayn 🕮 Marwan told Walid that Husayn should be killed on the spot as he would not get a better opportunity to do so.

Upon hearing this comment from Marwan, Imam Husayn 🕮 responded in a raised voice: "*How dare you ask for my head?*" Upon hearing this the Hashemite youths, taking it as their signal immediately stormed through the closed door with their swords drawn. Walid and Marwan were now helpless to do anything and Imam Husayn 🕮 returned to his own home. However, he decided that with this new ever-present threat of being assassinated, his remaining in the city of Madina would be impossible from now onward. With a heavy heart, he started to make plans for abandoning the city of his Grandfather (Madina); constantly reciting the holy verse from the Quran which Hazrat Musa 🕮 had recited when he had left his hometown in the way of Allah 🕮: "*So he went forth therefrom, fearing, awaiting; and he said, 'My Lord deliver me from the unjust people.'* [Surah Qasas: 28:21].

He reached Mecca on a Thursday night on the 2nd of Shabaan 60 AH, where he camped at a site known as '*Sheib-e-Ali'*. Upon arriving here, he recited the next verse of the same 'Surah Qasas': "*And when he turned his face towards Madyan he said: 'Maybe my Lord will guide me in the Right Path'* [28:22]. Secure in the belief that 'theologically' it is forbidden for anyone to shed blood in the precincts of the holy Kaaba, Imam Husayn 🕮 resided in Mecca for three months in relative peace.

However, as the season for the pilgrimage of *Hajj* started approaching, he began to receive sacksful of letters sent to him from the people of Kufa urging him to assist them in throwing the yolk of Caliphate of a sinner like Yazid from off their shoulders and help free them from his persecution. They even went to extent of stating that if Imam Husayn 🕮 withheld his help from them they would hold him responsible for their troubles on the Day of Judgment! Yahya bin Hakam the Governor of Mecca had a lot of respect for Imam Husayn 🕮 and did not wish to harm him in any manner. When Yazid became aware of this lenient attitude of Yahya toward Husayn 🕮, he removed him from his office and installed Umer ibn Saeed ibn Aas as the new Governor of Mecca, with instructions that Husayn 🕮 was to be assassinated by his henchmen disguised as pilgrims, killing him during his performance of the *Hajj* rites. When this intelligence, confirmed beyond any doubt, reached Imam Husayn 🕮, he changed his intention of *Hajj* to that of *Umra*, and after performing its rites, he left Kaaba with his family and friends on the 8th of Zilhaj and proceeded towards Kufa. While leaving the city of Mecca he supplicated in the following manner which confirms that he was now aware of the fate and destiny which awaited him: *"Death clings to the neck of the son of Adam in the manner of a necklace strung around the neck of a young maiden. My desire to meet my ancestors is as intense as was the desire of Jacob 🕮 to meet his son Joseph 🕮.* **That** *place is preferable to me where I will meet my martyrdom. I can envisage the scene when those inhumane people will dismember my body and tear my limbs apart. There is no escape from what has been preordained; and the Day that has been destined for me. The desire of us Ahlul Bayt is in accordance with Allah's Will and we are patient in our trials and (content to) attain the rewards which He has kept for the 'patient ones.' The Prophet 🕮 cannot be separated from his body parts (members of his Ahlul Bayt). If our wishes coincide with the Will of Allah, then we will thank Allah and seek help from Him to fulfill His Will. When the Will of Allah coincides with the wishes of a person, then this is sufficient to demonstrate that he is striving in the Path of Allah."*

There were sixteen stages in the journey of Imam Husayn ﷺ from his start in Madina to Mecca and finally to his ultimate destination in Kerbala, Iraq. These were as follows:

1. Manzil-e-Safah
2. Manzil-e-Taigham
3. Manzil-e-Zaat-e-Iraq
4. Batan-ur Ramah wa Hajar
5. Manzil-e-Zurood
6. Manzil-e-Thalabiya
7. Manzil-e-Zabalah
8. Batan-e-Aqeeq
9. Manzil-e-Siratah
10. Manzil-e-Sharaaf
11. Manzil-e-Zujasm
12. Manzil-e-Baidah
13. Azeeb-ul-Hajanaat
14. Qasr-e-Bani Maqatil
15. Manzil-e-Nehnava
16. KERBALA.

At the sixth stage of his journey in *Al Thalabiya* Imam Husayn ﷺ learnt that his cousin and emissary Hazrat Muslim bin Aqeel ﷺ and his old friend Hazrat Hani ibne Urwah ﷺ had been brutally beheaded and their bodies been dragged through the streets of Kufa. Members of the Tribe of Bani Asad who were accompanying him, advised him not to proceed towards Kufa as he no longer had anyone left there in that city (Kufa) whom he could rely upon; and his own life now would be endangered. The Imam ﷺ recited the Quranic phrase: *"Inna Lillahey wa Inna Ileyhey Rajeoon – We are from Allah and to Him is our eventual return";* further adding: *"Allah has the final accounting of our true supporters. Those who claimed to be our supporters from the Ummah have now abandoned us. Muslim bin Aqeel and Hani ibne Urwah have been martyred. Whoever from amongst you wishes to turn and go back is free to do so; and will not be held accountable for their departure...."*

At the eighth stage of their halt at *Batan-e-Aqeeq* a traveller named Umer ibne Lauzan from the tribe of Akrama brought the news that the roads between Qadsiyah and Ghadeer had been closed by the orders of ibn Ziyad and soldiers had been placed everywhere. Apart from swords and armaments he said, there was **nothing** visible in those areas and he entreated the Imam ﷺ to turn back, pleading in the name of Allah ﷻ. Imam Husayn ﷺ thanked him for his kind sentiments but continued with his plans.

When he arrived at the eleventh stage of his journey at *Manzil-e-Zujasm*, he encountered a battalion from the army of Yazid lead by Hurr ibne Riyahi who stopped him from going towards Kufa, saying that he was under strict orders to keep Husayn ﷺ confined to a desolate place, and prevent him from going towards any inhabited cities where he would have access to food and water! He too pleaded with the Imam to have pity on himself and his family and return to Madina to save his own life. Imam ﷺ responded by asking: *"Are you trying to frighten me with death?"* Then turning to his companions, he addressed them saying: *"The world has rapidly changed its colours and honorable deeds have disappeared from its face. Life has become subservient to tyranny where poison is spreading all around. I regard death to be a blessing and hate to live among such unjust people even for a single day! Whoever stays with me will most surely die. I have withdrawn my pact of allegiance with you; and you are no longer bound by your oath of fealty to me. You are free to leave at any time to save your own lives."*

At this juncture we will record in brief a few of the responses given to Imam Husayn ﷺ from some of his faithful companions:

Zohair ibn Qain who had only recently joined the Imam ﷺ [as he had previously been aligned with the party of the third Caliph Uthman] was the first to speak saying: "O Son of the Prophet! We have heard your speech, but by God, even if we were to live forever in this world, we would still prefer to sacrifice our lives for your sake, choosing death with you in preference over this world!"

Then **Nafe ibn Hilal-e-Jamali** stood up and addressed the Imam ﷺ saying: "O Son of the Prophet! You understand even amongst the companions of your revered grandfather; there were hypocrites who would promise to render help but used to devise plans against him. They spoke sweet words but bore bitter malice in their hearts up to such time that the Apostle of Allah passed away from this sordid world. Then your noble father Ali ﷺ had to confront similar types of people, to the extent that he had to fight the *'Nakiseen, Qasiteen and the Mariqeen'* till he also achieved his martyrdom. Now, *we* are also being faced with a comparable situation. So, whoever among us breaks his promise will work toward his own loss. Allah will protect you from these kinds of people. Do not pay heed to this situation. Let us proceed ahead in the name of Allah ﷻ; be it to the East or to the West. We are neither against your decision, nor are we afraid of death. We are steadfast in our belief. We place our trust in Allah. We are friends of those who are your friends and an enemy of those who are your enemies!"

Burair ibn Khazeer Hamdani then stood up to say: "I swear by God, O Son of the Prophet, that it is the greatest mercy of Allah Almighty upon us that He gave us the opportunity to fight alongside with you, and that our limbs will get severed in assisting you; and that your revered Grandfather will be our intercessor on the Day of Judgment. He will grant us deliverance for this reason alone because salvation will never be for those who have slaughtered the grandson of the holy Apostle. They will never be able to face their Lord; and what a horrible fate awaits them when they will be thrown into the fire of Hell!"

At the thirteenth stage of *Azeeb-ul-Hajanaat* the Imam ﷺ was joined by Tarmah bin Adi who was accompanied by five others willing to join the caravan of Imam Husayn ﷺ. Their names are given as: Umer ibne Khalid Asadi; Saidawi and his slave Saad Majma bin Abdullah-e-Aaizi along with the son of his slave named Ayad bin Majma; and lastly Junada bin Harris-e-Sulaimani. Hurr objected to this saying that since these people are from Kufa, he could not allow them to join the Imam ﷺ's caravan and he would have to arrest them or send them back to Kufa. Husayn ﷺ however said that since they had reached him, they were now under his protection and were included among his friends and supporters; and he was duty bound to take care of them! These five persons informed Imam Husayn ﷺ of the prevailing conditions in Kufa saying that the important people in Kufa had all been paid hefty bribes and been silenced. 'Their hearts may be with you, but their swords are unsheathed in support of Bani Umayyah!' They also related news of the torturous death of Qais bin Mas-haar for his support of the Imam ﷺ. Upon hearing this Imam Husayn ﷺ quoted a verse from the Quran stating: "*There is one who has achieved his martyrdom while the other yet awaits! And neither of them has broken their pledge!*"

Tarmah bin Adi who had joined Imam Husayn ﷺ at the thirteenth stage suggested to the Imam that he take shelter in a safe-guarded fort known to him nearby which was well protected by a force of twenty thousand soldiers. Imam Husayn ﷺ thanked him for his kind offer of support but politely refused and continued to proceed on his journey. The fourteenth and fifteenth stages of his journey were also traversed, intercepted with minor incidents and eventually accomplished in similar arduous conditions. Upon finally reaching the 16th stage of their journey on the 2nd of Muharram 61 AH, a commander from the army of Hurr announced that Husayn ﷺ's caravan would not be allowed to advance any further. Additionally, they announced a prohibition to him from setting his camp anywhere close to the waterfront. Imam Husayn ﷺ enquired about the name of this location where they had halted; and upon being told that among some of its other names, one of it was "**KERBALA**" he dismounted saying: "*I seek protection from 'Kerb' and 'Bala'* [Trials and Tribulations]. *This is our destination.* **We have reached our Goal!"**

He then made inquiries as to who was the owner of this land. Upon being told that it belonged to the tribe of Bani Asad who were located some short distance away, he sent for their chiefs and leaders, and upon meeting them, he bought a section of land needed for his tents, along with some surrounding area, for 7,000 Dirhams. He then bequeathed the land back to the Bani Asads but *took a pledge from them that after his martyrdom, they would bury the bodies of the martyrs from his group of companions.* Then he turned to the womenfolk of the tribe and told them: "*In case your men do not perform this task out of fear of the 'Authorities' you should make them conscious of their sense of honour in fulfilling their promise*". He further added: "*Even after this, if they still could not or would not do so, then you should instruct and* **encourage your children** *to throw handfuls of sand on our dead during the course of their playful frolics, so that our bodies will get hidden from sight!"*

The purpose behind the purchase of the land was to ensure that eventually his burial would take place on a land which belonged to him and was not usurped or belonged to some others.

We can gauge the degree of Faith, Resolve and Determination of Imam Husayn ﷺ from the foregoing, that even in the face of certain death, being faced with a huge army of thirty thousand (or according some reports even up to a hundred thousand) soldiers of a blood thirsty enemy, he still proceeded with complete calm and trust in Allah ﷻ with a small band of 32 horseman and 40 foot soldiers; while in a similar situation of being faced with death, even

Jesus 🕮 in spite of being a prophet of high calibre, at the time of his crucifixion had lamented: *"Alia! Alia! O Lord, O Lord! Why have you forsaken me?"* [Bible]

Once the camps were set up at a fair distance from the waterfront, negotiations continued back and forth between the two sides to resolve the situation. On the 7th of Muharram however, the enemies decided to cut off the water supply to the tents of Husayn 🕮 in its entirety, resulting in further constant skirmishes which mostly proved unfruitful in delivering water to the camps over the protracted distance. On the night of the 9th of Muharram 61 AH the army of Yazid came forward with their battalions to attack the camp of Husayn 🕮. Imam 🕮 sent word through his brother Hazrat Abul Fazl Abbas 🕮 to the enemy army to grant them a respite for the night so that they may spend their (last) night in prayers to the Almighty Lord; to which the enemy agreed. As the night progressed and while they were each engaged in their acts of worship, it is reported that the sound of prayers emanating from their camp was like the deep "humming sound" of honeybees around their hive!

Shortly after daybreak on the 10th of Muharram 61 AH, the commander of the Yazidi forces Umar ibn Saad ibn Abi Waqqas shot the first arrow towards Imam Husayn 🕮's camp and proclaimed: "O People! Be witness that I have shot the first arrow at Husayn's army". As soon as this first arrow was dispatched, thousands of additional arrows were rained down upon the small band of Husayn 🕮's army. The Imam 🕮 calmly addressed his companions with the following words:

"Stand up to welcome the inevitable death which is certainly coming towards you! May Allah shower His blessings upon you. These are not mere arrows but a message of death being sent by the enemies towards you!" He then recited a small prayer out aloud: *"O Lord! You are my Shelter in my Adversity, and my Hope in all my Travails.*

I rely only on You in this great Calamity that awaits me now! How many are the tragedies that disheartened humans and how many are the hearts that are set to tremble when they find no succour. How many are the catastrophes that close all avenues and life appears to be bleak and stark. Friends abandon you and enemies taunt you. I turn solely to you because I know no other recourse. It is only You Who removes the adversities and compensates evil with good. Surely You are the Owner of all good, and the Origin of all Favours and the Best Guide towards the Ultimate Destination."

After this he mounted a camel and holding the Quran in his hands, he proceeded to the enemy's army and addressed them as follows:

"O group of People! Do not rush towards destruction! I wish to give you some advice which will be of benefit to you in both this world and in the Hereafter......." He then continued his sermon along the same lines, in which *he first introduced his own connection to the holy Apostle Muhammad Mustafa ﷺ, and further warned them that they were going on a path of perdition due to their misguidance and advised them to change their path even at this late stage.* All this however, fell on deaf ears and the enemy nonetheless commenced their attack as planned; and the battle began to rage in earnest.

By the midday prayers 40 of Imam Husayn's 72 companions had already achieved their martyrdom! At that time, he requested a short spell of halt in the battle so that the Noon prayers could be performed. This request was denied, with one Haseen bin Tameem from Yazid's army daring to taunt the Imam ؏ saying: "O Husayn! Your prayers will not be acceptable anyway, so why bother stopping [?]; and they continued to shower arrows on the remaining companions of Husayn ؏ even as they prepared to stand up for their midday prayer!

The prayers began on Imam Husayn ؏'s side with his two faithful companions Zohair ibn Qain and Saeed ibn Abdullah standing in front of those performing the prayers and taking any and all arrows coming in their army's direction from the enemy upon themselves; to such a point that as soon as the prayers were completed, Saeed ibn Abdullah fell to the ground from the excessive wounds from those arrows and achieved his martyrdom.

After the midday prayers, the remaining companions in Imam Husayn ﷺ's camp went into battle on an individual basis, attacking the enemy hoards until, by the time of the *'ASR'* [late afternoon] prayer, almost all of them were martyred brutally: sons, brothers, nephews, friends and helpers; including his six-month-old infant son Ali Asghar ﷺ! Imam Husayn ﷺ was now alone and the **sole** survivor among the 'able-bodied' men in his camp albeit himself completely exhausted and wounded, not to mention being denied of food and water for three days! The enemy anticipating that the end was now imminent moved forward, intent on attacking the tents in his camp; but Imam Husayn ﷺ called out in a raised voice saying: "*O Enemies of God! I am still alive! Attack me if you must, and refrain from going toward the women and children or plundering their tents!*"

At that moment, the raised voices of children from Husayn ﷺ's camp could be heard clearly, yearning, and crying out for a drop of water. Taking leave from his family, in a final courageous attempt Imam Husayn ﷺ now entered the battleground with his unsheathed sword *'Zulfiqar'* in hand; and single handedly mounted several daring attacks deep into the enemy ranks. Fighting like a champion warrior and according to the documented reports, "scattering the enemy soldiers like thistle-seeds being blown about in the wind"! But even at the height of his battle when the enemy soldiers were running helter-skelter seeking protection and pleading for mercy from him shouting: *'Al Amaan! Al Amaan (Protection, Protection!) Ya Husayn'* Imam Husayn ﷺ looked up toward the sky and seeing that the time for the *'Asr'* prayer was departing, he put his sword back into its sheath and prepared to offer the last prayer of his life! Since by now his chest and body were riddled with arrows, he could not bring himself to bend into the position of a normal prostration; so, gathering the sand of Kerbala into a small mound to enable him to prostrate; he began his prayer. The accursed Shimr on orders from Umar ibn Saad realizing this to be an ideal moment, advanced with his poisoned sword in hand and severed the head of Imam Husayn 🕮 while he was absorbed in deep communion with his Lord![118] Immediately after the beheading, his noble head was mounted on top of a lance and displayed to the enemy forces as a sign of their triumph. But even as the drumbeats of their victory began to sound all around, the very sky and earth resounded with loud sounds of wailing. Dark clouds gathered all around obliterating the view; and intense winds gushed around bemoaning the brutal killing of the Grandson of the most beloved Prophet of Allah 🕮! However, the enemies of Allah remained immune to these signs of 'wrath' from the Lord and continued to rejoice and went on a bout of pillage and destruction of the tents of Imam Husayn 🕮, subjecting his family members [now comprising mostly of women and children], to untold brutalities and torture.

11.13: Some Miracles of Imam Husayn 🕮

There are a great many miracles attributed to Imam Husayn 🕮, but for the sake of brevity we will recount just a few of them. The very first miracle to be recorded was at the time of his holy birth on the 3rd of Shabaan 4 AH and is listed as follows:

1. It is mentioned in 'Rauza-tus Shohada' by Mulla Husayn Wayez Kashafi that an angel by the name of 'Fitrus' had lost his

---

[118] *"O Lord! What has he lost who has found You? And what has he gained who has lost YOU?"*

ability to fly due to his having incurred the displeasure of Allah ﷻ; because of which his wings had been singed, and he had been cast in an isolated valley where he remained for a lengthy period of time. Upon hearing from Angel Gabriel about the birth of Imam Husayn ﷺ, he requested to be taken with him so he could offer his felicitations to the Prophet ﷺ on the birth of his second grandson. When he arrived in his presence with Angel Gabriel, after offering his salutations Fitrus apprised the holy Apostle of the infirmity which was descended upon him due to the wrath of Allah ﷻ; and pleaded for his intervention in granting him pardon and the restoration of his wings on this happy occasion. The Prophet ﷺ ordered him to rub his body against the feet of Husayn ﷺ (some say cradle) as an expression of his contriteness and implore for Allah ﷻ's Mercy in the name of this newborn infant. Immediately upon doing so, as a gift of this auspicious birth, his ability to fly was restored and he triumphantly flew away proclaiming phrases in praise of Imam Husayn ﷺ. It is said that Fitrus now, along with 70,000 other angels has been appointed to stand guard on the mausoleum of Imam Husayn ﷺ till the Day of Judgment.

2. In one of his other books 'Aknazul Gharayeb' Mulla Husayn Wayez Kashafi records another incident from the childhood of Hasnain ﷺ that one day a hunter presented a baby deer to the holy Prophet ﷺ while his elder grandson Imam Hasan ﷺ was seated with him. The Prophet ﷺ accepted the gift and gave it to Hasan ﷺ as a pet. When Imam Hasan ﷺ went home with the baby deer, Imam Husayn ﷺ asked as to how he got it? He replied that their grandfather had given it to him. Imam Husayn ﷺ ran out to the Masjid and being at the point of bursting into tears he asked: "*O Grandfather! Where is my baby deer?*" Simultaneously at that very moment a commotion was heard in the Masjid as a female deer entered with a fawn in tow. Unafraid of the human congregation she approached the holy Prophet ﷺ and after offering her

salutations, she said that one of her two baby fawns had been trapped by a hunter while she was feeding the other. But even as she was worried for her lost fawn, she added: "I was commanded to instantly rush with my other baby and present it to you **before a tear fell from your child Husayn ﷺ's eyes**"! So, saying, she offered her second baby to the holy Apostle ﷺ who in turn presented it to Imam Husayn ﷺ! Both children played happily with their pets for some time and then returned the two fawns back to their mother!

A third miracle which we have listed is one of the many that occurred after his martyrdom. When the severed head of Imam Husayn ﷺ was mounted on a lance by the enemies and taken around to various places; it was noticed by one and all that it was always heard to be reciting verses from the holy Quran. This was clearly witnessed and recorded in Kerbala, Kufa and Syria. Various books have recorded that there were visitations of the angels wherever his noble head was kept during the journey from Kufa to Damascus. Even to this day, there are numerous miracles that keep occurring in connection with the *'Alam'* [Standard or Banner] raised in the name of Imam Husayn ﷺ. Not only Muslims but also non-Muslims have derived benefits from these miracles. This is quite common and prevalent to this day in the Indian sub-continent.

11.14: Prediction by the Prophet ﷺ Regarding the Martyrdom of Imam Husayn ﷺ and the Manifestation of the Wrath of Allah ﷻ After This Tragic Event:

There is a tradition related by Ibn Abbas and recorded in various authoritative Islamic books[119] that he, Abdullah ibn Abbas saw the Prophet 🕮 in his dream in a condition that he had discarded his head turban, his hair was dishevelled, and his body was covered with dust. He had a bottle in his hand which contained some blood. Ibn Abbas enquired the reason for his distraught condition, and he said he was coming from that fateful spot in Kerbala where his grandson Imam Husayn 🕮 had just been martyred; and the bottle in his hand contained some blood spilled from his decapitation.

There is another similar tradition related by the Prophet 🕮's widow Hazrat Umme Salama recorded by Baihaqqi, Ahmed ibn Hanbal and Abu Naeem wherein she states that once the holy Prophet 🕮 awoke from his afternoon nap and came to her in a very disturbed condition. He had some grains of sand in his hand which were red in colour which he was turning over between the palms of his two hands and examining them minutely. When she asked about the significance of the sand which seemed to have caused him such consternation, the Apostle of Allah replied that Angel Gabriel had just paid him a visit and apprised him that his grandson Husayn will be martyred in Kerbala and said that this was a sample of the soil which he had brought from the spot where Husayn will meet his martyrdom in the Iraq.

Abu Dawood and Hakim have a similar tradition related from Umme Fazal bint Harrith and Dailami has a tradition related from Ammar ibne Yasser that the Prophet 🕮 used to say that the skies had wept over the martyrdom of John the Baptist [Yahya bin Zakariya] and they will also weep after the martyrdom of my son Husayn. The sky will turn red and remain in this condition for 40 days.

---

[119] 'Al Mustadrak' by Hakim; Vol IV, Pg 398; 'Musnad Ahmed ibn Hanbal' Vol I, Pg 242/43; 'Mishkaat' Vol 8 Pg 140.

Tirmizi records a tradition from a lady by the name of Muslima who went to visit Hazrat Umme Salama and found her to be crying excessively. Upon enquiring the reason, she said: "I just saw the Apostle of Allah ﷺ in my dream in a condition that his hair was dishevelled, his beard was drenched with his tears, and his clothes were covered with dust. I asked: O Apostle of Allah! What is this condition I see you in? And he replied: '*I had gone to Kerbala, and there I witnessed the martyrdom of my son Husayn!*'" This same tradition is recorded in two other books.[120]

Suyuti records some of the signs of Allah ﷻ's wrath which were manifested on the entire earth following the martyrdom of Imam Husayn ﷺ. He writes: "After the martyrdom of Husayn ﷺ the environment turned black, and the world remained shrouded in darkness for seven days. The sunlight when reflected from the walls had an orange and saffron hue; and the stars were seen to be falling and tumbling down from the skies for several days and there was an excessive display of meteorite showers following this great tragedy! In the sanctified area of Jerusalem (*Bait ul Muqaddas*) whenever any stone was overturned, there appeared to be fresh blood underneath at its base. Indeed, it appeared as if the entire universe had been affected by this astounding natural phenomenon."

Ibne Asakir narrates from Minhal ibne Umer that he was present in Damascus and saw the head of Imam Husayn ﷺ mounted on a lance being paraded at the front of a procession. A person was walking ahead of him reciting the Chapter of '*Kahaf*' from the holy Quran. When he reached the verse relating to the sleeping companions of the Cave as being one of the astonishing signs of Allah ﷻ, his amazement knew no bounds when he heard the severed head of Imam Husayn ﷺ stating in a very clear and

---

[120] 'Mustadrak,' Vol IV, Pg 19; 'Mishkaat' Vol 8, Pg 139.

eloquent voice that "*his being beheaded and raised on the lance was a greater and more wonderous sign of Allah* ﷻ *as an admonishment for the people to ponder upon; more so, than the story of the Companions of the Cave!*"

Abu Naeem has written about another remarkably chilling and fright-instilling occurrence that took place on the way to Damascus while some of the perpetrators of Yazid's army were engrossed in drinking and merry-making when suddenly an invisible hand miraculously appeared holding a pen and wrote the following script on a wall in blood: "*Can those people who were responsible for the assassination of the Prophet's Grandson ever hope for salvation at his hands on the Day of Judgment?*"

Countless books of history and tradition are replete with details about extraordinary events that occurred following the martyrdom of Imam Husayn ﷺ; and are filled with predictions about the dire consequences which would engulf his killers both in this world and in the Hereafter. In 'Sawahiq-e-Mohriqa', 'Hayatul Haiwan', 'Rauzatul Ahbab' and Thalabi have all recorded that Yazid, Khooli, ibn Ziyad, Umar ibn Saad, Shimr and other key perpetrators survived only a short while after the Battle of Kerbala; and all of them met with a drastic and woeful end. The other participants who had been under the command of these figures were embroiled in afflictions of various kinds of debilitating diseases such as leprosy, leukoderma, madness and mental degradation and many other horrible ailments; and their dreams of acquiring wealth and estates promised to them by their superiors in this world came to naught and were never fulfilled!

11.15: Mourning for Husayn ﷺ AND the 'Mourners': Both are a Sign from Allah ﷻ

My late uncle Ali Basheer Saheb who authored several books on Islam, believed that the *ritual of mourning* for Imam Husayn ﷺ in every generation for over hundreds of years is no less than a 'Sign' of Allah ﷻ (*Shayer Allah*). In his book 'Hayaat-us-Sayyedus Shohada' he has put forth the following viewpoint:

"The ritual of mourning for Husayn ؏ generation after generation most certainly is one of the 'Signs of Allah ﷻ'. It is incumbent upon us to perpetuate this ritual in every generation so that the supreme principles of Islam such as *'Tawheed'* [Unity of Allah ﷻ], *'Risalat'* [Prophethood], *'Imamat'* [Leadership of the people], Truth and Morals, Virtue and Honesty, Patience and Perseverance, Principle and Steadfastness, Obedience to Allah ﷻ and Acceptance of His Will, Forbearance and Sympathy; Reward and Punishment, Contentment and 'Bravery in the face of Trials', and several other higher upright qualities are inculcated not only in the Muslim Ummah but also among Humanity at large. These exemplary qualities that were displayed by Husayn ؏ and his companions are all recounted in the annual ritual gatherings of 'Mourning' and lead us to a better understanding of the Divine purpose of our own creation by Allah ﷻ; and form a universal message for all mankind.

The criticisms and objections of those who are against these rituals are due to their lack of understanding of the higher principles behind this great tragedy; due to their being devoid of the true knowledge behind this; and their own lack of 'depth of observation'. In blindly objecting to these rituals, they display a complete ignorance of the historical, religious, political, and moral aspects of true Islam which are depicted in this supreme sacrifice. Those who believe that the 'Message of Islam is Eternal' should also know that the ritual of mourning has always been associated with Islam. It is neither a Jewish tradition nor an 'Innovation' (*Bidat*) by the Muslims. This practice has been in Islam from the very beginning of time; whereas an innovation (*Bidat*) is something that was or is, introduced into Islamic practices by later generations.

The earlier prophets of Islam also adhered to this principle and were aware of the importance of mourning because their fundamental beliefs were also based on this same Divine philosophy. Even our own Prophet ﷺ when first apprised of this tragedy of Kerbala by Angel Gabriel ﷺ, wept profusely; as also did Ali ﷺ, Fatima ﷺ and Hasnain ﷺ; even though the actual tragedy of Kerbala had not yet transpired!

Hence for those who claim to be following the *Sunnah* of the Prophet ﷺ it becomes incumbent upon them to observe this tradition and commemorate this tragedy, more so now, when we have become aware of all its gory details. Human nature is such that we are always affected by any tragic incident; and in so long as we are expressing our grief and sympathy for this tragedy in whatever way or form, we are following the tradition of the previous prophets. Regardless of who observes this ritual or does otherwise, the fact is that Allah ﷻ has *etched this tragedy with His Divine Pen on the Pages of Time!* It is now beyond human capacity not to be affected by this tragedy.

Since the love of these holy personalities has been made mandatory by Allah ﷻ on all Muslims (Quran; 42:23)[121] and loving them has been ordained as "True Belief" (*Eman*), then those who love them will be affected by their tragedy. Those who do not love them but only pay lip service and verbally express their attachment and are not affected by their tribulations and calamities are manifesting a grudge in their hearts against these noble personalities. Lest we become sceptical about their stance, that 'to bear a grudge against these personalities is not possible', we

---

[121] "*Say, I do not ask of you any reward for it, but love for my near relatives...*" Holy Quran, 42:23.

maintain that it is **not only possible but is an actual fact**; for, the holy Prophet ﷺ being aware from his prophetic knowledge that these sort of persons would sprout within his Ummah, announced ahead of time in the well known tradition that: "*he loves those who love these personalities and will be an enemy of those who are inimical toward them'*.

All tragedies no matter how severe or heart rending, are forgotten with the passage of time. But this Tragedy is eternal, and its effect will never change, just as Allah ﷻ has stated in the Quran: '*There is no change in the Sunnah of Allah'* (48:23). In support of this there is also a tradition from Allah ﷻ in the scripts referred to as '*Hadith e Qudsi'*[122] wherein Allah ﷻ states that: '*He will create a nation who will mourn for Husayn in every Era and every Age; and they will expend their resources in their ongoing generations to perpetuate this tradition.'*"

Recognizing the truth of the foregoing 'adherence to the special status of Kerbala' by those who are truly attached to the family of the holy Prophet ﷺ, a Sunni scholar Dr. Sir Sultan Ahmed while presiding in a conference held on 15th April 1940 had this to say in his opening address: **"The Tragedy of Kerbala is an integral part of the Shia faith which colours and governs all aspects of their lives. For someone to try and interfere in this belief is akin to robbing them of their dearest treasure, for which, to safeguard and protect, they are even willing to sacrifice their own lives...!"**

---

[122] "Hadith e Qudsi": Traditions and narrations from Allah ﷻ to the holy Prophet ﷺ which are in addition to the Quranic revelations and do not form part of the holy Quran.

11.16: The 'Alam' (Insignia) of Imam Husayn ☝

The *'Alam'* [Banner or Insignia] of Imam Husayn ☝ is a replica of the banner used by his grandfather the holy Prophet ☝ in various defensive battles of Islam during his lifetime. He invariably gave this banner to Ali ☝ and occasionally to others such as Ja'far-e-Tayyar ☝ and others of similar calibre. In Kerbala, Imam Husayn ☝ elected to give this to his brother Abbas ibn Ali ☝ and appointed him as his official Standard Bearer. To this day the followers of Husayn ☝ install an *'Alam'* in their places of gatherings held for mourning the Tragedy of Kerbala. It is also their belief that on the Day of Judgment there will also be a Banner known as *'Liwaa-ul-Hamd'* which will be accorded to Ali al-Murtaza ibne Abi Talib ☝ by the holy Prophet ☝ on the orders of Allah ☝; and those who are gathered under this *'Alam'* or banner will be the ones to have achieved salvation. All prophets and saints will also be under the shadow of this same banner.

From times immemorial to the present day, all countries have a banner or a flag which represents their nation or country, and due respect is accorded to it. Showing profound respect to it is a mark of an individual's allegiance to his country. Even in the sports arena like in the Olympics and other International Games, countries carry their own flags, and due deference is given to this insignia by all. No self-respecting nation objects to this practice, even to the extent of crying under this banner as a display of their attachment to their nationalities.

Similarly, the *'Alams'* installed in the present day in the name of Imam Husayn ☝ and his martyred companions *are* in effect, an ongoing reminder of the banners that were upheld by Imam Ali ☝ and the Prophet ☝ in perpetuating Islam. As such, offering respect to these 'Alams' is just a manifestation of the attachment to a *'Sign of Allah'* and it is NOT any form of Idol worship; but rather, a demonstration of respect to the memory of those past bold-spirited, valorous luminaries, and the events and incidents which they were embroiled in; and which are considered to be 'Milestones' in the establishment of Islam.

To commemorate any important event is quite normal and part of human nature. In fact, in certain important cases it is even mandated by Allah ﷻ Himself. For instance, to commemorate the sacrifice of Hazrat Ismail ﷺ certain rituals have been included and prescribed as being mandatory during the performance of *Hajj* (pilgrimage). Not only were the actions of the two prophets Abraham ﷺ and Ismail ﷺ decreed as being among the 'Signs of Allah' (*Shayir Allah*), but also the action of Hazrat Hajera ﷺ the wife [*as well as a mother*] of a prophet running back and forth between the two hillocks of Safa and Marwa in search of water for her infant son, were also mandated as a necessary ritual for the Muslims for the acceptance and completion of their own *Hajj* rituals (Quran; 22:32-36). The animals purchased for the sacrifice, *along with the ropes that are tied around their necks* are also all regarded as being *'Signs of Allah* ﷻ*'* (5:2). The one who respects these signs as being in line with the decree of Allah ﷻ inculcates within himself a spiritual cognition worthy of achieving a state of piety known as '*Taqwa*' for the sake of Allah ﷻ in his heart. Hence, the respect accorded to the '*Alam*' is not an innovation (*Bidat*) but a tradition that is being followed as a continuation of a practice ordered by Allah ﷻ and observed by His Apostle ﷺ.

Here we will note an opinion expressed by a renowned Hindu thinker and writer by the name of Girdhari Lal Anand Kashmiri who states the following about the survival of the Shia faith because of their adherence to the *'Azadari'* (mourning) of Imam Husayn ﷺ:

"It is a sign that a nation which commemorates its Heroes who sacrificed their lives, is one that will remain alive and vibrant in opposing Evil. This is what Husayn did in the battlefield of Kerbala by drawing a line between Good and Evil. That nation which forgets the sacrifices of its heroes and hurtles along, is in fact, displaying its moral bankruptcy. It is a pity that many people in various Muslim countries have chosen to ignore these great sacrifices and refrained from expressing their own feelings because of fear of repercussions from their governments. These people in due time will forget the heroic sacrifices that had been given in the past for preserving the Message of Truth over Falsehood and the lofty ideals associated with their sacrifices."

11.17: Justification for the Rituals of Mourning for Imam Husayn ﷺ

Some people object to the mourning for Imam Husayn ﷺ. In this connection we shall quote some reliable traditions, as well as the views of the scholars from the Sufi School of Thought (Aka: *Ahle Tariqat*). To weep over a tragedy is a natural phenomenon. The earlier prophets are also recorded as having wept over different calamities or tragedies inflicted upon them, right from Adam ﷺ, Noah ﷺ, Job (Ayyub) ﷺ, Jacob (Yaqoob) ﷺ and Joseph (Yousuf) ﷺ. Instances associated with the mourning of these prophets over what befell them are frequently recorded in the holy Quran; for example, in: *Surah Najm*: (53:43); *Surah Isra*: (17:109); *Surah Marium*: (19:59); *Surah Dukhan*: (44:29) and *Surah Yousuf*: (12:84) to mention only a few. In cases of severe calamities which befall the saints or pious servants of Allah ﷻ, the very elements of nature like the sky and the earth, and seas and the wind etc., all weep over their misfortunes by His command. Several reliable and creditable historians and authors have recorded that after the martyrdom of Imam Husayn ﷺ fresh blood rained from the sky and dripped from the tree leaves; and collected in small puddles on the ground, to the extent that whenever any stone was turned over, it revealed fresh blood underneath! [A similar phenomenon had occurred after the martyrdom of Imam Ali ﷺ].

When Husayn ﷺ was barely four months old the Prophet ﷺ had wept upon being informed by Angel Gabriel ﷺ of the impending 'Shahadat' (martyrdom) of Imam Husayn ﷺ which would happen many years later the plains of Kerbala! After the Battle of Ohad not only did he, ﷺ and his companions weep over the martyrdom of his Uncle Hazrat Hamza ﷺ, but he also requested the women from various tribes of Madina to mourn over him; and when they complied, he blessed them for their actions. He himself personally eulogised and recounted the goodness and piety of his Uncle Hamza ﷺ making the others cry over his loss in death.

Ibn Abdul Birr in 'Istiyaab' narrates from Hazrat Jabir ibn Abdullah Ansari and Allama ibn Abil Hadid has also reproduced the same from Waqidi, that when Hazrat Safiya the sister of Hamza ﷺ used to weep for her brother, the Prophet ﷺ would join her in her mourning. In addition to this, several acknowledged books like 'Sahih Bukhari' and others[123] record that not only did the Apostle of Allah ﷺ mourn over Hamza ﷺ's death but also did likewise on the news of the martyrdom of Hazrat Ja'far-e-Tayyar ﷺ and Hazrat Zaid ibn Harith.

To counter the argument of some people who believe that it is improper to grieve over a martyr who has achieved eternal life by his martyrdom, [while on the contrary they add that it should be regarded as an occasion for *celebration* for having gained the pleasure of the Lord]; the actions of the Prophet ﷺ related in the foregoing clearly mandate that *mourning **must be** observed for the martyrs.*

---

[123] Ibn Saad in 'Tabaqat'; Abu Dawood and Hakim from Umm Fazl bint e Harith; Baihaqqi in his 'Dalayel' from ibn Abbas; Sahih Bukhari in his 'Kitabul Janayaz', Pg 3.

As previously mentioned, generations of Sufis and 'Ahle Tariqat' in the Indian subcontinent have been commemorating the martyrdom of Imam Husayn ﷺ from time immemorial by abstaining from any other kind of festivity or celebration during the first ten days (*Ashra*) of Muharram; and hold gatherings for mourning over the martyrdom of Imam Husayn ﷺ and his companions. There is an established belief among them that one of their very pious persons, a noted Sufi saint once saw a dream two days before the 10th of Muharram in which he saw the *Lady of Light* Fatima Zahra ﷺ along with the wives of some previous prophets, sweeping the ground in a certain depression in the land of Kerbala, while tears were flowing profusely from her eyes which she kept wiping with the corner of her cloak. In his dream this saint asked her the reason for her tears and agony; and she replied: "*This is the spot where my son Husayn will be martyred in two days time!*" This narration is recorded in more than one book of their traditions.[124]

Dr. Zakir Hussain the past President of India, had written in a paper[125] published some time ago that: "Humanity when it deviates from the True Path is pulled back into the right fold when it gets exposed to, and reflects upon, the finer points of the supreme sacrifice of Husayn ﷺ at Kerbala." Countless other references [numbering over 80] from scholars of various schools of thoughts supporting the concept of mourning for Imam Husayn ﷺ and its spiritual beneficial effects upon humanity at large, are listed on pages 886 - 888 in the original Urdu version of '*Kalematul Haqq*' for those who are interested in checking this out further.

It is ironical however, that in spite of these numerous traditions upholding the ritual of mourning for Husayn ﷺ, there are people

---

[124] Khwaja Qutubuddin Bakhtiar Kaki: 'The Saint" – Pg 223/224; 'Tarikh e Ahmedi' by Sheik Ahmed Husayn.

[125] 'Husayn and Humanity'- Moharrum Edition 1382 AH.

to this day who claim to be from the posterity of the killers of Husayn ﷺ and his companions; and who actually hold gatherings on the eve of 'Ashoora' to celebrate the 'victory' of Yazid and even claim to have the very dagger that was used by Shimr to severe the head of the Imam ﷺ while he was prostrated in prayer to his Lord!

On the other hand, there are several Sunni households who have a genuine attachment to the Prophet ﷺ's family and who subscribe to an entirely opposite view. For instance, Maulana Sibghath Ullah Shaheed Ansari so writes in his thesis titled 'The Ugly Scar on the Face of Islam' published in 1383 AH:

"By God! Tell me in all honesty that is it not an utter shame that those who benefitted from the lofty ideals of the Prophet ﷺ and his family would resort to such a heinous crime? Was Husayn not propagating the Message of Peace and Harmony, and 'Forbidding the Evil' and 'Advancing the Good'; and was he not a True Representative of his grandfather's religion? I regard the commemoration of this major event as a *tonic to revive the sick body of Islam,* and I consider this heinous crime as an admission of the guilt by the entire Muslim Ummah! I am convinced that the great position attained by the noble sacrifice of Imam Husayn will remain alive forever; and that there will be countless persons having a live conscience, who will be proud to be associated with this remembrance of the Tragedy of Kerbala."

Allama Shahabuddin ibn Hajar-e-Makki who was the chief 'Mufti' of Mecca and the author of the famous book 'Sawaiq-e-Mohriqa' has this advice for the people on page 110 of his book:

"Save yourselves from the Fire of Hell and take care that you do not adopt the pernicious habits of the 'Nasibis' who are against the Ahlul Bayt of the holy Prophet, lest you get destroyed in the Hereafter! Do not indulge in any sort of merry-making or celebration on the Day of 'Ashoora' taking this as a festive day of an 'Eid'! Do not wear new clothes or dress up or use any makeup or apply collyrium to your eyes. Be aware that giving up such practices in observance of the mourning for Husayn ﷺ is no less than following the Sunnah of the Apostle ﷺ himself!"

An eulogy written by Allama Sharfuddin Busairi in praise of the holy Ahlul Bayt ﷺ still forms a part of the curriculum of the Sunni Deobandi School in India under the title of 'Burdah Shareef' along with an elegy by him on the tragedy of Kerbala titled 'Hum Zia' wherein he emphasizes that one *should* weep on the Tragedy of Imam Husayn ﷺ for this, he says, is *incumbent* upon the Muslims because it is part of the Prophetic traditions. This mourning should not be restricted for the Day of '*Ashoora*' (the 10th Day of Muharram) alone, or only in the vicinity of the land of Kerbala, but it should become part and parcel of your natural habit in whichever part of the land you live in. He further goes on to add that this practice is not to be restricted for the '*Rafadis*' alone, but every Muslim rich or poor, should inculcate this habit and adopt this practice.

Numerous reputed Sunni scholars such as Sulayman Balkhi Qandoosi Nakshbandi [author of 'Yanabi al Muwaddah' Vol 2, which has a special chapter dedicated to the importance of 'Azadari' states on page 357]; Mulla Husayn Waiz Kashafi [author of 'Rauzataz Shohoda']; Sheik Suhail ibn Abdullah Tastari; Khwaja Bande Nawaz Gesu Daraz; Khwaja Hasan e Basri; Shah Abdul Haq Dehlawi; Baba Fareed Gunj Shakkar; Maulana Hafiz Shah Mohammed Faiq Hanafi; Wasti Hanafi Nizami; Ahmad Shaybani Qadsara *and* many others have high-lighted and emphasized upon the mourning for Husayn ﷺ and written about the great reward that awaits the mourners in the Hereafter; while some even express the view that those who do not cry for Husayn ﷺ carry a stone in place of their hearts! The followers of many of the above-mentioned saints and/or scholars to this day practice the observance of the mourning ceremonies including placing '*Tazias*' [facsimile of the tomb of Husayn ﷺ] around the tombs of these revered personages.

In connection with the ritual of self flagellation there are some who object to this practice. On this issue we wish to draw the attention of the reader to a parallel in the early Islamic period, with the behaviour of a noteworthy companion of the Prophet ﷺ by the name of **Owais e Qarani** RA.

At the time of the Battle of Ohad he was a young man 27 years old living in Yemen spiritually attached to the holy Prophet. When he got news that the Prophet ﷺ had lost some teeth during the battle of Ohad in Medina, he was so agitated by the thought of pain suffered by the holy Prophet ﷺ that in sympathy, he broke four of his own teeth!

Then upon reflection, it is recorded that since he did not know *which four of his teeth the Prophet ﷺ may have lost,* he broke *all his front teeth in empathy for the Apostle*! When the Prophet ﷺ heard about this behaviour of Hazrat Owais Qarani RA, *far from chastising him,* he ﷺ, **praised** the level of his attachment and 'love for his Prophet'! Hence if the lovers of Imam Husayn ﷺ in memory of the dismemberment of his body after his martyrdom; and its being trampled under the hooves of horses by the enemies, display their grief by beating their chests or flagellate themselves, it should not be taken as a reason for criticism or objection by any.

A Sunni friend of mine once remarked to me that non-Muslims find the Shia rituals of 'Matam' (beating of chest) and self flagellation to be a laughable matter; and hence it would be proper for the Shias to desist from such practices. It would be better for them to stay home and recite the Quran for the blessings of the soul of Imam Husayn ﷺ instead, rather than following this ritual. To this my answer is that every ritual in any religion should be judged according to its philosophy.

A similar criticism could be levelled by the non-Muslims against the rituals of *Hajj*. A case in point is that some of my non-Muslim friends after watching a documentary on *Hajj* told me in a sarcastic manner that it was interesting for them to see Satan being depicted into three categories of 'Large, Medium and Small' allotments! Thereafter they were quite diverted at watching the Muslims, (especially the older ones), grinding their teeth and throwing stones and slippers at these monuments; and in the process, inadvertently also showering these articles on pilgrims gathered in the same assemblage, thereby inflicting harm on others during this process! Also amusing to them was the sight of old men trotting along like camels between the hillocks of Safa and Marwa. Finally, the ritual of kissing the Black Stone of the Kaaba which to them, was reminiscent of the original 'Idol Worship' of the earlier statues that had been installed within its four walls!

Notwithstanding such criticisms, it is essential that these rituals *must be completed* by Muslims to have their Hajj accepted according to the commands of Allah ﷻ and His holy Prophet ﷺ. So, my point is that criticism from any quarter should not be an influencing factor in the performance of any ritual. Therefore, if the lovers of Husayn ؏ choose a certain form or ritual to express their attachment to him, they should be free to do so based on certain philosophies and personal values and should not become a subject of criticism by any others. In fact, even the highest authorities among the Shia Jurists in all ages, when questioned, have refused to criticize this practice or pass judgment against it!

A famous Sunni scholar by the name of Badshah Husayni, an ex-President of the Sunni Jamaat, made this declaration after his last *Hajj*: "I have learnt two things after my last *Hajj*. The first is that after the holy Prophet ﷺ, Ali ؏ is the 'King' - and all the rest are his subjects. Secondly, in whichever form or whatever way the martyrdom of Husayn ؏ is celebrated, it cannot be criticized or condemned; especially in the light of the fact that the 'love of Ahlul Bayt' has not only been endorsed by the Quran but this love acts as the 'passport' which enables one to attain salvation in the Hereafter!"

11.18: Reconstitution of Traditions with the Change of Times

To conclude, several Sunni scholars of high calibre have supported and upheld the various forms and rituals of mourning that have evolved over the ages in different continents wherever the mourning for Imam Husayn ﷺ has been conducted. For further details pages 895-899 can be referred to of the original Urdu text, as different countries and distinct cultures have evolved their own ways and forms of Mourning the Tragedy of Kerbala and commemorating the unique sacrifice of Imam Husayn ﷺ in his bid to preserve the 'Deen of Allah and (his grandfather) Rasoolallah'!

11.19: Summary

In their biases people are so blinded that they overlook the obvious miracles happening even today before their very own eyes! For instance while on the one hand they accept the miraculous incident of Abrahim ﷺ being unscathed by the fire lit by Nimrod, yet when faced with the everyday occurrences of people walking barefooted under the 'Alams' of Imam Husayn ﷺ on large areas of burning beds of charcoal fires **without sustaining any burns** to their feet whatsoever, they seem unwilling to accept this as being a supernatural or a miraculous occurrence!

For the edification of the reader, this practice of walking barefoot over fire beds while carrying the banners of Husayn ﷺ is very prevalent in the Indian subcontinent where not only Muslims, but also many Hindus celebrate Muharram; and walk over live charcoals chanting the name of Imam Husayn without coming to any harm; or even sustaining a blister on their feet! The behaviour of such obtuse persons who fail to recognise the significance of such miracles and do not believe in them are like the persons mentioned in chapter (6:25) in the Quran: "*We have cast veils over their hearts lest they understand it*" as against those mentioned in (22:32): "*...Whoever respects the signs of Allah, this surely is (a sign of) the of piety of their hearts.*" This now concludes our discussion on this subject, and we need not delve any further into this matter.

11.20: Miracles Exhibited by Alams of Imam Husayn ﷺ During the Reign of the Moghul Emperor Aurangzeb

After the conquest of the State of Hyderabad Deccan by the Moghul Emperor Aurangzeb, an orthodox Sunni by faith, he issued an edict that all 'Ashoor-Khanas' (Centres where the *Alams* are installed for mourning) should be closed and no one be allowed to install the *Alams* to commemorate the mourning of Husayn during the month of Muharram. Nor were they to take out any processions on the streets with these *Alams* (as was the usual custom) on the Day of *Ashoora* (10th day of Muharram, the date on which Imam Husayn ﷺ achieved his martyrdom)[126]. At this point it was brought to his attention that there were certain long established old *Alams* installed in various *Ashoorkhanas* spread out over the city which were known to exhibit miraculous feats. Lending an ear to these suggestions, he made an exception that only those ancient *Alams* of longstanding duration would be permitted to be installed but with the restriction that they should not be taken out on the streets; and should only remain confined within their respective boundaries.

---

[126] 'Tarikh-e-Alamgir' by Prof. Sale Chand.

It is recorded in a book of history by Sale Chand titled 'Tarikh e Alamgir' (History of Aurangzed) that an old woman defied this order and decided not only to install the *Alam* which had been in her family for generations and known to be associated with many miracles over the ages; but she also dared to take this out on the street accompanied by her grandchildren, reciting eulogies about Imam Husayn's tragedy. She then deliberately walked past the residence of Aurangzeb with the children in tow. Upon hearing the commotion of the wailing sounds of the mournful procession, Aurangzeb ordered the arrest of the old woman. However, it is recorded that no sooner did he glance at that procession from his balcony, he immediately abandoned his seat; and to the surprise of his courtiers and subordinates, he ran after the old woman discarding his shoes and his head turban. Then, taking the *Alam* from this old lady, he placed it on top of his own head and joined in her march! Later, when questioned about his unusual behaviour and reversal of attitude, he replied that when, with an intent to punish the old woman, he glanced at her small procession, he was **amazed** to see that the **holy Prophet ﷺ himself** was walking behind the procession, beating his chest, throwing sand over his bare head and bewailing his grandson Husayn ؑ's martyrdom! He added that he could not help but pay homage to the *Alam*!

Shortly after this episode, Aurangzeb wrote a letter[127] to his younger son Moazzam Jah in which he categorically stated that the true path was only that of Husayn ؑ: "My son! This world is short-lived and lasts but a few days and it somehow passes away. The reality is the Hereafter which is forever; and to benefit and be successful there, one <u>must</u> be attached to Husayn ؑ!" Soon thereafter he withdrew his order (*Farman*) about the ban on *Alams* and *Azadari* and in fact, made arrangements to move an

---

[127] Ibid, Letter dated 4th Rajab, 1110 AH.

auspicious, historically famed and sacred *Alam* associated with the holy fourth Imam Zainul Abideen as-Sajjad ﷺ, known as the *'Alam of SAR-TAUQ'* which used to be installed in a relatively humble locality known as *'Ettebar Chowk'* and he, Aurangzeb from then on arranged to have it set up in a more prominent location in the heart of the Old City of Hyderabad (India).

The entire area of this new venue of the *Alam* later came to be known as the locality of *'Daar-ul-Shifa'* (House of Cure) because of the countless miracles achieved through the blessings of this *Alam;* particularly in connection with the curing of illnesses and chronic ailments of different sorts. The site or place (which still exists and is visited by thousands) in which this Alam got installed, became famously known as *'Alawa-e-Sar-Tauq':* **The Shrine of The Shackle Collar Lock of Imam Sajjad** ﷺ where many a prayer invoked is granted, and the sick regain their health! The unique feature of this *'Alam of Sar-Tauq'* is that it contains the 'lock' which was part of the Iron Collar that had been placed around the neck of the holy fourth Imam Sajjad Zainul Abideen ﷺ, [the only surviving son of Imam Husayn ﷺ[128] after the Battle of Kerbala], when he was taken as a prisoner by the Yazidi forces and marched through the streets of Kufa and Damascus.

Several earlier attempts by Aurangzeb (prior to his change of heart in favour of Shias) to have this miraculous *Alam* removed and put away in some remote corner had been repeatedly unsuccessful. In an initial attempt towards this, on his orders an elephant was brought in to cart this grand and heavy *Alam* and its accompanying paraphernalia out of the city limits. But when it was

---

[128] Not only was he vested with this strangling collar, but he was also weighed down by heavy iron chains and shackles from his neck to his handcuffs; along with a constricting iron waistband, and iron anklets that were attached and chained with links to heavy Iron Balls which he was forced to drag along, with every movement of his steps!

laden with all the items to be relocated, the elephant ended up with a broken back and the move had to be abandoned! A second elephant was brought in some days later, and to the surprise of all present, this phenomenon of the *second* elephant also ending with a broken back got repeated! When two elephants suffered this same unfortunate fate, Aurangzeb was convinced that there was some Miraculous Power associated with this relic of the "***Lock***". After his change of faith, he subsequently ordered that this *Alam* be moved to a new location which eventually came to be known as *'Daar-ul Shifa'* (*The House of Cure*) where it is still lodged and serves as a Blessed Shrine for one and all in seeking cure for ailments and blessings and fulfillment of their wishes.

Maulana Abul Kamal Syed Ahmed Shamshi Kazmi *Mufti-e-Azam*, Taunk, upon research presented a dissertation on the beliefs and practices of the Sunni Sect. On page seven of this chronicle published in 1385 AH he writes that among the Sunni Sultans who ruled India, Aurangzeb was the most bigoted and intolerant of them all. But during his research, *Mufti* Shamshi Kazmi states that he discovered that despite being extremely prejudiced earlier, Aurangzeb in his later life imposed no restrictions on the mourning ceremonies for Imam Husayn ﷺ. This change he writes occurred after the incident of the old lady followed by her grandchildren carrying an *Alam* and going past his residence; to such an extent that he even had this practice eventually established in the Agra Fort in North India (which is in the vicinity of the famous Taj Mahal); where he had the *Alams* and other rituals of *Azadari* observed on a regular basis during the remainder of his rule. These relics associated with his mourning assemblages are still preserved in the Agra Fort by the present governments.

The *Mufti* further elaborates about a dispute which arose when the Sunnis of Burhanpour objected to the processions being taken out by the Shias during the month of Muharram. The case was eventually presented in the court of Aurangzeb who not only ruled in favour of the Shias, but he also further announced that these processions should be allowed to continue without disturbance, and none could raise any objections against these rituals.

In his last days, Aurangzeb made a will in which he instructed that upon his death his shroud and his grave should both be sprinkled with the sand and dust of Kerbala in order that he may attain salvation. This he said was because of his belief that most certainly the last resort for forgiveness of sins committed by sinners is none other than Husayn ﷺ! To support this view he quoted the Quranic verse from Surah *al-Shura,* Chapter (42:230: *"Say, I do not ask of you any reward for it (my services to Islam) but the love for my Qurba (near relatives);"* and went on to endorse that the attachment to the holy Prophet ﷺ and his Immaculate progeny was the best incentive and guaranty for securing the hereafter. He also instructed his own family and other relatives that the descendants from the progeny of the Prophet ﷺ through his daughter Fatima ﷺ: the *'Alawis* and *Sayyeds'* should be respected and left free from harassment.

During the latter part of his life, Aurangzeb had taken to transcribing the Quran, making prayer caps, and selling them for a small price; with instructions that this money should be used towards the purchase of his own shroud and his burial expenses. Furthermore, he also strictly forbade that the income of the 305 rupees realized from his transcribing of the Quran should not be used for his benefit, but rather, it should be given out in charity, as in the **Shia** Jurisprudence (*Fiqh*) it was forbidden to charge money for either teaching or writing the holy Quran.

As an aside, it is interesting to know that in the various battles that he fought, Aurangzeb used to carry a sword which was inscribed with the words: **"Ya Allah! Ya Ali."** To this day this sword is preserved in the Red Fort Museum, New Delhi India.

11.20a: Additional Accounts of Miracles Related to the Holy Prophet ﷺ and his Ahlul Bayt ؏

Farishta in his 'History of The Deccan'[129] has recorded an incident with respect to the Sunni 'Nizam Shahi Dynasty' which was founded by Ahmad Nizam Shah in the late Ninth century AH. His son Burhan Shah ruled the city of Ahmed Nagar India, from 914 AH up to 961 AH. He had a son called Abdul Qader who was beset by a malady which had no cure. No amount of medical aid rendered by the '*Hakeems*' and doctors of his time had any effect, and his death was imminent. The king was distraught with grief and asked for help from any source available.

An Iranian Shia scholar named Syed Shah Taher who had been living in the same city, but for fear of being ostracized and/or killed, had been living under dissimulation (*Taqiya*) without revealing his true faith, now approached King Burhan Shah and said that if the King would grant him safety of his life, he would suggest a cure for his son Abdul Qader which would most certainly be successful and guarantee his son's cure! Upon receiving the assurance from the King about his own life's safety, Taher Shah stated that he would be invoking the cure for the Prince in the names of the Prophet ﷺ, his beloved daughter Fatima Zahra ؏, Ali ؏ and his progeny up to the 12 Imams of the Ahlul Bayt ؏; provided the King had no objection.

Burhan Shah responded by saying that when he had no hesitation in going to the Temples and Churches to seek a cure, how could he object to the blessed names of the Prophet ﷺ's family? Shah Taher was emboldened by this response and made an agreement that if the youth recovered, the King would accept the Shia faith. The latter acquiesced. Shah Taher said that since this

---

[129] 'Tarikh e Farishta'- Vol 2, Pg 115.

exchange of dialogue between the two of them had taken place on the night preceding a Friday morning, it was the ideal moment to invoke the prayers for the cure through these Holy Personalities. He directed the King to remain by the side of his ailing son, who to all intents and purposes, appeared to be in the throes of death, tossing and turning, bemoaning, and constantly kicking off his blankets.

During the night Burhan Shah fell asleep and just before dawn he states he saw a vision in which he saw an imposing personality whose face was radiating a heavenly light. On his right hand were 12 other personalities also of shining faces. In his dream he stood up in awe and greeted him, whereupon he was told by someone that this impressive person was none other than the Prophet Muhammad ﷺ and that the 12 others were the Imams from his holy progeny. The Prophet ﷺ addressed him in his dream with words to the effect that: "*O Burhan! Your son Abdul Qader has been cured through the blessings of Ali and his Eleven Immaculate Sons. Now it is up to you to keep your part of the bargain that you made with my son 'Taher' and not go back on your word!*" When he awoke from his dream, the King was overjoyed to see that his son was indeed completely cured and the nurse who was present by the side of the youth also attested to the fact that he had regained his normal health! The King fulfilled his promise, adopted the Shia faith, and instructed that the names of the Twelve Imams ﷺ should be recited in all the mosques in town, and ensured that these were always included in all his own sermons and edicts that were issued thenceforth.

On a somewhat similar note, an interesting anecdote which was voluntarily recounted to me by my Sunni friend Abdul Rasheed Siddiqi who was the Secretary of the Education Department in Nizmabad India, was that during his youthful days when he was acquiring his education at the Aligarh University, he never paid any importance to the month of Muharram. One year, on the 10th of Muharram (*Day of Ashoora*) out of curiosity, he decided to join the onlookers to view the procession of the *Alams* and the relics connected with the mourning processions. He said that since he had a brand-new pair of shoes which he had bought earlier but never used, he thought it would be a good occasion to put them on.

Wearing these shoes for the first time on the *Day of Ashoora,* he approached the spot where the procession of mourners was beginning their walk on the flaming charcoals. When he arrived at that area, he said that he was absolutely baffled to see that without his **ever being conscious,** his new pair of shoes had somehow come off his feet *somewhere;* and he *somehow* also found himself *standing barefoot in the middle of the fire pit* [!] resulting in the soles of both his feet being badly scalded! He confided to me that he later repented his action and vowed that he would never again initiate the use of any new item during the first ten days of Muharram! On the contrary, as time progressed, he eventually came to respect this mourning period to a point that he himself started to hold a mourning ceremony in his own house annually every year during the month of Muharram; and furthermore, he also started composing elegies on the tragedy of Kerbala!

On a personal note, my own respected mother had several dreams over the years during her lifetime in which she had the privilege of seeing visions of many of the Holy Personalities from the household of the Prophet ﷺ such as the holy Prophet ﷺ himself and the exalted Lady Khadija ﵇; as well as her beloved daughter Fatima ﵇ and some of the Imams descendent from her progeny.

On one such occasion many years ago just before the advent of the month of Moharram my mother saw the holy Prophet ﷺ in her dream, being ridden on an elephant and holding *two Alams* in his hands, from which, leaning down towards her, he gave her one saying: "*This is Husayn's Alam, keep it with you.*" Then pointing to the other *Alam* in his own hand, he told her in her dream: "*And this is Fatima's Alam which I am keeping for myself!*" When she related this dream to me, I asked her to sketch the *Alam* which she had seen in her dream. In comparison to other *Alams*, this one turned out to be in an unusual shape of a 'Crescent' with the words "*Ya Husayn*" inscribed in Arabic in its centre. I immediately arranged to have such an *Alam* designed and handmade for me; but by the time it took the Silversmith to craft it and 'made to order,' the delivery was delayed, and we finally got possession of it on the 4th date of Moharram. Without further loss of time, we immediately installed this new *Alam* in our personal household *Ashoorkhana*. Ever since that date, regularly every year on the 4th day of Moharram *in all subsequent years that followed*, I and my family have always been *blessed with some good tidings or the other*, including monetary benefits and/or bounties of other kind. Even outsiders who have invoked prayers at this *Alam* in our house, in the name of Imam Husayn ﷺ have had their wishes invariably granted!

Once during my tenure as a Judge in a district known as Warangal in South India, a case was presented before me in which a prominent and honest young police officer was charged with malfeasance. His name was Abdul Majeed Subhani a follower of the Sunni Faith. Based on the evidence forwarded and the witnesses' statements, I decided to issue a judgement against the accused for the alleged crime. Before the case was finalized however, the month of Moharram intervened and I went on leave as was my usual habit and decided to postpone my Verdict till my return after the first 12 days of Muharram. A notice to this effect was sent to his advocate Mirza Shukur Baig who was pleading on behalf of the accused. Unbeknown to me, before our departure from Warangal to our *Ashoorkhana* in Hyderabad, [and I say this on oath before Allah ﷻ] this young man's mother also a Sunni by faith, visited my wife and asked her to intervene and convince me about her son's innocence.

My wife responded that she does not interfere in my official matters but told her that if her son was indeed innocent, then why not visit our *Ashoorkhana* in Hyderabad and plead at our *Alam* in the name of Husayn 🕌 and ask for his freedom. In desperation, the mother of the accused, unexpectedly arrived at our *Ashoorkhana* in Hyderabad coincidentally also on the 4th of Moharram, and invoked her prayers through the intercession of Imam Husayn, to save her innocent son from jail or any other related harsh sentence for a crime which she believed he had not committed.

Without having any knowledge of the mother's actions of having visited our *Ashoorkhana* either, their lawyer Shukoor Baig upon my return to court requested a reopening of the case and a further review of the witnesses, which I duly granted. When this happened, one of the key witnesses Saith Kanhiyya Pershad now excused himself and withdrew his evidence; owning up to the fact that he had been overawed by the atmosphere of the court and the presence of many prominent police personnel, some of whom were themselves involved in the crime! Seeing this, other witnesses also came forward corroborating with the new evidence which proved the youth's innocence. Based on these new facts I amended my earlier judgement of a possible death sentence and released the youth as being "**not guilty**". This had a two-fold effect: First of freeing an innocent person and secondly, protecting **me** from delivering an unjust decision!

It was only a year later when the mother of this youth [Abdul Majeed Subhani] returned to our *Ashoorkhana* in the month of Moharram to fulfill her vow made earlier and her pledge to join in the commemoration of the martyrdom ceremonies of Muharram *in thankfulness for the release of her son*, that I became aware of her earlier involvement and the resultant outcome. She proceeded to inform everyone present of the turn on events after her 'Dua' made by her at this *Alam* which had resulted in not only freeing an innocent person from being falsely charged but also prevented the real culprits from getting away Scott free!

As far as my own individual experiences are concerned, I have been blessed in seeing the holy Prophet ﷺ and many members of the holy Ahlul Bayt ؑ, as well as several of their companions, including some of the Martyrs of Kerbala in my dreams on several occasions which still stand out clear and distinct in my memory. I also had the good fortune of asking countless questions to the holy Prophet ﷺ in my dreams in connection with the compilation of this book, which he answered gracefully without any sign of impatience! In one such dream I recall seeing the holy Prophet ﷺ surrounded by several companions, and someone rebuked me in my dream for harassing the holy Prophet with a multitude of questions; to which the Prophet ﷺ responded saying words to the effect: *"Let him ask, for how will he know if he does not ask, for who else is there to answer them?"*

On another occasion while this book was still in a manuscript form, I saw the Prophet ﷺ in my dream, again surrounded by some companions; and pointing to me in my dream he told his companions: *"He is dear to me, and also dear to me are the papers that he is writing upon!"*

11.21: Expression of Faith by a Hindu for Imam Husayn ؑ

We refer to an article written by an Intellectual Hindu person named Vishvanath Parshad Mathur a resident of Lucknow; printed in Moharram 1383 AH under the title of "Bharat and Husayn". In this article the writer states that the universe belongs to Husayn; and at another place he says 'Husayn belongs to us Hindus'. In his poetry he says that Husayn is embedded in his heart, and 'Hindustan and Hindustanis (India and Indians) love Husayn'.

The article begins by tracing the journey of Imam Husayn 🕮 from Mecca to Kerbala and progresses to the point where Imam Husayn 🕮 was confronted by the forces of Yazid's army who insisted upon blocking the Imam 🕮's progress any further. Refusing to compromise with the Yazidi forces, Husayn 🕮 to avoid a situation which could lead to unnecessary bloodshed asked that he be allowed to go away in peace towards the "land of Hind" (India). *The writer finds it significant that Imam Husayn 🕮 did not mention any of the surrounding Muslim states like Ethiopia, Egypt, Iran or Syria; but rather, a country which did not have a single Muslim person*: [i.e. India]! This leads him to believe that Imam Husayn 🕮 must have had a spiritual attachment for the people of India! He must have loved them as he must have known that these people would also love him in return! Upon research, he writes that even before the advent of Islam the Indian priests and monks used to recite rosaries known as *"Husayn Poti"* on the peaks of the Himalayan Mountains. As there were *no* Muslims in India during that period, the writer reasons that it *had to have been Hindus* that followed these practices as Hinduism was the prevalent religion of the Subcontinent. On further research he goes on to write:

"These high priests and monks were from a sect of Brahmins who were following some ancient Edicts mentioned in their old Scriptures and who have since come to be known as '**Husayni Brahmins**'. To this day these 'Husayni Brahmins' are found all over India, but their population is concentrated around Jammu and Kashmir. Not only are they proud of their attachment to Husayn 🕮 but also are still faithful adherents to his creed. We cannot say who was originally responsible for instilling the love of Husayn 🕮 and the 'Ethos and Pathos' displayed for his martyrdom in their mournful attachment to his sacrifices in the virgin land of India.

We can only assume that it was a *Super Natural phenomena* and that it was the *'Hand of Destiny'* which to this day ensures that not only the Muslims but a large number of Hindus also mourn for Husayn ﷺ every year during Moharram, in reverence to Imam Husayn ﷺ's wish to have been allowed to come to India to avoid bloodshed by engaging in any battle with Yazid.

When the crescent moon of Muharram is sighted, it is again not just the Muslims but we Hindus who also find our eyes welling up with tears in remembrance of the sacrifice of Imam Husayn ﷺ. India has now undergone a change of face, but up to 30 to 50 years ago when India consisted of different states ruled by Hindu 'Maharajas' like the State of Gawaliar and the State of Indore for example: their Maharajas were renowned for the Moharram ceremonies respectfully observed by their subjects. There are several mausoleums of Imam Husayn ﷺ (*Imam Badas or Ashoorkhanas*) built by a lot of Hindus for conducting the mourning rituals, for instance the 'Thakurganj *Imambada*' built by Raja Mevaram in Lucknow. Similarly, Raja Chawlal had also done the same, and Raja Takat Rai had set up an '*Imambada Trust*' for the same purpose of commemorating the tragedy of Kerbala. Hindus have not restricted themselves merely to the construction and maintenance of these mausoleums but have also done extensive literary work in praising and propagating the great personality and sacrifices of Imam Husayn ﷺ by their prose and poetry. As a famous Indian poet Josh Malahabadi has written:

'Since when did Muslims lay exclusive claim to Husayn?
Let the masses awake from their drowse and dream,
*Every Nation will cry out: **Ours is Husayn!**'*
However, according to me Imam Husayn ﷺ is:
The Universal Star of Humanity!"

With respect to the foregoing views expressed by the esteemed writer Vishvanath Parshad Mathur, we have attempted to translate a quatrain which he composed (in Hindi) after giving considerable thought to the '*Wish expressed by Imam Husayn* 🕮 *to be allowed to migrate to Hind*' before he got embroiled in the Tragedy of Kerbala. He writes:

"Upon my eyes do I place him, and in my heart he resides.
This Earth belongs to Husayn, and to him belong the Skies.
*Ever since he stated **before** Kerbala, his wish to go toward India,*
*This Land of "**Hind**" from thence has been,*
*The **Exclusive Domain of HUSAYN, The King!**"*

Vishvanath Prashad Mathur, Lucknowi.

11.22: Fourth Imam: Ali ibn al-Ḥusayn Zainul Abideen 🕮

Imam Zainul Abideen was the eldest son of Imam Husayn 🕮 and he was the 4th Imam of the Ahlul Bayt 🕮. His mother was Sheher Banu, the daughter of King Yazdjad ibne Shehriyar, Shah of Iran; and her grandfather was the famous king known for his justice as "Nau-Sherwan-e-Adil". There are different accounts with respect to her arrival in Madina. According to Sheik Mufid Ali 🕮 during his Caliphate sent Jabir ibne Harith as his Governor of a province in Khorasan, Iran. After the defeat of the ruling dynasty of Iran, the two daughters of the last king Yazdjad ibne Shehriyar were taken as captives by Muslims and presented in the court of Jabir. He in turn sent them on to Imam Ali 🕮 in Kufa. Their names were Sheher Banu and Gehan Banu. The former was also known as '*Shah-e-Zanaan*' because of her imposing personality. Imam Ali 🕮 got **her** married to Imam Husayn 🕮 in the year 36 AH and she gave birth to Imam Ali Zainul Abideen 🕮 in 38 AH. Eighteen months after giving birth to the 4th Imam 🕮, tragically she passed away.

As for her sister Gehan Banu, Imam Ali 🕮 got her married to his adopted son Muhammad ibne Abu Bakr whose mother was Asma bint Omais. Asma had first been married to Imam Ali 🕮's brother, Ja'far ibne Abi Taleb 🕮, (**aka** 'Jafar e Tayyar' 🕮). She had migrated to Ethiopia from Mecca with him and returned to Madina in 7 AH with Jafar 🕮. Unfortunately, Hazrat Jafar was martyred a year later in the 'Battle of Muta' in 8 AH. Subsequently Abu Bakr married her; and she gave birth to a son Muhammad around the year 9 AH. When Abu Bakr died in 13 AH, Asma bint Omais got betrothed to Imam Ali 🕮 and brought her son Muhammad along with her as a child of four years. Imam Ali 🕮 consequently adopted the young Muhammad as his own son. This lends credence to the fact that when Muhammad bin Abu Bakr was wed to Gehan Banu he was around 25 years old in age, [and **not** a mere 7-year-old groom as some historians have erroneously stated!] While Sheher Banu gave birth to Imam Ali Zainul Abideen 🕮, her sister Gehan Banu gave birth to her son Qasim bin Muhammad bin Abu Bakr at around the same time.

The tradition that the two sisters were brought to Madina during the reign of Umar in 16 AH is not credible as only a small portion of Iran was conquered by Umar in 16 AH and Muhammad bin Abu Bakr would have only been around 7 years old at that time, making it impossible for him to have married Gehan Banu at that early age! In this connection Shibli Nomani has categorically stated in his book[130] as follows:

"It is false that Sheher Banu and Gehan Banu were brought to Madina in the time of Umar. Zamakshari is by no means an authentic historian. Iran was not fully conquered during the reign of Umar; and the family of the Iranian King Yazdjad was not taken prisoner by Umar's army. I doubt very much whether Zamakshari

---

[130] 'Al Farouq'- Vol 2, Pg 139 – Shibli Nomani.

even knew when King Yazdjad was assassinated! Many other historians confirm the fact that the daughters of King Yazdjad were brought to Kufa during the Caliphate of Ali 🕮 in 36 AH. All other traditions related in connection with Umar's role and intervention in the disposal of the two princesses in marriage to Husayn 🕮 and Muhammad bin Abu Bakr 🕮 appear to be weak and unreliable; since Husayn 🕮 would have been only 12 years in age at that time, while Muhammad bin Abu Bakr would have been a mere seven-year-old!"

Leaving aside the earlier discussions about the marriages of Imam Husayn 🕮 and Muhammad bin Abu Bakr to the two sisters from the royal family of Iran, we now turn our attention toward the attitude of the Muslims in connection with the progeny of the holy Prophet 🕮. Several Sunni scholars who are not inimical to the progeny of the Apostle 🕮 state that it is incumbent upon the Muslims to express their love for the Ahlul Bayt 🕮. For example, Data Ganj Baksh, the great Sufi scholar of India has noted the following in his book 'Kashful Mahjub':

"Imam Zainul Abideen 🕮 was not only the successor of the Prophet 🕮, but he was the 'Chief of the Oppressed' and a 'Guiding Light' for all the believers". Another leading Sunni scholar Abu Uthman Umer has written: "There is no doubt about the greatness of Zainul Abideen 🕮. Despite the differences within the various sects of the Muslims, the Caliph Umar ibn Abdul Aziz used to say that 'if you want to observe the best of the human race, then look at Ali ibn Al Husayn 🕮'". It is recorded in 'Tarikh e Nisai', 'Huliyat e Awliya' and by Abu Naeem that as long as Imam Zohri was alive, he used to praise Ali ibn Al Husayn 🕮 in the words: "I have not found anybody better than Ali Zainul Abideen 🕮 in this world!"

When Hisham bin Ismail was the Governor of Madina he used to mistreat Ali ibn al-Husayn 🕮. Walid who was the then Governor of Hijaz had Hisham removed from his office and made him stand in the central marketplace where people were urged to condemn his behaviour and hurl their abuses at him! When Imam Zainul Abideen 🕮 himself happened to pass by this place, he asked his companions to refrain from abusing Hisham. The latter observing this, shouted in a loud voice: "No doubt this behaviour comes natural to him as he is the Light from the family of the noble Prophet 🕮!"

Ali ibn al-Husayn 🕮 was also known as '*Sayyedus Sajideen'* and '*Zainul Abideen'* because of his excessive prostrations and piety in prayers, respectively. He was a replica of his grandfather Ali 🕮 in the performance of his prayers and fasts. He used to say, *"Be it little, but let me be regular in performing acts of charity on a daily basis."* Among his countless acts of charity are mentioned the fact that he used to carry heavy sacks of food items on his back distributing food to the needy during the darkness of the night, and heavy loads of water bags to the thirsty by the day. These prolonged activities left scars on his back which were only uncovered when he was given the ritual bath at the time of his funeral. It is related through Abu Hamza Thumali a constant companion of the Imam 🕮 that Imam Zainul Abideen 🕮 would advise him that going to the market to buy provisions for one's family has a reward equivalent to freeing a slave in the way of Allah 🕮! Prior to part-taking of his own meal, he used to give away an equal amount of food to a needy person to gain the pleasure of Allah! It is reported from his illustrious grandson Imam Jafar-e-Sadiq 🕮: *"My grandfather preferred to travel alone and incognito because he used to say that due to his close relationship to the holy Prophet 🕮, his fellow travellers would give him a high degree of respect and not allow him to do any work himself. Concealing his identity, he would urge his co-travellers to freely ask him to do any task for them which they required."*

There was one camel which was very attached to him on which he had performed twenty trips for pilgrimages of Hajj and Umrah. At the time of his death, he willed that his son Imam Muhammad al-Baqir ﷺ should also treat this animal with the same kindness and love, as he himself had never so much as ever applied a single stroke of his whip upon its body during their years of association!

While performing 'Wudoo' [ablution for his prayers] he used to turn pale with the 'Awe of Allah ﷻ' and when asked about the reason for this he would say *"Do we not know Whose Presence we are going to be standing in when we perform our prayers?"* In the book 'Sawaiq-e-Mohriqa' by ibn Hajar-e-Makki it is stated that he used to perform 1000 units of prayers every night in the legendary way of his grandfather Ali ibn Abi Talib ﷺ. After the martyrdom of Imam Husayn ﷺ at Kerbala, Hazrat Muhammad e Hanafia, the surviving son of Imam Ali ﷺ thought that because of his age and senior years and his relationship with his father Imam Ali ﷺ, he could now be the present Imam of the Age. But Imam Zainul Abideen ﷺ told him: *"O Uncle! I am the Imam of the Time as my father had invested me with this Authority prior to his martyrdom in Kerbala. If you are in any doubt, then let the 'Hajar-e-Aswad'* [the Black Stone of the *Kaaba*] *bear witness to this fact."* Accordingly, they proceeded to Mecca and entered the precincts of the holy *Kaaba* and stood in front of the Black Stone; whereupon a sound was emitted from it reciting the Quranic verse: *'Kulla Shai-in Eh Saiy-Naho Fee Imamim-Mubeen'* and then adding that *"Imam Zainul Abideen ﷺ was the Imam of the Time and it was incumbent on Muhammad-e-Hanafia to obey him!"*

It is recorded in several reliable books that he undertook to perform the journey of Hajj on foot at the tender age of nine years without the using as his means of transportation any animal of conveyance such as a mule, horse, or camel. He also, neither had any items of provisions for eating or sleeping enroute. On the way he met up with a caravan of other Hajis whose leader was surprised to see a young lad of nine alone on his way to Mecca! He enquired as to why a boy of such tender age would undertake such a trip alone, and on foot! The Imam ﷺ replied: "*I do it because if I were to die early, I would be denied the reward of the Hajj.*" Unable to resist, the Leader of the Caravan enquired "Where are your provisions for the journey?" Imam Zainul Abideen ﷺ replied: "*For a man the best provision is his piety.*" He was then asked: "Where do you propose to stay, and who will take care of you?" Imam ﷺ replied: "*The Host Whom I am on my way to visit will look after me.*"

So saying, he proceeded on his way, even as the caravan Leader stood by astonished. Shortly thereafter, the leader of the caravan saw that the young boy was approached by a good-looking young man of an impressive gait, who stood before the boy and after kissing him on his forehead, engaged him in some conversation; then offered his salutations and departed. The leader could not contain his curiosity. He ran up to the young Imam ﷺ and asked him as to **who** he was and, as to who was that mysterious visitor who had appeared out of nowhere and then disappeared as quickly! The Imam ﷺ replied: "*I am Ali, the son of Husayn, and that was Nabi Khizr; and it is habitual for him to come to visit us Ahlul Bayt periodically, to pay his respects.*"

Hafiz Abu Naeem in his book 'Huliyatul Abrar' records an incident during the time of Hajj when Hisham ibn Abdul Malik who was the son of the Caliph of the time [and later became a Caliph himself], was performing Hajj in Mecca. He attempted to kiss the Black Stone of Kaaba but was unable to even get close to it due to the excessive congregation of Hajis around it, no matter how much he tried. He then ordered a chair for himself and sat down surrounded by his courtiers from Syria. Presently he saw Imam Zainul Abideen ﷺ approach the holy Kaaba. Immediately the crowd dispersed and made way for him so that he easily reached the '*Hajar-e-Aswad*' and kissed it, then departed. One of the Syrian courtiers asked Hisham as to who this impressive youth was to whom the people paid such immense respect. Hisham feigned ignorance and pretended not to know his identity. However, Abu Faraaz 'Farzdaq' a famous poet who was present nearby immediately composed and recited a lengthy poem extempore in praise of Imam Zainul Abideen 🕮, starting off with the words:

"If you do not know, I will tell you who he is....
I know him extremely well, as do these surroundings of the Kaaba
*For they are familiar with the **very** Sound of his Footsteps...."*

Hisham was annoyed no end and had Farzdaq arrested and imprisoned! To this day this poem is cited and quoted in the Arabic literary circles, and it has also been translated from Arabic into the Persian and Urdu languages.

Imam Zainul Abideen 🕮 was imprisoned twice during his lifetime. The first time was after the Battle of Kerbala which he could not part-take in due to being afflicted with a serious illness during that period. It was due to this reason of being confined to bed with an ailment, that he was saved from being slaughtered by Yazid's army. Regardless, he was handcuffed and shackled in heavy iron chains by them and taken as a prisoner and brought into the court before Ibn Ziad, the Governor of Kufa. When questioned by Ibn Ziad as to who he was he replied: "*I am Ali the son of Husayn.*" When Ziad heard this, he said: "But Ali ibn al-Husayn was killed in Kerbala." The Imam replied: "*That was my younger brother with the similar name; I am the older son of Husayn.*"

He was then sent to the court of Yazid in Damascus with the rest of his family members [who were now mainly comprised of ladies and children] as prisoners, along with some relatives of the other martyrs. Initially they were imprisoned in an old desolate downtrodden house within the city of Damascus. It was in this house that his four-year-old little sister Sakina ◈ (**aka** Ruqaiyya) eventually passed away due to the harsh conditions of their imprisonment. The Imam ◈ buried her in the same dilapidated quarters; and her grave is still present to this day at this same location. A grand mausoleum now stands over her tiny grave, and people flock in large numbers for visitation to this site in the same manner as their visitations to the grave of Imam Husayn ◈ and other holy places. When news about the pitiable death of the little girl Sakina ◈ became public, the situation in Damascus immediately changed dramatically and became tense and hostile towards Yazid, to such a point that he was forced to eventually release these prisoners of the Prophet ◈'s family.

After being released from prison in Syria in 63 AH, Imam Zainul Abideen ◈ took the severed head of his father Imam Husayn ◈ with him and buried it alongside his holy body in Kerbala. It is recorded in all reliable books that while being transported, the head of his father ◈ was constantly busy with the recitation of *Surah Kahaf* (Ch 18) of the holy Quran. The atrocities inflicted on Imam Zainul Abideen ◈ and his family members during their sojourn in Damascus were of such severe degree, that he would say later that Allah ◈ had ordered the Ummah of his Prophet to love his family, but the treatment meted out to them in total contradiction was such that had He ordered them *to hate and oppress them instead*, they could not have done any better! Whenever he was asked as to **where** he had suffered the most torture, he always replied: "*Ash-Shaam! Ash-Shaam! Ash-Shaam! (In Syria, In Syria, In Syria!)*

Eventually, after completing the rituals of burial of his martyred relatives in Kerbala, Imam Sajjad ◈ returned and settled in Madina. However, he was once again recalled to Syria by Caliph Abul Malik ibn Marwan who had succeeded Yazid; but nonetheless, he was released after a brief period and once again sent back to Madina. He was 22 years old when the event of Kerbala took place and he survived 35 years after this tragedy and was never known to *even smile* after his heart-rending experiences. Whenever water was brought to him to drink, he would cry so profusely that often his tears would mingle with the water, and it would become undrinkable so he could not slake his own thirst which would often remain unquenched! He was eventually poisoned by the Caliph Walid ibn Abdul Malik and achieved his martyrdom on 25th Muharram 95 AH.

11.23: Some Miracles of Imam Zainul Abideen

It is recorded in 'Shawahid' by Mulla Jami that the Fourth Imam was imprisoned along with his aunts and relatives by Abdul Malik ibn Marwan in an old and dilapidated prison which was infested with snakes and scorpions. It was noted in amazement however, that rather than sting him, the deadly creatures would be prostrating at his feet in a manner of paying their respects to him!

In the same book it is written that the Imam had such power and control over his own captivity, that at will, he could make the chains around his neck and body fall to the ground and release him from their constrictions. When ibn Ziad the Governor of Kufa witnessed this, he was frightened no end and arranged the captives' speedy exit out of Kufa to Damascus.

After the martyrdom of Imam Husayn his stepbrother Hazrat Muhammad-e-Hanafia Ibne Ali as mentioned earlier, erroneously conceived himself to be the next Imam of the Time. Imam Zainul Abideen differed with him pointing out that though he was his senior in age, as well as his uncle, he was nonetheless mistaken in his assumption. Thereupon they agreed to go to the holy Kaa'ba and stood before the Black Stone (*Hajr e*

Aswad) which not only invoked greetings upon but also testified to the fact that Imam Zainul Abideen ﷺ was the new Imam!

During his second confinement in prison, when one of his companions by the name of Zohri, who was an ardent admirer of the Imam, visited him in prison, he started shedding tears in profusion at the sight of the Imam ﷺ being tied up in iron chains and heavy shackles around his neck, waist and ankles; as well as restrictive handcuffs around his wrists! Imam Zainul Abideen ﷺ consoled him saying that this was one of the tests that Allah ﷻ had designated for them Ahlul Bayt ﷺ, and out of their extreme degree of love for Allah ﷻ it was easy for them to bear these travails. He then added: "*If we wish to release ourselves from these shackles the Almighty has given it within our power to do so at our will!*"

Zohri says that no sooner had these words left the lips of the Imam ﷺ he saw the chains and shackles fall off from the Imam ﷺ's neck and body; and the Imam was leaning back against the wall and continuing the conversation with him quite normally! He then instructed Zohri to return to his home, content in the knowledge that his Imam was free to exercise his own will whenever he chooses. When Zohri left the Imam and went back into the city he says the town was buzzing with the news that the Imam ﷺ had miraculously freed himself leaving his shackles lying in the prison and was nowhere to be found by the 'search parties'!

After this incident, Zohri went and met Abdul Malik ibn Marwan and told him not to inflict any pain on the progeny of the holy Prophet ﷺ. Abdul Malik in turn replied: "As soon as I imprisoned him, I saw him appear in the private quarters of my palace which are not accessible to anybody! I was frightened and was left speechless! He addressed me saying: '*Why are you tormenting the progeny of the holy Prophet?*' and then he disappeared!" After this incident Abdul Malik was overawed by the experience and decided to release him.

Several incidents are recorded in numerous books wherein they state that the Imam ﷺ used to communicate with various animals: (notably the deer and antelopes, and even the big game animals like the lion) many a time in the presence of others, which used to leave the audience dumbfounded!

It is stated that once an admirer of the Imam ﷺ requested him to partake a meal in his house but his wife was not quite in favour of this, commenting that though her husband often went 'out of pocket' in arranging a meal for the Imam, she questioned him as to what *his Imam* had done for him in return? The man persisted anyhow and did end up inviting the Imam ﷺ. After the meal was over the Imam requested his host to bring water for him to wash his hands. The host returned with a filled jug and a container to collect the falling water. As he began to pour water over the Imam ﷺ's hands, the Imam ﷺ intstructed his host to closely observe the contents of the water that was falling into the basin. To his utter surprise, the host was astounded to see that as the droplets of water fell off his hands, they were turning into rubies and emeralds and other precious stones! The Imam ﷺ then asked the man to give these Basin-full of jewels to his wife on his behalf!

There are many such miraculous incidents mentioned in connection with the 4th Imam Zainul Abideen ﷺ in the book 'Shawahed e Nabuwah' out of which for the sake of brevity, we have only selected these few.

11.24: Fifth Imam: Muhammad ibn Ali al-Baqir ﷺ

Imam Muhammad al-Baqir ﷺ was the son of the holy 4th Imam Zainul Abideen ﷺ, and his mother was Fatima, the daughter of the holy second Imam Hasan ﷺ. Her title was 'Umme Abdullah'. Thus, he was the grandson of both Imam Hasan and Imam Husayn ﷺ. He was born on the 1st of Rajab 57 AH. He was barely 3 or 4 years old when he too was present with his revered father and grandfather at the Tragedy of Kerbala. Though very tender in age, he also went through the extreme hardships of thirst and hunger for three days in the burning sands of Kerbala. After the battle was over on the 10th of Muharram 61 AH, along with the rest of the holy Prophet ﷺ's family, he was also taken as a captive and paraded in the streets of Kufa and Damascus and confined for a length of time to a prison with the rest in Damascus.

Ibne Madani relates from Jaber ibn Abdullah-e-Ansari himself that when in his old age he was beginning to lose his eyesight he, Jaber, would often sit in the Masjid of the Prophet ﷺ (*Masjid e Nabawi*) chanting the name "*Baqir, Baqir!*" People were bewildered at his strange behaviour, putting it down to senility in his advanced age. One day Imam Baqir ؏ happened to walk past him in close vicinity. Jabir immediately addressed the Imam ؏ and asked him to come close to him. When the young Imam ؏ complied, Jabir asked him to retrace his steps backwards and then forward again!

Finally, unable to contain his excitement he exclaimed: "By Allah! This is the *exact* way the noble Prophet ﷺ used to walk!" He then asked the Imam ؏ for his name and his father's name to which the Imam ؏ replied: "*I am Muhammad, the son of Ali ibn Husayn ؏.*" Jabir responded emotionally saying: "May my parents be sacrificed for you! Are you indeed Baqir?" The Imam ؏ replied in the affirmative and then added: "*O Jabir, why don't you deliver that which has been entrusted to you by my grandfather the holy Apostle?*" Upon hearing this Jabir kissed the Imam ؏'s forehead and said: "O my young Master Baqir! Your Grandfather the holy Prophet ﷺ had foretold me that *I would live long enough to meet you and had asked me to convey his salutations to you!*"

The people who witnessed this incident started to marvel and wondered as to how all this was possible? Jabir explained that one day he was sitting in the company of the holy Prophet ﷺ while Imam Husayn ؏ as a child was playing in his grandfather's lap. At that moment, the holy Prophet ﷺ turned his attention to his companion Jabir and remarked: *"O Jabir! You will live long enough to meet a son born to my son Husayn whose name will be Ali; and he will be so superior in piety and Ibadat (worship) that on the Day of Judgment when a Caller will ask for 'Zainul Abideen to arise' my son Ali ibn al-Husayn will step forward! And O Jabir he Ali, will have a son called Muhammad who has been referred to as 'Baqir' in the Torah. O Jabir! You will live long enough to meet him; and when you do, convey my Salutations to him!"*

Abdul Rauf Monadi has mentioned in his 'Tabaqat' that the reason the 5ᵗʰ Imam ﷺ was known as 'Baqir' was because this name implies "the one who splits open (Knowledge)' and he did this by disseminating knowledge on various subjects to his companions and disciples. Among his well-known disciples were Attar ibn Jari, Imam Zohri, Imam Vaziri, Abu Hanifa and Abu Sufiyan-e-Soori.

Allama Shibli attests in his book 'Seeratul Nauman' that Imam Abu Hanifa, Imam Malik, Imam Shafei, Imam-e-Waziri ibn Mubarik and Ziyad ibn Manzer are also among those who benefitted from Imam Baqir ﷺ's teachings and expounded on the 'Usool-e-Fiqha' (Islamic Jurisprudence) as taught by this Imam ﷺ.

Both Sunni and Shia scholars accept the fact that Abu Hanifa gained a major portion of his knowledge from being in close association as a student of Imam Baqir ﷺ and later from his son Imam Jafar al-Sadiq ﷺ. It was during the lifetime of these two Imams: Muhammad al-Baqir ﷺ and Jafar al-Sadiq ﷺ that the study of Islamic Jurisprudence was organized and expounded; so that people began to study the *traditions of the Prophet* ﷺ and *verses of the holy Quran* in a disciplined format. Most issues were contemplated and deliberated upon in lengthy discourses and usually resolved within the guidelines of the above-mentioned two sources. However, when there were no relevant traditions in connection with certain problems, and no related verses of the Quran could also be identified in their limited knowledge, some scholars began to use their own conjecture to settle those issues. Imam Muhammad al-Baqir ﷺ forbade the people from resorting to conjecture (*Qiyaas*) because *"conjecture could sometimes guide one, but often times mislead them!"* Hence he ruled that conjecture cannot be the right solution, because in matters related to 'True Faith' and the 'Hereafter'; a wrong interpretation of a significant issue, could jeopardize the outcome of a person's 'Salvation' in the 'After Life'!

It was for this very reason that the holy Prophet ﷺ had left behind the two '*Heavy Entities*': the **Quran and his Ahlul Bayt** for our guidance; as only these holy persons from the Ahlul Bayt were the ones who knew the meanings of every verse of the glorious Quran as well as the traditions of the Prophet ﷺ; and could therefore give the correct interpretation and true guidance. Unfortunately most of the Muslims had turned away from Ali ﷺ, the true heir of the holy Prophet ﷺ, and hence were unable to derive any real benefit from the Prophetic traditions, nor could they understand the true meaning of the Quranic verses; and thus ended up relying on their own conjecture (*Qiyaas*) which often resulted in leading them to incorrect interpretations.

In the book 'Manaqib of Ibn Shehr-e-Aashub' it is mentioned that a person once approached Abdullah ibn Umar and asked a certain question related to some issue on Islamic Jurisprudence. Abdullah ibn Umar could not give an answer but pointed to a young man (Imam Baqir ﷺ) and said, "Ask him". The person did as recommend and came back to Abdullah ibn Umar saying that his problem was resolved; to which ibn Umar responded saying: "He is the repository of knowledge, as Knowledge has emanated from their house!"

On another occasion Khazi Shareek, a government appointed Magistrate of State was approached by a couple of people who asked questions pertaining to the Jurisprudence applicable in the cases of "shortening of the obligatory prayers during travel" and secondly, "under what conditions does the Friday Congregation Prayer become mandatory?" They further added that the answer should be backed by authentic traditions of the Prophet ﷺ and not given by his own opinion or interpretation (*Qiyaas*). The sheik was flustered and unable to answer these questions; whereupon these two persons informed him that they had heard from one Muhammad bin Muslim Thaqafi who in turn had asked these very same questions to Imam Muhammad al-Baqir ؑ who had unhesitantly given the correct answers with relevant references of the Quran and traditions going back from his father to his forefathers all the way back to his great Grandfather, the holy Prophet ﷺ himself that: upon completion of 'two stages' of travel a 'four cycle' prayer could be shortened to 'two cycles' whereas for the Friday Prayer, if a group of five people congregate together out of whom one is willing to lead the prayers, then the Friday Prayer can be established.

The Imam ؑ was always known to be very refined and meticulous in his dressing. In later years of his life, he was known to dye his hair to maintain his neat and well-groomed appearance. At about this time, a group of Muslims had adopted an ascetic lifestyle by giving up the good things in life: eating dried bread and wearing coarse clothes and sporting a lifestyle much below their standard. People became impressed by their outward piety and began to pass comments about the Imam ؑ to the effect that 'the grandson of Ali was living in a style more lavish than this group of pious Muslims.' Imam Baqir ؑ took this with a smile and countered their criticism by saying: "*There is no blame on people for living in a decent lifestyle, eating, and dressing well. During the times of Ali ﷺ the conditions of life were different: the general standard of living was extremely low, and many persons could not afford to even have a meal of dried bread. As such, Imam Ali ﷺ used to lower his own standard to a level such that even the poorest person could not point a finger at him. These days the standards are much improved, and it is far easier to obtain the good things of life. To live well and eat well now without indulging in excess is completely permissible in Islam. To deny yourself the use of the blessings of Allah ﷻ would be tantamount to being ungrateful to Him for His blessings. There is one section of society who pretends to be pious and refrains from living well. To adopt an austere lifestyle to impress others could become a sin of 'showing off' (Riya); in the same way as going in the opposite direction of 'overindulging' and living a lavish lifestyle. Both such lifestyles would be wrong. A medium path is recommended as the best to be adopted."*

During the time of Imam Muhammad al-Baqir ﷺ there was a person named Muhammad bin Makandar who followed the Sufi faith and was regarded by most people to be a very pious man who spent his entire day and night in prayers. He never worked to provide for himself or his family but lived on handouts from his friends and associates and the common people. One day he saw the Imam ﷺ toiling in the intense heat of the day, working in his garden alongside his two workers. Smug in his concept of considering himself to be a 'pious person' due to his own excessive worship, he criticized the Imam ﷺ saying: "You are the son of the Prophet ﷺ and Islam originated from your household. It is not befitting for you to go toiling in this heat in pursuit of a livelihood to acquire the goods of this world (*Maal-e-Duniya*)! If the Angel of Death were to visit you now, how will you explain yourself to Allah?" The Imam ﷺ calmly replied: *"Working for and earning a just living for yourself and your family is **an act of piety** designated by Allah. If death comes to me now in this condition, then His Angel* *will find me serving Allah ﷻ in obedience to His command of supporting my family! It is religiously incorrect and not proper to burden others with your own responsibility of supporting yourself and your family while sitting idle yourself. This is against the precepts of Islam."* Upon hearing this, the Sufi exclaimed: "I had wanted to teach you, but instead **you** have taught me the true meaning of Islam through your actions and words!"

The Imam was known to be such a lenient master that his slaves used to long for; and eagerly await an opportunity for the Imam ﷺ to ever ask them to run an errand for him or perform a task on his behalf. But they hardly ever got a chance; rather, it was the Imam ﷺ who used to end up doing the tasks for them! Prior to eating himself, he would personally ensure that all his slaves and household members had eaten before he partook of any food himself. Praying, fasting, and instructing the community was his normal day to day way of life. Eventually, like his revered father, he too was poisoned by the ruler of his time Hisham ibn Abdul Malik in the year 114 AH (733 AD). Hisham was a mortal enemy of the Imam ﷺ and would call him repeatedly to Damascus from the city of Medina simply to harass him; and tried many a time to imprison him on various occasions on any feeble pretext.

On one occasion there was a display of the skill of archery by many persons held in the court of Hisham. He turned to Imam Baqir ﷺ and tauntingly challenged him to try his hand and shoot some arrows himself. The Imam ﷺ declined saying he was now old and did not feel up to indulging in this sport anymore. But Hisham insisted, whereupon the Imam ﷺ shot nine arrows consecutively all as in 'bull's eye' right on target, to the point that the preceding arrow was being split by the next arrow, all landing dead on at the same spot! Hisham's wish to belittle the Imam backfired and evaporated, and he quickly called a halt to the activities and promptly dismissed the court!

Some time later however, succumbing to the intense hatred of the Imam ﷺ which he carried in his heart, Hisham presented him with a saddle for his horse which had been laced with a deadly poison; with the order that this saddle was meant for the exclusive use of Imam Baqir ﷺ alone! Upon receiving this, the Imam ﷺ remarked: *"I know that this saddle will prove injurious to my well being and health, but it is decreed that I should attain my martyrdom through this means!"* He subsequently died due to this form of poisoning.

Like his late father Imam Sajjad ﷺ, Muhammad al-Baqir ﷺ also used to weep profusely for his grandfather Imam Husayn ﷺ; and the great tragedy which engulfed him. When questioned as to how long he will cry, he used to quote the verse from the Quran and say that *"Prophet Yaqoob (Jacob) ﷺ cried for years on end for Yousuf (Joeseph) ﷺ; I have seen 18 'Yousufs' of my family slaughtered before my eyes!"*

11.25: Some Miracles of Imam Muhammad al-Baqir ﷺ

In the book "Shawahed" by Faiz ibn Mathar, he relates that one day he personally went to Imam Muhammad al-Baqir ﷺ to ask a certain question regarding the performance of Salaat during a journey which he intended to undertake. But before he could voice his question, the Imam ﷺ gave him the answer, quoting a tradition from the Prophet ﷺ! The author further writes that he also witnessed the Imam ﷺ conversing with and instructing the *Jinns* in matters of Islam and answering their queries, though he, Faiz himself could not see anyone visibly present before his eyes!

Data Ganj Bakhsh for the general edification of the *Ahle Tareeqat* Sufis, writes in his book 'Kashful Mahjoob' that Imam Muhammad al-Baqir ﷺ was from the household of the holy Prophet ﷺ and as such he held an honoured and esteemed position. In matters of Divinity, he was an absolute authority. On page 95 of this book, he records a related incident as follows: One day the Caliph summoned the Imam ﷺ to his court with the intention of killing him by sleath. But when the Imam ﷺ arrived, the Caliph welcomed him with great respect and honoured him with extreme courtesy and sent him off by giving him several gifts before he departed. When questioned by his courtiers later about the reversal of his behaviour in showing such great respect and showering expensive gifts on the Imam ﷺ as he bid him farewell, the Caliph replied that when the Imam ﷺ entered his Court, he saw two ferocious lions accompanying him on either side, threatening to kill him if he so much as harmed a single hair of the Imam ﷺ! Data Gunj adds that the miracles and special qualities and traits of the holy Ahlul Bayt ﷺ are so numerous that if he were to recount even a portion of them, no book would ever be ample or sufficient to enlist them; and people would undoubtedly get wonderstruck that these holy personalities possessed such great merits and were of such Divine calibre!

It is recorded from the Sixth Imam Jafar al-Sadiq ﷺ that once Imam Muhammad al-Baqir ﷺ was riding on his horse through a wilderness when a mountain goat approached him and after invoking salutations, asked him for his blessings to which the Imam ﷺ responded in kind.

He also said that his revered father addressed him one day and predicted that there were five years remaining in his own life and this later turned out to be true.

Once, a person set out from his own hometown toward the city of Medina with a sincere desire to meet Imam Muhammad al-Baqir ﷺ. But by the time he arrived in Medina it was late in the night, raining and bitterly cold. He reached the house of the Imam ﷺ and stood hesitantly by the door, wondering whether it was proper to disturb the Imam ﷺ at this late hour of the night. However, to his great surprise he heard the voice of the Imam ﷺ from within the house asking his servant to open the door and grant entry to his guest on his behalf, referring to him by his name!

Once someone enquired from the Imam ﷺ as to: 'what are the rights of a True Believer upon Allah ﷻ?' The Imam ﷺ replied that *"if he is a True Believer, Allah will endow him with extraordinary powers; for instance, if the Believer were to point to a tree and order it to move from its place, it would do so".* To demonstrate this, the Imam ﷺ pointed to a tree and asked it to come forward and it started to uproot itself and move towards him. Imam ﷺ again ordered it to return to its original spot and it duly complied!

One day Imam Baqir ﷺ happened to walk past a Palace that was being constructed for the Caliph Hisham ibn Abdul Malik. He remarked that this palace would soon be destroyed and razed to the ground. People were amazed at this statement and wondered as to who could destroy a palace which was being built by the Caliph himself! However, very shortly thereafter, when Walid became the Caliph, one of his first acts was to have the palace demolished and levelled to the ground!

Prior to his death Imam Muhammad al-Baqir ﷺ instructed his son Imam Jafar al-Sadiq ﷺ that he should give him his burial bath and conduct his funeral rites, because only an Imam can do this for another Imam. He also predicted that one of his other brothers would come forward to do this and would also contest the Imamate. He bade Imam Jafar al-Sadiq to be patient because the other son would not succeed in his plans and would himself not survive too long after him. This prediction also proved to be true.

Abu Baseer, who was blind, relates that when he met Imam Muhammad al-Baqir ﷺ he asked him: "Are you from the progeny of the holy Prophet ﷺ?" He said *"Yes".* Then he asked: "Had not the Prophet ﷺ inherited the knowledge of the previous prophets (*Ambiya*)? He said *"Yes."* Then he again asked: "Have you also inherited this knowledge from the Prophet ﷺ?" He replied *"Yes".*

Then he, Abu Baseer again asked: "Can you then also raise the dead back to life like Nabi Esa (Jesus 🕮), or give sight to the blind and cure the lepers?" He replied *"Yes"*. He then asked: "Do you also know what is stored in other peoples' houses?" The Imam 🕮 replied: *"Yes! By the Power entrusted to us by Allah, we can do all these things, but for reasons of decorum we do not do these as a normal practice."* Then Abu Baseer says that the Imam 🕮 asked him to come near and he ran his hand across his eyes upon which he could immediately see everything with a sharp vision! The Imam then brushed his hand across his eyes once again and he was returned to his state of blindness. The Imam 🕮 then asked him: *"Which of the two would you prefer: to regain your sight and be questioned about your actions on the Day of Judgment; OR remain blind and enter heaven without any questioning?"* Abu Baseer opted for the latter and remained blind for the rest of his life.

To conclude this section, we record one last episode wherein it is said that the Imam 🕮 was travelling with his entourage when he spotted two persons. He turned to his servants and said, *"these two are thieves and should be arrested"*. They went and caught them, after which Imam Baqir 🕮 asked one of his slaves to go towards a nearby hill where he would find a cave; and hidden inside this cave he would find the stolen goods bundled up in two bags. He told him to bring these bags back carefully. When the bags were brought back as instructed, Imam Baqir 🕮 said that one of the two bags belonged to a person who resides in Medina, while the owner of the second was an outsider. When the Imam and his entourage arrived in Medina, they found that two persons innocent of the crime had been arrested on charge of this robbery and were being walked towards the Magistrate's Office for a ruling. The Imam 🕮 arranged for the falsely accused persons to be released from their custody and the real culprits handed over for their sentencing. The first bag was then given back to its rightful owner. As for the second bag, Imam Muhammad al-Baqir 🕮 said that it belonged to a non-Muslim person who, unaware of the theft of his goods was waiting for its delivery outside the precincts of Medina. Imam 🕮 personally had his bag returned to him; and when this man realised that even without opening the bag the Imam 🕮 had described its contents in detail he was astonished and overawed and immediately accepted Islam.

A Sunni scholar named Mustahsan Farooqi writes that were someone to recount all the miracles of this Imam 🕮 alone, it would require a whole lot of super-sized books to compile them.

11.26: Sixth Imam: Jafar ibn Muhammad al-Sadiq 🕮

The holy sixth Imam 🕮 was the son of Imam Muhammad al-Baqir 🕮, and as such he was a direct descendant of Imam Ali 🕮. He was born on 17th Rabbi Al Awwal 83 AH [702 AD] while some traditions say it was 80 AH or 699 AD. His mother was Farwa bint Qasim [Ibne Muhammad bin Abu Bakr]. Qasim himself was born of a Persian princess called Gehan Banu who was brought to the court of Imam Ali 🕮 as a captive, along with her sister Shehr Banu 🕮. Seeing that they were descendants of a noble family, Imam Ali 🕮 had arranged to get princess Shehr Banu married to his own son Imam Husayn 🕮, and Gehan Banu married to his adopted son Muhammad bin Abu Bakr.

Imam Jafar al-Sadiq 🕮's appellation was 'Abu Abdullah' while he was also known by many other titles such as 'Sadiq, Sabir, Fazel and Taher'. Hafiz Abu Naeem in his book 'Huliyatul Abrar' quotes a tradition from Umar bin Al Maqdam wherein he says: "Whenever I look at Jafar e Sadiq 🕮 I immediately get reminded that he is a noble descendant from a lineage of the previous prophets!"

Imam Malik ibn Anas, the Imam of the Maliki sect says that: "No eyes have seen a better person, nor any ear has heard from a more superior person; nor any heart has felt the heartstrings being pulled towards him as much as by the personality of Imam Jafar e Sadiq ☙. He was the most knowledgeable person in the entire world! He was the one who spent his night in prayers and fasted during the day!"

Hazrat Khwaja Bande Nawaz Gesudaraz Husayni writes on page 67 of his handwritten manuscript that: "After Ali ☙, he possessed the most knowledge on the holy Quran and knew the secrets and inferences of the Almighty's Words. He used to explain the hidden and inner meanings of the Quranic verses. This knowledge was gifted to him by Allah ﷻ in the same way as it was to Imam Ali ☙. His exposition and reasoning which he exhibited, completely enthralled his audience and left them mesmerized and dumbfounded!"

The famous Sunni Egyptian scholar Fareed Wajdi writes: "Imam Jafar al-Sadiq was descended from the holy Prophet ﷺ and in fact he was one of the most prominent among the Ahlul Bayt ☙. He was endowed with the title of 'Sadiq' because his speech was always based on truth. He was distinguished by his superior knowledge amongst all the people of his time".

We will quote a couple of the Imam ☙'s sayings as a sample of his wisdom and faith in Allah ﷻ: He said: "*Whenever I fell into straitened circumstances, I used to trade with Allah by giving out a little in charity and gaining a lot of beneficence from Allah ﷻ in return!*" He also used to advise his children: "*There is a key for every Treasure; and the Key for Sustenance (Rizq) is Almsgiving and Charity in the Way of Allah ﷻ.*"

On one occasion when Imam Jafar ☙ had engaged some workers to till the land in his garden and it was time for the 'Asr Salaat' (afternoon prayer) the workers stopped their tasks. The Imam ☙ immediately instructed his agents to pay the workers their wages *before the sweat of their brows could dry!*

Muawiyah ibne Wahab says that once while in a state of travel he found the Imam ﷺ prostrating himself in submission. When ibn Wahab enquired the reason for this, he replied that he had just been granted a blessing from Allah ﷻ and he had bowed down instantly in a 'Prostration of Thanks' (Sajda e Shukr).

Once a relative of his spoke to the Imam ﷺ in a very rude manner, but the Imam ﷺ on the contrary, remained kind and courteous to him. When asked about his fortitude in such matters, the Imam ﷺ replied that "Being kind to ones' relatives reduces the punishment of sins from Allah ﷻ."

A Christian person by the name of Zacharia bin Ibrahim had converted to Islam and when he met Imam Jafar al-Sadiq ﷺ he said that all members of his family were still followers of the Christian faith; and in addition, he said that his mother was also blind. The Imam ﷺ told him to be especially careful toward his mother and to be kind to his relatives. After some time his mother remarked that even though he had always been a good son, he was now showing an extraordinarily kind behaviour with respect to her, which he had not displayed prior to his becoming a Muslim. She asked the reason for his change in attitude, to which he replied that the Imam of the Muslims had ordered him to be especially kind and careful about her well being because of her high status as a mother. Upon hearing this, she was so impressed that she also converted to Islam!

Imam Jafar al-Sadiq ﷺ was the embodiment of kindness and tolerance toward everyone especially his slaves, whom he used to treat as his equals. If anyone of them was belligerent, he would release them from his bondage. It is recorded that one day he sent one of his slaves to run an errand for him and when he was unusually late in returning, he personally went out in search of him and found him fast asleep at a certain spot under the shade of a tree. The Imam ﷺ sat down next to him, and rather than waking him up, he began gently fanning him to keep him cool from the heat of the day. When the slave eventually woke up, the Imam 🕮 simply remarked that "*The day was created for work; and night was meant for rest.*"

In the matter of the emancipation of his slaves, Imam Jafar 🕮 used to actually write up documents of their release duly attested by witnesses, with the stipulation that, upon their release from bondage, they would perform their daily ritual prayers, observe the fasts, perform the Hajj and pay the Zakaat provided they could afford it; and in general follow all other Islamic practices! In addition, he also endorsed a specific condition that they love the Prophet 🕮's family and abstain from the company of unrighteous persons.

He very often invited guests while eating his meals, offering them with the best of food while he himself would simply restrict to his normal diet of bread and vinegar. On special occasions however, like on the days of feasts or festivals, he would not hesitate to eat of the good food that was usually offered on such occasions. When any guests stayed over in his house, he would not allow them to do any work saying: "*Our Grandfather, the Prophet 🕮 would never allow his guest to do any work, saying that it was the duty of the host to do all the work in his own house.*" It is also said that he would often go out in the dead of the night to distribute food to the poor and the needy.

It is further recorded from one Abu Jafar Khasshami who states: "One day Imam Jafar 🕮 gave me a purse full of money and directed me to deliver it to a certain person but instructed me not to reveal his identity to that person. When I delivered the money as instructed, the man took it and gratefully thanked me and raised his hands in prayers for the generous person who had sent it". Abu Jafar Khasshami adds that after accepting the charity, the man being totally unaware that this help was from the Imam Baqir 🕮

[who regularly used to help many indigent persons while choosing to remain incognito], turned to him and complained that while others offered help to him in his hour of need, Imam Jafar al-Sadiq 🕮 seemed to ignore him!

Another follower of the Imam 🕮 by the name of Fazal ibn Marra remarks that this trait of doing charity while remaining incognito so as not to make the recipient person feel embarrassed or indebted, was so ingrained in Imam Jafar al-Sadiq 🕮's character that he often used to send gifts and presents to the needy amongst his relatives (as well as other indigent persons within the society), conveying the impression that these gifts were being sent to them from far off locations. This act of kindness, however, would often result in his own relatives complaining that while "others from far off places like Iraq" were displaying kindness towards them and sending them help, Imam Jafar 🕮 himself, despite being in their proximity, appeared to be indifferent to their needs and their state of destitution!

When such remarks were circulated back to him, Imam Sadiq 🕮 used to go into a *'Sajda-e-Shukr'* (prostration of thankfulness to Allah 🕮 and implore: *"O Allah! Grant me patience in the name of my parents and my ancestors, to bear this with fortitude and not be offended by any criticism!"* He used to say that *"doing 'good' to your relatives was the essence of charity and Allah 🕮 would forgive one's sins because of these acts."* He also used to say: *"I hasten to fulfill the needs even of my enemies."* He would often caution and advocate that *"your neighbours have a great right over you; and stated that one's neighbourhood could include up to 40 houses around one's own dwelling!"* Among his numerous other sayings, a few are given below as a sample:

1. There is nothing better than piety (Taqwa).
2. There is nothing better than silence.

3. Criticism breeds animosity. Revealing others' secrets belittles one in the eyes of the people and causes a loss of self respect.

4. If someone obstructs another person from helping, then be aware that he can easily behave similarly against you!

5. The best person is he who has these three qualities: Controls his Anger; Forgives the mistakes of others; and serves and benefits others with his wealth and time.

6. One who gives up mischief and sedition attains honour; one who gives up pride and arrogance attains a high status and one who gives up miserliness gets respect.

7. Knowledge, Piety, and Good Manners are essential qualities for all humans, and it is incumbent upon every person to inculcate these traits.

8. Regard that person who, despite getting upset at being subjected to any form of ill treatment from you on as many as three occasions but **still** did not cut off relationship with you, as being entirely trustworthy; and take him for your sincere friend!

9. Charitable deeds are accepted when you perform the following: Fulfill the monetary obligations of a needy person **without delay.** Consider your own donation as meagre even though it may be great. Give the donation in secrecy (incognito).

10. The one who spends his wealth carefully, Allah causes an increase in his wealth, and those who spend it carelessly its blessings will diminish.

11. Do not look for a friend who is devoid of defects, as this is not possible.

12. Befriending people is a good trait, but to be tolerant of their shortcomings is even better!

13. A likeable person is one who makes people get attached to him due to his good behaviour.

14. If you befriend a person for more than 20 days, then he becomes like one of your relatives.

15. The one who is satisfied upon receiving small blessings from Allah, Allah Himself gets pleased with a little of his virtuous deeds!

16. Beware of the wailing of an oppressed person because he appeals for his rights to Allah and Allah never denies anybody their just rights.

17. Beware of the Wrath of Allah ﷻ, but not to the extent of giving up hope in His Mercy!

18. The winter season is "Springtime" for a true believer because the 'True Believer' will spend its long nights in prayers to his Creator, and its short days in fasting.

Regarding the trusts that are given among each other, Imam Jafar al-Sadiq ﷺ would at times say: "I will tell you what my father Imam Muhammad al-Baqir ﷺ said about his own father Imam Zainul Abideen ﷺ: that he used to say that 'even if the murderer of my father Husayn ﷺ had given me the very sword with which he had killed my father, to hold it in safe-keeping', even so I would have returned it to him in the same condition as that in which I had been entrusted with!'"!

One time it is recorded that someone before starting his prayers in the mosque had placed his money bag by his side. When he finished his prayers, he saw that the bag was missing. Upon looking around he noticed that none other was present in the mosque except for Imam Jafar al-Sadiq ﷺ who was absorbed in prayer in a remote corner of the mosque. The man not knowing the identity of the Imam ﷺ began to accuse him of having stolen his bag. Imam Jafar ﷺ calmly asked him as to what was in the bag and he replied that there were 1000 Dirhams in it. The Imam ﷺ

took him to his own house and gave him the 1000 Dirhams. When the man later returned to the mosque, he found that his bag with the money was in fact there intact! He felt ashamed and went back to apologize and return the money to Imam Jafar al-Sadiq ☉, who however replied that once they give anything away in the way of Allah ☉ they never take it back.

Some people during his lifetime were beginning to incline towards Sufism and Mysticism; but the Imam ☉ in keeping with the tradition of his forefathers and by his own exemplary behavior, succeeded in bringing them back to the right path.

It is recorded by Kulayni in his treatise 'Al Kafi' that one day Abu Sufiyan Suri entered the mosque and saw that Imam Ja'far al-Sadiq ☉ was extremely well dressed. He approached the Imam and said in a critical manner that the Imam ☉'s forefathers, the Prophet ☉ and Imam Ali ☉, were never known to have worn such elegant clothes; and how was it that he did not follow in their tradition? The Imam ☉ replied in the same vein as his revered father Imam Baqir ☉ had responded to his own followers saying: "*In those days there was not enough wealth, and people could not afford such attires. But things are different now and people are economically well off; and it is incumbent upon them to partake of this bounty from Allah and display it as a sign of their thankfulness. It is to thank Allah ☉ and display His bounty that I have dressed accordingly.*" He then lifted a corner of his outer garment and showed the coarse inner garment which he wore to deny himself the feel of luxury of a smoother material against his skin. He then lifted the outer garment of Abu Sufiyan Suri and revealed the fine inner garment that the latter was wearing next to his body and remarked: "*This is the difference between you and us the Ahlul Bayt!*"

Ibne Hajar Askalani writes in his book 'Sawaiq-e-Mohriqa' that many scholars from various parts of the world used to attend his lectures and discourses. Some of the countries mentioned are Iraq,

Iran, India, Syria and some European places such as Greece and Rome; from where students used to attend his classes and take notes on an ongoing basis. The Imam 🕮 used to instruct them to preserve these notes and pass them on to their posterity to ensure that the knowledge would reach their new generations even after they themselves were gone.

In the book 'Minhajul Miqaal' it is said that at certain times the number of students attending his lectures were as many as four thousand! It is said that when Imam Jafar e Sadiq 🕮 gave his discourse, *it appeared as if an Ocean of Knowledge was surging forth from his lips and students would be sitting with their pen and paper in fascination, taking detailed notes and the Imam 🕮 used to tell them to take good care of their writings, for this would be the best inheritance that they would leave for their children!* He also used to insist upon them that while taking these notes to be careful about their grammar and enunciations so that the TRUE meaning of the traditions will remain intact and not be distorted because of any slight or minor misrepresentations recorded by them in error. Approximately 4000 traditions have been attributed directly to him!

Some 400 of his prominent students are known to have compiled a total of 400 books which have come to be known as *"Usool-e-Arba Miah"* (Four Hundred Principles of Jurisprudence) and these books cover the entire rules of Islamic *Fiqh* - Jurisprudence! These books remained in their original condition until 448 AH and were collected and stored in a library in 'Karkh' near Baghdad. This library was owned by Abu Sasr Shahpur bin Ardarsheer who was the Vazir of Baha-ud Daulah. When Tuglaq Beg Seljuki attacked the city he burnt this library, but some selected books were saved by the revered scholar Naimatullah Jazairi and preserved until his death in 1112 AH. [Ref: Anwaar-ul-Naumaniyah].

The great scholar Syed Murtaza Alam-ul-Huda who was of the same era is said to have possessed 400 books which contained a total of 5000 articles on *'Usool'* (Principles) and these were preserved until the era of Ibn Idris; but unfortunately, now there are only 30 of these books which have survived to the time of our generation! In two of these books written by Imam Jafar al-Sadiq ﷺ under the titles of *'Al Jame'* and *'Ilm e Jafer'* in addition to dealing with the subject on hand, the Imam ﷺ has also recorded the biographical information of all the 'Shia Imams' and their sayings and predictions about events to occur to the end of time.

The Sunni scholar Sahebzada Mustahsin Farooqi writes that apart from being the ultimate model of piety and one of the most authoritative exponents of *'Irfan'* he was also one of the greatest traditionalists of his time. The list of his students is extensive; and to name but a few who were the cream of the jurists and traditionalists of their time, we have names such Yahya bin Saeed, Yahya Al Qathan, Shouba, Sufiyan ibne Ainiyyah, Ibn Jareeh, Abu Ayub-e-Bahastani, Imam Sufiyan Suri, Imam Malik and Imam Abu Hanifa, were all among those who were taught by him. Abu Hanifa was often heard to admit and say: "Had I not spent the two years of my life with Imam Jafar al-Sadiq ﷺ I would have perished, and no one would have known about me!" Abu Hatim, another of his students used to say that the Imam ﷺ was so perfect and pious that whenever he said something, no body could dare question his knowledge on any subject! He was so honest and truthful in his speech and statements that he was called *'As Sadiq'* (The Truthful) by all.

Hafez Abdul Aziz bin Akhzar Junabazi relates from Saleh ibn Aswad that he personally heard Imam Jafar ﷺ declare several times amidst a large audience, [in the same style as his great Grandfather Ali ibn Abu Taleb ﷺ]: *"Ask me whatever you wish to ask, before you lose me."*

Allama Sheik Mufeed in his book 'Kitab ul Irshad' has quoted Imam Jafar al-Sadiq ﷺ as saying: *"We have been given (endowed with) the Knowledge of all the 'Seen' and 'Unseen'. We have the books of 'Ilm-e-Jafer Ahmer' (Red) and 'Ilm-e-Jafer Abyad' (White), as well as the 'Mushaf-e-Fatima' (*The Chronicles of Fatima Zahra ﷺ*) which contains the predictions of all that is to happen in future, as well as the names of all persons who have special knowledge and possess the Divine Authority. We also have the book 'Jame' which was dictated by our grandfather the holy Prophet ﷺ to Imam Ali ﷺ; and this contains all the information that people would like to know till the Day of Judgment."*

The second Abbasside Caliph Mansur Dawanaqi, due to the rising popularity of Imam Jafar al-Sadiq ﷺ and fear for his own position, had the Imam ﷺ moved from Medina to Baghdad where he could keep a close watch on him and his activities. Many a time he summoned the Imam ﷺ to his court with the intention of having the Imam ﷺ killed; and the people would often be fearful that this would be the last day of the Imam ﷺ's life! But Mansoor would get so over-awed by the Imam ﷺ's personality, while also being fearful of losing favour with the populace, that he held his hand and desisted from conducting his devious plots. As an alternative course, he later had the Imam ﷺ sent to Basra under the care of a person known as Aamel Kufi where to his consternation the Imam ﷺ became extremely popular among the masses; so Mansoor had him again sent back Medina where he was eventually poisoned.

In the book 'Tazkeratul Khawas-ul-Ummah' by ibn Sabbagh Al Maliki it is recorded that Mansur Dawanaqi had Imam Jafar al-Sadiq ﷺ poisoned through grapes infested with a deadly poison and sent by his orders through a person named Muhammad bin Sulaiman. This led to the demise of the Imam ﷺ on the 15th of Shawwal 148 AH. His eldest son Ismail had died in the year 128 AH during own lifetime; so, his younger son Musa al Kazim ﷺ

became his successor. However, the present Ismaili Sect of Muslims continues to regard Hazrat Ismail as the spiritual successor of Imam Sadiq even though his death had taken place 20 years before the demise of his father Imam Sadiq 🕮!

11.27: Some Miracles of Imam Jafar al-Sadiq 🕮

The Abbasside Caliph Mansoor called Imam Jafar al-Sadiq 🕮 to his court and accused him of causing sedition among the Muslims. The Imam 🕮 denied the charge, but Mansoor said he had a person who could testify to this fact. Imam 🕮 asked that this person be brought before him so he could have a face-to-face confrontation. The person arrived and said that he had heard the Imam say a few things that could be deemed as being seditious; whereupon the Imam 🕮 asked him to repeat the same charges under an oath in the same manner as the Imam 🕮 dictated. At first the person baulked but when pressed by the Caliph he eventually did take the oath as instructed by Imam Jafar 🕮 and instantly fell to the ground and was pronounced dead! Mansoor had his corpse disposed without any qualms.

Mansoor nonetheless, continued in his nefarious plans to have the Imam 🕮 killed by any means possible. Toward this end, one day he ordered the doorkeeper of his palace to kill the Imam 🕮 as soon as he entered his court. The Imam 🕮 came in, and going past the doorkeeper, sat by the side of Mansoor; and upon ending his visit, left by the same door past the same doorkeeper. After his departure Mansoor asked the guard as to why he did not kill the Imam as instructed? The doorkeeper replied under oath that he never saw the Imam 🕮 enter or leave the palace!

One of the courtiers of Mansoor recounts that he saw Mansoor sitting deep in thought one day and asked him the reason for this. Mansoor replied that he had killed many Alawites (Shias of Ali 🕮) but was not able to kill their leader! When asked as to who their leader was, Mansoor replied it was Jafar e Sadiq 🙼. The courtier said it was so because the Imam 🙼 was always busy in prayers and worship and did not care for this world. Mansoor told him that he suspected him of being partial to the Imam 🙼; but nonetheless he said that he had taken an oath that he would not rest till he had put Imam Jafar 🙼 to his death! He then called his executioner and told him that when Jafar ibne Muhammad 🙼 arrives, I will place my hand on my head and that will be a signal for you to kill him.

When the Imam 🙼 arrived in the court, the courtier reports that he was near the Imam 🙼 when he arrived; and he saw his lips move while he said a few words. Instantly the walls of the palace began to shudder and quake! When Mansoor saw this phenomenon, he rushed toward the Imam, took him by the arm, and made him sit on his own throne! Then he humbly asked: "O Son of the Prophet, what is the reason for your visit?" The Imam replied: *"You sent for me"* to which Mansoor asked: "What is your wish and how may I fulfill it?" the Imam 🙼 responded: *"I wish that you do not invite me into your presence so often!"* When the Imam 🙼 departed, the courtier asked Mansoor the reason for his unexpectedly courteous behaviour toward the Imam.

He replied: "When Jafar al-Sadiq 🙼 arrived, I saw a huge serpent standing alongside the Imam with its mouth wide open, and said it was ready to swallow me and destroy my entire court if I brought any harm to Imam Jafar 🙼!" The courtier was amazed and said this was sheer magic, but Mansoor replied: "No, this is the 'Power of The Greatest Name of Allah 🙼' (*Isme Azam*) which is the protective shield for his grandfather, the Prophet of Islam and his progeny!"

Once the companions of Imam Jafar al-Sadiq 🙼 asked him about the miracle of Hazrat Ibrahim 🙼 when he killed four different species of birds, mixed their body parts, and then revived them back to life. The Imam 🙼 stated that the miracle was true and added that he too could perform the same. He then proceeded to do so with a pigeon, a peacock, a crow, and a hawk. After killing and dismembering these birds, he mixed their flesh and feathers together, and upon calling each by its name, the bird of each species came back to life! Many other miraculous incidents are found in books with respect to this Imam ﷺ but only a few have been recorded by us for the sake of brevity.

11.28: Seventh Imam: Musa ibn Ja'far al-Kazim ﷺ

The holy 7th Imam ﷺ was the inheritor of Imamate from his noble father Imam Jafar e Sadiq ﷺ, though he was not his first-born son. He was in fact about 20 years younger than the first-born son Ismail ﷺ who passed away in the month of Shawwal 128 AH. Imam Musa al Kazim ﷺ was born about 9 months earlier in that same year on the 7th of Safar 128 AH. His patronymic filial appellations were Abul Hasan, Al-Kazim, As Sabir, Saleh, and Amin. It is noted in the book 'Tabaqat al Huffaz' that because of his excessive worship and piety he was also referred to as 'Abdus-Saleh'. In another book 'Fusool Mohimma' it is stated that he was recognized as the most eminent exponent of Islamic Jurisprudence of his era and recognized as being the most pious. Apart from this, he was known to be the most generous among his age and was especially kind and concerned towards the needs of the beggars and the poor among the society who had no knowledge about their benefactor: a fact which was only revealed after his death.

Allama Ibne Hajar Asqalani has recorded that the people of Iraq used to refer to this Imam ﷺ as 'Baab ul Hawayej' – 'The Door through which the Wishes are Fulfilled' because of their wishes being granted and needs being fulfilled through him. Even at the tender age of 5- or 6-years people were impressed by the knowledge that he imparted. It is stated that Imam Abu Hanifa once visited the holy sixth Imam Jafar al-Sadiq ﷺ to get some clarification on certain issues with respect to the Islamic Jurisprudence. Imam Jafar ﷺ instead of answering himself, referred Abu Hanifa to his young son al-Kazim ﷺ who was about 5 or 6 years of age; and yet he answered all his questions to his complete satisfaction leaving him totally amazed at the intellectual capacity of this 5- or 6-year-old child! [Ref: 'Manaqib' Pg 69].

The Caliph Haroon al Rashid was a bitter enemy of this pious Imam ﷺ and not content with having him imprisoned for no less than 35 years in all; he simultaneously had an order issued for his execution; and eventually did have him poisoned. Imam Musa al-Kazim ﷺ was martyred under Haroon's orders on the 25th of Rajab 183 AH, while he was still confined in one of his prisons.

In his bid to belittle Imam Musa al-Kazim ﷺ Haroon once asked him as to how and on what basis did, he classify himself as the progeny of the Prophet ﷺ, because he was a direct descendant of Ali ibn Abi Taleb ﷺ? In reply the Imam ﷺ quoted two verses of the holy Quran: 3:61 and 27:16. *In the first instance he explained that this verse was revealed during the actual confrontation of the Prophet ﷺ with the Christians of Najran; at which time in keeping with Allah ﷻ's injunction to "take his sons" (Abna Ana) the Prophet ﷺ took Hasan and Husayn ﷺ under the category of his sons, though they actually were the children of Ali ﷺ and Fatima ﷺ. Ever since then they were referred to as "the sons of the Prophet ﷺ" - and I am their direct descendant!*

As for the other verse, Imam Kazim ﷺ proved through the verses of the holy Quran that *although Hazrat Esa ﷺ had no father, yet he is regarded as a "descendant from Hazrat Sulayman ﷺ" through his mother's connection; because his revered mother Hazrat Mariam ﷺ was from the progeny of Hazrat Sulayman ﷺ, and thus he, Esa ﷺ, is linked through the lineage from his mother's side! Similarly, Imam Musa al-Kazim ﷺ's lineage is linked to Prophet Muhammad ﷺ through his daughter Fatima ﷺ.*

The eminent Sunni Sufi scholar Syed Jamal Alishah Chisite wa Husayni writes in his publication 'Kashaful ghita Al Usool Al Mawta' printed 6th Safar 1334 AH, wherein he quotes a couplet from Imam Shafei who said that "The Grave of Imam Musa al-Kazim ﷺ is the best place for the acceptance of any prayer!"

One day Haroon Rashid was sitting in the precincts of the holy Kaaba where he saw Imam Musa al-Kazim ﷺ sitting in a corner where a large crowd had surrounded him paying their respects and kissing his hand. Haroon became bitterly jealous at this display of respect and affection being showered on the Imam and voiced his objection to the Imam for tolerating such behaviour of the people. To this Imam Kazim ﷺ replied: "*You rule over them as your subjects, while I rule over their hearts.* (The difference is that) o*n the Day of Resurrection when we see the Prophet ﷺ you will greet him as 'O Son of my uncle' while I will greet him as 'O my grandfather'!*" This ignited the fire of hatred in Haroon even more and resulted in having the Imam ﷺ arrested and confined in an old and dilapidated prison in Baghdad.

From there after some time, he had him moved to Basra where he instructed his Governor Esa ibn Jafer ibn Mansur with orders to keep the Imam ﷺ in solitary confinement and under strict surveillance. A brief time later he wrote again to have Imam al-Kazim ﷺ put to death while he was still in prison! But seeing the piety and patience of the Imam ﷺ where he would often be seen praying and worshipping and thanking Allah ﷻ in words to the effect: "*O Lord! I used to always ask you to give me the time and opportunity to worship You in seclusion without other distractions; and You have answered my prayers and provided me with time to pray to You in an undisturbed state of solitary isolation;*" Esa ibn Jafer refused to follow orders to kill him!

This prompted Haroon to recall the Imam ﷺ back to Baghdad where he was imprisoned under the watch of Fazal bin Rabee with the same instructions that he was to be executed while still in prison under his eye. Fazal bin Rabee also refused to conduct this dastardly deed, whereupon another person Fazal bin Yahya was appointed for this heinous task; but seeing the Imam's personality and piety he also refused to carry out Haroon's orders! In frustration Haroon then searched out a hardhearted person with a brutal reputation named Sindi ibn Shahek and bluntly told him that "years have elapsed with al-Kazim being confined in prison with no end in sight" and ordered that something should be done to finalise this without further prolongation! Sindi then took it upon himself to sneakily feed some heavily poisoned grapes which resulted in the Imam 🕮 being in extreme pain for three days before succumbing to the poison and achieving martyrdom on the 25th of Rajab 183 AH at the age of 55 years.

The prolonged period of incarceration over so many years had taken its toll on the health and well being of the holy Imam 🕮 to such an extent that he had become totally emaciated due to lack of food, sunshine, and freedom of movement within the constricted quarters of his prison cells. This fact was brought to light upon the public when word got around that Imam al-Kazim 🕮 had died; and people were sent to remove his body; but returned from the prison saying that there was only a sheet of cloth spread on the floor of the cell, but no dead body! The Jailor recalled them and pointed to the same sheet of cloth lying on the floor and said *that* was the body [!], thereby exposing the fact that except for his skin and bones, there was no flesh left on the Imam 🕮's form and physique due to the rigours of his prolonged imprisonment. It was a dark dungeon with only one small hole in its wall to let some light and air in. The two pieces of bread offered to him were made from the husk of wheat and a small pitcher of water for the entire day! Very often, even this he did not consume fully. He spent all his time in prayer and worship until he was called back to his Lord.

In the book 'Fasal Al Khataab' Khwaja Muhammad Parsa has noted the following tradition: "Caliph Mamoon Rashid once said that his father Haroon Abbasi called all his sons together on one occasion and told them all that: "Musa al-Kazim was the Imam and Proof of Allah over all people. I was just a leader of a group of people, but I obtained this position **by the force of arms**. I swear to God that Musa Kazim was the descendant and true successor of the Prophet of Islam and was more worthy and capable of the Caliphate than me. But when it came to 'Power and Pelf' and the worldly Caliphate of governing the people, I was adamant to obtain it. Even if anyone of you, *my sons*, had opposed me in this matter, I would have gouged out your eyes and put you to death!" This narration is also recorded by the famous Sunni scholar Hafiz Abu Naim Isfahani in his 'Musnad' and he has endorsed it as being a "true" and reliable tradition.

11.29: Some Miracles of Imam Musa al-Kazim ﷺ

Among the various miracles performed by Imam Musa al-Kazim ﷺ was his uncanny prediction of his own death a few days ahead of its occurrence. Before his actual demise, he had foretold that he would be poisoned one day, be sick the next day and die on the third day. That was how it happened.

On one occasion he was seen to raise the water level of a dried-up well to the brim. This was someday when he was attempting to let down a pot down at the side of the well to obtain some water; but the pot slipped and fell into the well along with the string tied to it. The Imam ﷺ raised his hands in an invocation and the water rose to the top along with the fallen pot. He then took the water needed for his ablution!

Caliph Haroon once presented his Minister Ali bin Yaqteen with a set of expensive clothes along with some money. The latter being a secret follower of Imam sent these gifts over to Musa al-Kazim

🕮. The Imam 🕮 kept the money but sent the garment back with instructions that he should take particular care of this garment. Some days later, another courtier within his court told Haroon Rasheed that those clothes presented by him to Ali bin Yaqteen had been given by Yaqteen to the Imam 🕮 and he said that he suspected that Yaqteen was essentially a Shia of Musa Kazim. As a result of these instigations, Haroon sent for Yaqteen and asked him to bring the garment that had been given to him earlier. Ali bin Yaqteen had no problem producing the garment in question and was saved from the wrath of Haroon!

In connection with Ali bin Yaqteen the narrator describes another incident that once he sent some presents and letters [containing queries on various subjects] from different persons to Imam Musa al-Kazim 🕮 through a courier. When the courier reached the Imam 🕮 he accepted the gifts, then without having read any of the communications sent to him, he put his hand in his pocket and brought out some letters of his own which he handed to the courier saying that those were the replies to the various questions that had been sent through Ali bin Yaqteen by the people!

It is recorded[131] that one day a group of Shias visited Imam al-Kazim 🕮 from the province of Khorasan bringing with them some gifts as well as sundry amounts as "*Khums*" money which had been sent by different persons from his followers in that area. Amongst these gifts, there was a length of a hand-woven cloth, along with seven (some say *two*) Dirhams from an old lady as part of her annual "*Khums*" amount for the Imam 🕮. Soon as the contingent arrived in his presence, Imam Kazim 🕮 first *asked for the package sent by this old lady. He accepted her presents, but simultaneously he*

---

[131] Translators Note: The source of this is taken from a book by P. E. Trust, Karachi Pakistan.

returned the cloth as well as her money [to which he added some of his own] back with the delegation, instructing them to give these to her on his behalf and to advise her that she would die within seven days of receiving this from him. She was to use the cloth for her shroud and the money for her funeral expenses! It happened exactly as the Imam had predicted, and her shrine still exists in a Northeast part of Iran [Khorasan] where many people come to pay their respects. It is known as the 'Shrine of Bibi Shatita'.

Miracles are performed every year at the shrines of all the holy Infallible Imams; but one year in 1349 AH there were numerous such miracles observed in Kufa, Samarrah, Mashed, Kazemain and Kerbala. But most of these miracles appeared to occur in Kazemain in the shrine of Imams al-Kazim 🕮 and Muhammad al-Taqi al-Jawad 🕮 where the blind, the handicapped and paralytic persons who, though they were pronounced medically incurable, were totally cured. The news was so extraordinary that the Baathist government in Baghdad installed a committee to investigate this phenomenon. This group of persons recorded at least 50 cases from the city of Baghdad alone that had been completely cured of all ailments that were deemed incurable. This news was circulated all over the Islamic world, so much so that an eminent scholar Ali Naqi Saheb from India travelled and visited the shrines listing the names along with the photographs of several people that had been miraculously cured. He then published a book in 1380 AH listing these miracles to which both Sunni and Shia scholars have attested as being true.

11.30: Infallibility of Imam Musa al-Kazim 🕮

Caliph Haroon Rasheed left no stone unturned to hurt, insult and deride the reputation of Imam Kazim 🕮 and to bring down his honour and respect in the eyes of others. Towards this, he contrived all sorts of cunning measures and evil designs. In one well known incident it is recorded that to falsely accuse the Imam ﷺ of indecent behaviour, he cajoled, bribed and threatened a beautiful slave girl of dubious reputation to spend an entire night in the prison quarters of the Imam ﷺ. To achieve his lowly plan, he had her locked up overnight in the cell with the Imam ﷺ with an understanding that on the following morning when Haroon and his men enter the prison cell she would wail and lay false charges of [God forbid] an immoral behaviour by the Imam ﷺ. But, contrary to the arranged plan, when the girl entered the cell, she saw that the Imam ﷺ was completely impervious to her presence and was totally absorbed in prayer and prostration in worship to his Lord all night; and the calm and soothing sound of his prayers was resounding all around the cell. This prolonged act of worship of the Imam ﷺ had such a devastating effect on her that it resulted in a state of a complete 'change of heart', and she herself went into prostration praying to the Lord and repenting for her sins!

Next morning when the officials designated by Haroon arrived at the prison to vilify the Imam ﷺ they found both inmates of the prison deeply absorbed in prayer, and the very walls of the cell were echoing the words *"Subbuhun, Quddusun"* in praise of Allah ﷻ! The Imam ﷺ is known to have stated: "*We Ahlul Bayt are the Fathomless Oceans of Purity, and even when anything impure associates with us, it gets purified!*" (Quran: 33:33).

11.31: Eighth Imam: Ali ibn Musa al-Raza ﷺ

Imam Musa al-Raza ﷺ was the son of Imam Musa al-Kazim ﷺ. He was born on the 11th of Zilqaada 148 AH in the city of Medina. His patronymic filial appellation was Abul Hasan; and he was also known as Wali, Zaki, Saber and al-Raza[132]. His famous

---

[132] Friend of Allah, Pure, Patient and The Agreeable.

contemporary Ibrahim ibn Abbas is known to have said that he had not seen a more learned person than Imam al-Raza ﷺ.

It is also recorded that like his forefathers, he used to sleep for a brief while at nights spending long hours in worship and used to fast during most of his days. Mamoon Rashid the son of Haroon who was the Caliph during Imam al-Raza ﷺ's lifetime, to pacify those people who were favourably inclined towards the House of the Prophet ﷺ, had appointed Imam al-Raza ﷺ as his heir and successor to the throne of his Caliphate after him. But nevertheless, the Imam ﷺ being least interested in his maneuvers, continued to sit on a simple straw mat in a humble manner. All his slaves and servants used to partake of their meals with him on the same mat. He was incredibly soft spoken and was a person of very few words. No one dared speak aloud in his presence. He never sat with his legs stretched out even in the company of one or two persons; and he also never rested his back against any bolster, or cushion, or a wall while in the company of others.

Jalaluddin Suyuti in his treatise 'Tarikh ul Khulafa' has collected several traditions in praise of the Imam al-Raza ﷺ. In summary, the conclusion of his findings shows that Mamoon Rasheed had gathered many prominent scholars around himself and had deep and lengthy discussions with them, to the extent that he himself had become quite knowledgeable [and an expert to some extent] in matters of Islamic Jurisprudence. In 201 AH he appointed Imam al-Raza as his heir apparent and even minted a coin in honour of the Imam ﷺ. He also issued an order that nobody should praise Muawiya Ibne Abu Sufiyan in their sermons or else face the consequences of his wrath and the loss of protection of any official support from him. Furthermore, he also had the names of the first three Caliphs banned from the Friday sermons; and on the contrary, he insisted that only the name of Ali ibn Abi Taleb should be mentioned on a regular basis. At this new trend of his behaviour his family members from the Abbasside dynasty convinced him that it would be a matter of time before he would lose his own position if he continued in like manner; and the Caliphate would be passed down into the hands of the Ahlul Bayt ﷺ. Eventually these instigations had their effect in poisoning his mind and shaking him out of his 'benign mind-set' towards the house of the Prophet ﷺ. Mamoon realizing that to retain the throne in his hold rather than let go of the reins of Power, he turned against the Imam ﷺ and eventually had him killed by presenting him with poisoned grapes in the month of Safar 203 AH.

A detailed review of history leads us to conclude that Mamoon Rasheed was influenced by political considerations prevailing in that period; and decided that the most expedient way to pacify the revolting factions under his sway would be to associate himself with the Alawites by nominating Imam al-Raza ﷺ as his 'Heir Apparent'. His decision was forced upon the Imam ﷺ despite his consistent refusal to accept a position involved with dealing with any political matters.

Mamoon's first capital city was Merv in which he chose to establish his seat of Caliphate. Imam al-Raza ﷺ was brought to this city with great pomp and respect. Allama ibn Hajar e Makki in his book 'Tarikh e Naishapour' mentions that when the entourage of Imam ﷺ was passing through the city of Naishapour thousands of people getting wind of his arrival, thronged around him making it difficult for the caravan to proceed even at a snail's pace!

The Imam ﷺ was mounted on a mule with an umbrella held over his head. Hundreds of historians and traditionalists where amongst the huge crowd, anxious to speak to him, while the crowds were insisting upon seeing their Imam and hearing him speak. At their insistence Imam al-Raza ﷺ dismounted and removed the umbrella so that the masses could get a look at him. His hair was long up to his shoulders in the tradition of his Great

Grandfather the holy Prophet ﷺ; and his face was bright and glowing with the Light of Piety. The people started crying at the sight of his magnificent stature and their eyes were cooled by his grandeur. Many started kissing his feet and even the very mule which the Imam ؑ had used for his travel! It is recorded that there were thousands of traditionalists present with their pen and notepaper ready to document the Gems of Knowledge which they hoped to receive from a member of the progeny of the holy Prophet ﷺ. They insisted upon the Imam ؑ to relate some traditions, and in response he acceded to their request and recited a tradition which has become famous and unanimously been acknowledged by scholars from *all school of thoughts* and known as the '*Hadith-e-Silsila uz-Zahab*' – 'The Tradition of the Golden Chain of Links'. Imam Musa al-Raza ؑ began as follows: *"I have heard it from my father Musa al-Kazim ؑ, who heard it from his father Jafar e Sadiq ؑ, who in turn heard it from his father Muhammad al-Baqir ؑ, who heard it from his father Zainul Abideen ؑ, who heard it from his father Husayn ibn Ali ؑ, who heard it from his father Ali ibn Abi Taleb ؑ, who heard it from Prophet Muhammad Mustafa ﷺ, who heard it through Angel Gabriel ؑ who in turn said that Allah ﷻ The Almighty (Jalla Jalalahu) has stated that: 'There is no peer against Me, and there is none worthy of prayers except Me! O People! Obey Me and worship Me. Whoever remains true to his belief in My Oneness (Kalema-e-La-Ilaha-Illallah) 'with all the essential **pre-conditions (be sharteha, wa shurooteha) attached to it'**, then indeed he has entered My Fortress and obtained his security and saved himself from my Wrath!"*

The Imam ؑ then withdrew himself under the shade of his umbrella and re-emerging shortly after a brief pause, he added: "…. *And **I am** one from among those designated as **an 'Essential Pre-condition'!**"*

The people then asked as to how they could remain true to their fealty (*Shahadah of La Ilaha Illallah*) he replied: "*By being obedient to Allah ﷻ and His Prophet ﷺ and being truly committed to the love of us Ahlul Bayt ؑ – The People of The House*".

Mamoon Rasheed insisted upon and offered the Caliphate to the Imam ؑ saying that when he was engaged in battle with his elder brother Ameen to protect his throne, he undertook a vow that if he is victorious, he would hand over the Caliphate back to the rightful heirs among the *Bani Fatima*. He then further added that "among the *Bani Fatima* I do not find anyone more worthy than you!"

To this Imam al-Raza ؑ replied: "*If this Caliphate has been given to you by Allah ﷻ then* **you have no right** *to give it away. But if it has* **not been given to you** *and was meant for someone other than you, then* **also, you have no right** *to give it away!*" This sort of discussion continued to swing back and forth between them for several days. Khwaja Muhammad Parsa in his book 'Faslul Khitab' writes that: "Mamoon kept the pressure on the Imam ؑ to accept the designation, but Imam al-Raza ؑ used to insist that he preferred to be by himself as a humble and obedient servant of God; and for him this was more prestigious than a position entailing the pomp and pelf of this world. His ongoing prayer to his Lord was to keep him protected from the temptations of worldly glamour and to enable him to rekindle and rejuvenate the traditions of the holy Prophet ﷺ. Nonetheless this 'to and fro' sway of arguments continued to such an extent that Mamoon's Prime Minister Fazal bin Sahl was driven into saying: "I have never seen the status for the 'Throne of Caliphate' being so denigrated as to become lower than the most menial position which is unacceptable by any!"

Mamoon eventually resorted to threats and high-handed tactics wherein he issued an ultimatum that either Ali ibn Musa al-Raza ؑ accepts his nomination or faces certain death by execution! The Imam ؑ then reluctantly and under duress accepted the designation of being his 'heir apparent' **upon the condition** that he will **not** interfere with matters of the State; and if at all he is asked for any advice, he will strictly adhere to the Quranic injunctions and the traditions of the holy Prophet ﷺ. This acceptance of nomination of heir apparency occurred on the seventh day of Ramadhan, Monday 201 AH; and since the *Eid ul Fitr* was anticipated to occur about three weeks later, Mamoon sent word to the Imam ؏ that he should lead the *Congregation Eid Prayers* so that the public in general could benefit from his noble presence; to which, though initially reluctant, the Imam ؏ finally agreed.

Consequently on the Day of *Eid ul Fitr* Imam al-Raza ؏ dressed himself in the manner of his forefathers: the holy Prophet ﷺ and Imam Ali ؏: wearing white robes with a white turban on his revered head, with one end of it falling over his right shoulder; a short vest over his midriff and his trousers somewhat upturned; a staff in his hand and walking barefooted. His entire entourage was dressed in glittering, scarlet-coloured robes and walking barefooted behind him. When the people saw the simple attire of the Imam ؏, they also took off their shoes and started following him walking barefoot toward the *Eidgah* (Place where congregational *Eid* prayers are usually held). When the Imam ؏ stepped forward and recited *'Allah ho Akbar'* in his resounding voice, the entire procession began to reverberate with the electrifying cries of "*Allah ho Akbar*"!

When news of this reached the Prime Minister Fazlal bin Sahl, he came out post haste and seeing the reaction of the masses, he became extremely insecure for his own position. He immediately went to Mamoon and warned him that if he allowed the Imam ؏ to continue his walk to the *Eidgah* and perform the act of leading the prayers, his own government will go away from the control of the **Abbasside's** to that of the **Alids.** He urged that if he wished to safeguard his position, he was well advised to stop the Imam 🕮 from proceeding any further in this venture. Mamoon panicked and personally went over to the Imam 🕮 on the pretext of concern for the Imam, saying that he did not wish to inconvenience the Imam 🕮 any further with the 'burden' of this task; and added that the person who normally conducted these prayers would take over and carry on this duty as usual; and with a false show of solicitation he added: "I request you to retire back to your quarters and rest!" Imam al-Raza 🕮 abandoned his walk and returned to his quarters, fully realizing the reasons for Mamoon's deceptive tactics.

After this incident and the political move adopted by Mamoon, the Imam 🕮 barely survived for eighteen months. It also so happened that other Abbasside's were also forcing Mamoon to withdraw his support for Imam al-Raza 🕮 as some of them had already paid their allegiance to one Ibrahim bin Mahdi as the next in line of Caliphate. Mamoon was in a quandary, being 'caught between a rock and a hard place' so to speak. He could neither afford to upset the Bani Fatimids by cancelling Imam al-Raza 🕮's heir apparency, not could he afford to upset the Abbasside's by retaining him in that position. He then made up his mind to have the Imam 🕮 removed by assassination!

Simultaneously Mamoon also started having doubts about his Prime Minister Fazal bin Sahl's loyalty to himself. Consequently, he decided to undertake a journey from Merv towards Baghdad taking with him the Imam 🕮 and Fazal. Upon reaching a station called Sarkhas for resting at night, he convinced four of his trusted confidantes to assassinate Fazal bin Sahl; and this was duly conducted in the darkness of the night! The caravan then proceeded to a place called Toos in the county of Sanabad. Imam al-Raza 🕮 by his divine knowledge confided to one of his chosen companions that Mamoon in his evil intentions was now also planning to have him, Imam 🕮 himself poisoned!

Shortly thereafter a messenger arrived from Mamoon with word from him that he was inviting the Imam 🕮 to come and meet him; adding that if the Imam was unable to do so for any reason, then he Mamoon himself, would come over to meet him. Imam al-Raza 🕮 donned his cloak over his shoulders and went to meet him. Mamoon arose from his seat in apparent respect to receive the Imam 🕮 and made a show of making him sit on a special place of honour. After the exchange of a few pleasantries, he ordered the attendants to bring the out the grapes which had been specially kept aside for the Imam 🕮. Upon his insistence that he try this special strain (of grapes), the Imam 🕮 ate a few of them which had stealthily been laced with a deadly poison. These heavily poisoned grapes produced the desired effect of causing his death within a very short while.

Prior to his demise while he was still residing in Khorasan, Imam al-Raza 🕮 was worried for his nine-year-old son Muhammad al-Taqi 🕮 living in his hometown in Madina and who would become the next Imam after him. He had written a brief letter to him, an extract of which is as follows:

"O Soul of your Father! I have heard that when you leave the house the servants constrain your exit and entrance from the house by a small side door. This is with a desire to restrict your access to your relatives and the public in general, so that people may be denied the benevolence of your personality. I advise you to always leave and enter by using the Main gate, and when you go out, always carry sufficient money with you so that no person is denied from your liberality when they ask. Give preference to your relatives over the rest and ensure that enough is given to meet their needs. When your uncles ask for help do not give anything less than 50 Dinar; and when your aunts approach you for help, do not give them less than 25 Dinars. If you wish to give them anymore, it will be up to you. Never be afraid of being impoverished by your acts of charity because Allah

the Almighty has promised to replenish those who give in His way with an ample reward." [Ref: 'Musnad-e-Ahlul Bayt'].

11.32: Miracles of Imam al-Raza 🕮

When Mamoon appointed Imam al-Raza 🕮 as his successor, the courtiers and other notables resented the appointment and decided among themselves to belittle him by their irreverential behaviour of neither having the curtain of the door lifted to facilitate his entrance in deference to his position; nor rising to greet him or paying any special respect to him upon his arrival. Subsequently, when the Imam 🕮 arrived, as per their plan, they remained rooted to their spots; but at the same moment a strong gust of wind wafted through the court causing the curtains to be raised as the Imam entered; and the courtiers themselves awed by his presence, involuntarily rose to their feet and greeted him by offering their salutations

One day a traveller is said to have come from Kufa to Khorasan to meet Imam al-Raza 🕮 and had certain questions in mind which he intended to get answers for from him 🕮. However, due to certain limitations of time he could not pose those queries and departed from Imam's presence without getting an opportunity to clarify his doubts. But much to his surprise a servant of the Imam 🕮 came after him as he left and handed him an envelope saying that this contained all the answers from the Imam 🕮 to the various queries he had in mind!

One person from India known as 'Abu Ismail Hindi' knew no Arabic but nonetheless came to the Imam 🕮 to converse with him on certain subjects. The Imam 🕮 recited a brief prayer and put his finger against his lips. Abu Ismail Hindi started conversing in fluent Arabic!

Another very well-known episode is recorded by several well known and reliable traditionalists and historians that Mamoon in yet another attempt to dishonour and embarrass Imam al-Raza ﷺ, tried to take advantage of a visiting magician from India, who was reputed to perform exceptional tricks using his skills in the art of conjuring Magic. Mamoon offered him a handsome reward of One Thousand Dinars if he could perform one of his tricks to ridicule the Imam. The magician agreed. Imam ﷺ was invited for food and the guests began to serve themselves. Every time Imam Raza ﷺ stretched his hand toward the platter of bread, it would float away from him. Upon repeatedly being subjected to this embarrassment by the magician, which was causing a lot of amusement among those present at the dinner gathering, Imam al-Raza ﷺ raised his eyes toward a carpet embroidered with an image of a Lion that was hanging on the opposite wall. He looked at it and ordered the lion to come down and deal with the magician; whereupon the guests saw to their utter amazement that the picture came to life and the lion jumped off the wall and attacked the magician and devoured him! The Caliph and his guests were shocked by this spectacle and abandoning their food they ran out of the room seeking the nearest exit! Later when Mamoon pleaded with Imam ﷺ to return the Magician back to life, Imam al-Raza ﷺ responded that: *"Had the 'Asa' (Staff) of Moses regurgitated the snakes that it had swallowed in the Court of Firon, he too would have ordered this Lion to do the same;"* thereby clearly demonstrating in light of the Quran, that Allah ﷻ does give the power to perform such amazing miracles to His selected and chosen Personages by His command.

Another interesting incident is recorded that one day a small bird came in the presence of Imam ﷺ and began fluttering its wings. The Imam ﷺ looked toward his companions and said that the little bird was telling him that a snake had come and occupied its nest and she was seeking protection against it from the Imam! He then asked his servant to go and remove the snake from the bird's nest; and upon investigation it was found indeed to be true!

Hakim has documented in his works that one day a person by the name of Muhammad Ibn Esa saw the holy Prophet ﷺ in his dream, seated in the local mosque with a tray full of dates in front of him. When Ibn Esa approached the Prophet ﷺ (in his dream), he ﷺ gave him a handful of dates which were 18 in count. Muhammad Ibn Esa remained baffled as to what could be the significance of his dream. A few days later when he entered the local mosque, he was surprised to see that Imam al-Raza ﷺ was sitting exactly in the same spot as he had seen the holy Prophet ﷺ sitting in his dream; and more surprising still was the sight of a tray full of dates in front of the Imam ﷺ! When Muhammad Ibn Esa approached the Imam ﷺ offering his salutations, the Imam also gave him a handful of dates, which upon counting **were also all of 18**! When Ibn Esa asked the Imam ﷺ for a few more, and he replied: "*Had my grandfather the holy Prophet ﷺ given you anymore, I too would have done likewise!*"

Mulla Jaami relates in his book 'Shawahed-e-Nabuwah' that Imam al-Raza ﷺ once instructed his servant Aba Saltt Hirvi to go to a certain place and fetch the sand from there. He did so and when the Imam ﷺ received this he smelled it and said this is from the spot of the earth where my grave will be dug. He then instructed Aba Saltt that after his death at the time of his burial, he should stand at the head of the grave where he will find a moist area and recite a specific prayer which he now taught him. The Imam ﷺ further said that upon recitation of this prayer the grave would open and become filled with water to the brim. He will see tiny fish swimming inside this grave which the Imam ﷺ said should be fed by the pieces of bread which he was giving him. After being fed, the fish would disappear. He then told him to recite another prayer, upon which the water would also recede and the grave will be empty. The Imam ﷺ then *specifically instructed* Aba Saltt to ensure that he conducted all these activities in the presence of Mamoon Rasheed. He then predicted his own impending death saying that Mamoon will invite the Imam ﷺ the next day and poison him. He further added that if Aba Saltt sees the Imam ﷺ returning from Mamoon's quarters with a cloth over his head and his face covered, he could take it as a sign that he had been poisoned and that it was time for his departure from this earthly abode. He then added: "*When you see me returning in this condition, do not speak to me!*"

Aba Saltt states that the next day the Imam ﷺ rose early, bathed, and donned a change of apparel, then appeared to be waiting for the inevitable call from Mamoon to come. The call arrived in the form of a messenger send by Mamoon. Imam al-Raza ﷺ accompanied him to Mamoon's residence where the latter greeted him with a false air of sincerity and made a great show of respect by kissing him on the forehead and offering him an honoured seat. A brief time after, Mamoon offered him the poisoned grapes which he insisted were unique and had been specially sent for him. The Imam ﷺ said that the "*the grapes of Heaven were far superior to any found on this earth!*" Upon Mamoon's persistence Imam ﷺ partook of a couple of the grapes and got up to leave. Mamoon enquired as to where was the Imam going, to which Imam al-Raza ﷺ replied: "*To the place where you have sent me!*"

He then covered his head and face with a cloth and re-entered his own quarters. Aba Saltt now knew that the end of the Imam ﷺ was imminent and became extremely sad and sorrowful. At this moment he saw a handsome youth appear in the room bearing a strong resemblance to Imam al-Raza ﷺ in his looks. Aba Saltt asked in surprise as to how he had arrived there as the doors were all closed; and the youth replied: "*By the help of The One who made me traverse from Medina to here in an instant!*" He then introduced himself as Muhammad ibn Ali, the young son of Imam al-Raza ﷺ.

Aba Saltt states that he saw the youth enter the Imam 🕮's room and lay his face cheek to cheek on this father's face. They then continued a whispered conversation for an extended length of time which he, Aba Saltt could not comprehend. When their communion ended, Muhammad ibn Ali 🕮 instructed Aba Saltt to bring the container of water and a wooden plank which he would find in the next room. Abu Saltt deferentially disagreed, saying that they never stored any water in the other room. But upon the youth 🕮 repeating his orders, Aba Saltt entered the room and to his surprise saw that indeed there was a water container as well as a wooden plank placed in the room!

The young Imam 🕮 then asked him to go back and bring the shroud and coffin, as well as other essentials which he would again find in the same room. He went and brought the required items and then offered his help in giving the ritual burial bath. Muhammad ibn Ali 🕮 declined his help saying he already had others (Angels) to assist him in this task. After the rituals of the bath and shroud were over, the Imam 🕮's body was placed in the coffin, and his young son offered the funeral prayers. At the conclusion of his prayers, the roof over the room miraculously appeared to open and the coffin ascended into the sky. Aba Saltt was amazed and asked as to where had the coffin been taken.

The young Imam replied that Imam al-Raza 🕮's soul had gone to pay his respects to holy Prophet 🕮's soul in Madina before being confined to his grave! Mamoon arrived at about this instant and tried to enter the Imam 🕮's quarters but the door was locked; and the young Imam 🕮 bade him to wait a while before unlocking the door. A short while after, the coffin containing Imam al-Raza 🕮's body was returned to the room, and the door was opened for Mamoon. He entered and immediately began to weep in a loud and hypocritical manner. He then ordered that the body should be taken to the graveyard where Aba Saltt (said that) he then did all that he had been bidden earlier by Imam al-Raza 🕮 to do at his grave in Mamoon's presence: *specifically reciting that special prayer over his coffin within Mamoon's earshot.* Mamoon was amazed and dumbfounded at the sights that unfolded before his eyes upon the recitation of these prayers, including the appearance of water and the tiny fish in the grave and their ultimate disappearance!

After the burial of Imam al-Raza 🕮, Mamoon asked Aba Saltt to teach him the special prayers that he had recited at the grave. To his utter consternation Aba Saltt had completely forgotten the prayers and could neither recall or recite nor repeat them! Mamoon disbelieved him and had him sent to prison where he remained confined in isolation for a year praying desperately for release. His supplications were granted wherein he saw the same youth Imam Muhammad ibn Ali 🕮 appear before him in his prison cell one day consoling him that his prayers had been accepted. He then moved his hand over the handcuffs and iron shackles fell apart and the young Imam 🕮 led him out of the prison to his freedom!

11.33: Ninth Imam: Muhammad ibn Ali al-Jawad 🕮

Imam Muhammad al-Taqi 🕮 was the only son of Imam al-Raza 🕮 and he was born on the 10th of Rajab 195 AH. His name was **Muhammad,** and his other titles were **Taqi** and **Jawad**. His patronymic was *Abu Jafar,* and his other appellations were *Al Qane* (The Content one) and *Al Murtaza* (The Elevated one). His revered mother was known by various titles such as Sabika, Khairzaan, Rehana and Sakina. Her ancestry was from the same lineage as Maria the Coptic lady who was one of the wives of the holy Prophet 🕮 and the only other wife beside Hazrat Khadija 🕮 to have borne the Prophet 🕮 a son called Ibrahim 🕮. Imam Muhammad al-Taqi 🕮 was barely 8 or 9 years old at the time of his revered father Imam al-Raza 🕮's death; but nonetheless despite his tender years, he was very knowledgeable on every subject

In the book 'Sawaiq Mohriqa' by Ibn Hajar e Makki it is recorded that one day he was playing with some children of his age in a street of Baghdad. Caliph Mamoon Rasheed happened to pass through this street with his Entourage. Seeing the Caliph's approach all the children ran away clearing the path, but the young Imam 🕮 remained at his spot. Mamoon stopped and asked the Imam as to why he had remained in the street without any apprehension when everyone else had run away? The young Imam 🕮 replied: *"Why would I run away when the road is wide enough for your procession to pass while I remain on **my side** of the street? The only other reason I would run away would be if I were guilty of some crime; but I am not guilty of any wrongdoing and I assume that **you** would not punish any innocent person without a just cause!"* Mamoon was astounded by this response and enquired as to his name and that of his father's. Imam 🕮 replied: *"I am Muhammad bin Ali, the son of Ali Ar-Raza 🕮"*. Mamoon was thrown into a pensive mood as he continued with his plans of going outside the city limits and hunting with his Falcons. To his surprise one of the falcons returned with a small fish in its beak; and he was puzzled as to how the falcon could have caught a fish in mid-air when there was no lake nearby, nor any 'pond of water' around the outskirts of the city!

As he returned past the street where the young Imam 🕮 was still playing, he asked him as to what he, Mamoon was holding in his fist. The Imam 🕮 unhesitatingly replied: *"Allah 🕮 has created small fish in the seas which sometimes due to strong gush of winds get sucked up into the atmosphere and the Caliph's trained falcons at times hunt them and bring them back to their master. The master then comes trying to test the sagacity and wisdom of the family of the Prophet 🕮!"*

Mamoon was further impressed and amazed at the erudite responses of the young Imam 🕮 and then and there he decided to take the Imam 🕌 with him to his Palace to keep him under his wing in a highly favoured position. With the passing of time, the more Mamoon was exposed to Imam Muhammad al-Taqi 🕌's Intellect and Knowledge, his respect and reverence towards him increased more proportionately; to the extent that he eventually gave his daughter Ummul Fazl in marriage to the Imam 🕌.

Mamoon started paying a lot of respect and attention to Imam Taqi 🕌 which in turn caused a great deal of jealously and resentment among his close associates. The Abbasside's began to be apprehensive at the possibility of Mamoon appointing him as his successor in the same way that he had appointed his father Imam al-Raza 🕌. A great deal of conspiracies started springing up, and to suppress the intrigues, Mamoon announced that he was according to such respect to the young Imam 🕌 due to his superior knowledge and wisdom over **everybody** else in his realm. The Abbasside's countered by saying that they would put him to the test by bringing one of their own learned scholars to debate with him. Eventually a day was chosen, and all the courtiers, scholars and noblemen were gathered in the court of Caliph Mamoon to witness this formal discussion between two learned personalities. Their most senior and venerable scholar by the name of Yahya bin Aksam was chosen for this assignment by the Abbasside's.

In honour of the occasion, Mamoon had a special Dias constructed which was draped with an expensive cloth and on which the Imam 🕌 was seated radiating his brilliance! Yahya was asked to take his designated seat close by. The contest began by Yahya putting forward many complicated questions on diverse subjects to which the Imam 🕌 replied with ease and proper references to the Quran and Hadiths from the Prophet to support his answers. After these preliminaries were over, Yahya bin Aksam then asked the Imam 🕌 the following question (which he, in his own opinion, deemed to be a very complicated one, and *precisely* designed to confuse the young Imam 🕮. His question was: "If a person is in the condition of an *'Ehram'*[133] and goes hunting, then what is the penalty for such an act?"

With the appearance of being in complete control of the situation, the Imam 🕮 replied with confidence:

"Your question is 'Vague and Incomplete'. To determine the Penalty, you have to first clarify whether the hunter was a mature person or a minor, male or female? Was the hunt conducted during the day or night; within the precincts of the 'Haram' or out of it's bounds; whether this was a Free person or a Slave; whether it was a Bird or an Animal; whether it was done solely for 'sport' or with a need to eat; whether after committing the hunt the person was remorseful of the act or jubilant; whether the 'Ehram' was with the intent of Hajj or an Umra; etc etc etc..." which the Imam 🕮 kept listing one after another as being the myriad possibilities to this hypothetical question.

When Yahya Bin Aksam heard the list of the numerous possibilities that could be mushroomed out of his simple query, he was aghast and totally nonplussed! Mamoon Rasheed applauded the young Imam 🕮 for the superb way he had responded to the senior scholar! Since Aksam seemed lost for words, Imam Muhammad al-Taqi 🕮 proceeded to give elaborate answers regarding the various penalties associated with each individual scenario. Mamoon completely taken up by the erudite and impromptu response of the Imam 🕮 requested him to pose a question [however insignificant], to his senior opponent Yahya Bin Aksam. Imam Muhammad al-Taqi 🕮 thereupon turned towards Yahya and asked the following: *"What would you say about a man*

---

[133] When a Muslim dresses up in a specific attire (two pieces of unstitched cloths) with the intention of performing the Greater or the Lesser pilgrimage [*Hajj* or *Umra*] of the House of Ka'aba and is prohibited from any worldly activities including hunting.

who looked at a woman in the morning and she was unlawful [Haram] *for him. After sunrise she became lawful* [Halal] *to him. Then at noontime* [Zohar] *she again became unlawful; by mid-afternoon* [Asr] *again became lawful but at sunset* [Maghreb] *she was unlawful* [Haram] *and by night-time* [Isha] *she once again became lawful; but by midnight she was unlawful and then at dawn* [Fajr] *of the next morning she was once again lawful for him as his spouse?"* Yahya was completely bewildered and said that this question was *totally beyond his knowledge,* and he had no answer whatsoever!

He then requested the Imam 🕮 to illuminate him on the intricacies of this knotted issue. Imam Taqi 🕮 gave the following clarification: *"A stranger looked at a slave girl in the morning and she was unlawful for him. He purchased her at Sunrise and she became lawful. At Noon he set her free so she became unlawful to him. At Asr time he married her, and she again became 'Halal'. At Sunset, he compared her to his mother* [Izhaar] *and she became 'Haram' for him. At night* [Isha] *he paid the obligatory expiation to atone for this act, and she once again became lawful to him. At Midnight, he divorced her, she became unlawful yet again. At Fajr he reconciled with her and took her back in* **'Ruju'** [remarriage] *and she once again became Halal for him!"*

Upon hearing this Mamoon was delighted beyond words and turned to the Abbasside's present in the assembly saying: "Did I not tell you about the excellent qualities of this knowledgeable person? Are you now convinced about his ability and Intellect?" They in turn could not help but admire his sharp wit, and all agreed in unison that indeed the young Imam 🕮 was exceptionally gifted.

Shortly thereafter Mamoon conducted the marriage of his daughter Umm Fazal with Imam Muhammad al-Taqi 🕮. A strange quality of Caliph Mamoon was that on the one hand, he would get impressed by the Imam 🕮's unlimited knowledge and offer him worldly honour, while on the other hand, out of insecurities for his own seat and dwindling popularity, he would be consumed with jealousies and would start plotting to have him removed by assassination! Eventually due to the intrigues of the Abbasside's and their apprehension, that if left to mingle with the general populace, the Imam ﷺ would clearly win the majority over in his favour, he had Imam Muhammad al-Taqi ﷺ poisoned in like manner of his revered father Imam al-Raza ﷺ; with the marked difference that Imam Muhammad al-Taqi ﷺ was only 25 years old and at the peak of his youthful bloom when he was martyred by his enemies! The date of his demise is recorded as being the 29th of 'Zilqaad' 220 AH in the city of Baghdad. He was buried in the suburb of Baghdad at a place called 'Kazemain' next to his Grandfather Imam Musa ibn Jafar al-Kazim ﷺ.

11.34: Some Miracles of Imam Muhammad al-Taqi ﷺ

After his marriage to Mamoon's daughter Umm Fazal, one day while travelling to Madina with his Entourage, Imam Muhammad al-Taqi ﷺ halted at a station on route, to offer his prayers. He performed his ablutions [Wudu] at the base of a dried up and withered fruit tree. In like manner of his grandfather the holy Prophet ﷺ's miracle, the tree immediately got revived and in a matter of moments not only flourished with lush leaves but fresh fruits to the extent that the companions started eating them saying that they had rarely tasted such delicious fruits!

It is narrated that a certain person once visited a mosque in the city of Damascus in which the severed head of Imam Husayn ﷺ had once been kept overnight. When he became aware of this fact, he was deeply saddened and overcome with emotion and grief. Just then another person with an impressive bearing entered the mosque and asked him to rise. When the person stood up, he found himself in the city of Kufa Iraq, inside the Masjid e Kufa alongside this noble stranger. From Kufa he was next transported to Medina and then to Mecca and back again to the mosque in Damascus! This happened two years in a row; and the second time this amazing occurrence took place the man mustered enough courage and asked the nobleman as to his identity, to which he replied: *"I am Muhammad ibn Ali Al-Raza!"* When this man upon learning about the identity of the miraculous person started talking about his unusual experience to others, some people who were inimical towards him, falsely accused him of claiming himself to be a prophet with supernatural powers, and launched a complaint with the township Governor, which resulted in him being arrested and imprisoned. When the people who were sympathetic to the plight of this man, wrote to the Governor to have the man released from the prison as he was not guilty of any crime, the Governor responded that "the one who had taken the man to visit the various *Masajids* in different lands and brought him back to his hometown, could also release him from prison if he so desires!" On receiving this news from the authorities, the people were very disheartened. However, a few days later, when one of them went to visit the prisoner, to his surprise he found that the cell was empty although it was locked from the outside and under strict security! They realized that the prisoner had indeed been miraculously released from his incarceration by his benign saviour!

Once a pious lady sent a messenger to Imam Taqi ﷺ requesting him to send a piece of cloth from him, which she said she would keep with her and include it with her burial shroud. When the messenger arrived and relayed this message, Imam ﷺ replied that this was now not needed. When the messenger returned to convey the Imam ﷺ's response he learnt that she had indeed died a couple of weeks prior to his return!

As discussed in the previous section on Imam al-Raza ﷺ, his servant and close confidante Abu Saltt had been quite unjustly imprisoned by Mamoon Rasheed. Abu Saltt invoked his prayers to Imam Muhammad al-Taqi ﷺ who miraculously appeared in his prison cell and taking hold of him by hand removed him bodily from the prison to his freedom!

11.35: Tenth Imam: Ali ibn Muhammad al-Naqi ﷺ

Imam Ali al-Naqi ﷺ was the son of the 9th Imam Muhammad al-Taqi ﷺ. He was born on the 5th of Rajab 214 AH. His patronymic filial appellation was *Abul Hasan*. His other titles were Al Murtaza, Al Naaseh (Advisor), Al Faqih, Al Ameen, Al Tayyaeb, Al Naqi (Clean and Pure) and Al Hadi.

He was summoned by the Abbasside ruler of his time and taken away from his hometown Medina to a place called *'Surre-man-rah'* which later came to be commonly known [to this day] as *'Samarrah'*. As this city was also the headquarters of the Abbasside cantonment with many battalions of soldiers stationed there, the area also came to be known as *'Askaria'* [place of Armoured Personnel] and for this reason the Imam ﷺ was also referred to by some as *'Ali-e-Askaria'*. Upon being brought to this town, Imam al-Naqi ﷺ was confined to house arrest and kept under constant surveillance by the ruling authorities. His knowledge was legendary like that of his forefathers, and his generosity was known far and wide; and whoever approached him for help received far more than what they asked for.

It is recorded that in the court of the Caliph of the Billah clan, Mutawakkil-e-Abbasi, a woman once presented herself claiming to be a descendant of Imam Husayn ﷺ and demanded special recognition of her status. The courtiers were confused as to how to confirm the veracity of her claim. Some advised their Caliph Mutawakkil to approach Imam al-Naqi ﷺ for a solution to this enigma. The Imam ﷺ was consequently brought to the court and asked to resolve their dilemma. The Imam ﷺ promptly stated that the flesh of the descendants of Imam Husayn 🖫 was protected by Allah 🖫 from being devoured by wild animals. If she were indeed truthful in her claim, the wild animals kept in the Caliph's Zoo could be brought to court in her presence and the truth of her claim would be established! The woman panicked and immediately withdrew her false demand!

Seeing this, some people present in the court of Mutawakkil incited him to challenge the Imam 🖫 to be subjected to the same test and see if he could withstand the truth of his own statement! Mutawakkil immediately agreed and Imam al-Naqi 🖫 was ordered to go to the arena where three ferocious lions were released from their cages for this test. Mutawakkil himself ascended to the rooftop to watch this spectacle from afar. To his great amazement, when the three hungry roaring lions were released from their cages, they initially bounded out in anticipation of mauling their quarry; but immediately upon seeing the Imam 🖫, they began to purr in submission like kittens and started to go around him in circles, rubbing their nose and eyes on his feet and on the sleeves of his garments! Finally, they bent their knees and sat down before him in obedience much as an obedient pet animal does before its' master!

Mutawakkil was awed beyond words but being a sworn enemy of the progeny of the holy Prophet 🖫, he ordered this news to be suppressed and not made known to the public. Some people around him however, suggested to him that perhaps to establish his own lineage he too should put himself to such a test, whereupon he angrily rebuked them by asking: "Are you from among those who wish to see me dead?"

Caliph Mutawakkil due to his political reasons resorted to a lot of pomp and ceremony in the matter of having Imam Ali al-Naqi 🖫 transported from Medina to Sammarah. For fulfillment of this mission, he sent one of his Commanders Yahya bin Harsima along with a contingent of his soldiers to escort him. When the Imam realized that it would be futile to offer any resistance to this 'official invitation' he ordered the people who were accompanying him to 'pack enough blankets and warm clothing' for their journey. Yahya who was *not* a follower of the faith of the Imam 🕮, silently wondered as to how the Shias could believe in such a person to be their Imam [?] when he had *no idea* of the weather conditions prevalent, nor did he seem to have any knowledge of the geographical areas around him, in asking them to pack warm clothes for an area known for its hot climate!

Yahya records that during their travel they broke journey to rest and halted at a desolate place where there was no herbage or vegetation, nor any sign of human inhabitation. After putting up their tents and while resting within it at night, one of his Sunni companions from the contingent sarcastically remarked that among the Shias there is a tradition from Imam Ali 🕮 that '*there is not a single piece of land on this earth where a dead person is not buried and will be resurrected from it on the Day of Qiyamah!'* Then he went on to add: "Now **who** can believe that in **this** desolate and unpopulated place there can be a grave of any human being?"

Yahya recounts further that shortly thereafter, a severe storm began to brew seemingly out of nowhere, with howling winds and hailstones and the temperature dipped down to such an extent that they were all shivering from the cold with **no warm clothes or blankets** to protect them! Yahya states that he lay there in a sorry state being frozen to near death! At this instance he heard someone asking permission to enter his tent. When he looked up, a person entered carrying a bundle in his hand and said that Imam al-Naqi 🕮 had sent these for him and his companion. Upon opening the package, he found two sets of warm clothing and two blankets which he and his companion thankfully utilized and saved themselves from being frozen to death! He adds: "I thanked the Imam 🕮 for his consideration and repented in my heart for my earlier disbelief and ridiculing thoughts about him, and *then and there* I secretly acknowledged him as my Leader and the rightful Imam 🕮

In the morning upon daybreak, they discovered that half the contingent of Yahya had perished due to the severe cold, including the person who had mocked the saying of Ali 🕮. Seeing this horrific condition of the death of his soldiers Yahya says he went to see the Imam 🕮 who was engrossed in prayers and reciting the holy Quran. Seeing us, he finished his prayers and after enquiring about us he asked us to prepare for the burial of our companions and then added: "*Be aware that this is how the graves are dug in all places whether they be in populated cities or in desolate areas. The sayings of our revered ancestors are never wrong!*"

Mutawakkil was an extremely hard hearted and cruel person. After inviting Imam al-Naqi 🕮 from Medina to Sammarrah he did not even bother to receive him upon his arrival. On the contrary, he had him imprisoned immediately and placed in the custody of a military officer named Zaraqi with explicit instructions to be very severe and harsh when dealing with the Imam. Zaraqi however, over a period mellowed in his behaviour towards the Imam 🕮 as he saw him always engrossed in prayers and supplications. He further saw that the Imam 🕮 had a grave dug in his cell close to his place of prayer, and upon questioning he explained that the grave served as a reminder to him of the eventual end of all beings and helped him to develop a greater sincerity in his invocations to Allah 🕮.

The personality of the Imam al-Naqi 🕮 was such that Zaraqi was overcome by his piety and started treating him with utmost respect. He eventually took him away from the prison and started keeping him in his own house under a 'sort of a house arrest'. One day Safra ibne Abi Alaf who was a Shia, came to visit the Imam ﷺ in the house of Zaraqi. The latter then confided to Safra that he too had become a Shia and was now completely turned against Mutawakkil and had even started cursing him for the kind of behaviour he adopted against the Imam ﷺ. When Safra entered Imam Naqi ﷺ's room to meet him, he saw him seated on a straw mat engrossed in prayers. Upon seeing the pitiable condition of the Imam ﷺ, Safra began to weep uncontrollably. Imam ﷺ assured Safra that regardless of his atrocities against him, no great harm would come to the Imam ﷺ from Mutawakkil.

When Mutawakkil became aware that Zaraqi had become extremely lenient with the Imam ﷺ, he had the Imam transferred under the care of a well to do person called Ameer Sayeed who immediately adopted an atrocious behaviour towards the Imam ﷺ. Periodically other followers of Imam al-Naqi ﷺ used to come to visit him and finding him under the harsh conditions of imprisonment would weep out of their love for the Imam ﷺ. One such person Ibn Rodhmah came to Sammarrah on some errand and when he heard that Imam al-Naqi ﷺ was kept in captivity in the house of Ameer Sayeed, he arrived at the house to pay his respects to the Imam ﷺ. Upon seeing him Sayeed mockingly asked: "Have you come to visit your Lord?" Ibn Rodhmah replied: "God forbid! My Lord is One Who Cannot be seen by any eye! My intention is only to pay homage to Ali al-Naqi ﷺ who is my Imam in this world and in the Hereafter. Most certainly this is my reason for my visit." Ameer Sayeed then told him to hurry up and finish his visitation as he had been given orders by Mutawakkil to execute the Imam by the next morning! When Ibn Rodhmah entered the room he too like the previous visitors before him, was appalled by the surroundings; as the Imam ﷺ had been put in solitary confinement in a dark and dingy room with no amenities or creature comforts to ease him. On seeing the uncontrollable grief of Ibn Rodhmah, the Imam 🕮 assured him that no harm will come to him and he predicted that Mutawakkil would himself die before the Imam 🕮!

This trend of keeping Imam al-Naqi 🕮 rigorously confined in the worst of conditions in solitary isolation, led even his worst enemies to wonder at the degree of patience and fortitude which the Imam 🕮 displayed; and never ever showed by his attitude that he was stressed by his surroundings. He was a model of good manners, always displaying a smiling face and polite deportment whenever he greeted his visitors. His patience never gave way to despondency; and no one ever got the impression that he was suffering any mental agony while confined to his solitary and darkened cell with none to converse with! He remained the 'Guiding Light' and a source of inspiration for all Muslims, spending his nights in prayers and his days in fasting. This clearly demonstrates that these godly persons, whether they are in captivity or free in their homes or elsewhere; even though they may be alone, confined in dark quarters or among the elite in bright surroundings, their personalities never waver. They are steadfast in being a model of *Exquisite Behaviour* par excellence!

One day to belittle the Imam 🕮, Mutawakkil invited him to his court where music and dancing were in full swing and wine was flowing like water! Upon Imam al-Naqi 🕮's arrival Mutawakkil offered him a goblet of wine. Imam 🕮 politely refused saying neither he nor any of his revered ancestors had ever touched such a drink or been near it. Mutawakkil then asked him to watch the musical dances which again the Imam 🕮 declined saying that he had no interest whatsoever in such frivolous activities. Mutawakkil then said: "As you are proficient in poetry, could you recite some for our benefit?" Imam 🕮 agreed saying that he would recite some verses which had been recited by his great Grandfather Imam Ali ibn Abi Taleb 🕮. The gist of that poetry which he recited on this occasion is as follows:

"They used to spend their nights in their Mansions on the Lofty Heights of Hilltops; Guarded by their minions. Masters of All that they Surveyed! But these Lofty Hills proved to be of no help to them; and the Pomp and Pelf of their Well-Built Abodes availed them naught! They were made to descend from their High Palaces and lowered into their Ignoble Graves. What a transformation from their Former Lives! Loneliness of the Tight Graves, and a 'Caller' asking: 'Whither have your Thrones and Regal Robes now gone? Where are those Faces which used to be covered in Veils of Silk and Satin?' And the Grave replied: 'Where once these faces were covered with silk, and partook of their Delicious Meals, they have now themselves' become Edible items for the Worms! Insects are crawling over those Delicate Countenances; and the Lips which drank from the Cups of Wine are now themselves the food of Crawling Parasites!"

The effect of this recitation had such a profound effect on Mutawakkil, his courtiers and his audience that many that were present began to wail in loud voices, while many others smashed their wine glasses and swore never again to indulge in such superficial frivolities! Imam al-Naqi ☙ returned to his confined quarters, having the tables turned on the Caliph, and all his nefarious plans brought to naught!

Imam al-Naqi ☙ was imprisoned for a lengthy period of 13 or more years by Mutawakkil. Towards the latter part of his imprisonment, Fateh Bin Khaqan despite being a Shia was appointed by Mutawakkil as his Prime Minister because of the many extraordinary talents, foresight and efficiency in administrative reform; as well as for the control he wielded over the people at large. Using his influence, Fateh Bin Khaqan managed to convince Caliph Mutawakkil to release the Imam ☙ from prison but put him under 'House Arrest'. Towards this end Fateh bought a piece of land in the name of Imam al-Naqi ☙ and had a small house constructed for him and eventually moved the Imam ☙ to this house. Mutawakkil nonetheless, still ordered strict security guards to keep a watchful eye on the activities of the Imam ﷺ.

Soon after this, it was seen that Mutawakkil was struck with a serious and life-threatening ailment which defied medical cure. Calling upon all the well-known physicians and notable medical practitioners of his time for help, [in diagnosing and/or finding a cure for him], proved to be futile. At long last the mother of Mutawakkil approached Imam al-Naqi ﷺ and implored him to cure her son. The Imam ﷺ complied and wrote a simple prescription which resulted in his complete recovery within a few days! As a gesture of her gratitude Mutawakkil's mother sent a pouch full of Ten Thousand Dinars which the Imam accepted but immediately had it distributed among the poor. Word soon spread far and wide about the generosity of the Imam ﷺ and his benevolence even towards his enemies. His popularity among the general masses soared higher. This led Mutawakkil to fear for his own position and his declining popularity even more; to the extent that one night in a drunken stupor he decided to have the Imam ﷺ killed and permanently removed from his horizon. Towards this end he ordered four Turkish slaves to assassinate the Imam as soon as he entered the court. He then sent word to Fateh to produce the Imam to his court immediately.

When the Imam ﷺ arrived accompanied with Fateh the four Turkish slaves who were hiding behind the doorway came forward with their naked swords in hand. But Imam al-Naqi ﷺ neither showed any signs of fear nor unease, but rather, reciting some prayers under his breath proceeded calmly toward Mutawakkil. Observing him to be close at hand, Mutawakkil jumped off his throne in a panic and respectfully asked the Imam ﷺ to sit on his own throne asking him his reason for visiting him at such a late hour! Imam ﷺ replied that he had been summoned by his courier. Mutawakkil responded that the courier had lied, and he ordered

Fateh Bin Khaqan to accompany the Imam ﷺ and take him back to his abode with due respect!

After Imam al-Naqi ﷺ's departure Mutawakkil asked the four slaves the reason why none of them had even attempted to execute the Imam as instructed. They all replied in unison that when they saw the Imam ﷺ enter, he was preceded by a giant of a man holding a drawn sword in hand announcing that whoever takes a step towards the Imam will be instantly beheaded by him! Mutawakkil concurred that he too had seen the same vision!

Consumed by the flames of jealously against the Imam ﷺ, Mutawakkil thought of yet another way to try and humiliate him in public. This happened to be on a day of *Eid* when in a fit of intoxication, he ordered that he take a tour of the city by being carried in a Palanquin seated on his throne, while his courtiers would follow him on foot. He summoned Imam al-Naqi ﷺ and also ordered him to join his entourage on foot. Once the tour commenced, Mutawakkil ordered those carrying his throne to hasten their speed and start running, thereby causing everyone else on foot to start running to keep pace with him! Likewise, the Imam ﷺ also ended up having to run the entire distance like a 'commoner' along with the rest of the foot soldiers. Toward the end of the tour Imam ﷺ started reciting a verse from the holy Quran: *"Fas bir Jameel Wallaho Musta'ano Ala ma'a Tasse-foon"* [implying that Allah ﷻ is with those that are patient]. He was then heard to say: *"Mutawakkil has done this to belittle my position, whereas my position with Allah is far from being any less than the sacred 'she camel' of Prophet Saleh ﷺ."*

Zaraqi who was also in this procession overheard him and was extremely saddened by this occurrence. Upon returning to his house he related the incident to his family and a religious scholar present on the occasion warned him to **beware** that there will be a drastic occurrence in the city within the *"next three days"* because the Imam 🕮 had compared himself with the '*she camel*' of *Nabi Saleh* 🕮; and the people of that era had been destroyed on the third day for having scoffed and mistreated a '*Sign*' that was designated by Allah 🕮 as being venerable, and had harmed and killed it.

Sure enough, within three days after this incident, Mutawakkil was murdered by his own son Muntasir Billah, who after assassinating his father ascended the throne as the next Caliph from the Billah 'dynasty'! However,[134] he only survived for six months and died suddenly at the young age of twenty-five years. He was far from inimical to Imam al-Naqi 🕮, giving his followers the liberty to have unrestricted accessibility to all the Shia shrines which was very much appreciated by the public at large.

After his death, a series of coups and Palace revolts took place which were orchestrated by the Turkish [Roman] slaves who held the *de facto* power and kept appointing various Caliphs one after another from the 'Billah' family of the Abbasside's. Finally, when Motaz Billah ascended the Caliphate, he committed the heinous crime of assassinating Imam al-Naqi 🕮 also by having him poisoned. He died on the 3rd of Rajab 254 AH.

11.36: Some Miracles of Imam al-Naqi 🕮

Though like every other Immaculate Imam of the holy Household of the Prophet 🕮, Imam Ali al-Naqi 🕮 also has several episodes recorded which were attributable to his miraculous powers, but again, in the interest of brevity we shall restrict ourselves to documenting only a few of these unusual incidents.

Once Mutawakkil acting on some false rumours about Imam al-Naqi 🕮, sent one his guards by the name of Sayeed to go and ransack the Imam 🕮's house in the middle of the night; and bring

---

[134] Extract taken from: 'Biography of Imam Ali un–Naqi AS' complied by Peer Muhammad Ibrahim Trust, Bahadurabad, Pakistan.

back the wealth that he would find therein; because he had received reports that the Imam 🕮 had accumulated a lot of money given to him by his followers. When this man stealthily entered the Imam's abode in the darkness of the night with no lamp or light to be guided by and was groping in the dark, he heard the Imam 🕮's voice addressing him by his name and asking him to wait till he brings him a torch to assist him in his search! Imam 🕮 then put forward a pouch empty of any wealth; and simultaneously he also picked up a sword from under his prayer mat and gave these to Sayeed to give it to his master; telling him that *that* was the extent of wealth in his possession which he had falsely been accused of hoarding! Sayeed was ashamed of his own presence in the Imam 🕮's house in the middle of the night and astounded that not only did the Imam 🕮 identify him by name in the dark but was also aghast at his ability to know the reason for his own nocturnal visit!

When the Imam 🕮 was summoned by Mutawakkil to come from the city of Medina to Iraq, the escorts accompanying him halted at a stark and desolate place for rest. It happened to be an old, ruined house which had neither any flora nor forest. The narrator says that when he saw this dilapidated place, he was shocked and saddened to realize that it was due to their enmity that these people chose this kind of a rundown place to make him uncomfortable. But to his amazement he records that the moment Imam al-Naqi 🕮 stepped onto this spot it appeared to have gotten transformed into a lush and beautiful garden; and every room that he stepped into was also turned into the most comfortable of quarters!

Once a person came complaining to the Imam 🕮 about the brutality of a certain Magistrate located in the city of Kufa. The Imam 🕮 told the person to be patient about the situation for two months and he would see the result. Exactly two months later, the official was dismissed from his position.

Mutawakkil had a personal zoo in his palace with many species of birds and animals which used to create a lot of commotion, to the extent that ordinary conversation would be drowned in their joint twitters. None could calm or stop these creatures from making their sounds, nor suppress the resultant high level of noise. However, it was a normal sight for all to see, that whenever Imam al-Naqi ※ happened to pass by or entered the area, all creatures would be silenced instantly and remain quiet for the entire duration of his stay; only resuming their lively prattle after his departure!

11.37: Eleventh Imam: Hasan ibn Ali al-Askari ※

Imam Hasan al-Askari ※ is the son of the holy 10th Imam al-Naqi ※. He was born on the 10th of Rabbi-us-Thani in 232 AH. His titles were *Abu Muhammad, Al Siraj-Al Khalis, Al Zaki* and *Al-Askari*. It is recorded by Hajar-e-Makki in his book 'Sawaiq-e-Mohriqa' that even from the tender years of his childhood, Imam Hasan al-Askari ※ was extremely pious and God fearing. To illustrate this, he has recorded an incident about an interaction between Bahlool Dana and Zaid-e-Majnoon: two well known ascetic and godly persons of their time, once within earshot of this Imam ※ when he was still in his early years of childhood. These two seniors got engrossed in reciting poetry in praise of Allah ※ and quoting verses describing some of the horrific scenes of the Day of Resurrection. Despite his tender age, Imam Hasan Al Askari started weeping from the fear of God!

The Caliph of his time was Motamid Billah who was true in the tradition of his ancestors in carrying the hatred in his heart towards the progeny of the holy Prophet ※. Like his forefathers, he too had Imam Askari ※ confined to an extremely narrow and dark cell in a basement with no windows, or any other source of light and air. The height and length of this cell were so diminutive that the Imam ﷺ could neither stand upright nor sleep fully stretched out on its floor! The food was rationed out to him in the form of two small pieces of 'flat bread' and two small bowls of hot water as a drink! The water given was so little that he could not perform even the ablution (*wudu*) for his prayers and had to resort to the '*Tayyamum*' (the alternate way of purification) before prayers.

In a state of rage Motamid once ordered his slaves to cast Imam Hasan Al Askari ﷺ into the den of hungry lions in hopes that they would rip him apart and devour him. But contrary to his expectation, in the tradition of the Imam ﷺ's forefathers before him, whenever they too were subjected to this kind of 'perceived torture' by the Caliphs of their time, the lions in this instance also, were seen to immediately become submissive before the Imam ﷺ, purring around him like pet cats, rubbing their eyes and foreheads on his feet!

Such displays of the Imam ﷺ's miraculous powers were hushed up by Motamid, while his own open acts to humiliate the Imam ﷺ in some form or the other in his court for the public at large, [wherein he and his courtiers would burst out into unbecoming laughter] continued as a normal form of mistreatment towards the Imam. The Imam ﷺ however, steeped in his noble heritage took it all in his stride and was never heard to have rebuked anybody!

A notable and famous incident recorded during the time of the holy 11th Imam ﷺ is that of Samarrah and its surrounding areas being caught up in the grip of a severe draught with its accompanying famine-like conditions due to lack of rainfall for three consecutive years! During this period Motamid ordered the nation to all gather and collectively pray in a mass outcry of pleading for the blessing of rains from Allah ﷻ; but all to no avail!

Hearing about this, some time later a Christian monk from the nearby area came forward, along with a group of other Christians, and congregating in a public area of the city he started to pray for rain. Immediately clouds gathered on the horizon and the rain started to descend from the skies! Many of the people present were impressed with this occurrence and began repeating the prayers shown by the Christians; and each time it resulted in bringing a bout of rain and causing many a Muslim to turn toward the Christian faith! Motamid was perplexed and called upon all his pious 'men of cloth' to explain this baffling phenomenon. The learned Muslim scholars admitted their own inability to tackle the problem and advised him to consult the 'one whom he had imprisoned' because *he alone,* they said, would be able to unravel this mystery through the knowledge of his revered ancestors which he had inherited, being a descendant of the holy Apostle!

Following this advice, Motamid had Imam Askari ﷺ brought out from prison; and with a great deal of hypocrisy and a false show of respect he addressed the Imam ﷺ saying: "O Son of the Prophet, the followers of your grandfather are turning away from his religion, and now it is up to you to save them!" He then apprised the Imam ﷺ of the entire situation about the monk's ability to bring down rain to their parched lands through his special invocations; and entreated the Imam ﷺ to help resolve this mystifying situation. Imam Askari ﷺ responded by asking Motamid to assemble the masses outside the city limits and order the monk to come and invoke his prayers under the open sky. When the monk began his invocation and raised his hands high toward the sky in prayers, the Imam ﷺ went up to him and took away a small object from his hand and then asked the monk to resume his prayers.

But none of the number of prayers invoked by the monk or his companions now had any resultant rainfall. On the contrary, all clouds dispersed from the horizon leaving the people perplexed yet again as to the truth at the bottom of this entire episode! Motamid asked Imam 🕮 as to what was it that he took away from the monk? Imam Askari 🕮 showed them a small piece of bone which he said belonged to some previous prophet which the monk had somehow acquired. He explained it was not unusual that when a bone of any prophet is exposed to the sky it always results in the prayers being answered. Imam 🕮 had the bone duly buried; but Motamid asked as to what was to be done to bring forth the rain? Imam Askari 🕮 replied that he would personally pray the next day for the rain under the open sky; and asked Motamid to instruct the people at large to join behind him in a congregation prayer. This was duly carried out the next day, and after Imam 🕮 offered his 2 cycles of prayers and raised his hands toward the sky, rain clouds began to gather from every direction, and the heavens opened up with the rainfall coming down in such abundance that the entire effects of the draught were erased and they were released from the famine that had gripped this land for many months. Those Muslims that had become Christians reverted to their own *Deen*, while many of the Christians also ended up adopting the faith of Islam.

After this incident, the popularity of Imam Hasan al-Askari 🕮 soared to new heights, to the extent that Motamid could no longer confine him in dark dungeons and was forced to also release all the followers of Imam 🕮 who had been imprisoned. The Imam 🕮 was now allowed to live in his own house albeit under constant surveillance. It was during this brief period of respite that the miraculous birth of the holy 12th Imam 🕮 took place on the 15th of Shabaan 255 AH.

While all Shias were implicit in their belief that there would be 12 Imams from the holy House of the Prophet 🕮, all Muslims in general were also aware of the several traditions which had been quoted amongst them generation after generation. In this connection they also all believed that when the 12th Imam 🕮 arrived, it would signal the end of the brutal rule of the usurper

Caliphs who would be toppled, and their cruel rule would come to an end. This was the very reason why each despot Caliph had kept the Imams 🕮 of their times imprisoned or under house-arrest and eventually had them all poisoned and put to death to prevent the 12th Imam 🕮 from being born!

Bearing the above conditions and reasons in mind, Imam Hasan al Askari 🕮 did not reveal the birth of his son the holy 12th Imam 🕮 to *anyone except a few* of his dependable followers and not more than a couple of his own relatives. Motamid who was also privy to such traditions and afraid for his own throne, relentlessly tried his best to ascertain whether the predicted birth of the 12th Imam 🕮 had taken place, but to no avail! Finally, he too resorted to the nefarious act of his ancestors and had Imam Hasan al Askari 🕮 poisoned at the youthful age of 29 years! The holy Imam 🕮 was martyred on the 8th of Rabi ul Awwal 260 AH.

When the news of Imam Hasan al Askari 🕮's demise spread through the city Motamid himself also showed up wearing a false expression of grief and pretending to mourn the loss of this great Imam! The Imam 🕮's brother by the name of Jafar ibne Ali al-Naqi 🕮 was also present alongside with the rest of the mourners, claiming to be the next Imam after Hasan al-Askari 🕮. When preparations had been made for the Imam 🕮's burial, and his funeral prayers were about to be led by Imam Askari 🕮's brother Jafar, a young and strikingly handsome youth emerged from behind the curtain and stepping forward addressed Jafar saying: *"O Uncle step back, for it is my right to lead the funeral prayers of my revered father!"*

Jafar was so overawed by the spiritual grace and grandeur of the newcomer, that he at once stepped back conceding the responsibility of leading the prayers to this noble youth. Soon after conducting the prayers and leading the funeral procession, the youth calmly retired to his chamber and disappeared from public view!

Imam Hasan al-Askari 🕮 is buried in the same house in which his revered father Imam al-Naqi 🕮 was buried.

11.38: Knowledge of Imam Hasan al-Askari 🕮

It is related in the book 'Manaqib ibn Sheher Ashoob' that during the lifetime of Imam Hasan al-Askari 🕮, there was a noted scholar by the name of Ishaq e Kindi. In the later stages of his research, he appeared to have gotten deviated in his thinking and started writing and expressing his own opinion on certain verses of the holy Quran which he considered to be discrepant and/or incompatible in their content and context. This news reached Imam Hasan al-Askari 🕮; and coincidently it so happened that one day some of Ishaq's students came to pay homage to him. The Imam 🕮, addressing them enquired as to whether there was no sensible person among them to dissuade their teacher from going in this misguided direction. He then quoted some verses from the Quran which according to Ishaq e Kindi would have been 'incompatible;' and gave them the interpretation of the latent meaning of those verses according to his superior knowledge. He instructed them to present these arguments before their tutor. Of these, though most of them were hesitant, one student was bold enough to muster the courage to approach his teacher Ishaq e Kindi and counter his claims by the arguments he had imbibed through the Imam 🕮's instructions. Ishaq immediately responded by saying that what he was saying was *way beyond* his [this student's], capability; and asked him as to where and how he had obtained this information. Upon being told that it was Imam Hasan al Askari 🕮 who had imparted it, Ishaq instantly stated that apart from that household, there was *no one* in the world who had this kind of knowledge! Realizing his shortcomings, he called for some firewood and immediately burnt all his manuscripts which contained incorrect conclusions in his personal treatise!

Once a person known as Abu Hashim Jaferi says that he was in the presence of Imam Hasan al-Askari 🕮 when a noted scholar of the time Abu Mohammed Janfaki who had gained a reputation for high learning and erudition came in and put this question before the Imam 🕮 as to why the women who are weak in physique should be entitled to one share in an inheritance from the parents, whereas men who are stronger and more robust in their constitution should be entitled to two shares? Imam Askari 🕮 responded to this spontaneously saying:

"Women are exempt from taking part in a war and have also not been burdened with earning a livelihood, whereas the men have been made liable for both these responsibilities. Therefore, this Divine Ordinance is based on Justice and Equity; and it is only those persons who due to their bias and lack of wisdom are misguided by their rebellious instincts and attempt to find fault with the Divine set up."

At one time he was asked to clarify the meaning of a Quranic verse which referred to *"...a particular descendant from amongst certain progenies."* The Imam 🕮 replied with utmost serenity: *"I am that superb descendant"* and then he detailed his pedigree tracing it back up to the holy Prophet Muhammad 🕮!

There is an exegesis of the Holy Quran attributed to the holy Eleventh Imam 🕮 which has been under constant study and observation by the scholars for hundreds of years in Arabia, Egypt, Ethiopia, Iran, Palestine, Syria, Tripoli, and particularly in Cairo. All the erudites from these countries are unanimous in acknowledging this as being a superb faculty of learning even up to the very present generation.

For the sake of being concise, we have restrained ourselves from presenting any more examples to illustrate his exalted status in the arena of knowledge and God-given wisdom.[135]

11.39: Some Miracles of Imam Hasan al-Askari 🕮

One Muhammad bin Ali ibn Ibrahim ibn Jafar al-Sadiq 🕮 relates that once he and some of his friends were in dire financial need. After consultation among themselves they decided to approach Imam Askari 🕮 for monetary assistance. When they arrived in his presence, even without being asked, the Imam 🕮 advanced them the exact amount of money that they each needed.

Mustaeen Abbasi had an unruly horse which could never be controlled by anyone. Any attempt to ride it resulted in the riders all being thrown off and sustaining severe injuries. The Vazir of this Caliph suggested that an easy unsuspected way to have the Imam 🕮 killed was to make him mount this animal. With this nefarious plan in mind Imam Askari 🕮 was "respectfully" presented with this horse and asked to ride it. The Imam 🕮 accepted the gift unhesitatingly and asked for the horse to be saddled. To the surprise of all present, the horse remained docile and calm upon the Imam 🕮's arrival and gave no sign of its unruliness as long as the Imam 🕮 remained astride on it. Thinking that the horse had now been tamed, Mustaeen took the horse back into his own stables and then ordered one of his own select persons to ride it. The horse promptly threw the rider off which resulted in his severe injuries including the loss of all his front teeth!

Once a follower of the Imam 🕮 says he approached the Imam 🕮 and expressed his indigent condition and his inability to meet his daily expenses to him. The Imam 🕮 dug a small hole in the

---

[135] The last two paragraphs were taken courtesy of Peer Mohomed Ebrahim Trust, Karachi Pakistan.

earth with his whip and retrieved a pouch which had Five Hundred Dinar in it which he handed to him; and which was exactly the amount needed by him to meet all his expenses.

Once a non-Muslim person (a *Majusi*) who was in jail wrote a letter to Imam Hasan al Askari 🕮 describing his plight; but was shy from asking for any monetary help. Upon receipt of his letter, the Imam 🕮 wrote back saying that he would be freed from jail by noontime of that day. As indicated by the Imam 🕮, the person was indeed set free, and upon stepping out from his confinement he was greeted by a messenger from the Imam 🕮 who handed him One Hundred Dinars to tide him over, with instructions from the Imam 🕮 not to hesitate in asking for his help in future when in difficulty.

11.40: Twelfth and Last Imam: Muhammad al-Mahdi 🕮

The Twelfth Imam 🕮 was the son of the holy 11th Imam Hasan al-Askari 🕮. He was born on Friday the 15th of Shabaan 255 AH. He was the only child of his parents. His revered mother's name was Narjis Khatoon, but she was known by several other names such as: Maleka, Saiqhal and Susan. She was the granddaughter of the last Ceasar of Rome (Constantinople), whose army had been defeated by the Muslim forces; and their ladies had been taken as captives to be sold as slaves. Her lineage traces back to that of Lady Mary (*Marium bint Imran* 🕮) the mother of Jesus 🕮. She was also distantly related to the family of Simon Peter (*Shamoon*) the chief disciple of Jesus 🕮.

It is a belief among all Muslims that when the Twelfth Imam 🕮 (The Mahdi 🕮) will reappear in this world towards the End of Time, Jesus 🕮 will also descend from the Heaven and pray behind him. The world will then be filled with Peace and Justice, just as it will be filled with wars and strife before their advent. Many Sunni scholars including Mulla Jani in his book 'Shawahed', Abul Fida in his book 'Tareeq', Abi Dawood in his 'Sunan' and ibn Hajar e Makki in 'Sawaiqe Mohriqa' and many others have all written that the son of Imam Hasan Al-Askari 🕮 was born on the 15th of Shabaan 255 AH and is miraculously still alive till today!

Another prominent Sunni scholar Mulla Ali Muttaqi in his book 'Muntakhib Kanzul Aamal' Vol 4, Page 40, has recorded a tradition that *"The Earth can never be without the 'Proof of Allah' (Hujjatullah), regardless of whether the people recognize him or not."* In another book titled 'Mukashifaat-e-Mumami' written in 1119 AH by a notable Sunni scholar who states a similar tradition that *"For **its very existence**, it is incumbent for the world to have the 'Proof of Allah' (Hujjatullah) to exist within this Earth, till the end of time."*

Sheik Mohiuddin writes in his book 'Al Futuhat' that it is most essential for the Imam Mahdi 🕮 to appear and announce his presence to set the affairs of the world aright; but this will not happen till such time as when the world is burdened with injustice and oppression. The Mahdi 🕮 will appear at such a time and he will be from the progeny of the holy Prophet 🕮 and a descendant from the line of his daughter Fatima 🕮.

Allama ibn Hajar e Asqalani in his book 'Al Isaba' writes on page 124 that the Mahdi 🕮's name is Muhammad, and one of his titles is *'Abul Qasim'* - also like that of the holy Prophet 🕮. His other titles are *'Al Muntazir'* - The Awaited One; *'Saheb uz Zaman'* – The Master of Age and *'Khalaf-e-Saleh – The Virtuous Son'* of the Prophet 🕮. He further writes that "the Mahdi 🕮 disappeared and is hidden from sight by the Will of Allah 🕮 and no one knows as to when he will reappear. He was 5 years old at the time of his revered father's death, but even at this early age Allah 🕮 had bestowed him with complete knowledge."

Sheik Abdul Haq Muhaddis Dehlawi, Mulla Abdur Rahman Jami in 'Shawahed al Nabuwah', Malakul Ullema Shahabuddin

Daulatabadi in 'Hidayatul al Sa'ada' – all these Sunni scholars have recorded the details of the birth of Imam Mahdi ﷤ and are agreed upon the date of his birth as being on Friday the 15th of Shabaan in the year 255 AH in the city of Sammarah in Iraq.

Khwaja Mohammed Parsa in his book 'Fasal al Khitab' and Imam Qandozi in his famous book 'Yanabi al Muwaddah' write that his father was Imam Hasan al-Askari ﷺ and his mother was Narjis Khatoon ﷤. He was the only son born to the Imam and is last in the line of the 12 Imams from the progeny of Prophet Muhammad ﷺ. He was born on 15th Shabaan 255 AH and was 5 years old when he lost his revered father. Allama Qandozi Balkhi further writes in the same book that a servant of the Eleventh Imam Hasan al-Askari ﷺ by the name of Abul Qasim stated that after the birth of the 12th Imam ﷤, Imam Askari ﷺ named him 'Muhammad' and after three days he brought him out on his hands and showed him to all his close and intimate followers with these words: "*This is your future Imam and Calipha and I have named him Muhammad. He will be your Imam after us, and he is that very Imam and our Caliph for whom you will await and look forward to his reappearance after the earth will be filled with strife, war, cruelty, and injustice. He will fill it with Justice and Equity.*"

Imam Qandozi further records that Jafar ibn Maalik relates that Muawiya ibn Hakam, Mohammed ibn Ayyub and Muhammad bin Uthman all state that they went in a group of 40 people to visit Imam Hasan al Askari ﷺ. He showed them his newborn son and said: "*After me he is your Imam and your Caliph. Obey him and do not dispute his authority after me.*"

Hamdan Inqilanasi states that he asked Umer bin Uthman Al Amawi if Imam Hasan al Askari had passed away? He replied yes, he died but has left his son as his successor and his allegiance is (still) binding on us.

Kamal-Ibne-Ibrahim-e-Madani says: "I once visited Abu Muhammad Hasan al-Askari ﷺ. I noticed that the door of the adjoining room was draped with a curtain. While I sat within the room, a gust of wind blew the curtain aside at which time I observed a young good-looking boy inside the other room. Imam Askari ﷺ told me: *'You have just seen your future Imam and Calipha'*."

Another Sunni scholar Sheik Husayn Dayar Bakri has noted the following excerpt in his book:[136]

"The Twelfth Imam is Muhammad ibn al-Askari, ibn Ali, ibn Muhammad, ibn Ali al-Raza ﷺ. His patronymic or filial appellation is 'Abul Qasim' (same as that of the holy Prophet ﷺ). The Imami sect refers to him as *'Hujjat al Qaim al Mahdi Al Muntazar* and *Saheb-uz-Zaman.'* According to their belief he is the last of their Twelve Imams. They also believe that he entered a cave in Sammarrah and disappeared while his mother looked on, and he did not return."

Imam Ahmed bin Yousuf Damasqi who is also known as 'Imam e Qurbani' reports this same information in his book 'Tarikh-e-Akhbarul Awwal Fee Asarul Awwal' with the added comment that the Imam ﷺ though barely 5 years at the time of his father's death, was endowed with Divine Wisdom and Knowledge similar to the way that Prophet Yahya bin Zakaria (John The Baptist ﷺ) was blessed with at that same age. He was of normal stature of children at that age but had an extremely beautiful countenance which gave the impression of a 'Light' radiating from within. The Shias refer to him as *"Al Qaim, Al Muntazar* and *Saheb-e-Saif".* They believe that he will have two Occultations: 'Minor' - (*Ghaibat-e-Sughra*) and Major (*Ghaibat-e-Kubra*). During the Minor Occultation he will appoint four successive scholars as his representatives in the

---

[136] 'Tarikh al Kahmis' – Vol 3, Pg 331

years immediately following his disappearance from the public eye. After the death of the fourth representative, he will go into the Greater Occultation and only reappear towards the end of Time.

Sibte Ibn Jauzi, another prominent Sunni scholar also emphasizes and confirms the miraculous birth and lineage of the 12th Imam ﷺ in the comparable way as the other foregoing writers.

Khwaja Mohammed Parsa, in addition to the statements recorded from him earlier, has also written the following in his same book (Fasal al Khitab):

"The traditions are numerous on this topic of the Mahdi. He is the 'Master of The Age' and is hidden from our eyes; and yet present among us. His noble and superior qualities are countless. All scholars are unanimous in their views about his miraculous birth, his exalted personality, and his ultimate reappearance when he will reinstate the Jurisprudence of his grandfather the noble Prophet Muhammad ﷺ. He will rid the world of the Evil that would be prevailing. During his era, his followers will be the most pious, and free from doubts or evil traits. They will follow him implicitly without question and will not dissent or contravene him. The Imamate and Caliphate will end with him. He has been 'The Master of The Age' since his revered father's death and will remain so till the 'Day of Doom'. Jesus ﷺ will also reappear and pray behind him, confirming his exalted status."

Abu Abdullah Mohammed ibn Yousuf ibn Muhammad-e-Kanji Shafaei in addition to confirming the foregoing in his book 'Kitab-ul-Bayan Fee Akhbar-us-Saheb-uz-Zaman' also writes that Imam Mahdi ﷺ is the son of Imam Hasan al Askari ibn Ali al-Naqi ﷺ; and is alive from the time of his father's death to this day. The proof of his long life is the very same as those which are accepted for Prophets Jesus ﷺ, Khizr ﷺ and Ilyas ﷺ.

Allama Dhahabi who has denied several traditions with respect to the exalted status of the Ahlul Bayt of the Prophet ﷺ, nonetheless quotes a tradition from Imam Ali ؑ which many Sunni scholars[137] have also endorsed. The tradition goes as follows:

"God is the Witness that his Earth will never be devoid of the Proof of Allah; so that the Evidence of Allah ﷻ can never be refuted. These exalted personalities (Imams) are few but their status with Allah ﷻ is Exalted and Lofty. It is only through them that Allah ﷻ sends his Arguments and Justification so that these may be presented to the people through them as they are the ones who possess knowledge. It is through them that True Knowledge reaches the people. Although they are in mortal forms, their souls are in Exalted Places. They are the True Caliphs of Allah, and they are the ones who beckon people toward His True Path. They are well known to the people in their true status or hidden from them due to the fear of oppressive environment."

Earlier in this book in Chapter IV we have already cited 20 traditions from the holy Prophet ﷺ which were taken entirely from Sunni sources, and these need not be repeated here again. In the earlier stages of his Lesser Occultation, Imam Mahdi ؑ was guiding his followers through his appointed deputies because the political conditions were such that he could not appear in person. The Caliph Motamid was aware that Imam Hasan al Askari had left an issue behind; and that his son was alive and had conducted the funeral rites of his revered father. On the one hand he could not deny the existence of the 12th Imam ؑ while on the other hand he could not refrain from his efforts to trap and remove (kill) him for good.

---

[137] Allama Muttaqi in 'Kanzul Amaal', Vol 5, Pg 231; Sulayman Balkhi Hanafi – 'Yanabi al Muwaddatah' Istanbul Edition year 1523; Ahmed ibn Hanbal in his 'Musnad', Vol 4, Pg 400; Hafiz Abu Naeem – 'Hulayatul Awliya' Vol 1, Pg 80.

Towards this end, in order to get more information about the young Imam, Motamid invited the step brother of Imam Hasan al-Askari ﷺ called Jafar ibn Ali al-Naqi ﷺ (who was also referred to by many as 'Jafar-e-Kazzab' [*Liar*]); and after paying him a great deal of respect he endeavoured to extract a false tradition from him to the effect that Hasan al-Askari ﷺ had died without leaving any issue, and that the rumours circulating about the birth of the 12ᵗʰ Imam ﷺ were false. He further had him promote a rumour that the Mahdi ﷺ will be born closer to the Day of Judgement. This was done by him in the hope of convincing the people to accept him, Motamid, as their Caliph and live in peace and harmony under his reign.

The Shias of Ahlul Bayt ﷺ were accustomed to sending their donations and gifts to the Imams of their time, which the Imams used to distribute among the poor. Accordingly, after the death of Imam Hasan al-Askari ﷺ the Shias of Qum arrived in Samarrah looking for their next Imam. Jafar the stepbrother of Imam Askari ﷺ tried to obtain these donations by implying that he was the next Imam of the Time; but they refused to give in, asking for the proof of his *Imamate* in like way Imam Hasan al-Askari ﷺ used to demonstrate. Jafar took this group of people to the Court of Motamid and complained that these people were refusing to give him the donations which by rights were his due share as their Imam. When Motamid questioned the reason for their refusal they said: "We are only the bearers of these funds and trusts which belong to others. We have been instructed by them to hand over these trusts only to him who will be able to tell us the names, amounts and identities of the senders. In the past up until now, all previous Imams used to do this and establish their authenticity as our Imam."

Jafar was unable to satisfy and fulfill these conditions; and this group of people left the court and started on their journey back home. They had barely left the precincts of the city when they were hailed by someone, calling them by their names saying: "Come this way, your Imam is calling you." They turned and followed this person to a house where they saw the 12th Imam مَيِّة in person, with their own eyes! The Imam مَيِّة identified the amounts and the senders along with their names and addresses. Hearing this, the group fell upon the feet of the Imam مَيِّة and handed the amounts over to him. After enquiring about the rulings on certain issues from him, they took their leave to return to their hometown well satisfied. In parting, the Imam مَيِّة told them that in future they should refrain from coming to him as it endangers his position with the Caliph. They should instead go to the deputies appointed by him for dealing with their problems and issues.

Meanwhile, Motamid continued in the pursuit of his nefarious plans to arrest the Imam ﷺ. Towards this end, he continuously sent his spies and police to raid his house and catch him unawares. At times, these spies would be successful in entering his house when the Imam مَيِّة was present within his house and though they could *hear him* reciting the Quran in his melodious voice, yet they could not *see him*! The Imam مَيِّة in the manner of his Great Grandfather the holy Prophet ﷺ who left before the very eyes of his enemies on the night of *Hijrat* (migration), the Imam also similarly recited a few verses of the Quran and walked past the spies unnoticed by any!

During the next few years, the Imam مَيِّة continued to meet with certain select group of his trusted scholars in the basement of his house to discuss various issues of Knowledge (*Ilm*) and Jurisprudence (*Fiqh*). However, as the vigilance of the spies increased this regular habit of meeting was abandoned. Now only his most trusted deputy was given the privilege of meeting him in a certain cave located in the western portion of the city. When the conditions of spying became even more stringent, the Imam ﷺ

eventually left the city of Samarah with his mother and kept changing destinations to dodge the surveillance of the government. The Imam ﷺ continued to reside in and around the precincts of the city of Hilla where to this day a Mausoleum stands erected in the spot where he is believed to have resided and finally gone into occultation.

Mulla Mohammed Baqir Majlisi in his scholarly treatise of 'Bihar ul Anwar' Vol 13, writes about the special deputies appointed by the Imam ﷺ during the period of his Lesser Occultation; and these persons became the 'medium' of approach for the people to reach their Imam. All matters relating to various issues would emanate through them for his followers. The first of these chosen deputies was **Uthman Bin Sayeed-e-Amari**. He was a contemporary of both Imam Ali al-Naqi ﷺ and Imam Hasan al-Askari ﷺ; and he had also been deputised by these two Imams ﷺ during their own turbulent times. Uthman Bin Sayeed died in 295 AH and after him his son **Abu Ja'far Mohammed** became his next deputy. He died in 305 AH, whereupon this mantle was passed on the lot of **Husayn ibn Rooh**. He passed away in 329 AH and after his death the secret meetings came to an end. Only under extraordinary circumstances one very venerable and pious person named **Ali ibn Muhammad-e-Samari** was allowed to have an audience by the Imam ﷺ. The pressures of the government were now intensified and the hounding of his followers by the government officials among the public had also increased to new heights. The Imam ﷺ ordered them to refrain from *even mentioning* his name in public, and only to refer to him in an indirect way as '*Naaji-e-Muqaddas*' – *the Sinless Pious Person*".

During the period of the Minor Occultation people used to send written queries to the Imam ﷺ through his deputy; and in return they used to receive a handwritten reply from the Imam ﷺ. These documented inscriptions from the Imam are known as "*Tauquee-e-*

Mubarak" (Blessed Signatures or Autographs); and these are mentioned in several famous and authentic books. These are a collection of questions and replies on various issues and topics that were posed to the Imam 🕮 by his followers. The last deputy of the Imam 🕮: **Ali ibn Muhammad Al-Sameri** received the final instructions sent to him in the Imam 🕮's own handwriting while he was in the very end moments of his life and breathing his last. A summary of these instructions is as shown under:

"In the Name of Allah The Beneficent and The Most Merciful: O Ali ibn Muhammad Al Samiri, may Allah grant Great Rewards to your Companions in Fatih. You will expire in six days, so get your affairs in order. In respect with a 'deputy' after you, appoint NONE; as the period of the Major Occultation has now begun for me. My reappearance will now be after a prolonged period by the Will of Allah 🕮. Hearts of the people will be hardened in that period, and the Earth will be filled with Injustice and Oppression. There will be many people during those times who will profess to be in 'contact with us and claim to be in regular conversation with us'. Anyone claiming to meet us in this way **before** *the advent of 'Sufiyani'* **and** *the 'Proclamation from the Heaven about our Reappearance' would be an outright liar.* **There is No Power but that of Allah 🕮!"**

Ali ibn Muhammad-e-Samiri circulated this letter among the Shias whereat it soon became public knowledge. To avoid confusion in the minds of the public the *Ulema* opine that by his statement about "not openly meeting with anyone" the Imam 🕮 meant that he would NOT be meeting anyone in an **obvious** manner where he would be recognized as such. Nonetheless, the Imam 🕮 does meet the people on various occasions such as during Hajj or Ziyaraats, but the people do not recognize him and only become aware of their encounter *after* the Imam 🕮 disappears from their sight!

Sunni and Shia scholars have both testified to the fact that they have seen and met with the Imam ﷺ during his Major Occultation; and claim to have also gained the benefit of his knowledge on various intricate and complicated Islamic issues. In this connection, following is a concise list of books that record various incidents of encounters with the Imam ﷺ:

1. Anqa-e-Maghreb – by Sheik Mohiuddin, Al Arabi
2. Al Waquiyat Wal Jawahir by Imam Abdul Wahab Sherani
3. Sibatah-al Marwayed – by Sheik Abdul Lateef Halabi
4. Mataleb-us-Su'ool by Mohammaed ibn Talha ash-Shafei
5. Al Bayaan Fee Akhbar Saheb-uz-Zamaan by Mohammed ibn Yousuf ibn Knaji Shafei
6. Farayad-Al-Musta'een by Imam Humveni
7. Fusool-e-Muhimma by Nooruddin ibn Mohammed Mali

Some Sufi scholars of the *Ahle Tariqat* have reported in their own autobiographies that they acquired their knowledge both, in the 'physical and spiritual' fields through the guidance of Hazrat Imam Saheb-uz-Zamaan ﷺ.

Accordingly, Allama Abdul Rehman Chisti in his book 'Maraeth Madary' has recorded various incidents about a Sufi scholar by the name of Badi Uddin Qutub. This manuscript was written in 1064 AD and is still housed in the Library Section of the 'Salar Jung Museum' in Hyderabad India. In this manuscript it is mentioned that Badi Uddin Qutub was a descendant from the family of Prophets Moses and Aaron ﷺ. His father had seen a dream in which Prophet Musa ﷺ had prophesied to him about a son's birth; and given him the good news of his future achievements.

Badi Uddin Qutub in addition to becoming proficient in his knowledge of the holy *Quran* was also an extremely well-versed scholar of the *Taurah, Bible* and the *Psalms.* But despite this he was not satisfied; and in his search for additional understanding and awareness, he proceeded to the holy City of Madina, where, while in proximity of the shrine of the holy Prophet ﷺ he had an inspired vision wherein the Prophet revealed the true Islamic Faith to him and 'assigned' him into the care of Imam Ali ؑ for further guidance.

As a result of this experience Badi Uddin Qutub proceeded to the Mausoleum of Ali ؑ in Najaf, Iraq where he began to pursue his quest for further enlightenment in the library of 'Aastaan-e-Quds' located in that holy city. After his extensive search Allama Abdul Rehman Chisti writes that Badi Uddin Qutub concluded that the "Twelfth Imam ؑ is present in this world, though in Occultation; and is ready to help those who seek his guidance. In brief, he further acknowledges that Muhammad, al Mahdi ؑ, the son of Hasan al-Askari ؑ is a descendant of Lady Fatima ؑ the daughter of the holy Prophet ﷺ. He will physically reappear on Earth when ordered to do so by Allah ﷻ."

Imam Malik, one of the four Imams of the Ahle Sunnat has confirmed the above-mentioned tradition. So also, have done many others, included among them is the illustrious Sunni scholar Sheik Mohiuddin Arabi, who has documented in his book 'Futuhaat' that Imam Mahdi ؑ **has been born** to Imam Hasan al Askari the son of Imam Hadi ؑ from the progeny of the holy Prophet ﷺ; and will emerge from his Occultation along with Jesus ؑ when commanded to do so by Allah ﷻ. There are several other authentic books that corroborate the foregoing assertions in connection with the present Imam ؑ's birth and existence.

There are some Sunni traditions which confirm the belief that Jesus ؑ will descend from the Fourth Heaven after the *Zuhoor:* (reappearance) of Imam Mahdi ؑ and acknowledge him as his Leader and join the Imam ؑ. On the other hand, there are some other Sunni traditions for instance in 'Dar-e-Mukhtar' that 'Jesus *will* make his reappearance but follow and obey Abu Hanifa'! Then again, in the same vein, there are some other traditions which state that 'Prophet Khizr ﷺ was under the tutorship of Abu Hanifa for 30 years [!] and that even after the latter's death, Khizr ﷺ continued to visit his grave to receive guidance and inspiration on several matters'!

This line of reasoning is amazing because Khizr ﷺ was endowed with Divine Knowledge *directly by Allah* ﷻ as stated in the holy Quran: *"Then they found one* (Hazrat Khizr) *from among Our servants whom We had granted Mercy from Us, and whom We had taught Knowledge from Ourselves."* Surah *Kahf* (18:65). Moreover, this is a prophet and a *Nabi* regarding whom Allah ﷻ mentions in the Quran as being the one who imparted knowledge on various issues to none other than "one of the Five" Exalted (*Ulul Azm*) Prophets - Hazrat Musa ﷺ! In comparison, Abu Hanifa was no more than a 'mere' Jurist; and traditions such as these that contravene Quranic statements cannot stand up against a microscopic investigation of Logic and Reason.

Notwithstanding such illogical traditions as mentioned above, we have other authenticated traditions from one of the 'Six True Books': 'Sunan-e-Abu Dawood' which states that: "The Imam Al-Qaim ﷺ will be sent by Allah ﷻ to establish Peace and Justice on this Earth; and he will be from the *Ahlul Bayt* of the Prophet ﷺ." These sorts of traditions are also supported by other notable Sunni scholars such as Ibn Hajar-e-Makki in 'Sawaiq al Mohriqa' along with a few more who believe that the last Imam Mahdi ﷺ has been appointed by Allah ﷻ and will make his reappearance towards the End of Time.

At this point it is worth reflecting that when many Sunni scholars are agreed upon the fact that the last Imam ﷺ will be appointed **solely** by Allah ﷻ, then why is this 'Reason and Logic' not applied with regard to the First Imam Ali ﷺ and to **all of the other** Eleven Imams ﷺ of the Ahlul Bayt ﷺ as being the ones appointed by Allah ﷻ?

Some self opiniated persons *question the validity of the belief* that a person can be alive and in hiding, for *hundreds of years* and will make his reappearance close to the Day of Judgement! They question as to how it is possible for any living being to be alive for such an extended period? To this we refer to various incidents recorded in the holy Quran for instance, in Chapter 18 about the "People of The Cave" (*As-haab-e-Kahf*) and their dog who awoke from their slumber after 300 years; and then after sending one of their companions into the town's marketplace to buy some provisions, subsequently upon his return, have all gone back to sleep again, and will remain in this state till the rise of the Mahdi 🕌 at end of time.

Prophets Khizr 🕌 and Ilyas (Elias) 🕌 too are mentioned as being alive, as is also Jesus 🕌 kept in a state of sojourn on the "4th Heaven" till such time as he makes his reappearance on earth with the Mahdi 🕌. Similarly, Satan has not only been granted a tenure of life close to Eternity, but he has also been given the power of misguiding humans by leading them into temptations and spreading evil among the people. In the same manner "Dajjal" – another evil character is mentioned in the Quran and said to be in existence from time immemorial and will make his appearance in society close to the 'End of time.' So, it begs the question that while these various personalities are alive, why should there be any doubt that Allah 🕌 will not grant an equally lengthy life to a "son from the progeny of the holy Prophet"🕌 to be able to guide the people in their lives during the absence of any other prophets. If this were not so, it would not be the Justice of Allah 🕌 that he has given freedom to Satan to *misguide* the people, while not granting the same privilege to some *other 'Entity'* to counteract the Evil influence of Satan and guide them towards the Right Path over such a prolonged period in time!

Another irrefutable proof from the Quran in connection with the existence of the Living Imam ﷺ was given by none other than the Living Imam himself [!] when a challenge was issued by some Sunni brothers to their Shia counterparts in an Interfaith Group meeting. This incident was recounted in the mid 1970s by a reputed Shia scholar in a large 'open-forum type' of a gathering which we [translators] were privileged to hear his speech.

Apparently a discussion between the two groups got to the point with Shias insisting on their belief in the longevity of life granted by Allah ﷻ to their 12th Imam ﷺ, versus the Sunni group's demand to prove *from the Quran*, that anyone could live this long; with the added stipulation to not give examples of Satan or of Prophet Jesus ﷺ, since they were an 'exception to the rule' and were granted a special lease of life by God.

The challenge was accepted with a request that they be given a certain time-limit within which to produce their proof. Time was granted, and the Shias immediately started going through the holy Quran, and several books of references, and every other religious tome at their disposal to find such proof and attestation, with no success. Finally, in their despondency, close to the eve of their deadline date, they decided to invoke the help of the 12th Imam ﷺ himself. To this end, they all went *out of the city limits to a quiet and deserted area;* then, standing as a group under the open skies in the darkness of the night, they desperately started invoking the Imam ﷺ for help. Finally, into the small hours of the night close to a short time before the advent of dawn, they noticed a figure coming towards them in the dark. Upon approaching them, without any preamble he told them to look up Ch 37, Sura *Saffat,* verse 144. On enquiring his identity, he said: "*Your Imam*"! When one of them mustered enough courage to ask as to why he had not come to their help till the last hours of the challenge, he replied that *had they called upon him earlier and not relied on their own prowess, he too would've come to their help earlier!*

The Shias were elated beyond words and came back to the table armed with the Quranic reference about the incident of Prophet Jonah (Yunus 🕮) as guided by the Imam; thereby proving [from the Quran] that if Allah had so wished, he would have kept not only Yunus 🕮 but also the fish that swallowed him alive till the Day of Resurrection!

"*So, the fish swallowed him while he did that for which he blamed himself. But had it not been that he was of those who glorified us, '***he would certainly have tarried in its belly to the Day when they are Raised.***"* (37: 142-144).

In the face of such water-tight evidence, the Sunni scholars and their group acknowledged the fact that indeed it is beyond debate that those whom Allah 🕮 wants to grant a long life to, can be, (and *are*) *alive* till the end of Time!

Reverting to our original text, Chap 97 (Surah *Al Qadr*) of the holy Quran states that "*on the Night of Qadr Angels and Souls all descend towards the Earth by the permission of Allah 🕮 and bring Tidings of Every Affair*". So, where do all these Angels go? And "whose" attention do they bring these "Tidings" to? There must be "***some personality in charge***" on Earth to accept and review the "Affairs" that are being brought down by the Angels *every year* on the "Night of Qadr"; and *that* "***personality***" obviously is the "Link" between Allah 🕮 and His creation!

In a similar vein, in Chapter 36 (Surah *Yasin*) Allah 🕮 clearly states "*All affairs are recorded (and entrusted) to a Manifest Imam*" *(36:12)*. Since this verse is not restricted to any period in history, but is for "all times", and it is also 'grammatically recorded in the present tense', it stands to reason that in *every age* there has to be a manifestly appointed Imam. To support this point further, we have the famous tradition of the Prophet 🕮 known as: "The

Tradition of The Two Weighty Entities" (*Hadith e Thaqelain*) in which he ﷺ stated: "*I leave behind you Two Weighty Entities: The Book of Allah and my Ahlul Bayt. They will **never be separated** from each other till they meet me at the Pool of Kauther on the Day of Judgement."* Since the holy Quran is still present among us in its original text and form, it again stands to reason that as both are inseparable from each other, an Imam from the progeny of the Prophet ﷺ must also always be present in every Age and Era.

Accordingly, the Twelver Shiites believe that the last of the Twelve Imams is still present among them by the Grace and Will of Allah ﷻ but hidden from sight for a specific purpose. And these believers who have faith in the "*Unseen*" (Ch 2:3), do not consider it important or necessary to physically see their Imam! After all, they argue, "Who has seen God?" They are confident in their belief that this is their Imam who gives the Shias their moral support and makes them spiritually strong; and they in turn resort to him with supplications and prayers when faced with any insurmountable difficulties. The respect they have for him is such that when he is mentioned by name, the Shias stand up in respect and pay their salutations as though they are seeing him, and as if he is actually present in their midst.

As per the following Quranic verse in Surah *Baqirah*: "*Wa Kazaleka Ja'alnakum Ummatan Wasatan le Takoonu Shohada-ey Alan-Naas Wa Yakoonal Rasoolo Alaikum Shaheeda...Thus we have made you a 'Middle Nation' that you may be witnesses over (the deeds of) the people; and the Apostle may be a witness over you*", (2:143), the Mahdi ﷺ is also one of the persons from that particular "Select Group" who have been ordained by Allah to be a witness over the deeds of the people. Also, like his forefathers, he ﷺ too is one of the designated "True Successors" of the holy Prophet ﷺ ordained by Allah ﷻ; and a "Caliph" appointed by Him on this Earth. The Quran additionally states in Surah *Bani Israel*:

"*The Day We shall summon every group of people **along with their Imam**....*"(17:71), and considering this, the Shias believe that in the Hereafter, they will all be raised under the banner of **this** Living Imam when called to justice.

All Muslims, irrespective of their affiliations believe that when the Mahdi ﷺ reappears to establish "Peace and Justice" on this Earth after it has been filled with strife and injustice, Jesus ﷺ will also descend from the Heaven and follow and assist him in this endeavour. Apart from their spiritual attachment to the Living Imam ﷺ while he continues in his state of "*Ghaibat*" (Great Occultation), the Shias resort to several recommended prayers which they recite in times of difficulties whereby they have their wishes granted, and even in rare cases, meet with their Imam ﷺ in person!

A well-known incident is recorded in history about two persons named Muhammad Jamal and Ali Qazwini who were both lovers of the holy Ahlul Bayt ﷺ. The actual name of the former was Muhammad, but since his trade was hiring out camels (*Jamal*, in Arabic) he came to be known as Muhammad Jamal. One day he approached Ali Qazwini who was the Vazir of the Caliph of his time, to help with a certain request of a needy person. Ali Qazwini sent word that he was too busy to meet him. Muhammad Jamal returned disappointed and disheartened that he could not resolve the needy person's problem.

Some time later Ali Qazwini set out for the pilgrimage to the shrines of the Imams of the holy Ahlul Bayt ﷺ. During this journey he unexpectedly found himself in a garden where he met a young handsome man with a bright countenance and an imposing personality. To his surprise the young man addressed him by name saying: "*You had a visitor called Muhammad Jamal whom you refused to meet, making him return very sad and disappointed. Of what benefit is this pilgrimage that you are now undertaking? You should first go and apologise and make amends with him."* Ali Qazwini was completely over awed by this personality and said, "I will most certainly obey your orders, but please tell me who you are?" To this he replied: *"Have you **Not** recognized the Imam of your Time?"* So saying, he disappeared from his sight!

When Ali Qazwini recovered from the shock of this encounter, he once again found himself on the road leading to the shrines. He immediately abandoned his plans of visiting the shrines, turned back, and proceeded directly to the house of Muhammad Jamal. There, after knocking on his door, he lay down on the ground resting his cheek on the doorstep and called out to Muhammad Jamal to come out and step on his face! The latter upon encountering this scene, resisted, but on repeated pleas and insistence by Qazwini on Oath of Allah ﷻ, Muhammad Jamal reluctantly did as he was bid. Qazwini then stood up, apologized to Muhammad Jamal, and related the entire incident which had taken place between him and the Imam ul Asr عليه السلام!

In Kufa Iraq, there is a mosque known as the *'Masjid-e-Sehla'* where people have seen the present Imam عليه السلام on many occasions. Many a time the Imam عليه السلام has also been seen in the company of Hazrat Khizr عليه السلام and Hazrat Ilyas عليه السلام walking behind him at a respectful distance. Upon consideration, why should it not be so? Considering the famous tradition of Prophet Mohammad ﷺ: *"Awwalona Muhammad, Ausatona Muhammad, Aqhirona Muhammad, Kullona Muhammad! - The First of us is Muhammad, the Middle of us is Muhammad, the Last of us is Muhammad; We All of us are Muhammads,"* this Imam عليه السلام *is* also a "**Muhammad,**" and as such, commands a higher status than the that granted to the other prophets granted a lessor position in comparison to the holy prophet of Islam , peace be upon him and his family. This Imam عليه السلام is the "Last" of the Muhammads and obviously for this reason he was also named as Muhammad!

11:41 Some Miracles of The Twelfth Imam ﷺ

Regarding his miraculous birth there are several confirmed traditions that his revered mother Lady Narjis Khatoon ﷺ bore no signs of his pregnancy till the very end, in a manner like that of the mother of Moses ﷺ. Hence *no one*, even to the extent of the members of his own household, were aware of his impending birth! One day when his Aunt Lady Hakima Khatoon came visiting his revered father the holy Eleventh Imam ﷺ, he, Imam Hasan al Askari ﷺ requested her to stay behind saying: *"Today Allah ﷺ is going to bless me with the birth of my son!"* In surprise his aunt commented that she saw no signs of pregnancy on his wife Narjis ﷺ! To this the Imam ﷺ replied: *"Yes indeed! Narjis is also like the mother of Musa ﷺ; and the signs of her pregnancy will only be apparent just prior to the time the birth of my son!"*

Shortly after the midnight prayers, Hazrat Hakima Khatoon states that she ﷺ entered the room of Lady Narjis ﷺ where she noticed the signs of her imminent delivery. She immediately began to recite various chapters of the holy Quran: Surah *Ikhlas, Qadr* and the verses of *'Ayaatul Kursi'* to ease the pangs of birth; and she further relates that whichever Surah of the Quran she started to recite, the child within the womb of Narjis Khatoon ﷺ repeated the same!

Shortly thereafter, she saw the whole house suddenly lit up with a brilliant light and the newborn child immediately went into prostration before Allah ﷺ! At that very moment Imam Hasan al-Askari ﷺ was heard to call out from the adjoining room, asking his aunt to bring his infant son to him! When she took the child over to him, Imam Hasan al-Askari ﷺ kissed him on his mouth and gave him his tongue to suck on. Then addressing his newborn son, he said: *"O My son, speak by the Grace of Allah;"* upon which the child recited the following verse: *"Bismillah hir Rahman ar Raheem. Wa Nureedona Anna Munna Alal Lazeena as-Tazefu Fil Arzey wa*

*Najalahum Aaimmatah, wa Najalahumul Waritheе.... And We
desired to bestow a favour upon those who were deemed weak in the
land; and to make them the Imams, and to make them the Heirs."*
(Surah *Qasas*: 28:5).

According to Lady Hakima Khatoon there were several other
unusual occurrences that took place immediately after the birth of
this miraculous child. She saw some unknown "beings" with a
green hue, descend into the house. She asked Imam Askari 🕮 as to
who these were, to which the Imam 🕮 replied that these were
Angels sent by Allah 🕮 to felicitate him upon the birth of *The
Mahdi* 🕮; and included among them was Angel Gabriel 🕮! She
also states that a Quranic verse was imprinted on his right arm:
"*Wa Qul Jaa'ul Haqq wa Zahaq al Baatil; Innal Baatilo Kana Zahuqa
.... And say: The Truth has come, and Falsehood has vanished; Indeed,
Falsehood was bound to vanish."* (Surah Bani Isreal 17:81).

It is recorded that one day a devotee of Imam Hasan Askari 🕮
visited him and enquired as to who would be his successor after
him. Imam 🕮 led him towards an adjoining room and parted the
curtains whereupon a good-looking boy of about three or four
years old emerged and greeted him. Imam Askari 🕮 then sent the
child back. The person relates that when he raised the curtain again
a little later, he did not find anyone in the room!

Tradition further relates that the Twelfth Imam 🕮 was seen
collectively by a large group of people when his revered father
Imam Hasan al-Askari 🕮 was martyred; and subsequently very
soon after again, when his last rites were being conducted. Just as
the ceremony was about to commence, and the brother of Imam
Askari 🕮 was about to lead the congregation, a young boy came
forward and asked his uncle to step aside saying that it was his
right to lead his father's funeral prayers! But immediately after
conducting the formal rituals, he disappeared.

The ruling Caliph instantly sent his security guards all over town to search out and bring the youth to him, but none succeeded. He was seen later on and off by many persons in the most amazing circumstances; like offering his prayers on a Mat spread over the water of River Tigress (*Dajla*), in the manner of prophet Jesus ﷺ walking on water [!]; but none were ever able to pursue or apprehend him!

Instances and incidents of his followers and devotees sighting him in various lands and in varied places, his coming to their aid in difficulties etc., abound in numerous Annals of Miracles recorded about the Imam of their Time. He is referred to by his followers by several titles such as: *Saheb uz Zamaan, Imam ul Asr, Imam ul Waqt; Al Hujjat, Al-Mahdi, Al Muntazir* and so forth; and the last of them being: *Al QAIM – THE ONE WHO WILL RISE!*

To his faithful followers he is the "**Awaited One**" who has been born hundreds of years ago and is patiently awaiting God's Command to take his Rightful place on Earth.

May Allah ﷻ hasten his appearance ﷺ!

Bibliography

1. The Holy Quran – Urdu and English Translations
2. Nahjul Balagha: Sermons of Ali Ibne Abi Taleb ﷺ

Books On Quranic Interpretations – 'Tafseer-E-Quran'

3. Tafsir-e-Kashful Bayaan – by Abu Ishaq Imam Ahmad Thalabi
4. Tafsir Shawad-ut-Tanzeel – by Hakim Abul Qasim Al Baghavi
5. Tafsir Maalim-ut-Tanzeel – by Shamsuddin Nujumee
6. Tafsir Asbaab-al-Nuzool – by Abul Hasan Al Wahidi
7. Tafsir Kashaaf – by Jaraullah Zamakhshiri
8. Tafsir Majmu-ul-Bayaan – by Ibne Jareer Al Tabarri
9. Tafsir-e-Kabir – by Muhammad bin Omer Fakhruddin Raazi
10. Tasir-e-Mafati-ul-Ghaib – by Muhammad bin Omer Fakhruddin Raazi
11. Tafsir-e-Neshapuri – by Allama Nehsapuri
12. Tafsir Durre-Manthur – by Abdul Rahman Jalaluddin Suyuti
13. Tafsir Baidhavi – by Baidhavi
14. Tafsir Jaamae-Al Quran – by Qurtavi Andulisi
15. Tafsir-al-Naar – by Sheik Abdu
16. Tafsir Baihaqqi – by Abu Bakr Abdul Rahman bin Husain Al Baihaqqi
17. Tafsir Ibne Abi Hatim – by Ibne Abi Hatim
18. Tafsir-e-Kathir – by Ibne Kathir
19. Tafsir Abu Yusuf – by Abu Yusuf Yaqoob bin Hassaan
20. Tafsir Muqarrazi – by Muqarrazi
21. Tafsir-e-Tabarsi – by Tabarsi
22. Tafsir-e-Fateh-ul-Qadheer – by Shokani
23. Tafsir Abu Hayyaan – by Abu Hayyaan
24. Tafsir A'alusi – by A'alsusi
25. Tafsir Abu Masood – by Abu Masood
26. Tafsir Nas'fi – by Nas'fi

27. Tafsir Khazin – by Al Khazin
28. Tafsir Ibne Al Hijaj – by Ibne Al Hijaj
29. Tafsir Mujahid – by Mujahid
30. Tafsir Maqatil – by Maqatil
31. Tafsir Marduwiyah – by Abu Bakr Marduwiyah
32. Manazil-min-Quran-fee-Ali – by Hafiz Abu Bakr Shirazi
33. Nuzool-al-Quran-fee-Ali – by Hafiz Abu Naeem
34. Nazalat-fee-Ali – by Naqqash
35. Tafsir Husayni – by Nooruddin bin Ali bin Husayn, Mullah Vahez Kashafi
36. Tafsir-al-Manazir – by Rashid Raza Wahabi Misri
37. Ahkam-al-Quran – by Sheik Mohiuddin Ibne Arabi Andulusi
38. Ahkam-al-Quran – by Abu Bakr Muhammad bin Ali Raazi Hanafi
39. Tafsir Fateh-ul Aziz – by Shah Abdul Aziz Mohaddis Dehlavi
40. Tafsir Fateh-ul-Bayaan – by Siddiq Hasan Khan Bhopali

Books Of Traditions

41. Sahih Bukhari – by Abi Abdullah Muhammad Ismail Bukhari
42. Sharah-e-Bukhari – by Ainee
43. Faiz-ul-Baari – Translation of Sahih Bukhari by Faqirullah
44. Taisarul Bukhari – Trans of Sahih Bukhari by Waheed-uz-Zaman, Viqar Nawaz Jung
45. Tarjuma Sahih Bukhari – by Abdul Da'em Al-Jalaal Al-Bukhari
46. Sahih Muslim – by Abul Hasan Muslim bin Hujjaj Taqshari
47. Sharah Sahih Muslim – by Abdul Ali Behrul Uloom
48. Ja'mae Tirmizi – by Abu Esa Al Tirmizi
49. Sunaan-e-Kabir – by Abdul Rahman Ahmad bin Shoaib Nisai
50. Khasayas-e-Nabuwah – by Abdul Rahman Ahmad bin Shoaib Nisai
51. Sunaan-e-Abi Dawood – by Abi Dawood Tayyasi

52. Sunaan Ibne Ma'aja – by Abi Abdullah Muhammad bin Yazeed bin Ma'aja Quroyeni

53. Musnad-e-Shafe'i – by Abu Abdullah Muhammad bin Idris Shafe'i

54. Musnad-e-Ibne Hanbal – by Abdullah Ahmad bin Muhammad bin Hanbal Shaibani

55. Zawaid-e-Musnad – by Abdullah Ibne Ahmed

56. Sunaan-e-Darami – by Abu Muhammad Abdul Rahman bin Rahman Al Darami

57. Mu'watta – by Imam Malik Ibne Anas

58. Al Mustadrak – by Al Hakim

59. Talkhees Mustadrak – by Hafiz Mohammed bin Abdul Rahman Al Dhahabi

60. Al-Isti'ab – by Ibne Abdul Birr Qartabi

61. Sunaan-e-Baihaqqi – by Hafiz Abu Bakr Ahmed bin Husain Al Baihaqqi [Fiqh- Shafe'i]

62. Dalayel-e-Nabuwah

63. Khasayas – by Tabrani

64. Moa'jim-e-Salasa – by Tabrani

65. Ausa't –by Tabrani

66. Tabaqaat-ul-Kubra – by Mohammed bin Saad Katib Waqidi

67. Sunaan Darqatni – by Abul Hasan Ali bin Omer Darqatni

68. Jama-e-Ba'in Al Suhaha – by Abd Ra'iy

69. Jama-e-Ba'in Al Suhaha – by Zareeni

70. Jama-ul-Ba'in-e-Sohaheen – by Hameedi

71. Jawama-al-Jama' – by Sanjani

72. Naqad-al-Sahih – by Mujaduddin Ferozabadi

73. Moa'jim-al-Kabir – by Tabrani

74. Riaz-un-Nazzarra – by Mohibuddin Tabarri

75. Zakha'er-ul-Uqba – by Mohibuddin Tabarri

76. Yanabul Muwaddah – by Sheik Sulayman Balkhi Qandusi Hanafi

77. Firdous-al-Akhbar – by Dailami

78. Muwaddath-ul-Qurba – by Sayed Ali Shahabuddin Hamdani, [Fiqh-Shafe'i]

79. Urwatul Wusqa – by Alla-ud-Dawlah Ahmed bin Muhammad

80. Mohahib-ud-Duniya – by Ahmad bin Muhammad bin Abu Bakr Al Qastalani

81. Irshaad-al-Baari – by Ahmad bin Muhammad bin Abu Bakr Al Qastalani

82. Sharah-e-Mohahib-ud-Duniya – by Allama Rasqani

83. Mohahib-al-Mohahib – by Mohammad Al-Naqvi Al Jaffer

84. Sharah-e-Mohahib – by Zareeni

85. Faizul Qadeer - Sharah Jama'e Al Qadeer – by Munadi

86. Sunan-e-Hamuyeni – by Hamuyeni

87. Asnaad-al-Mutaalib – by Al Beroni

88. Sunaan Ibne Maghazi – by Ibne Maghazi

89. Sunan-e-Dul'aabi – by Dul'aabi

90. Mishkaat-ul-Masabih – by Waliuddin Makki

91. Marqat Sharah-e-Mushkawat – by Mulla Ali Qari

92. As-hatul-Mu'ath – Sharah-e-Mushkawat – by Abdul Haqq Muhaddis Dehlavi

93. Talkhisal-Sahih-fee-Sharah-e-Masabih – by Muhammad Idris Hanafi

94. Mazaher-e-Haqq [Tarjuma Mishkaat] – by Maulana Qutubuddin

95. Tarjuma Mishkaat – by Maulana Shujauddin

96. Tarjuma Mishkaat – by Maulana Ashiq Elahi Meeruti

97. Misbah-ul-Sanath – by Abul Qasim Lakhvi Shafe'i

98. Jama'e-ul-Usool-fee-Ahadis-Al-Rasool – by Ibne Atheer Mubarak bin Muhammad Shaibani

99. Jama'e-Al-Jawamah – by Abdul Rahman Jalaluddin Suyuti

100.   Jama'e-al-Sagheer – by Abdul Rahman Jalaluddin Suyuti

101.   Ahyaar-al-Mayyat – by Abdul Rahman Jalaluddin Suyuti

102.   Kunooz-al-Haqaheyq – Sharah Jama'e Sagheer – by Abdul Rahman Jalaluddin Suyuti

103. Kunooz-al-Daqaeq – by Munadi Misri

104. Safar-us-Saadaat – by Mujajuddin Ferozabadi

Books Of History

105. Tarikh-e-Tabarri – by Abdul Razzaq Ibne Hameed Ibne Jareer Al Tabarri

106. Tehzeeb-Al-Aasaar – by Abdul Razzaq Ibne Hameed Ibne Jareer Al Tabarri

107. Zakhair Al-Uqba – by Abdul Razzaq Ibne Hameed Ibne Jareer Al Tabarri

108. Tarikh Assim Kufi – by Khwaja Ahmed bin Asif Kufi

109. Wafa-al-Wafa [Translation of Assim Kufi] – by Ahmad bin Muhammad Hanafi

110. Tarikh Kamil – by Kamil Ibne Atheer Al Jazri

111. Tarikh Al-Khamis – by Sheik Hussain Dayaarbakri

112. Tarikh Al-Khulafa – by Abdul Rahman Jalaluddin Suyuti

113. Akhbar Al-Mahdi – by Abdul Rahman Jalaluddin Suyuti

114. Tarikh Al-Jama'e Baladhuri – by Ahmad bin Yahya bin Sabir Baladhuri

115. Tarikh Baghdad – by Hafiz Abu Bakr Al-Khateeb Baghdadi

116. Tarikh Al-Madina – by Samudi

117. Akhbar-al-Awwal-fee-Aasaar-al-Awwal – by Imam Ahmed bin Yousuf Damashqi

118. Tarikh Ibne Khaldoon – by Ibne Khaldoon

119. Tarikh Ibne Khalkhan – by Ibne Khalkhan

120. Tarikh Waqadi – by Waqadi

121. Tarikh Abul Fida – by Abul Fida

122. Tarikh Ibne Asakir – by Hafez Kabeer Abul Qasim Ibne Asakir

123. Tarikh Yaqubi – by Yaqubi

124. Tarikh Al-Fakhri – by Al Fakhri

125. Tarikh Ibne Al Wardi – by Ibne Al Wardi

126. Tarikh Ibne Sha'hr Ashoob – by Ibne Sha'hr Ashoob

127.   Tarikh Salfi – by Al Salfi
128.   Mushkil-al-Aasar – by Al Tehtawi
129.   Akhbar Al-Akhiar – by Mulla Abdul Rahman Jami
130.   Rauzatul Shouhada – by Mulla Husain Wahiz Kashafi
131.   Kanzul Gharayab – by Mulla Husain Wahiz Kashafi
132.   Rauzatus Safa – by Khawind Shah
133.   Tarikh-e-Tamaddun Al Islam – by Jorji Zaidan
134.   Noorul-Ain-fee-Mashad – by Al Husayn Qazi Sibghatullah
135.   Tarikh-e-Ahmadi – by Nawab Ahmad Husain Khan
136.   Tarikh Al-Islam – by Ehsanullah Abbasi Ghorakhpuri
137.   Tazkeratul Karaam: Tarikh-e-Khulafa-e-Arab-wa-Islam –
        by Syed Shah Muhammad Kabir Abul Ullai
138.   Tarikh Hindustan – by Dr Sail Chand

Various Books

139.   Malal-wa-Nahl – by Abul Fatah Abdul Kareem Shahrastani
140.   Al-Badaiya-wa-Al-Nahayya – by Abul Fida Ibne Atheer
        Damashqi
141.   Rabi-ul-Abraar – by Jajurallah Zamakhshari
142.   Rawaey Al-Mustafa – by Sadruddin
143.   Sharaf Al-Mustafa – by Hafiz Abu Sayeed Nishapuri
144.   Sharaf Al-Mustafa – by Abu Hamid Shafei
145.   Mithalab – by Abul Manzar Hisham Ibne Sayab Al-Kalbi
146.   Mizan-al Etedaal – by Muhammad bin Abdul Rahman Al
        Dhahabi
147.   Mizan Al Kubra – by Imam Shahrani
148.   Lisaan Al Mizan – by Ibne Uqdah
149.   Fitnatul-Kubra – by Dr Taha Hussain
150.   Amali – by Abu Abdullah Naishapuri
151.   Amali – by Sheik Sudduq
152.   Wafi-bil-Wafiyat – by Salahuddin Khaleel Ibne Aibak Al
        Safdi

153. Fawateh – by Abul Hassan Al Wahidi
154. Tajreed Al-Tamheed – by Ibne Abdul Birr Andulisi
155. Darj-ul-Daar – by Aseeluddin Shafei
156. Abtal-al-Batil – by Fazl Ibne Rozbhan Shirazi
157. Haqayeq-al-Ahqaq – by Shaheed Shaheed-e-Thalis Qazi Syed Noorulallah Shooshtari
158. Saif-al-Malool – by Qazi Sana Ullah Panipati
159. Ahqaq-al-Haqq [Tarjuma Haqayed-al-Ahqaq] – by Hasan Abbas Al Musawi
160. Kashaf-ul-Haqq – by Hassan bin Yusuf bin Mutahir [Allama Hilli]
161. Matalib-al-Su'ool – by Kamaluddin Mohammad bin Talha Shafei
162. Kifayat-al-Talib – by Abu Abdullah bin Yusuf bin Mohammad Al Kanji Shafei
163. Kitab-ul Bayaan-fee-Akhbar-e-Saheb-uz-Zaman – by Abu Abdullah bin Yusuf bin Mohammad Al Kanji Shafei
164. Kitab al-Mua'ref – by Ibne Qutaiba Denavari
165. Al-Imamt wal-Siyasat – by Ibne Qutaiba Denavari
166. Al Aqhad – by Ibne Abdullah
167. As-Seerah – by Ibne Hisham
168. Fasal-ul-Khitaab – by Khwaja Mohammad Parsa
169. Al Tarwaaj – by Sheik Al Askari
170. Mohazerat-al-Adba – by Abul Qasim Husain bin Muhammad [Ragheb Isfehani]
171. Usni-al-Matalib – by Ibne Atheer Jazri
172. Fusool-al Mohimma – by Nuruddin Ibne Sabagh Maliki
173. Noorul Absaar – by Nuruddin Ibne Sabagh Maliki
174. Shifa-e-Al Sudoor – by Ibne Sabah Maghrebi
175. Al Asaaf be-Sharah-Noor-Al Absaar – by Sabban Misri
176. Thamarat-al-Awraaq – by Yaqut Hamavi
177. Madinatul Al-Mo'ajiz – by Allama Barsi
178. Manafae al-Aulad – by Mulla Fayazuddin Sunami

179. Kitab al-Shifa – by Qazi Ayyaz
180. Shahed Ainea – by Allama Alusi
181. Bulugh al-Arab – by Allama Alusi
182. Zakhair al-Mu'aad – by Allama Uja Ali
183. Zakhair-al-Mu'aad – by Ibne Qeem Jauzi
184. Taraq al-Hikmiyah – by Ibne Qeem Jauzi
185. Darasat al-Baib – by Mulla Muhammad Moin
186. Seerat al-Halabiya – by Ali bin Burhanuddin Shafaei
187. Al-Moa'fiqah – by Ibne Saman
188. Arbayeen – by Jamaluddin Muhaddis
189. Arbayeen-fee-Usool-e-Deen – by Mohammad bin Ibne Omer Fakhruddin Raazi
190. Awarif-ul-Moa'rif – by Shahabuddin Suharwardi
191. Ahyaa-el-Uloom – by Zainuddin Abu Hamid Mohammad bin Mohammad Al Ghazzali
192. Sirr-ul-Aalemeen – by Zainuddin Abu Hamid Mohammad bin Mohammad Al Ghazzali
193. Mathoolal Ilm-ul-Usool – by Zainuddin Abu Hamid Al Ghazzali
194. Mazaaq al-Arifeen [Tarjuma Ayya-ul Uloom] – by Ahsan Siddiq Nanunavi
195. Farayed-ul Samteen – by Muhammad bin Ibrahim Jouveni Shafei
196. Daar-ul Samteen – by Sheik Al Hafiz Zarandi
197. Hulayatul Awliya – by Hafiz Abu Naeem
198. Nisa-e-Kafiya – by Hafiz Abu Bakr Shahab
199. Al Kashaf ash-Shaafi-fee-Takhrij Al Kashaf – by Ibne Hajar Asqalani
200. Fateh-ul Baari – by Ibne Hajar Asqalani
201. Al-Isaba – by Ibne Hajar Asqalani
202. Sharah-e-Maqasid – by Saad Uddin Tuftazani
203. Sawaiq-e-Mohriqa – by Shabudddin Ibne Hajar Makki, Mufti Azam, Makka

204. Al-Muwaqiyaat-wal-Jawahir – by Sheik Abdul Wahab Shurani

205. Kitab-al Wilayat – by Masood bin Nasser Seestani

206. Maghazi al-Rasool – by Mohammad bin Mohammad Al Waqidi

207. Isbaat-al-Waseeta – by Abul Hassan Ali Ibne Hussain Masudi

208. Al Futuhat-e-Makki – by Sheik Mohiuddin Ibne Arabi Andulusi

209. Durre-Maknoon – by Sheik Mohiuddin Ibne Arabi Andulusi

210. Anqwa-e-Maghrib – by Sheik Mohiuddin Ibne Arabi Andulusi

211. Ghaniyat-al-Talibeen – by Abdul Qadir Jilani

212. A'alam-ul-Vara – by Abu Ali Al Fazl bin Hasan Basri

213. Manaheej-at-Talebeen – by Qazvini

214. Sibtah-al-Marwareed – by Sheik Abdul Lateef Halbi

215. Asadul Ghaba fee Ma'refat Al Sahaba – by Ibne Atheer Jazri

216. Seerat Ibne Hisham – by Mohammad Abdul Malik bin Hisham

217. Hadiqatul al Haqaeq – by Hakim Sanaai

218. Haywatul Haywan – by Damiri

219. Insaan al Uyoon – Ali bin Burhanuddin Shafei Halbi

220. Khulasatul Wafa – by Nuruddin Ali bin Abdullah Samhudi

221. Jawahir-ul-Uqdeen – by Nuruddin Ali bin Abdullah Samhudi

222. Riyaz-us-Saleheen – by Sheik Mohiuddin Al Noori

223. Tanzeel-al-Abrar – by Al Boukhashi

224. Asaaf-al-Raghabain – by Sheik Muhammad Atquiyan

225. Rashfat-al-Saadi – by Abu Bakr Khizri

226. Tazkeratul Huffaz – by Al Dhahabi

227. Safwat-al-Safwah – by Sibte Ibne Jauzi (Abul Faraj Al Baghdadi Siddiqi Hanbali)

228.   Tazkeratul Khawas Al Ummah – by Sibte Ibne Jauzi

229.   Sawaneh Khwaja Badiuddin Shah Madaar – by Abdul Rahman Chisti

230.   Ma'refatal Sahaba – by Ibne Musnad

231.   Tohfatal Akhyar – by Maulana Abdul Hai

232.   Manaqib Al-As-haab – by Najmuddin Abu Bakr bin Muhammad

233.   Qasas Al Ullema – by Allama Tinka Baini

234.   Fazayal Al Sahaba – by Sumani

235.   Rooh Al Mu'ani – by Shahabuddin Alusi

236.   Subhey Sadiq – by Mulla Nizamuddin

237.   Kitab-ul Ashra – by Allama Baladhuri

238.   Basharatal Islam – by Syed Musleh

239.   Usool-al Akharat – by Musafir

240.   Miftah Al Najaat – by Mirza Ahmed bin Moatemad Khan Badakhshani

241.   Mashareq Anwaar al Yaqeen – by Rajab Ali Barsi

242.   Jawameh Al Kalam – by Syed Mohammed Al Husaini Khwaja Bande Nawaz

243.   Beher-al Mo'ani – by Syed Mohammed Al Husaini Khwaja Bande Nawaz

244.   Ganjal Asraar – by Moinul Haqq

245.   Malfuzaat Khwaja Gaan Chist – by Makhdoom Jehaniyan

246.   Raahat-al-Quloob – by Khwaja Nizamuddin Awliya

247.   Khash-al Mehjoob – by Abul Hassan Hajwari Data Ganj Baqsh

248.   Maktubaat Sheik Sir Hindi – by Mujadid (Alif Saani) Sheik Ahmad Farooqi Sir Hindi

249.   Zakhiratul Maal fee Sharah Aqd Jawahar Al Maal – by Shahabuddin Ahmad bin Abdul Qader Bakri

250.   Minhajul Tahqeeq – by Yahya Ibne Hasan Al Quraeshi

251.   Musnad Mu'ajim – by Abu Yaala

252.   Taiwaraat – by Sulfi

253.   Asfaar-e-Musa – by Sheik Mohsen Ahmad
254.   Rauzal Azhar – by Shah Naqi Ali Qalandar Kaakurawi
255.   Kitab-al Zeenateh – by Hafiz Abu Hatem Raazi
256.   Sharah-e-Tajdeed – by Mulla Qushnaji
257.   Hidayat al Saada – by Malik ul Ullema Shahabuddin Dawlatabadi
258.   Tawzih-ul-Dalayal – by Shahabuddin Dawlatabadi
259.   Seeratun Nabi – by Shibli Naumani
260.   Seerat-e-Naumani – by Shibli Naumani
261.   Al Ghazzali – by Shibli Naumani
262.   Al Farooq – by Shibli Naumani
263.   Ilmul Kalaam – by Shibli Naumani
264.   Abu Hanifa fee Siyasi Zindagi – by Maulana Manazer Ehsan Gilani
265.   Tadween-e-Hadees – by Maulana Manazer Ehsan Gilani
266.   Ummahaat-al Ummah – by Shamsul Ullema Hafiz Nazeer Ahmad
267.   Farayaz-al-Huqooq – by Shamsul Ullema Hafiz Nazeer Ahmad
268.   Roya-e-Sadiqa – by Shamsul Ullema Hafiz Nazeer Ahmad
269.   Sharafal Nabuwah – by Abu Sa'eed Abdul Malik bin Ibne Adi
270.   Shawahid al Nabuwah – by Mulla Abdur Rahman Jaami
271.   Madarij al Nabuwah – by Shah Abdul Haqq Muhaddis Dehlawi
272.   Jazbal Quloob – by Shah Abdul Haqq Muhaddis Dehlawi
273.   Akhbar-al Akhiyar – by Shah Abdul Haqq Muhaddis Dehlawi
274.   Manaqib – by Shah Abdul Haqq Muhaddis Dehlawi
275.   Manaqib – by Hakim
276.   Manaqib – by Abul Faraj Jauzi
277.   Manaqib – by Abu Abdullah Muhammad bin Idris Shafei
278.   Manaqib – by Khateeb

279.   Manaqib – by Sama'ani

280.   Manaqib – by Ibne Maghazil

281.   Manaqib Murtazawi – Syed Saleh Kashfi Tirmizi Hanafi

282.   Manaqib – by Abu Bakr Ibne Marduwiyah

283.   Manaqib – by Al Moeed Mawfiq bin Mohammad Khwarizmi

284.   Maqtal al-Hussain – Al Moeed Mawfiq bin Mohammad Khwarizmi

285.   Sharah Nahjul Balagha – by Ibne Abil Hadid Motazali

286.   Manaqib Ahle Bayt – by Mirza Mohammad Ali Mazbuta (Nizam Mazhabi Trust)

287.   Izalatul Khifa – by Shah Waliullah Mohaddis Dehlawi

288.   Tafmiyaat-al Ilahiya – by Shah Waliullah Mohaddis Dehlawi

289.   Hujjatul Balegha – by Shah Waliullah Mohaddis Dehlawi

290.   Qurratul Ain – by Shah Waliullah Mohaddis Dehlawi

291.   Tohfa-e-Athna Ashariya – by Shah Abdul Aziz Mohaddis Dehlawi

292.   Boostan al Mohiddisain – by Shah Abdul Aziz Mohaddis Dehlawi

293.   Fatawey Azizi – by Shah Abdul Aziz Mohaddis Dehlawi

294.   Sirrul Shahadatain – by Shah Abdul Aziz Mohaddis Dehlawi

295.   Maktu Nisbat Jawaz-e-Aza wa Buka – by Shah Abdul Aziz Mohaddis Dehlawi

296.   Maqatil as-Sibtain – by Abul Faraj Isfahani

297.   Shahadat Nama – by Syed Abdullah Shah Naqshbandi Qadri

298.   Fatemi Da'awat-e-Islam – by Maulana Khwaja Hasan Nizami

299.   Yazeed Nama – by Maulana Khwaja Hasan Nizami

300.   Tamacha ba Rukhsaar-e-Yazeed – by Maulan Khwaja Hasan Nizami

301. Maah Naameh Munadi – by Maulana Hasan Nizami wa Hasan Saani Nizami

302. Hayaat-e-Sayyedus Shohada – Maulan Sayyed Ali Basheer

303. Islam Ki Sher Dil Khatoon [Zainab AS] – by Asiya binte Taha Husain

304. Balaghat-un Nisa – by Syed Ahmed bin Abi Taher

305. Shehiraat un-Nisa – published by Matbu'ah Misr

306. Tazkeraat-al Awliya – by Sheik Fareed-Uddin Attar

307. Ruhaniyat key Tajdaar – by Sahebzada Mustasan Farooqi

308. Khazinatal Asifia – by Ghulam Suroor

309. Hidayat al Ummah fee Ma'refatal Aim'mah – by Ruhul Ameen bin Shamsuddin Mohammad Al Husain Sabzwari

310. Khusoos al Aim'mah fee Madah al Aim'mah – by Maliki

311. Hujfat al-Ahba – by Syed Al Mohaddasain Ataullah Husaini

312. Irja-al Matalib: Sawaan-e-Ali Ibne Abi Taleb – by Obaidullah Bismil Amritsari

313. Al Najm al Saqib fee Qazai Ali Ibne Abi Taleb – by Haji Mohammad bin Abdullah bin Nooruddin

314. Shah-e-Raahey Najaat – by Humayun Mirza [Barrister]

315. Bihar ul Anwaar – by Mulla Mohammad Baqar Majlisi

316. Hayaat ul Quloob – by Mulla Mohammad Baqar Majlisi

317. Irshad al Quloob – by Mulla Mohammad Baqar Majlisi

318. Kitab al Wilayat – by Masood bin Nasser Seestani

319. Isbaat al Wasiyat – by Abul Hasan Ali Ibne Husain Masoodi

320. Khasayes-e-Alwiya – by Abul Fatah Mohammad bin Ali bin Ibrahim Al Nazari

321. Noor-Ala-Noor Ma'muttahar Fitna Al Karamah – by Khaleel Ahmed Deobandi

322. Khilafat wa Mulukiyat – by Maulana Abul Ala Maududi

323. Haqiqat-e-Jihad - by Maulana Abul Ala Maududi

324. Ta'jeel al Manfehat – by Ibne Hajar Asqalani

325.   Fateh ul Baari – by Ibne Hajar Asqalani

326.   Kash-al Zunoon – by Haji Khalifa

327.   Minhaj al Usool – by Qazi Baidavi

328.   Ghayet al Maraam – by Imam al Behrain

329.   Misbah al Sunnah – by Baghavi Shafei

330.   Minhaj al Sunnah – by Ibne Thaymiyah

331.   Behar ul Najaat – by Abu Osman bin Omer

332.   Anwaar al Badayah – by Husain bin Sohail

333.   Aqayed wa Deeniya – by Zia Uddin Sareed al Jarjani

334.   Al Waraaj – by Sheik Al Askari

335.   Kitab al Bayaan wal Yaqeen – by Abu Osman Omer bin Jahez Basri

336.   Kitab al Saqifa wa Al Fadak – by Abu Bakr Ahmad bin Abdul Aziz Jawhari

337.   Radd-e-Munafaqat – by Maulana Sehvi Shah Kamali

338.   200. Masa'el al Khilafat fee Fiqha – by Sheik Al Taif Abu Jaffer Mohammad bin Hasan Tusi

339.   201. Ali And Ayesha – by Allama Umer Abu Nasr

340.   Naks al Shariat – by Abu Abdullah Mohammad bin Idris Shafei

341.   Kitab-e-Sulaym – by Sulaym bin Qais al Hilali

342.   Hadd-e-Tehqeeq ba Mashrab-e-Sunni – by Waheeduddin Khan

343.   Misbah al Zulm – by Syed Imdad Imam

344.   Manazer Al Masayeb – by Syed Imdad Imam

345.   Masalek Ibne Fadhlullah – by Ibne Fadhulullah

346.   Muslmanoun key Firqhey – by Maulana Ghulam Ahmed Wakeel Nizamabadi

347.   Do Islam – by Dr Ghulam Jeelani Barq

348.   Do Quran – by Dr Ghulam Jeelani Barq

349.   Bhai Bhai – by Dr Ghulam Jeelani Barq

350.   Islam Aur Banu Ummayyah – Dr Abu Bakr Khan Maleehabadi

351. Hazrat Ali Ibne Abi Taleb Aur Unkey Siyasi Hareef – by Syed Shahed Zaeem Fatimi
352. Al Ahdath – by Abul Hasan Ali Mada'eni
353. Fiqah dar al-Mukhtaar
354. Ghayat al Awtaat: Tarjuma dar al-Mukhtaar
355. Fiqah Fathawi Alamgir
356. Faqah Fathawi Qazi Khan
357. Fiqah Fathawi Azizi
358. Loghaat al-Quran – by Abdul Daaim Al Jalali Al Bukhari
359. Waheed: Al-Loghaat – by Waheeduz Zaman Viqar Nawaz Jung
360. Qamoos al-Loghaat – by Mujajuddin Ferozabadi
361. Islam Kyounkar Phaila? – by Dr Vishvanath Parshad Mathur
362. Humarey Hain Husain – by Dr Vishvanath Parshad Mathur
363. Bhagavad Gita
364. Krishan Binti – by Pandit Ramdhan Mazboot [Shakiri Pustakala, Delhi]
365. Ayodhiya ka Banbasi by Pandit Shanker Das [Pub Agra]
366. Budhiya Chamatkar – by L K Bhatnagar [Pub Alankar Pustakala, Kanpur]
367. Sarvar-e-Alam Jagat Guru – by Siddiq Deendar
368. Ja'ame Sipi – by Jamasap ba Ahad Gushtasip
369. Zan Zar Tasht

Books In English

370. Gospel of Barnabus
371. Historian's History of The World – Dr Henry Smith Williams
372. Chamber's Encyclopedia – 1950 Edition
373. Decline And Fall of the Roman Empire – Edward Gibbon
374. Comments On The 1887 Edition of Gibbon's 'Decline And Fall of The Roman Empire' – Dr Henry Smith Williams

375.   Heroes And Hero Worship – Thomas Carlyle
376.   Life of Mahomet – Washington Irving
377.   Lives of Successors of Mahomet – Washington Irving
378.   An Apology For Mohammad And The Koran – John Davenport
379.   Mohammad And Islam – Sir William Muir
380.   The Caliphate: Its Rise, Decline And Fall – Sir William Muir
381.   History of Mohammedan Empire – Major Price
382.   Makers of Arab History – Phillip Hitti
383.   History of Arabia And Its People – Andrew Chrechton
384.   Islam Under The Arabs – Robert Durie Osborne
385.   History of Islam – Dr William Durant
386.   Spanish Islam – Reinhard Dozy
387.   Spirit of Islam – Justice Amir Ali
388.   Politics In Islam – Khuda Bakhsh
389.   Hazrat Ali As An Ameer – Major General Akbar Khan
390.   Caliph Ali And His Times – Prof Abdul Ali
391.   Islam And Modern Challenge – Prof Abdul Wahab Bokhari
392.   Imam Ali – Sulayman Kattani [Trans I K H Howard]
393.   The Voice of Human Justice – Jorge Jordac
394.   Ayesha After The Prophet – Kurt Frischler
395.   Islamic Law 16th Edition – Chief Justice, Hidayath Ullah
396.   Mohammadan Law – Justice Babulal Varma
397.   Judgement In The Khoja Case – Justice Arnold – 1935 Indian Law Reports, Bombay
398.   Judgement In The Tabbarra Case – Special Judge Rai Thakur Parshad
399.   "Current Weekly": August 1968 – Dosi Fareedun Karaka
400.   A Miricle In Persia – Times of India, 25 March 1882
401.   Why I Became A Shia – Prof Sheik Ahmed Ameen Antaki
402.   Why I Adopted The Creed Of The Ahlul Bayt – Sheik Mohammad Marai Antaki
403.   Spiritualism And Islam – Prof M G Reynold

Books From French

www.ingramcontent.com/pod-product-compliance
Lightning Source LLC
Chambersburg PA
CBHW022112080426
42734CB00006B/95